Semper—Chai!

PAGE 564

Semper—Chai!

Marines of Blue and White (and Red)

Howard J. Leavitt

To order additional copies of this book, contact:
Xlibris Corporation
1-888-795-4274
www.Xlibris.com
Orders@Xlibris.com
17169-LEAV

Other book by author:

Footsteps of David – Common Roots, Uncommon Valor
(The Jewish Experience in the Military)

Book forthcoming:

Tales of Valor (tentative title)
The Return of the Maccabbis

Dedication

This book is dedicated to that group of men and women who are proud former Marines – the Semper Fi Marine Honor Detail of Riverside, California, and Riverside National Cemetery – a microcosm of our country, its diversity, and its strengths. They give so much. Yet, the gratification of service, the warmth and appreciation of the families and friends of the deceased veterans, and the privilege of continuing to participate in the Corps they cherish far exceed their input. As Marines, they consider it an honor and a privilege to serve their Corps and their country.

It is also a tribute to those of the Jewish faith who have served and continue to serve, honorably and well, for whom the words Semper Fidelis is not just a slogan, but a trust.

Semper Fi Marine Honor Detail
Riverside National Cemetery
Riverside, California April 2002

Comments by previewers . . . .

"The author, Howard J. Leavitt, has accomplished what would appear to be a daunting task – the telling individual story of members of a corporate institution. He provides a human face which emphasizes that it is the individual that counts in the progress of the nation . . .
    "Bravo Zulu for a job well done."

Charles D. Melson, Chief Historian, History and Museum Division, Headquarters, Marine Corps

"If the Marine Corps had an award for writing a book about the Corps, I am certain that you would be in consideration for receiving it."

Howard J. Fuller, M/Sgt, USMCR (ret)

Contents

PART IV

PART V

PART VI

PART XI

PART XII

The Marines' Hymn

From the Halls of Montezuma
To the Shores of Tripoli,
We have fought our country's battles
In the air, on land and sea.
First to fight for right and freedom,
And to keep our honor clean,
We are proud to claim the title of
UNITED STATES MARINE.

Our flag's unfurled to ev'ry breeze
From dawn to setting sun,
We have fought in every clime and place
Where we could take a gun.
In the snow of far off northern lands,
And in sunny tropic scenes,
You will always find us on the job
THE UNITED STATES MARINES.

Here's health to you and to our Corps
Which we are proud to serve.
In many a strife we've fought for life,
And never lost our nerve.
If the Army and the Navy
Ever look on heaven's scenes,
They will find the streets are guarded by
THE UNITED STATES MARINES.

The music was composed by Jacques Offenbach (1819–80)—
born as Jakob Eberst, the son of a synagogue cantor, in Cologne,
Germany—for the three-act version of his *opera bouffe* (a comic
opera of farcical character) *Geneviève de Bourbon*, first performed
on November 19, 1859. In the duet titled *Couplets des Hommes
d'Armes*, two comedians, Grabuge (baritone) and Pitou (tenor)
sang their words to the melody so well-known to the present.

Who wrote the words and when they were adopted by the
Marines remain unknown, their earliest appearance in print found
on an 1898 recruiting poster. The original three stanzas were
copyrighted by Major General John A. Lejeune, former Commandant, who approved a significant change in the time-honored
line, "We fight our country's battles on the land and on the sea,"
substituting, "in the air, on land, and sea."

Preface

"I think that, as life is action and passion, it is required
of a man that he should share the passion and action of
his time at the peril of being judged not to have lived."
Oliver Wendell Holmes, Jr. (1841–1935) in a
Memorial Day address, 1884

The genesis of *Semper Chai* occurred during a conversation with a non-Jewish acquaintance in the locker room of our sports club in Riverside, California. When this seemingly well-informed, well-intentioned, and educated businessman expressed surprise that Jews ever served in the U.S. Marine Corps, I knew the time had come to shed light on this ignored subject.

I made up a list of Jewish veterans of the Marine Corps from the rolls of the Jewish War Veterans of the United States, which became the nucleus of a larger list of veterans whom I tried to contact by mail or phone. Each of those who were reachable was sent a questionnaire I had prepared. My initial intent was to write a book based on the experiences of approximately fifty veterans, but that number soon doubled due to the amount of responses received. I expanded the project to include stories of Jewish veterans of the Marine Corps, deceased and living, through research in libraries and museum archives, and in firsthand accounts sent to me.

Of the 220 Marines presented in this book (including women and those in peacetime service) over 30 percent were killed or wounded in action. There may have been more: a number listed

neither wounds nor awards. The majority of those individuals whose stories
   are related or to whom references are made responded to my questionnaire. Virtually all expressed the same feeling regarding the purpose of this work: to impart that Americans of the Jewish faith are to be counted upon to defend their country, and that many have chosen to do so in the service of the U.S. Marine Corps.

   There are also those *not* of the Jewish faith who graciously volunteered to share information about their Jewish buddies and comrades in arms. They demonstrate in vivid terms the motto, spoken or unspoken, of Marine Band of Brothers.

   The information compiled in this book was gathered from extremely limited sources—responses from one organizational mailing-list inquiry, a brief advertisement in a few publications, and word-of-mouth leads.

   While historical research does not generally consist of such a narrow search, limited, to my knowledge, no records of the religion of Marines has ever been kept in historical repositories or elsewhere. Therefore, as no list of the Jews who served this country in the military at any particular time is in existence, the true extent of Jewish participation in the U.S. Marine Corps is impossible to determine. The participation described in this book, however, appears to be representative and goes a long way in confirming that *many* Jews were—and are—Marines, and that the basic and lofty precepts and spiritual underpinnings of the United States, the U.S. Marine Corps, and Judaism are one and the same, without any differences or conflict.

   The book contains frequent use of the word "Jap" and use of the word "Nip" and "gooks." One should understand that they were used in the context of the times: the Japanese, North Koreans, and Chinese were our enemies. Those terms, while not unacceptable then, are now considered insulting and demeaning. If an apology is required, it is so extended.

Foreword

It is with pleasure that I represent the Marine Corps' historical effort in this brief introduction to a valued contribution to the saga of America's own, the United States Marine Corps. The author, Howard J. Leavitt, has accomplished what would appear to be a daunting task–the telling of the individual story of members of a corporate institution. He provides a human face which emphasizes that it is the individual that counts in the progress of the nation. For those who choose to be Marines, it means to subordinate individual interests for the good of the whole, without relinquishing the key elements of their own identity in the process. In this, Mr. Leavitt has done well and has provided a reminder that the Marine Corps gathers strengths from seemingly diverse elements.

When I was growing up, there were three Jewish families in my California hometown and at my public school. Unique it was that all three families had fathers who served as U.S. Marines in World War II, providing a common heritage with my own family. In his book, I again meet familiar and new faces. As interested readers follow the portraits in this work, they should look for the common threads they recognize as friends, as fellow Marines.

"Bravo Zulu" for a job well done.

Charles D. Melson
Chief Historian
History and Museums Division
Headquarters, U.S. Marine Corps
Washington, D.C.

PART I

White Stars on a Field of Blue

Chapter I

Congressional Medal of Honor

"The Marines have landed and have the situation well in hand." Most of us grew up with this dramatic statement of the principal mission of the U.S. Marine Corps. And that's what President Wilson did on December 14, 1914, when a Marine detachment from the gunboat USS *Machias* landed on the northern coast to safeguard the last half-million dollars of the treasury of Haiti. Since open rebellion had not yet erupted, only a small number of Marines were landed, some later to be withdrawn.

By August 1915, a battalion of artillery landed at the capital city of Port-au-Prince to bring the strength of the 1ˢᵗ Marine Brigade under the command of Colonel W. T. Waller, USMC, to 88 officers and 1,941 enlisted men. At the end of September 1915, Major Smedley D. Butler, USMC, took command of those Marines who had moved to Gonaives, a seaport in the northeastern part of Haiti.

Major Butler was now a kind of roving battalion commander. Accompanying him was his orderly Private Samuel Gross (born Samuel Margulies, in Philadelphia, Pennsylvania on May 9, 1891 and died there on November 13, 1934. He is buried in the Har Nebo Cemetery, Philadelphia, Pennsylvania).

By September, Major Butler had moved north to Cap-Haitien. A hundred men, under one of Butler's subordinate unit commanders, remained at Gonaives and were attacked by a large

23

force of Cacos under the local commander, General Rameau. Butler—with his adjutant, Lieutenant Alexander A. Vandegrift, and his orderly Private Sam Gross—set out in a small boat for Gonaives, a distance of 160 miles.

In that small boat were three history-making Marines—destined to wear a total of six generals' stars and four Medals of Honor—including one who would become the Commandant of the Marine Corps: Major General Smedley D. Butler, USMC, two Medals of Honor; General Alexander A. Vandegrift, Medal of Honor and eighteenth Commandant of the Marine Corps, and Private Samuel Gross, Medal of Honor.

Samuel Gross received his Medal of Honor at the battle of Fort Riviere, the last stronghold of the Cacos. In his book, *Garde d'Haiti*, James H. McCrocklin, depicts the fierce combat which ensued between the Cacos bandits and the handful of Marines who stormed the fort:

"Fighting with rifles, bayonets, machetes, clubs, and rocks continued until the last Caco had fallen. More than 50, including several important leaders, were killed. The attacking Marines suffered only a few bruises and scratches. The first two to enter the fort and Butler were awarded the Congressional Medal of Honor. Butler brought up a ton of dynamite and had the walls of the fort demolished; it has not since been used by a military force. The destruction of Fort Rivière with its garrison broke the resistance of the Cacos."

General Butler completes the saga:

"The three of us, Iams, Gross, and I, were given the Congressional Medal for the Fort Rivière stunt. Iams came up through the ranks and was commissioned during the World War. He is now a captain of Marines. As for Gross, shortly after his gallant action at Fort Rivière, he developed epilepsy. When the attacks became more frequent, he was sent to a veterans' hospital. I lost track of him for twelve years. In 1930, I was speaking in Coatesville, Pennsylvania. I was telling my audience, some of whom were from the big veterans' hospital near the town, that a sergeant and a private of Marines had taken all the risk in the capture of Fort Rivière and that I always wondered what had become of the private. After the talk who should come on the stage with his hospital attendant but little Gross. He was partially paralyzed

and looked very ill. The attendant had not even known that Gross had won a Medal of Honor. I gave Gross my button (a small blue and white cloth rosette denoting the Medal of Honor) for wear on the lapel."

On November 17, 1915, the Marines, with Samuel Gross, attacked Fort Rivière in an attempt to cut off the retreat of the Cacos. "Gross was the second man to pass through the breach in the face of constant fire from the bandits."[1]

---

1 Brody, Seymour, *Jewish Heroes & Heroines of America*, Lifetime Books, Hollywood, Fla., 1966, p. 68.

PART II

Sketches

Chapter 2

A Lot of Good Men

Edwin Bernstein enlisted in the Marine Corps in May 1942 after receiving his discharge from the Canadian Army where he had been an American volunteer. He served with the 14th Marines, 4th Marine Division, participating in landings on Roi-Namur, Saipan, and Iwo Jima. He also served in Headquarters, Fifth Marine Division in the occupation of Japan, Sasebo, September–December 1945.

Discharged from active duty in March 1946, at Camp Pendleton, California, as a staff sergeant, he was recalled for the Korean War in November 1950. After two and a half years of service, he was released in June 1953, with the rank of technical sergeant. Ed contradicted me when I accused him of being a "former Marine." He corrected me with "the words of the Marine Corps League, 'Once a Marine, always a Marine.'"

Phil Bogatz's experience at Parris Island boot camp was not his greatest moment. He couldn't eat the food for two weeks and lived on chocolate bars, milk, and cigarettes. To make matters worse, his DI with the hairlip was his worst enemy. Living with seventy-five others provided real culture shock, and as he said, not so uncommonly, "the worst were from the South."

His experience was the usual routine of infantry training at Camp Pendleton, assignment with I company (rifle company), 25th Marines, and campaigns at Roi-Namur, Tinian, and Saipan. Phil was wounded twice, once on Tinian, and the other on Iwo Jima. In addition to his Purple Hearts, he received the Bronze Star Medal and two Presidential Unit Citations. After hospitalization in San Diego, he was discharged as a sergeant.

Phil noted that there were a lot of mistakes made. But, "When it came to combat, it all came together and we needed each other. It took a while until all respected each other and I was 'one of the boys.'"

Phil's modesty should come as no surprise. His wife related that "his second wound required his return to the States. He had skin from his heel grafted to his thigh. The first graft did not take and the procedure had to be repeated." And, "Phil has such respect for the Marine Corps. Even to this day, after being married fifty-three years, I still hear of little incidents that took place during the years he served in the Marines." Not only that, "The Marine Corps will always be a part of Phil's life."

People might question the surname of Joe Backfield. It is not exactly the one his parents had when they arrived in his country from the Ukraine in 1922. His family name was actually Barpel. But his brother used the name Backfield in school, and Joe did the same. However, when Joe went to enlist, his birth certificate bore the name, "Jerome Backfield," which is the name he used in the Corps till he had it legally changed to Joseph Backfield when he was in the Army till 1968 as a sergeant first class.

In addition to his combat experience on Bougainville, Guadalcanal, and Iwo Jima, a couple of incidents stand out in Joe's recollections. After a week on the firing range at Parris Island, his platoon had to pull one week of mess duty. Joe was assigned to pots and pans. His mess fed 1,800 troops. One day after noon meal, they marched to the medics for physical inspection. After a week, his mess detail became sick, vomited, had diarrhea, and fever. Men dropped out during the march. Fifty-six men out of the mess detail of sixty-nine were hospitalized. Of the thirteen, only Joe was able to report for duty. Of the 1,800 men, only three hundred reported for supper. Fifteen hundred men were sent to hospitals in South Carolina and Georgia. Joe said that the official excuse was E coli or salmonella. Almost all of the troops recovered within the next ten days.

Shipped overseas aboard the SS *George F. Elliott,* he landed in New Caledonia in October 1943. The following day, "the ammo dump on the dock was blown up with much loss of life. I was put on a burial detail. We were told 'unofficially' that a Jap sub came in under our ship through the defense nets and blew up the ammo. I don't know if this was the truth, but it seems feasible."

After the campaigns of Bougainville, Guadalcanal, and Iwo Jima, he returned to Guam to retrain for the invasion of Japan. "Thankfully, the atom bomb made the invasion unnecessary."

Sam Messing was more fortunate than his son: Sam survived World War II, but his son, Mitchel, was killed in Vietnam in 1959 while serving in the U.S. Air Force.

Sam joined the Marine Corps on October 5, 1942 and was assigned to platoon 901 at Parris Island, South Carolina. He became friends with actor Sterling Hayden who was a member of platoon 898.

After several assignments and training in the United States, Sam shipped out of Camp Lejeune in October 1944, and arrived on the island of Pauvuvu, the 1st Marine Division rest camp. In February, they arrived on Guadalcanal for maneuvers. Sam was assigned to the 2nd Battalion, 5th Marines, 1st Marine Division. Soon, they left for the invasion of Okinawa and hit the beach on Easter Sunday, April 1, 1945. While they met little opposition on the beach, "we made up for that when we got close to the airport. The battle of Okinawa produced more casualties than any other in the Pacific campaign. The American casualties were approximately 49,000 and the Japanese almost twice that number. It was here that he experienced one of the most unpleasant tasks of his duties—that of taking various kinds of ammo to the front lines and bringing back Marine casualties to graves registration.

After VJ Day, they were transferred to China to repatriate the Japanese troops still occupying that country. "The Chinese people were so happy to see us that they refused to accept any money for about a week. By that time, they had learned to say 'one dollar,' and everything was one dollar." Sam spent three months in Peking and three months in Tientsin, and although he was a corporal, he served as the acting platoon sergeant.

Sam Messing was discharged from the Marine Corps at Bainbridge, Maryland, on March 8, 1946. As a result of the malaria he had contracted in the Pacific, he was granted a small pension.

Jerry Levin served in Vietnam for eleven months as a member of 2nd ANGLICO and 3rd Medical Battalion. On his first night in Vietnam, he had nowhere to sleep due to the constant bombardment of incoming artillery. He managed to find a place in the dirt outside with just what he was wearing, and smoked Viet pot and drank beer. During that time, he kept throwing up and simply threw dirt over the vomit. "What a welcome."

Jerry was enraged with the behavior of some of the men from graves registration who were "dancing around like the devil or Indians, yelling, and screaming. They were about to cut off this North Viet's soldier's ears. It was awful–pure evil!"

Jerry Levin experienced no anti-Semitism. Every Sunday, while at San Diego, they were served bagels, lox and cream cheese by members of B'nai B'rith.

On October 19, 1983, the *Chicago Tribune* reported on the loss of two Marines who were shot while a part of the peacekeeping force in Beirut, Lebanon. One of them was Sergeant Allen Soifert, who was "slain on his second tour of volunteer duty." Soifert was "eulogized as a 'martyr' who died to help bring peace to the Middle East."

In a crowded synagogue of Nashua, New Hampshire, Rabbi Bela Fischer told "hundreds of mourners who packed Temple Beth Abraham, 'We pray that his dream of a sane and peaceful world will come true.'"

"Soifert, 25, was shot last Friday while on duty at Beirut International Airport. He was the fifth Marine to die in the strife-torn area."

Soifert went to Beirut in May. He had volunteered to go, after serving six months there starting the previous fall.

"Sergeant Allen Soifert was murdered by an Arab sniper–in a shot aimed at all efforts to bring peace," Rabbi Allen Weiss said. "The forces of hatred carried our bereavement here today. The shot that killed Allen was aimed at all of us."

"Allen died serving the country that he was proud of," Rabbi Weiss told Soifert's mother, Joan Romer, and her husband, Hyman.

Rabbi Shlomo Hochberg said of Soifert: "He was willing to sacrifice his own life for peace. He was a holy martyr, giving his life for his country."

"A white-gloved Marine honor guard carried Soifert's flag-draped coffin from the temple on its way to a small cemetery.

"Workers at nearby factories and warehouses looked through a chainlink fence as mourners filled the cemetery. They pressed their faces to the fence to hear the ceremony above the din from a nearby highway.

"Taps was played and a twenty-one gun salute sounded as Soifert's fellow Marines lowered his coffin by white rope into the ground.

"Hyman Romer shoveled dirt on to the coffin before ushering the family from the cemetery."

Despite his disclaimers to the contrary Benis Frank is indeed a man of distinction, having made his mark not only in the military, but as an author and historian as well.

Born in Amsterdam, New York, in 1925, he has lived most of his life in Stamford, Connecticut. He joined the Marine Corps as an enlisted man in World II, participating in the invasions of Peleliu and Okinawa, after which he served with the 1st Marine Division in the occupation of North China. Returning to active duty as a commissioned officer just before the Korean War, he joined the 1st Provisional Historical Platoon at FMFPac. Later, he returned to duty with the 1st Marine Division in Korea, where he was the division order-of-battle officer, and also served as battalion intelligence officer of the 2nd Battalion, 5th Marines.

Frank was released from active duty in November 1953, at which time he entered his second distinguished career–that of civilian historian in the Marine Corps Historical Program. He became chief historian in 1990 and retired in October 1997. He has written six major works on the Marines in World War II, a biography of General Holland M. Smith for *Men of War: Great Naval Leaders of World War II*, numerous articles and signed book reviews in the field of military and oral history, and made major contributions to dictionaries and encyclopedias. He is also a freelance indexer and copy editor, and has refereed a number of manuscripts in the field of military history.

His books include *Okinawa: Touchstone to Victory, Halsey,* and *Okinawa: The Great Island Battle.* He co-authored *Victory and Occupation,* the fifth and last volume of the official *History of the U.S. Marine Corps Operations in World War II.* He also wrote *A Brief History of the 3rd Marines* and *U.S. Marines in Lebanon, 1982–84.* He was general editor of the History and Museums Division's World War II Fiftieth Anniversary series of commemorative monographs, comprising twenty-five titles by the end of 1997.

His list of memberships in organizations and associations

includes the Company of Military Historians; the Oral History in the Mid-Atlantic Region; the Society of Military History; Virginia Scottish Games Association; the St. Andrews Society of Washington, D.C., and the Military Order of the Carabao. He is a Life Member of the 1st Marine Division Association.

Frank's personal stationery clearly demonstrates his passion and his pride. The return address displays in full color the emblem of the 1st Marine Division, and at the foot of the envelope is a listing of the theaters of war–World War II, North China, Korea, Vietnam, Southwest Asia, and the Cold War–in which the division participated.

A native Pennsylvanian, Sammy Davis turned seventeen years of age on March 15, 1942. With great difficulty he finally convinced his parents to sign the papers, and enlisted in the Marine Corps in August 1942. He was five feet six and three quarters and weighed one hundred twenty-two pounds.

After boot camp at Parris Island, South Carolina, he trained at Camp Eliot for six months before being shipped out to New Zealand. On arrival, he was assigned to King Company, 2nd Battalion, 2nd Marine Regiment, 2nd Marine Division. Although he was a "grunt," he was the kid of the company and was assigned to the captain as his runner.

The 2nd Marines was the first into action at Tulagi and Gavuto, and on Guadalcanal with the 1st Marine Division. When he was relieved, he shipped out to New Zealand, and with the 6th and 8th regiments, formed the 2nd Marine Division.

Like other Marines at the time, Davis was very impressed with New Zealand. "It was a beautiful country. The people honest, beautiful, and wonderful. At the time, the country was barren of men from sixteen to sixty–they were away fighting for England from 1939."

Davis was engaged in combat action on Tarawa at 18, Saipan and Tinian at 19, and at Okinawa at 20 years of age. With the end of the war in September, Davis was home in Pittsburgh, Pennsylvania, in November 1945–still twenty years old.

Sheldon Gross landed on Iwo Jima on D-Day with the fifth wave on February 19, 1945 and participated in combat action there as a private with the 3rd Battalion, 25th Marines. He remained there till relieved on March 16.

Gross was eighteen years of age at the time of induction. He came through the draft board and volunteered for the Marine Corps. Not only was he a college freshman at the time, but was an only child and entitled to a number of postponements, all of which he waived.

At boot camp at Parris Island, South Carolina, he says that he was the only Jewish Marine in the platoon although most of the men were from the New York metro area. He befriended an Italian immigrant who spoke very limited English, the result of which he became "the target of the DI when he did not respond correctly. I taught him the general orders. During periodic inspections, I would stand behind him and feed him answers. The platoon was commended for being well prepared. The DI was happy."

During one session on bayonet instruction, the DI slapped Gross for not responding quickly enough. The other Marines in the platoon were incensed at that action and wanted Gross to report the incident. But Gross refused to do so. At the conclusion of boot camp, the DI said, "Gross, you'll never make a pimple on a combat Marine's ass, but you got guts and got us through inspection."

His MOS qualified him to attend radar school at Hadnot Point at Camp Lejeune, North Carolina. After thirty days of mess duty, he was assigned to a twelve months radio school program. One month later, he was reassigned to Tent City to receive training as a .30-caliber light machine gunner. Gross enjoyed the assignment because he only had to carry the eleven-pound tripod while the assistant gunner had to carry the weapon and ammo weighing considerably more. After an abbreviated period of instruction due to the enormous number of casualties being suffered in the Pacific, they eventually arrived at the port of embarkation. They sailed the Pacific without benefit of a convoy. Upon arrival at Maui, Gross learned that they needed machine gunners and was assigned to L Company, 3rd Battalion, 25th Marines, 4th Marine Division.

One day, while walking down the company street, an officer approached and put his hand on Gross's shoulder. It was Father Hurley, the Catholic chaplain, who asked him why he had not seen him at Catholic mass. When Gross informed him that he was Jewish, he informed Gross that he would be expected to introduce himself to Chaplain Rosenberg that Friday. Dutiful as the Marine that he was, Sheldon faithfully attended services every Friday thereafter.

With the approach of the High Holidays, they were all preparing for the invasion of Iwo Jima. The 25th Marines was scheduled to go into the field for an extended period of training. Gross asked Chaplain Rosenberg if he could return to attend services. Father Hurley arranged transportation for Gross and the other Jewish Marines to attend both Rosh Hashanah and Yom Kippur services. As it turned out, Chaplain Rosenberg "somehow on his own was able to commandeer a bus, took us all to the summit on Yom Kippur. 'No hot dog stand, no sushi bars, no water, no nothing.' All the Jews in the 25th Regiment FASTED."

It was at Zenana, on New Georgia, that Sergeant Maier Rothschild, New York City, was wounded and won the Navy Cross for gallantry in action. As he and his company crawled ashore, he and another Marine volunteered to attempt to repulse an enemy counterattack. Although they were both anti-aircraft gunners, they set up two light machine guns in such a position as to command a good view of the expected Japanese attack. About one hundred fifty Japanese attackers in four columns appeared through the jungle that lined the beach close to the water's edge. Rothschild and his buddy were pressed to see the camouflaged Japanese as they merged with the green jungle foliage. "They waited until the crawling forms were clear of their protective coverage. At one time they were not more than five yards away. Then, their targets in the clear, they swept the converging lines with a withering fire that accounted for ninety-six of the enemy."[1]

With the final charge of the enemy, his buddy was killed. The one Japanese survivor charged his position. Rothschild pressed the trigger, but the gun jammed. However, he managed to catch the charging soldier on his bayonet. The beachhead was saved and Sergeant Rothschild received the Navy Cross and the Purple Heart awarded for the wounds he sustained.

Former Staff Sergeant Joseph C. Leifer's tour of duty in the U.S. Marine Corps was not brief. Three and a half years to be exact. He enlisted during the middle of December 1941, shortly after the United States entered the war against Germany and Japan. However, due to the huge influx of new recruits at the time, he did not report for duty till February 16 of the following year: Boot camp could not handle the thousands that joined.

Completing boot camp at San Diego, he was shipped to Jacksonville, Florida, for AMM school. There, "he found one of us in every barracks or class." By "us," presumably he means us Jewish-Americans. In November 1942, he sailed for Samoa, attached to VMF 111, 1st Marine Air Wing, later the 13th, then the 4th. After ten months in Western Samoa, he became crew chief, then was transferred to Fina Futi, Ellice Islands, then to Nuka Fatai, northern tip of Ellice, then landed at Betio, Kawajalein, Marshall Islands. After being wounded during an air raid on February 12, he was shipped to Pearl Harbor, then back to the States to Great Lakes Hospital, then to Klamath Falls, Oregon, for six months.

[1]Blumenthal, L. Roy et al., *Fighting for America*, Bureau of War Records and the National Jewish Welfare Board, Washington, D.C., 1944, p. 35.

Completing his active duty at Glenview Air Station he took a COG instead of finishing regular service. On August 16, 1945, he completed three and a half years in the Marine Corps.

When Leifer says that "one of us has been in the Corps since it began," presumably he means that "us" is us Jews of those of "us" of his family. His wife's uncle, by the name of Schneider, was in the Marine Corps in the twenties and served in Nicaragua in 1927.

The subject of Jewish-Americans in the Marine Corps has been an educational topic of discussion with many people for over fifty years, with the assumption that Jews do not join the Corps. Hopefully, the story of Staff Sergeant Leifer and so many others like him will lay that half-truth to rest.

Harris Zimmerman enlisted in the Marine Corps as a private, completed boot camp at Parris Island, had some raider training at Camp Lejeune, then went to Officer Candidate School at Quantico, where he was commissioned a second lieutenant.

Boot camp proved to be a very positive experience. "Most boots were too busy hating the DI to have time to hate Jews. It was a great leveling experience. Your background was nothing. Everyone was treated the same."

Following his commissioning, he attended a number of air-craft engineering schools, and served as squadron adjutant while still a ground officer. Whereupon, he applied for and was accepted for flight training, received his wings as a naval aviator in the Marine Corps, and began to fly operational aircraft when the war ended. Following his graduation from flight school, he flew TBFs and SBDs. As squadron adjutant, he served in an SBD dive bomber group. He "was thrilled to be able to fly combat aircraft."

His most unpleasant experience was the time he received an unfavorable evaluation from a Jewish officer at OCS.

Other than flying anti-submarine patrols over the Atlantic,

he had no overseas duty. Harris Zimmerman was released to inactive duty as a first lieutenant and made captain shortly afterward.

His overall evaluation of the Marine Corps is expressed in the following comment: "In all ways I was proud to be a Marine—and still am."

George Bernstein described the one anti-Semitic incident which occurred during his five years in the Marine Corps. While he was training with the 2nd Battalion, 26th Marines, one trainee did not believe he was a Jew even after seeing George's dogtags with "J" on them. He even wanted to go to the office and check the records. After all, George was blond. When he confronted George, he said, "You don't look like Hochberg (another trainee with black hair, etc.)." This was the only time he was even asked.

Following boot camp at MCRD, San Diego, he continued his training at Camp Mathews and then Camp Eliot, California. Completing training at intelligence school, he was assigned to Headquarters Company, 2nd Battalion, 26th Marines, at Camp Pendleton, then in the process of forming the nucleus of the 5th Marine Division.

After departure from the States, they arrived in Honolulu. There, Bernstein had an accident aboard ship. He fell from nets on deck trying to help sailors below. He fell across a winch and broke three bones in his back. Hospitalized in Hilo, the doctor wanted him to stay behind, but George refused and returned to his unit. They sailed from Camp Tarawa to Iwo Jima, and landed on February 17, and remained till March 26, 1945.

With the end of the war, he was shipped to Sasebo, Japan. There, he was assigned to count torpedoes and bombs located in caves.

It was on Iwo that George came the closest to losing his life. There, he experienced the unenviable task of seeing many of his comrades lying dead, and the place where he experienced the most memorable occasion of his life—the view of the American flag flying over Suribachi.

Though he survived combat in the Pacific during World War II, and made staff sergeant, Bernard (Ben) Anolik wasn't able to defeat heart disease at the age of forty-four. With that, he became a candidate for a new heart. He received a new heart, and thus was the first transplant patient in Pennsylvania. He lived for fifteen months after surgery and passed away at the age of forty-seven.

His sister related that he "was very proud—always talked about his time in service." Ben married while in service and had seven children. Now there are fifteen grandchildren and two great-grandchildren. "He is sadly missed."

Ivan E. Perlman, now Cantor Ivan E. Perlman, enlisted in the Marine Corps at the age of seventeen. He says that "My life was to be dedicated to the cantorate and which I have now been for fifty-four years. My wartime service was the only desire I had for the military." For Cantor Perlman, war may be necessary, but hardly something to enjoy. "I hate war and guns. There are *no* winners. Only Gold Star mothers."

Despite his aversion to war, not only was he engaged in combat as a radio operator on Iwo Jima and Guam, but received the Bronze Star for heroism on Iwo Jima. He had the most unpleasant experience of "seeing the bodies of my comrades piled up before we could give them a decent burial." Not only was he proud to do his part for the war effort, but "I was proud that I had the ability to be a Marine."

Barney Neff, Marine Corps pilot, enlisted in the Navy in 1942, and got his gold wings as a Marine aviator. Initially, he served as a test pilot for dive bombers and fighter planes. During that time, he won boxing championships in both heavy and lightweight classes.

Later, he was transferred to the Pacific theater of war as a fighter pilot. After his discharge from active duty in 1946, he continued to fly in the USMCR as a fighter pilot with the rank of major.

William "Bill" Schaefer enlisted in the Marine Corps in Albany, New York, at the age of seventeen and a half. Even before entering the Corps, he had learned the art of survival. His mother died ten days after giving birth to Bill and his twin sister, leaving a total of thirteen children. At the age of sixteen, he was already self-supporting, after living in orphanages and foster homes.

Artillery School at Quantico, Virginia, followed boot camp at Parris Island. However, not satisfied with being behind the infantry and front lines, he requested duty with the infantry "where the real action was." His request granted, he was assigned to the 4th Marine Division on Saipan. From then on, he saw plenty of action on Iwo Jima where he was shot in the right shoulder and bayoneted in the leg.

He was there when they raised the flag on Mt. Suribachi. This was one of his most memorable experiences in the Marine Corps. Following his return to the States, he was assigned to military police duty at Portsmouth Naval Prison, Portsmouth, New Hampshire.

His awards include the Purple Heart, Presidential Unit Citation, and Navy Commendation Medal.

At boot camp, he found no anti-Semitism to speak of. It was "boot camp that made a man out of me," he says. He attributes much of his success to "being intensely interested in any work he is currently involved in."

While the sight of the American flag flying over Suribachi was his most memorable incident of his military career, the most unpleasant were those in "seeing many of my buddies getting killed on Iwo." Schaefer credits the Marine Corps for enabling him "to face up to all problems." All in all, "the military was a good experience. I would do it over again if I had to."

As with so many others, told and unsung, Ben Leffler is a stern reminder that Jewish-Americans can be courageous in battle and be proud to be both Jews and Americans. He trained as a boot at Parris Island, where, for three months the DIs focused on indoctrination and intimidation. For a bonus, they were physically assaulted, fed poor food, and given a diet of inadequate sleep. The treatment culminated in the issuance of dress blues and an order for a full dress "field day." Unbeknownst to the likes of Ben Leffler and other unwary boots, it was not a picnic. Not only was there nothing to eat, but the day's bill of fare consisted of cleaning heads and barracks with toothbrushes.

However, he made a number of friends who shared common experiences. They marched to mess together, stood at attention waiting their turn to march in, and stood at attention "like little ramrods until told to sit."

Boot camp was followed by a number of assignments: Quantico, Panama Canal on a heavy transport (USS *Antares*) from the China station, "A most miserable voyage on a ship which could not move more than five knots. So we stayed aboard and were seasick for what seemed like a month and HOT! We slept on the metal deck on a bedding roll of maybe one-quarter which had to be rolled up in the morning for fear we would nap and be comfortable."

Leffler went through most of the enlisted ranks: Pfc., corporal, sergeant, staff sergeant, master sergeant, then into the officer ranks as second lieutenant, first lieutenant, captain, and finally, major. He was commissioned in the field to second lieutenant and received the Bronze Star with combat V and the Presidential Unit Citation.

There's little question that service in the Marine Corps was a positive influence in the lives of many Jewish-American Marines. The fact is that duty in the Corps had a salutary effect on many of them. One of them was Leo Weiner, now deceased. His wife writes that "he was proud to be a Marine and continued being an active member of the 4th Marine Division until he died. The Marine Corps was a positive and everlasting influence in his life." Also, "Leo was proud to have been a Marine and always felt he was still a Marine and I know he truly loved the Corps and lived his life in a most honorable way."

Leo was born in Masury, Ohio, in 1924. He joined the Corps after graduating from high school in 1942. After completing boot camp on the east coast, he joined the 4th Marine Division at Camp Pendleton for further training before going overseas. In February 1944, now overseas, he saw action on Saipan, Tinian, and Iwo Jima. In 1946, he was discharged as a corporal.

Leo was very reticent of his combat experiences. He told his family very little of what transpired in the foxhole. Although he did tell his wife of a few war experiences, he preferred not to go into detail with their children. He and his wife made a return to Iwo Jima in 1984. At that time, "he was very emotional as the memories of that battle returned and he remembered his lost buddies."

He attended religious services while in the Corps and became friends with Jewish chaplain Rosenberg. Anti-Semitism was never a problem with him. As Mrs. Weiner said, "In all the years in the Association, I never personally experienced anything but true friendship from the members."

Mark Haiman can make at least two or three well-deserved claims to fame, not the least is having achieved the rank of colonel in the Marine Corps. Another is the fact that in the absence of a chaplain during the Desert Storm operation, he conducted Rosh Hashanah and Yom Kippur services for several dozen servicemen in Saudi Arabia and thus "sang the first Kol Nidre heard in that area since the Expulsion some one thousand three hundred years ago."

But his achievements don't end there. He has a whole list of them starting with his commissioning as a second lieutenant after graduation from Columbia University School of Law in 1964, following Officer Candidate School of twelve weeks.

Colonel Haiman's illustrious career in the Marine Corps encompasses every level of legal officer, trial counsel, defense counsel, military justice officer, and deputy staff judge advocate. He was an instructor at the Naval Justice School and a student at the graduate course of the U.S. Army Judge Advocate General's School. He completed Amphibious Warfare School and Command and Staff College. He has also been the Staff Judge Advocate of the 1st and 3rd Marine Divisions, of I and III MEF, and of FMFPac. Colonel Haiman was a special court-martial judge and the Circuit Judge of the Keystone and Sierra Circuits. Not content with playing different legal roles, he has served as a company commander, executive officer of the Infantry Training School, and as Chief of Staff, I MEF (R) in Saudi Arabia during Desert Shield and Desert Storm.

His overseas service included two tours in the Republic of Vietnam, one in Japan, two in Hawaii, four years on Okinawa and in Newport, Rhode Island, New York City, Charlottesville, Virginia, Camp Pendleton, California, and the Persian Gulf. Colonel Haiman's personal decorations include the Bronze Star Medal, Meritorious Service Medal, Navy Commendation Medal, Combat Action Ribbon, and various campaign service and theater decorations. "He has no tattoos."

Goldie Sockol Schwartz has nothing but good to say of her service in the Corps. "In the service or as a civilian, it's not what you know, it's who you know."

She moved up the ranks quickly to become acting sergeant. "I was always proud of the service and now I'm color guard in Jewish War Veterans, Post 266, Delray Beach, Florida."

She was the squad room captain, which meant that "I went around with the officers inspecting hair length, bunks, duffel bags, etc. Also, I had to assign orders for cleaning heads and I always told them I would be in the heads and showers to help. Of course, I never got the 'head' till I had to inspect the jobs. We all fooled around and I got along with everyone."

Once she was thrown out of her bunk. "That was a bigger joke than anything (mattress and all). Those were the days."

"I was drum majorette in my platoon. And everyone yelled, 'Everyone's out of step but Goldie.'"

"We had fun wherever we were."

"Those were the days. I have wonderful memories of the Marines."

Goldie Sockol Schwartz served in the Marines from 1944 to 1946. Her principal station after recruit training was at Henderson Hall, Arlington, Virginia. There weren't many Jewish girls in the Marine Corps—at least where she was stationed. Now (1999) she is a member of a color guard at Delray Beach, Florida. "I am very proud to be an ex-Marine."

When Don Niederman was inducted into the Marine Corps he felt that he "had two strikes against me" at the very outset. "Being Jewish and coming from New York, the southern rebels hated both factors."

During the usual rigorous boot camp of twelve weeks, one incident remains fixed in his mind: a Polish kid from Michigan tried to get him into the ring. Niederman finally agreed, and felt he was really in for it. However, Don landed a blow to his jaw and his opponent didn't even blink. "But God was with me. A whistle blew and we heard, 'Mail call.' Everything stopped. He said, 'We'll finish this later.' I said, 'Sure, sure,' but made myself scarce after that." They went overseas later. "I was a tough kid from a tough section of Brooklyn. I was determined to take everything they could dish out."

As the war was coming to a close, he was sent to China for occupation duty. They were replacements sent there after the campaign on Okinawa. They departed from Norfolk, Virginia, passed through the Panama Canal, stopped at Pearl Harbor and Guam, and finally to China–his first ocean voyage.

He spent ten months in China–first in Tientsin, then Peking. Following China duty, he was sent home and discharged at the Brooklyn Navy Yard. His awards include the World War II Victory Medal and the China Service Medal. He was trained in the use of the M-1 rifle, the carbine, and the water-cooled and the air-cooled machine gun.

While on liberty in Tientsin he witnessed an argument between a rickshaw coolie and another Chinese man. The latter called a policeman who took out his pistol and shot the coolie dead. Niederman says that "This underscores the low value put on human life in most countries as compared to the high value in the United States."

According to Niederman, "The decision to drop the atomic bomb on Japan hastened the end of the war. The plan was to invade Japan in November 1945, with an estimate of about two hundred thousand casualties."

Most of the people with whom Lorraine Cooper worked with from 1943 to 1945 were intelligent, clean cut, and nice "except for my immediate superior, WO Joseph J. Miller, whom I will never forget. He was the only anti-Semitic person I came in contact with and he made my life miserable."

Lorraine went to Quartermaster School at Camp Lejeune and then to Quantico where she worked in the transportation department for the duration. She served in the Marine Corps a total of twenty-seven months.

Since the chain of command in the military dominates most everyone's career, and "he (Miller) was my immediate superior, I was doomed to be a corporal for two years while everyone around me was promoted." She blesses the day that the war ended and she was discharged. She still keeps in touch with some of her buddies. "It was an interesting experience."

For Alvin Wolf, other than the worst heat he had ever put up with—105 to 120 in the shade—boot camp wasn't too bad. Otherwise, no complaints other than the thoughts of the Marines who thought of the horns on his head the anti-Semites thought he should have had. "The Marine Corps made a responsible man out of me and taught me to be fair and honest." He particularly admired the platoon sergeant who "took me from a boy to a man." Other than a few rednecks at Parris Island and at the base in San Diego, he liked everyone.

During the war, he served in Tinian, Marshall, Pearl Harbor, and at Peleliu.

After being discharged from the Marine Corps in December 1945, he stayed in the reserve and was called back into active duty for the Korean War. During that time, he served at the Naval Gun Factory and at Camp Lejeune, North Carolina. His highest rank was that of staff sergeant. His opinion of the military is that it "was a very good experience," and in spite of being passed over for reasons he attributes to anti-Semitism, if he had to do it again, he would. On balance, he was proud to have served in the Marine Corps. He felt that he was doing something important to help his country.

Milton Burg recounts that he was nearly killed twice. As an eighteen-year old Marine just off the troopship, he landed on Guam with the second wave. He was carrying a carbine and communications equipment. On the first night ashore, he got caught in an artillery duel between American and Japanese forces. Every time a shell landed, he got splattered with dirt.

They were very close, and he couldn't move.

The second time, his unit was in a small gully and were surprised in an early morning raid by the enemy. They couldn't pinpoint the location of the snipers. Burg was lying on the ground with three other Marines. Two of his group were shot by one of the snipers. The others got up and searched for better cover. They joined some other Marines when they saw three Japanese soldiers coming around a hill. They opened fire, and all three went down.

Milton Burg attributes some of his success in the Marine Corps to his experience as a young man in the Boy Scouts. He found camping of great benefit. When he was placed in charge of ten other Marines on the train, he believes that he had learned some of his leadership qualities as a member of the Scouts.

As with many others, he was proud to have served his country in the Marine Corps. The experience was a very positive one—"The best in the world. I volunteered to go to Japan with the occupation forces but was denied because I had too many months overseas. Would I do it again (very gung ho)? The experience in the Marine Corps made me a stand-up-and-be-counted guy—kinda worldly attitude."

Martin Flaum was the first man to enlist in Syracuse, New York, after the attack on Pearl Harbor. As a private first class in C Company, 1st Marine Raider Battalion, he was killed in action on July 3, 1943 at the age of twenty. His father saw action in World War I.

Erwin Novy completed boot camp after enlisting from Newark, New Jersey. Nothing unusual at Parris Island. The old marching at four in the morning, fleas biting and making things miserable for everyone. Then three months of "fun" at the rifle range. One incident marred an otherwise pleasant stay at PI. During the first month of training, one recruit couldn't take it and blew his head off.

Erwin Novy was doubly fortunate in that he "never had a problem with anti-Semitism at boot camp or school." He "liked everyone—no special people." He entered the Marine Corps precisely because he was a Jew, in order to do his part in the war effort. He landed on Tinian on D-Day. During his stay on the island, manning a .90 mm gun, he had the opportunity of watching B-29s come and go. Five crashed while landing and five crashed while taking off. They burned for five hours in the water.

A couple of other incidents did tarnish an otherwise great tour of duty. On one occasion, his day was ruined when he learned that a Marine committed suicide by hara-kiri, or seppuku. On another occasion, while on patrol, his partner came across a starving cat which he promptly shot. Unfortunately, this act of inhumanity cost him five days in the brig for wasting ammunition.

Wilbur Franks' boot camp was rife with anti-Semitism. He spent much time "warding off the bigots in the Corps who came from the southern states. By standing up to them and not hiding my religion was the only way to keep them from putting me down. On a few occasions, the boxing gloves was the way to keep them off my back. But I stood my ground."

Wilbur's high school buddy was in the Army stationed at Hickam Field, Hawaii, the day of the attack on Pearl Harbor on December 7, 1941. He was buried there. He and the senior chaplain at Pearl Harbor were able to locate his grave. There, at the grave site, Wilbur and his brother took pictures, and when they returned home after the war, they gave the photos to his parents. They were also on hand when his remains were returned home for re-interment.

Despite the living hells which he managed to survive, Stanley Ryback, Brooklyn, New York, said that "I was and still am proud I was a Marine. If I had to tell my son what branch of service to go into, it would be the Marine Corps." Even given all the battles in which he participated, he says that "If there was anything bad I would tell you about it."

Typical of the urbanized middle-class Jewish family in which he was raised, when he told his mother he "was going into the Marines, her first reaction was that she fainted." He grew up in a middle-class Irish and Italian neighborhood and when "I saw all my friends go into the Marines, I followed suit not knowing what to expect. I found out soon enough when I reached Parris Island."

Completing boot camp, Ryback underwent the usual precombat training and conditioning at Quantico, Pendleton, the 4th Marine Division, Oahu, then on to combat in the Marshall Islands, Saipan, Tinian, and lastly, Iwo Jima.

Ryback had little trouble as a Jew in the Marine Corps. "They all respected me for my ability to do my work well. The only thing they did was give me the nickname 'Abe.'"

Many things remain vivid in Ryback's memory including "the respect we received from the Navy and the way they treated us. I'll never forget going down the rope ladders into the small landing craft that transported us to the beaches."

Stanley Ryback survived, is proud of his service in the Marine Corps. He "celebrated the 50th anniversary of the Iwo Jima Memorial in Washington, D.C."

Ed Heffron trained at boot camp for twelve days. He completed basic training in Panama because the U.S. government thought that the Japanese were going to attack the Canal Zone. Part of their job was to board any vessel except U.S. naval ships. He speaks highly of his comrades. "I had a good squad. I made corporal. We were an elite group. Any invaders would have had a bad time."

Returning to the States from Panama, he attended Engineer Camouflage School and became an instructor in personal concealment, scouting, patrolling, and sniper techniques.

Shipped overseas once again, he spent a few months in Hawaii, then entered into combat on Okinawa with the 1st Separate Engineer Battalion, III Amphibious Corps. With the surrender of the Japanese forces, he was sent to China and stationed in Tientsin, North China. Of the many places he visited during military service, North China was the most unusual.

Ed had some valuable words of advice. He said, "The military is the military. You kept your nose clean. Do whatever you are told. The service was ten times better than a college education." Other memorable occasions consisted of "riding the aircraft carrier *Essex* through the Panama Canal on its way to operations in the Pacific, being caught up in a two hundred mph typhoon on Okinawa which left nothing but the clothing on his back, his poncho, helmet, and rifle." He had the unforgettable experience of seeing "Chesty" Puller, holder of four Navy Crosses, at Camp Lejeune.

According to Ed Heffron, the best people he knew in the military were "the Marines who gave their lives."

As a member of the 1st Separate Engineer Battalion on Okinawa, he received the Navy Commendation Medal, the Good Conduct Medal, China Service Medal, American Theater Medal,

Asiatic-Pacific Theater Medal, World War II Victory Medal, and the Navy Occupation Medal.

Even now he remembers kissing the dock on the way to receiving his honorable discharge, "I never forgot that I was a Marine." Thirty years ago (1969), he bought an M-1 rifle–not to shoot–just to see if he could still take it apart. "It's still hanging on the wall."

———————

Arnold Kaplan enlisted at the age of eighteen, completed boot camp at Parris Island, trained at Cherry Point, North Carolina and El Centro, California, prior to his assignment to VMB-433 as ground personnel. His squadron flew the Marine equivalent of B-25 twin-engine bombers, the PBJ. They participated in bombing operations against the enemy at Rabaul, Kavieng, Truk, and other sites in the Southwest Pacific. Kaplan was stationed at New Hebrides, Espiritu Santo, Emirau, and in the Philippines. His squadron was instrumental in the consolidation of the Northern Solomons, Bismarck Archipelago, and the securing of Mindanao in the Philippine Islands. Following discharge, he remained in the reserve as a member of VMF-313 at Floyd Bennet Field, Brooklyn.

Arnold Kaplan's Marine Corps experience formed the foundation of his adult life and career. It had a direct and important bearing as a man of family, faith, and in his profession as a lawyer. The Corps instilled in him much the same qualities as so many others: "confidence, self-reliance, pride in myself, appearance (I still keep my wallet in my sock, no wrinkles in suits or shirts), and an ability to get along with all types of people."

He particularly admired his drill instructors who "showed me a new view of life outside of Brooklyn, New York. They made me a *mensch*."

There were thousands more. They all held in common certain values and aspirations. They were all dedicated to the defense and perpetuation of their country, the maintenance of our democratic institutions and ideals, and, for the most part, to uphold not only the honor and prestige of their country, but their faith and their people. And if this meant sacrificing their lives in quest and support of those goals, so be it.

Those Jewish-Americans who chose, or choose, to serve in the Marine Corps, endured the same privations, successes, failures, and jubilations and share the same pride and purpose. They served in the thousands, joined in the thousands, in the same, or nearly the same proportion of the population as their non-Jewish comrades-in-arms. They are far too numerous to mention. Space permits the mention of only some.

———

Some such as David Yush, of Hartford, Connecticut. He enlisted in 1942, leaving behind his job as machine operator, only to die in a hail of fire from a Japanese pillbox on Kwajalein, in August 1944.

Louis Slep, East Haven, Connecticut, turned down the chance to join the Air Corps as a pilot to enlist in the Marine Corps. After two years of combat, he was cut down on Eniwetok in the Marshall Islands.

Herbert Wolf, White Plains, New York, received the Purple Heart after being badly wounded on Eniwetok.

Captain David Zeitlin, of Connecticut, received the Silver Star and commendation from Admiral Halsey. In action at Vella Vella, directing landing operations, he saw a landing ship explode, setting fire to the fuel and ammunition. Assessing the emergency and taking charge of the situation, he swam to the rescue of wounded men through burning oil on the surface of the water and, disregarding the Japanese fliers overhead strafing the area, he organized and led a party of volunteers to rescue wounded from the deck of the burning ship, and supervised their rescue despite the face that the ship was hit again by bombs.

Major Martin Rockmore, New York, was also awarded the Silver Star for leading his men in a series of dashing, heroic

exploits on Cape Gloucester. His award was given "for conspicuous gallantry and intrepidity in action against the enemy."

Another Silver Star was won by Pfc. Norman Cohen of the
Bronx, who enlisted the day after Pearl Harbor, and "made a
specialty of wiping out machine nests single-handedly at
Guadalcanal, Cape Gloucester, and New Britain. "The boys got
to calling him 'Jap killer.'"

And, on D-Day minus 2 for Saipan, First Lieutenant Leonard
Wollman saw the island for the first time. He got his first look as
an observer in a torpedo bomber operating from a carrier. He
flew over the island from dawn to dusk, returning to the carrier
only to refuel.

He observed the defenses, the fortifications, the emplacements of the big guns which the Japanese had captured from the
British at Singapore. Further inland, he noted other artillery positions and locations of tanks and troops.

From his observations, he made detailed notes that day and
the next. With D-Day, he was in the air once again, spotting for
the artillery, reporting to units on the ground on the hits that
were accurate, as well as those off target. In particular, he was
observing the airstrip on Aslito.

On D-Day, while returning from an observation over Aslito, a
Zero dove on Wollman's plane, and riddled it with machine gun
rounds. Whereupon, Wollman's plane began to fall. Despite prodigious efforts to prevent crashing, it began to fall.

Five hundred feet above ground, the plane burst into flames
and crashed into an ammo dump. Although the pilot was killed,
Wollman managed to survive. Though he lost consciousness, he
was rescued and treated immediately in an improvised first-aid
station on a landing craft. Both of his legs were broken.

The wish to be of service runs deep in the family of Melvin
Krulewitch. Following in the footsteps of his illustrious father,
Peter Krulewitch not only followed him into Columbia Univer-
sity, but into the Marine Corps as well.

Peter Krulewitch joined the Marine Corps while at Columbia

and entered the Platoon Leader Program at Quantico. While in college, however, he got married and turned down a commission. Nevertheless, he became an enlisted man, as was his father in the early days of his military career. Peter served five years in the reserve and was honorably discharged in 1965, "with the exalted rank of corporal, E-4." While in the Corps, Peter taught Morse code for a time due to his previous experience as a ham operator.

Peter Krulewitch relates the story of the Passover Seder on Maui in 1943. Melvin Krulewitch, Norm Gertz's commanding officer, was seated at the head table of the Passover Seder wearing a *yarmulke*. He had had no idea before that that he was Jewish.

As for Peter Krulewitch, when he was in boot camp, he did not experience any overt anti-Semitism. However, he remembers the only other Jew in his company—Pinsky, from West Virginia. "He was smart, but a screwup, and I remember one day, a particularly angry gunny sergeant screaming at him, 'Pinsky, I didn't know they had a garment district in West Virginia.'"

PART III

Potpourri

Chapter 3

One of Many . . . Good Men

Jews have always served our country in our armed forces. Considerably more in wartime, but far from total absence during times of peace. Fortunately, quality is still more important than quantity. If it weren't, the Jews would have disappeared a long time ago.

If Gunnery Sergeant Al Adler is an example of the proud and the few, the Marine Corps is in good hands, we are well defended and represented, we can cease to fret about our future, and the Jewish community has every reason to be proud of him.

It would be difficult to envision a career, or life, more varied, exciting, meaningful, and dedicated than that of Gunnery Sergeant Al Adler. Once publicized, his life should be the envy of every young American, rich or poor, Jew or gentile, black or white. His life reads like an excerpt from the life of Walter Mitty, replete with contradictions, vicissitudes, service, and achievement. His person and life are exactly those to whom our youth of today, especially our Jewish youth, should look up to for inspiration and emulation. Could there be a better role model?

The fact that there has been a Jewish Marine gunnery sergeant with twenty years of service in all parts of the world should raise a few eyebrows among those who persist in bellowing that there ain't no such thing. But there is indeed such a person, not unlike Sergeant Alan Soifert, killed while on a peacekeeping mission, and for whom there is a parade ground and chapel named for him at Camp Lejeune, North Carolina.

His life is a paradigm of God, Country, Corps, and family. As Jews live, or should live, by a code, so does Gunnery Sergeant Al Adler. And it can be synthesized into one word, Honor. Nothing can nor will be done to sully it.

Jews, too, are "The Few, the Proud." Adler has "always felt that this phrase is equally relevant to the Jewish people. What else do Jews and Marines have in common? Consider the following:

"Both hold themselves to a higher standard.
Both adhere to special rules which we do not impose on the rest of society.
Both groups have produced a disproportionately high number of high achievers.
It is not easy to be in either group.
Both groups require a lifetime of study.
Both groups believe in setting the example.
Jews call it *Ahavat Yisroel*. Marines call it camaraderie.
Both emphasize history and tradition.
Every Jew knows the *Shma*. Every Marine knows the Marine Hymn.
Both have been in every clime and place."

With this dual, if not triple, pride, of being a Jew, a Marine, and an American in mind, Al Adler finds it disconcerting, to say the least, to discern a negative attitude in Jewish-American parents vis-à-vis the military, and, in particular, to the Marine Corps. He finds very disappointing the general apathy of the Jewish community towards its armed forces.

"This was particularly evident to me during my tour as a recruiter from 1987–1990. In the area where I recruited there was a sizable Jewish population. Unfortunately, I did not see them joining the Marine Corps in numbers proportionate to their population in my area. Most of the parents of the Jewish youth would actively discourage their kids from joining the Marines if they were even considering it. The irony of this is that I think that being a Marine has more in common with being a Jew than any other religion. The Marine Corps used the recruiting slogan, 'The Few, the Proud.' I have always felt that this phrase is equally to the Jewish people."

Adhering to his mutual calling as a soldier and a Jew, Al Adler joined the Marine Corps in 1981 at the age of nineteen. Boot camp at Parris Island was challenging. The difficulty and challenge of boot camp, however, is that which distinguishes the Marine Corps from other services and is "ultimately the first source of pride that a Marine feels in his Corps."

Although Al Adler had to join another boot platoon after the first phase of training due to illness, his new DI, Staff Sergeant Burd, a recon Marine and Vietnam veteran, was a reassuring force. Once, "while standing at attention in front of his desk as he looked over my training record, he noted that I was Jewish. He asked me about being Jewish and then explained to me that a Jewish Marine had saved his life, and lost his, in Hue City, during the Tet offensive." Adler believes that he was the second Jewish Marine he had known. He made it clear to Adler that it was important "to him that I graduate and become a Marine. He provided me the proper motivation that got me through boot camp."

The rest is history. And a history that should be publicized wherever the military and honor are esteemed—or should be esteemed.

He trained at Fort Huachuca, Arizona, to be an interrogator, of prisoners of war, and learned Arabic at the Defense Language Institute, Monterey, California, attended recruiter school, MCRD, San Diego, California, and staff NCO school, El Toro, California, Attaché Staff Operations Course, Bolling Air Force Base, Washington, D.C., and Jr./Sr. Drug Abuse Training Course, Leesburg, Virginia.

His MOS 0251 is Interrogator/Translator and his secondary

MOS is 8411, Recruiter. He was stationed at Camp Lejeune with G-2, 2nd Marine Division, and the 26th Marine Amphibious Unit, recruiter in New Jersey, attached to Intelligence Company, 1st SRIG, Camp Pendleton,

Consolidated Substance Control Center, MCB, Camp Pendleton, Headquarters, Marine Corps, Washington, D.C. His last duty station was at Camp Lejeune, with the 2nd CI/Humint Co., 22nd MEU.

Oddly enough, although logical from the point of view that he was trained as an Arabic linguist, he was assigned to the Defense Attaché Office, U.S. Embassy, Cairo, Egypt, 1995–98. This was definitely his most memorable assignment. "The Defense Attaché Office is a joint assignment, so I worked with Defense issues, not just Marine Corps issues. Additionally, working in an embassy allowed me to view military matters in the Middle East from the strategic perspective not just the tactical and operational." He was there during some momentous times, including that of the Rabin assassination, the wave of terrorism that followed, the Sharm-el-Sheikh anti-terrorism conference, and the Netanyahu years. A few of the highlights of being in Egypt included "re-enlisting on top of Mount Sinai, and organizing the Marine Corps School of Advanced War Fighting battle study of the 1973 Sinai battlefield. Being in Egypt also afforded me the opportunity to drive to Israel on a regular basis." There are few people who can say that they have celebrated Passover by leaving the Nile Valley, crossing the Sinai, then entering Israel. Adler did that twice.

Before joining the Marine Corps, Adler spent a year in Israel after graduating from high school. He spent the year on a religious kibbutz. He remembers that "During that trip, I remember standing east of the Suez Canal and looking towards Egypt. I remember thinking of them as the 'enemy.' I often thought of that time during my tour in Egypt, especially when at Egyptian occasions commemorating the October 6, 1973 Suez Canal crossing."

His long and illustrious career in the Marine Corps has included a number of combat assignments. He participated in Operation El Dorado Canyon (the bombing of Libya), the Gulf War, 1990–91, and Operation Restore Hope in Somalia, 1992–93. During the Desert Shield phase, he was attached to ANGLICO, which was attached to the 2nd Saudi Arabian National Guard Brigade. His mission was to assist the Saudi National Guard in coordinating air and naval gunfire support with the Marine Corps. Once Desert Storm started, Adler's assignment was to interrogate Iraqi prisoners of war.

From the Jewish perspective, Adler notes that he "was involved with the Rosh Hashanah and Kol Nidre that was held by Colonel Haiman at the port of Jubail. We figured that this had to be the first Jewish service held on the Saudi Peninsula in several hundred years. At the end of the Gulf War, I returned to my family on *Erev Pesach*. I really felt that I was delivered from the desert into freedom at a most appropriate time. It is also interesting to note that the cease fire on Iraq was called that year on *Pesach*."

Gunnery Sergeant Al Adler is indeed rightfully proud of his career in the Marine Corps. Not unlike other careers, he notes that his, too, had had its ups and downs. However, "In the end I feel that I have served my country in the world's finest fighting force. This is a special pride. I have put the Marine Corps needs above my own. There have been many times when this was hard. There certainly have been times when you wonder if it's worth it. Ultimately, I feel that every American enjoys the fruits of American society because a certain breed of people serve, and are willing to put serving a higher cause above their own interests. I would not trade it." Also, "Being a Marine has profoundly affected my outlook on life. Education takes many forms and being a Marine is a constant education. I have a deep appreciation for how good life in the U.S. has been to me and my family. The United States is the best country in the history of the world. Most Americans don't realize how good we really have it. Many of the Americans who don't realize this have never had to sacrifice as

Marines do. They have pursued lucrative careers, higher education, and enjoyed family stability. Marines sacrifice these things every day so the rest of our society can enjoy them. I am proud of my service to it."

Gunnery Sergeant Al Adler retired from the Marine Corps after twenty years of service and is currently (2002) residing with his family in Florida.

Chapter 4

Barney Ross, Hero of Guadalcanal

On January 19, 1967, the *New York Times* featured an article on
the life and times of Barney Ross. The headline, "Ross, Ring
Champion and War Hero, Dies at 57." "Barney Ross, the former
lightweight and welterweight boxing champion, died today of
throat cancer at the age of 57 in his apartment on Lake Shore
Drive (Chicago)."

He was a hero in more than one way. As the world's boxing
champion in two categories, he conquered a vicious narcotics
habit acquired as a result of his wartime experiences. As a role
model for the younger generations, he was a true hero as a Marine on Guadalcanal.

Born Barnet David Rosofsky on the lower East Side of New
York, his father Isadore was a Talmudic scholar from Brest-Litovsk
in Russia. They moved to Chicago where the elder Rosofsky
opened a tiny grocery store on Jefferson Street. The family—
father, mother, five brothers and one sister—lived in two and
half rooms on the same street as their store.

Small and skinny, Ross concentrated on religious studies,
and didn't participate in sports. He wasn't even a fan of boxing.
"His father thought violence between humans was shameful."
When his father was shot to death by two hoodlums attempting to
rob the store, Mrs. Rosofsky suffered an emotional breakdown,

some of the children were sent to an orphanage, and Barney and an older brother, Morrie, were taken in by a cousin.

Bitter and angry, Barney dropped out of his religious studies and became a troublemaker. The *New York Times* (June 19, 1967) reported that "His brother and he began to take various jobs, hoping to support the rest of the family. He even went to Al Capone, seeking a job. Tough as he was an experienced in street fighting, he began boxing as an amateur. He was an immediate success, overpowering opponents with fury and recklessness rather than skill. He pawned the gold medals he won at $3 each."

And Barney Rosofsky soon became Barney Ross. Barney Ross certainly rolls off the tongue more easily than Barney Rosofsky. But the real reason for the change of name is a little more touching. He didn't want his mother to learn of his pugilistic aspirations. He knew that she would be violently against his fighting in the ring or anywhere else for that matter.

It was thus to his surprise that she actually became a big boxing fan. "Ross later recalled the 'Ma and her gang' marching en masse across the city got to be one of the strangest features of Chicago's sports life."

In 1932, he beat Tony Canzoneri for the world's lightweight title, and two years later, "he stepped up in class and upset the hard-hitting Jimmy McLarnin for the welterweight title." McLarnin won the title back later that year, and Ross regained it from him in 1935. He held the title until May 31, 1938, when he was defeated by Henry Armstrong who "gave him a savage beating over fifteen rounds." Shortly afterwards, after a few unsuccessful bouts, he retired at the age of twenty-eight years.

With the attack on Pearl Harbor, at the age of thirty-three, Barney Ross, now overaged for enlistment, got a waiver and joined the U.S. Marine Corps as a recruit. Refusing an assignment as a boxing instructor, he hit the beaches on Guadalcanal in 1942 as a member of the 2nd Marine Division.

There, on November 20, 1942, Ross and his detachment encountered an advance party of the enemy. Close combat ensued during which time the Japanese managed to inflict heavy casualties on his patrol. First tending to the wounded men in his patrol, Ross single-handedly began to attack the enemy. "The fighting lasted till the morning when help arrived. He had used up his ammunition and had to use what was left of the wounded. He received the Silver Star for his bravery." Even then, "on the way back, LeBlanc told me he was promoting me to corporal on the spot and would recommend me for a medal. 'Give the other boys the medal,' I said. 'I just want a bed.'"[1]

With B Company, 2nd Battalion, 8th Marine Regiment, 2nd Marine Division, his CO was Captain O. K. LeBlanc, a tough, but popular officer. They moved up into the jungle. His first night on the island was a nightmare. As he described the situation, "There were ten of us in my platoon and we all tied strings around our fingers and then connected it one to the other, so we would keep alert. We agreed if we saw one fellow starting to doze, we'd yank the string and wake him up." As they had received orders not to shoot unless the enemy opened fire first, they kept their bayonets at the ready. However, some of the young kids in the company were nervous, scared, and jittery, so much so that they began firing. Two Marines actually shot each other in the confusion.

When the Japanese attack began the next morning, they flung themselves at the Marine positions wave after wave, screaming. The Marines stood their ground and cut down the attackers. Once they started firing, they lost their nervousness and forgot about being scared. Ross said that "When I saw my first Marine buddy get a bullet in his head and fall over dead, I felt so sick I had to vomit on the spot. But after a couple of days, I got hardened to dead, rotting flesh and to the sight of young kids with their arms blown off."[2]

Ross, with the other young Marines, watched dogfights that took place over Guadalcanal. Marine Grummans had dogfight after dogfight with the Japanese Zeros and "as each Zero went down I kept score from my foxhole. In two days, I saw thirty-one

[1] Ross, Barney and Martin Abramson, *No Man Stands Alone, The True Story of Barney Ross*, J. B. Lippincott Co., 1967.

[2] Ibid., p. 191–92.

Jap planes out of the thirty-two that were shot down, and not one of their pilots bothered to bail out."[3]

Barney Ross experienced the worst and the most intense of combat action on Guadalcanal. In one night, the Japanese launched a combined land and sea attack designed to drive the Americans out of the island. They poured out of their positions screaming, "'Die, you dirty Yankees.' But we stopped them with mortars, machine guns, and grenades, and their dead piled up like so many hunks of meat in a butcher store. We held them off for four days, then our company got orders to move up." The Army had arrived and was supposed to start a counteroffensive. The Marines' mission was to spearhead the attack, push the Japanese back, and let the Army take over.

Nearing the end of his tour on Guadalcanal, Christmas Eve of 1942 "was a night nobody who was on the 'Canal will ever forget. Jap planes raided us that night and the music and the prayers of the Christmas mass were often drowned out by the explosion of their bombs—Marines of all faiths came to the service—those who could get away from the lines, anyway."[4]

With the end of the mass, the priest asked a blessing from "the God who looks down on all of us." When he called on Barney to say a few words, he said, "'I've been thinking about my mother, too,' I said, 'and I've got a favorite song I'd like to play and sing in her honor. It's called *A Yiddishe Mama*.'"

As he sang it first in Yiddish, the tears started to run down his cheeks. Then he sang it in English. However, he changed *My Yiddishe Mama* to *My Wonderful Mama* and "when I finished there were a lot of other wet Marine faces in the crowd."[5]

With New Year's Day, things were quiet and they had a mass burial for the dead. Ross stood with about two thousand Marines watching the chaplains of the three religions hold services at the cemetery. He stood "for a long time at the graves of Whitey, Freeman, and other pals I had in the company and I felt as if my heart would break.

[3] Ibid., p. 193.

[4] Ibid., p. 200.

[5] Op. cit.

"I tried to go back to the lines one more time, but I collapsed. The malaria was eating me alive. A few days later, an aid man came in with a message. 'Get your gear right away. You've been ordered to be evacuated.'"[6]

With thirty others, he was taken by plane to the island of Ifati in the New Hebrides. His wounds plus malaria made it impossible for him to walk on his own. He had to be carried to the plane on a stretcher. After a stay in New Zealand, he was returned to the States. Barney Ross's war was over.

His next battle was against the malaria he contracted on Guadalcanal. Becoming more and more dependent on morphine to ease his pain, he was discharged as a hero—and as a drug addict.

Thus began his next battle. After plunging from celebrity to a pitiful addict, scrounging syrettes of morphine from doctors, and a divorce, he went to the district supervisor for narcotics in New York and said that his name was Barney Ross. He informed them that he was an addict and wanted to turn himself in.

In 1966, it was found that he had throat cancer. Most of boxing's celebrities attended a benefit held for him at Sunnyside Gardens in Queens in November of that year. It wasn't much help. He died shortly afterward, a war hero, a role model for everyone, a champion, and a Marine.

---

[6] Ibid., p. 201.

Chapter 5

Abraham Lincoln Marovitz, True Grit

To many Jews, especially immigrants from Europe, or the children of immigrants, the wish to serve their country was a highly motivating factor in their wish to join the armed forces. This was as much as in the Civil War right up to the Second World War. Judge Abe Marovitz said, "My parents taught me through their words and actions that we had a responsibility as American citizens to live honorable lives and help others as much as we were able."[1] The need to serve his country was so strong that in 1943 he set aside his profession as lawyer and state senator to enlist in the Marine Corps. His words were that "The legal profession had been very good to me. I had earned a nice living as a criminal defense lawyer and coming from an immigrant family and rising from poverty, I felt it only right to enlist."[2]

Abraham Lincoln Marovitz was born in Oshkosh, Wisconsin, in 1905, the son of Rachel and Joseph Marovitz, both immigrants, Rachel from Lithuania and her husband from Czarist Russia. She was so inspired by the words of Abraham Lincoln during her studies for citizenship that she named her son after him. The speeches, writing, and deeds of Lincoln "have given generations of Americans insights into the philosophies of a man who believed totally in equality and the greatness of the United States and its people."[3] Rachel

---

[1] Humble Beginnings, *Leatherneck* Magazine, Washington, D.C., May, 1991, p. 40.

[2] Op. cit.

[3] Op. cit.

Marovitz wished to carry on these aspirations in the person of her son to be born in the country of the man who saved the republic and freed the slaves.

In 1991, Senior Federal Judge Abraham Marovitz of Chicago, at the age of eighty-six said, "I come from humble beginnings. My father worked hard, yet he was not so fortunate in financial success. But he and my mother taught us through their words and actions that we had a responsibility as American citizens to live honorable lives and help others as much as we were able."[4]

At the time, living an honorable life and helping others as much as he could meant not only joining the armed forces, but enlisting in the service where he knew the action would be certain and heated, the U.S. Marine Corps. "The Marine Corps was an obvious choice for Abe Marovitz. With its traditions of honor, integrity, bravery, and his long-held beliefs in the American way."[5]

The need to serve was instilled in him by his parents, "who were immensely proud of American citizenship. The work ethic of his father also helped him decide there was nothing wrong with starting from ground up." Thus, he passed up the opportunity to be an officer. As a college graduate, lawyer, and a state senator, he could have received a commission very quickly.

Despite being slight of build, the Jewish kid from the Chicago ghetto had been a boxer. This was his way of earning extra cash while working as an office boy in the law firm of Mayer, Mayer, Austrian, and Platt. When one of the partners, Mr. Austrian, saw his face after one fight, he encouraged Kid Marovitz to forget about pugilism and enroll in night school at Kent College of Law. But the daunting tuition of a hundred and twenty dollars discouraged him from enrolling until Mr. Austrian offered "to raise my salary and he would finance my education while deducting the tuition from my pay. I don't think he ever took a cent back from me, though."[6] Graduating from law school in 1925 at

---

[4] Op. cit.

[5] Op. cit.

[6] Op. cit.

the age of nineteen proved to be a bit of a problem—he had to be twenty-one to practice law in Illinois. So he worked for Mr. Austrian until he passed the Bar exam.

In turn, Abe practiced law as an assistant prosecutor, later as a successful defense attorney in private practice.

With the onset of World War II, service to his country beckoned in defense of the adopted land of his parents. Abe Marovitz's journey to the Marine Corps was hastened by "his sense of integrity and a desire to return to his nation some of the good it had bestowed upon his family."[7]

"Both of my parents were extremely proud to have earned American citizenship. They always reminded us to appreciate our citizenship in America, a nation my father was convinced was the greatest on earth . . . I wanted to serve my country in the Second World War though I was thirty-eight years old."[8]

He managed to pull a string or two to get into the Marine Corps. When he took his physical, he was rejected because of color blindness. Unfazed by this temporary setback, he found a way to get in: "A psychiatrist friend of mine said he knew the doctor giving the military physical and offered to talk to him for me. So a few days later, I called this doctor and he told me to come down for another physical. He said my sight may have improved since last we met."[9]

At boot camp with recruits half his age, he kept up with those young lads. "I even finished fifteenth out of thirty-four when we went through the obstacle course. Some of them couldn't believe an old guy like me could do it."[10]

Despite his pleas for overseas duty, he was turned down twice. But his influence or the vast network of friends of Abe Marovitz again prevailed. One of Abe's friends at the time was Adlai Stevenson, then the Secretary of the Navy. When his CO learned of his plight, Marovitz said: "He told me that he would see about orders to the Pacific." Not long afterward, he and his command-

[7] Ibid., p. 42.

[8] Op. cit.

[9] Op. cit.

[10] Op. cit.

ing officer were on their way to Marine Aircraft Group 24 in the Philippines.

Marovitz was wounded, but refused to wear the Purple Heart. He felt unworthy to do so given that, in his words, so many others were injured far more seriously than he. "I saw Marines and soldiers who were wounded much worse than I had been," he said. "I couldn't convince myself to wear the same medal that those men had earned." At his discharge in 1946, he was a sergeant-major and had received shrapnel wounds during a Japanese artillery attack.

"One of the most important things the judge does that makes a difference is to swear in new American citizens . . . Where else could the son of Jewish immigrants rise from poverty to serve as a federal judge?"[11]

When Judge Marovitz thinks about the new breed of young Marines serving throughout the world, he hopes that they reflect upon the meaning of their motto, Semper Fidelis.

To him, it is an important symbol. He said, "To me, it means to be always faithful to our Marine Corps, but also to our family and friends. And especially to be faithful to this great nation of ours and its future generations. America is as my mother and father believed, the greatest nation in the world."[12]

11 Ibid., p. 43.
12 Op. cit.

Chapter 6

The Real Rosenbergs

Not only did the Leavitt brothers (I and my younger brother Ed) go into the Marine Corps from Brookline, but so did two-thirds of the Rosenberg brothers, our next-door neighbors.

Where the Rosenbergs' middle brother went wrong, we'll never know. He went into the U.S. Army.

The oldest of three brothers, Elliot Rosenberg, graduated from Harvard and joined the Marine Corps. He eventually became a platoon commander of Marines at Tarawa and other Pacific islands. He was seriously wounded, decorated, and departed from active duty as a captain.

One day in 1944, while my dad and I were taking a walk in our Brookline neighborhood, a husky, well-built man about five feet nine or ten, in green uniform, Sam Browne belt and all, with a few campaign ribbons, approached us. We stopped, and my father said, in so many words, "I see you are in the Army." I interrupted with, "No, Dad, he's in the Marines." He was wearing the bars of a first lieutenant or captain—I don't recall which. He had just returned from the Pacific. I believe he had recently fought on Tarawa. That happened to be Elliot Rosenberg.

The middle brother, Donald, went into the Army. Soon, he, too, was caught up in the thick of World War II, fighting the Germans in France and Germany.

With the outbreak of the Korean War, Ed, the youngest brother, with a mutual friend, went to the Air Force recruiting office and tried to sign up for pilot training. His friend found out that he was colorblind, and thus disqualified from flight training. Ed followed him out, unwilling to break up the bond that they had formed.

Instead, he followed in the footsteps of his oldest brother and joined the Marine Corps Platoon Leaders Class in 1951 while attending Northeastern University in Boston.

I even had the opportunity of seeing him that summer at Parris Island. Ed was commissioned a second lieutenant shortly after graduation in 1952. In early 1953, he completed the 16th Special Basic Class at Quantico and joined the 3rd Marines, 3rd Marine Division. Upon reporting for duty at Camp Pendleton, it was learned that Ed had been an economics major and since battalion staff officers were in short supply, he became both an S-4 (staff logistics officer) and supply officer.

Ed was eventually sent to Korea where he joined the 1st Battalion, 1st Marines and once again found the unit short on staff officers. The result, due to their knowledge of his previous staff experience, he was given a staff position instead of an infantry platoon command.

His Korean tour of duty ended in 1954, and he was transferred from the 1st Marine Division to return home for assignment to inactive duty. He was almost convinced, however, to remain on active duty as a captain, but he had other plans and returned to civilian life.

Elliot, Donald, and Ed Rosenberg—one soldier and two Marine officers—all successes, all Americans, all veterans.

Chapter 7

The Zimmermanns, A Study in Versatility

Colonel Jack B. Zimmermann's background is similar to that of my brother, Ed Leavitt: both graduated from the U.S. Naval Academy (USNA), went into the Marine Corps after graduation, served in Vietnam, achieved the rank of colonel, became interested in the law while in the military, attended law school while on active duty, served an almost identical length of military service—and the two became successful attorneys.

A native of San Antonio who currently resides (2001) in Houston, Zimmermann was commissioned as a second lieutenant upon his graduation from USNA in June 1964. Having completed the Basic School and Artillery Officer Orientation Course, he saw combat in Vietnam in 1965 as a forward observer with Battery G, 3rd Battalion, 12th Marines, and was attached to C Company, 1st Battalion, 4th Marines. In 1966, he served as Fire Direction Officer of Battery W, 3rd Battalion, and 12th Marines, also in Vietnam.

Returning to the United States after his first Vietnam tour of duty, First Lieutenant Zimmermann was assigned to the Joint Service Defense Atomic Support Agency at Sandia Base, Albuquerque, New Mexico. He served as course supervisor and platform instructor in several courses dealing with nuclear physics and nuclear weapons emergency-team operations.

In July 1968, Captain Zimmermann returned to Vietnam to assume command of Headquarters Battery, 1ˢᵗ Battalion, 13ᵗʰ Marines. He then commanded Battery K, 4ᵗʰ Battalion, 12ᵗʰ Marines, along the demilitarized zone. It was during this tour that he was awarded two Bronze Star Medals with Combat V for heroism and the Purple Heart for wounds sustained. His staff tour was as a member of the Marine Corps Wound Data and Munitions Effectiveness Team, studying combat casualties and equipment.

After receiving a Master of Science degree in Management at Purdue University (Indiana), he reported to Headquarters, Marine Corps, for duty in G-1, with responsibility for enlisted recruiting standards and the all-volunteer force. From 1972–75, Major Zimmermann attended law school at the University of Texas at Austin, under the Excess Leave Program. He graduated with a Doctor of Jurisprudence degree. During this time, he served as the assistant inspector-instructor, Company B, 1ˢᵗ Battalion, 23ʳᵈ Marines.

After graduating from the Naval Justice School at Newport in October 1975, Major Zimmermann was assigned as chief defense counsel, Force Troops Atlantic, Camp Lejeune. In June 1967, he was transferred to the 2ⁿᵈ Marine Division to serve as chief prosecutor and military justice officer. He resigned his regular commission in July 1978 to enter the private practice of trial law in Houston.

Upon leaving the regular service, he accepted his commission in the Marine Corps Reserve, serving from September 1978 to February 1981 as executive officer, 1ˢᵗ Battalion, 23ʳᵈ Marines, including duty in Norway during Operation Teamwork 80. From March 1981 to February 1982, Lieutenant Colonel Zimmermann served as S-3 of an MTU (Mobilization Training Unit) in Houston. From March 1982 to November 1983, he was executive officer of Headquarters Detachment 6, 4ᵗʰ Marine Division.

On December 1, 1983, Lieutenant Colonel Zimmermann assumed command of the 1ˢᵗ Battalion, 23ʳᵈ Marines, a Reserve infantry battalion, and served in that capacity during annual training duty at Pohakuloa, Hawaii, in 1984 and at Camp Ripley, Minnesota, in 1985.

On October 1, 1988, he was promoted to the rank of colonel. He subsequently served with MTU TX-5 in Houston and as staff judge advocate of the 4th MAW in New Orleans; Deputy Chief Defense of the Marine Corps in Washington, D.C.; and assumed command of Headquarters Detachment 6, 4th Marine Division, with responsibility for inspecting the mobilization readiness of Marine Reserve ground units throughout the country. His last duties were as group inspector for the 4th Force Service Support Group in Atlanta, Georgia, and as

Reserve general court-martial trial judge in the Navy-Marine Corps Trial Judiciary, presiding at trials in the Marine Corps and Navy when assigned to active duty at Camp Lejeune and NAS, Pensacola.

Colonel Zimmermann spent fourteen years in the active military and sixteen in the Reserve. At the retirement ceremony from the Reserve in Houston, he was honored with a parade consisting of an infantry battalion and a detachment. The keynote speaker was a three-star general. Unbeknownst to Colonel Zimmermann, his wife had contacted two enlisted men who had figured prominently during his tours in Vietnam: a Marine corporal and a medical corpsman, one from each tour. Both presented moving comments at the ceremony. The entire battalion with detachment passed in review of the colonel who had previously commanded both units.

In addition to his Bronze Star Medals and Purple Heart, Colonel Zimmermann received the Meritorious Service Medal, the Joint Service Commendation Medal, the Navy Commendation Medal with Combat V, the Combat Action Ribbon, the Presidential Unit Citation, two Meritorious Unit Commendations, and various service awards.

Following in the footsteps of her father, Colonel Jack B. Zimmermann, Major Terri R. Z. Jacobs of Houston graduated from the University of Texas at Austin in May 1989 with a bachelor of arts in government. In August of that year, she signed a Platoon Leaders Class (Law) contract and attended Georgetown University Law Center. She was commissioned a second lieutenant in August 1990 after completing OCS at Quantico. Of four women law student candidates, only one graduated: Terri. After graduation from law school in May 1992, First Lieutenant Jacobs passed the Maryland Bar exam and worked at a private law firm in Washington, D.C. until she entered the Basic School at Quantico in January 1993. She graduated with B Company in July 1993 and was transferred to MCAS, El Toro. Upon completing Naval Justice School, she became the civil law and review officer at the Joint Law Center. She performed these duties for nearly a year, and, after her promotion to captain on September 1, 1994, she moved to the prosecution section. Captain Jacobs was a trial counsel until she completed her active duty service in July 1996.

In August 1996, as a Reservist, she assumed the responsibilities of appellate defense counsel at the Navy-Marine Corps Appellate Review Board and currently performs these duties. As of May 1999, she was promoted to major. She currently practices law in Houston, and is the mother of Courtney and Benjamin.

Recruited by the Naval Academy as a football player, David Zimmermann, son of Colonel Jack B. Zimmermann, graduated in May 1992, elected service in the Marine Corps, and received a regular commission as a second lieutenant. In addition to his other honors, he was president of the Jewish Midshipmen's Club in his senior year at USNA. He was selected as a Marine Corps flight officer at graduation, completed the Basic School at Quantico in March 1993, and as a first lieutenant earned his wings from flight school at NAS, Pensacola.

In August 1993, he reported to MCAS, El Toro, designated as a weapons sensor officer on an F/A-18D fighter attack aircraft, and was promoted to captain in September 1996. He departed active duty in January 1997 to work as operations support officer for United Space Alliance, with an eye to the possibility of a flight-control position for future international space stations with NASA (National Aeronautics and Space Administration).

He then entered the FBI Academy at Quantico, received his credentials and badge as special agent in April, 1999, and reported to his first duty station with the FBI a month later in Oklahoma City, Oklahoma. He is the father of Melanie and Daniel.

David was the lay leader at Jewish services held at MCAS, El Toro. At the Naval Academy, he and his sister both attended Jewish services Friday evenings. It so happened that Rabbi Albert Slomovitz was the Jewish chaplain at the Academy. It is also ironic that Terri's husband Garrett proposed to her one evening at services. The rabbi then flew to Houston and officiated at Terri and Garret's wedding. In addition, Rabbi Slomovitz co-officiated by proxy at David and Sherri's wedding—a first for the temple, where they were married in a full-dress Marine military wedding on June 13, 1992, featuring an arch of swords. Coincidentally, Colonel Jack Zimmermann and his wife Ilene were married in an identical Marine Corps ceremony on the same day—June 13—in 1964.

Chapter 8

Band of Brothers

Although stories of anti-Semitic incidents abound among many Jewish-American Marines, there are not a few which illustrate just the opposite. A number of non-Jews indicated that some of their best friends, or acquaintances, were Jewish Marines whom they knew in the service. They held them in high regard. Ralph Butler, Wickliffe, Ohio, said that this inquiry of Jews who served in the Marine Corps "brought back memories of the fellow who I teamed up with the second morning on Tarawa."

They were both in the machine gun section of K Company, 3rd Battalion, 2nd Marines, but in different squads. As everyone was scattered and separated when the first wave of Amtracs hit the beach on D-Day, "this Marine and myself hooked up together on the second morning with a .30 cal machine gun and ammo.

"His last name was Horwitz, and he was one hell of a fighting Marine. I was his assistant gunner for this period of time, and he earned my respect. Forever."

H. R. Mitchell, University, Mississippi, actually sent an audio tape in which he recorded the story of one of his lieutenants, an Ira Goldberg, whom he admired very much and who was killed in action in the Pacific.

Mr. Mitchell, who described himself as eighty years old, does not write much these days, does not type, has no computer, but does read a lot. His narration demonstrates a well-educated man who is very articulate. He read my notice in the *Spearhead,* of the 5ᵗʰ Marine Division Association and wanted to convey the admiration he held for 2ⁿᵈ or 1ˢᵗ Lieutenant Ira Goldberg.

Goldberg was the Gas Officer for the 27ᵗʰ Marines, attached to Headquarters Company, 2ⁿᵈ Battalion, 27ᵗʰ Marines. Mitchell was a corporal in the same unit. Mitchell knew him from seeing him frequently. He was struck by the fact that Goldberg was good looking, personable, and knowledgeable.

Shortly before his death, the unit had suffered many casualties. As a result, Lt. Goldberg was reassigned as a platoon leader, a task in which he had no recent experience. He was ordered to return to the lines the next day.

The next time that Mitchell saw him, Goldberg was returning from the front on a stretcher en route to the beach. Mitchell recalls that Goldberg had a serene look on his face. While confronting the enemy, Goldberg was shot while leading a charge. As Mitchell said, "He did his duty and well," for which he subsequently received the Silver Star Medal.

Bob Brooks, Montana, also of the 2ⁿᵈ Marine Division, reported on two Jewish-Americans of his Company G, 3ʳᵈ Battalion, 28ᵗʰ Marines. He sent what has to be one of his treasured mementos—a large photograph of his entire company that was taken prior to the landing on Iwo Jima. He specifically mentioned in very complimentary language two sergeants, Top Sergeant Sam Winer, a pre-war veteran of China, and Sergeant Werner Heumann. He singled out Sergeant Heumann as one of the most courageous and loyal men of his company.

Howard Fuller, retired master sergeant, Riverside, California, spoke highly of "the only Marine that I can recall who was Jewish . . . Abraham A. Leon. We, who had the pleasure of knowing him always with affection called him 'Abe.'" Later, he was to recall other men of his squadron of the Jewish faith, including Captain (later Major) Al Clark, torpedo bomber pilot.

Insofar as concerned Abe Leon, "He joined VMSB-131,

Marine Scout Bombing Squadron in December 1941, shortly after we had moved from Brown Field at Quantico, Virginia, to the Naval Air Station at North Island, San Diego. His MOS was that of radio-gunner.

"He remained with the squadron and we departed for Hawaii in September in 1942, then we transitioned from a scout bomb squadron to become the first Marine Torpedo Squadron, being equipped with the TBF (Avenger) aircraft. Six weeks later we were at Henderson Field. Later, on Guadalcanal, Abe flew many combat missions during our eight months stay."

A lady from Neosho, Missouri, called to speak of a Jewish buddy of her late husband who served in the 2nd Marine Division. She was unable to remember his name, but was anxious to convey the message that her husband thought very highly of this man and wanted to be sure to remind everyone that "there was at least one gentile man who had such a friend in the Marine Corps."

Kingston Jones, Fort Myers, Florida, was a Marine who served on Saipan from 1944 to 1945, having arrived there with the 41st Replacement Draft. He was a "quite new second lieutenant." "Our first sergeant was named Feldman and popularly and customarily referred to as 'Top,' of course. Feldman reportedly had already served twenty-eight years. He was especially helpful to all of us who were young officers, particularly in familiarizing us with unwritten protocol and established routine—matters generally not a part of instruction that made for good and effective relationships."

Feldman taught Lieutenant Jones "to refrain from and avoid duties which my platoon sergeant would expect to perform. Feldman was our man on-the-job instructor in the crucial business of working with and relying upon NCOs. I was indebted to First Sergeant Feldman."

In addition to Werner Heumann, Bob Brooks speak highly of Sam Winer, first sergeant of G Company, 3rd Battalion, 26th Marines. In his letter, he said, "I have tried to summarize my feelings about two Marines of the Jewish faith. Both individuals were, in my opinion, outstanding Marines."

Werner Heumann was squad leader, 1ˢᵗ squad, 3ʳᵈ platoon. Before they were disbanded, he served as a Marine Raider behind Japanese lines on Guadalcanal for about thirty days. When they were disbanded, he joined G Company as leader of the 1ˢᵗ squad, 3ʳᵈ platoon. Although there was some resentment about him being from a big city, "Huey" was a dedicated and hard leader. However, that resentment disappeared as the Marines realized that his interest lay in preparing them for combat.

When G Company landed on Iwo with the ninth or eleventh wave, Heumann was instrumental in getting them off the beach. "He showed no fear of incoming artillery, mortar, or small arms fire." On D plus 1, their platoon advanced several hundred yards ahead of the main line with little or no resistance. When their platoon leader panicked under heavy enemy fire, he called upon Sergeant Heumann and asked him what they should do. When Huey responded, most of the men got back safely to the main line. On D + 2, after dark, the platoon was ordered to fill a gap in their lines. Under heavy enemy fire, Sergeant Heumann was severely wounded. Until he was evacuated, he continued to direct the squad.

Bob Brooks stated that "Sergeant Heumann was the best Marine that I served under and with during my time in the Marine Corps."

Sam Winer was first sergeant of G Company, 3ʳᵈ Battalion, 28ᵗʰ Marines. Prior to the war, he had served in China with the 4ᵗʰ Marines.

He "was as far and honest as any staff NCO I served under. Once the Iwo operation was concluded, a CS (chickenshit) gunnery sergeant joined our company." According to Brooks, he made a rather large number of irrational judgments. However, "the 'Top' interceded in the stupid decisions the gunny made. In my case, he twice overruled the gunny and saved my rear end from unwarranted discipline. All in all, a great Marine."

Other Marines wax enthusiastic over the professional and personal qualities of their comrades of the flock of Abraham. Lt. Colonel Tom W. Jones (now deceased) of Wisconsin wrote that a book on Marines of the Jewish faith "would not be complete without the biography of Colonel Arthur Friedman, USMC. I served with him as enlisted and as a Mustang, and there was none better."

Don Mollica, Fairport, New York, requested a copy of the manuscript to be sent to Marty Sucoff, with whom they "served together in the Pacific during WW2 and they were both wounded on Okinawa."

Lloyd Evans, officer in the 9,000 Badge of Honor Association USA-Taiwan Vets, wrote that "for years I have been seeking my two best boot camp friends, Barry Bond and Phil Stock. Both of these men are Jewish and like myself came out of the 'NYC experience.' They were members of Plt 407, PI, December 1956."

"Red" Kelly apologized for having forgotten to mention his good friend, Dick Jessor. Jessor, of New York City, now at the Institute of Behavioral Science, University of Chicago, has amassed an amazing record of accomplishment in a number of fields: He has written four books, climbed very high mountains of the world, and still runs the New York Marathon every October.

Jessor was a replacement after Saipan-Tinian to Kelly's tent and on his OP team. A sophomore at Yale prior to enlisting in the Corps, he returned after the war for his B.A., then his M.A. at Columbia, finally his Ph.D. at Ohio State.

And Lieutenant Ira Goldberg, previously cited by H. R. Mitchell, was also the focus of Howard Baxter's (California) praise. He wrote that "Right from the beginning, Lt. Goldberg began to inspire us by his example of leadership. Not by shouting or cussing at us, or pushing us forward, but by quietly, in an assured manner–*leading* us in the advance toward the enemy. Always at the head of the advance, *never* behind. He inspired a decimated Marine platoon . . . by example."

Baxter also cites Sgt. Murray Gold, machine gun section leader, killed in the recapture of the capital city of Korea, Seoul.

In a letter to the surviving members of the family of Lieutenant Leonard Sokol, James Buchanan, Ontario, California, says that "Most heroes die," and he proceeds to explain the circumstances under which the lieutenant met his death.

Lieutenant Sokol was the commander of a Marine combat company on Iwo Jima, in which Buchanan was a private first class and a runner for the company while at Pendleton. After the landing at Iwo, they fought their way to a final line near Kitano Point, the northernmost end. While there, Buchanan "got word that our lieutenant had been killed . . . for some reason I had to find out where and why."

After landing on Iwo, Sokol changed "from the quiet, reserved man to one with determination. 'You wouldn't believe, he was a tiger,' one observer said." As it happened, their company, Easy, had the "probable distinction of having the only Marine taken prisoner on Iwo. On March 3, Private Ralph Ignatowski was somehow dragged into a cave within a small canyon. What I tell you next is what I heard but did not see. He may have tried to rescue Ignatowski, but I don't know for sure."

"I walked into the canyon and found Lieutenant Sokol on a road, Ralph Ignatowski close behind. An officer approached me and said, 'Don't touch them. We may have an atrocity here.' I understand Ralph had been bayoneted numerous times; some punctures bled, some did not."

Buchanan continues, saying that "Leonard suffers no more, only his friends and relatives weep. Death is a wonderful release. He is missed."

John Bradley, one of the six Iwo Jima flag raisers, recalled the incident: (from Bradley, James, "Flags Of Our Fathers," Bantam Books, Division of Random House, 1540 Broadway, New York, New York, 10036, May 2000, p. 344-345)

"He said: 'I have tried so hard to black this out. To forget it. We could choose a buddy to go in with. My buddy was a guy from Milwaukee. We were pinned down in one area. Someone elsewhere fell injured and I ran to help out, and when I came back my buddy was gone. I couldn't figure out where he was. I could see all around, but he wasn't there. And nobody knew where he was.

"A few days later someone yelled that they'd found him. They called me over because I was a corpsman. The Japanese had pulled underground and tortured him. His fingernails . . . his tongue . . . It was terrible. I've tried to hard to forget all this."

"Many years later, in researching my father's life, I asked Cliff Langley, Doc's co-corpsman, about the discovery of Iggy's body. Langley told me it looked to him as though Ralph Ignatowski had endured just about every variety of physical cruelty imaginable.

"'Both his arms were fractured,' Langley said. 'They just hung there there like arms on a broken doll. He had been bayoneted repeatedly. The back of his head had been smashed in.'"

Just before Buchanan departed Iwo Jima, he attended services at the 5th Marine Division Cemetery at the base of Mt. Suribachi. He said, "As I looked at the grave markers one stood out in contrast . . . the Star of David above Lt. Leonard Sokol's body . . . My father's grandfather was a Jew and I felt proud to have some of that blood in my veins at that moment and to this day."

Thus, that hero died probably in a vain attempt to save the life of a fellow Marine. "Leonard was probably deserving of a posthumous award, but evidently no officers were present to see his outstanding bravery. It was a pleasure to have known him and he is a true hero in my book."

The comments made by gentile Marines about their Jewish comrades-in-arms were, with one exception, very favorable and complimentary: the exception being from a crank in northern California who badmouthed just about everybody, but especially the Jews and Jewish Marines, at that.

George H. Ward, a Mustang, of Soquel, California, was not that exception. He had some rather interesting observations about Jewish-Americans whom he had known while in the military. In fact, he made the same comment that Phil Laden made about there being 17,000 Marines in the world, and 18,000 policemen in New York City in 1937. However, in contrast to Laden, Ward seems to believe that there were more than two Jewish-Americans in the Marine Corps.

He says, "There were about seventy of us at the barracks at Washington Navy Yard. A Jewish Marine from New York named Alpert was one of the most likable, moochingest people I've ever met.

"Alpert would blithely take off for the Jewish holidays, then wanted leave for Christmas as well. As I say though, the guy was so damned likable you couldn't hold it against him."

He also made the acquaintance of Gunnery Sergeant Louis Greenberg. Ward is sure that "he's the guy who measured me for my greens at Parris Island. I later came under his control at Lakehurst NAS where I was post armorer after finishing school in Philly, and, as a second lieutenant, I met him at Quantico, where he was a captain."

Ward next came into contact with a certain Pfc. Alfred J. Drucker, "a Seton Hall graduate and a washout from OCS. He was a school teacher and was an excellent instructor in the Weapons School at Camp Lejeune. He was red-haired with blue eyes with freckled skin. He came back from a visit to report how his father, hanging from a subway strap remarked, 'Alfred, aren't these Jews terrible?'"

Ward surmised that Drucker washed out from OCS because of prejudice. One of his sergeants used to ride him constantly on his Jewishness, "most of it good naturedly. I recommended Pfc. Drucker for second lieutenant and Sergeant Norris for warrant officer. Both were approved."

"On Iwo Jima, I commanded the 3rd Prov Rocket Detachment with the 5th Marine Division as a first lieutenant. About ten days into the operation, I was on the extreme west flank with the Weapons Company commanded by Captain Saul Glassman to my right. We had agreed that our sentries would be coordinated, as the Japs were coming in from the water. When the time arrived for combining activities, no Marines had been sent out from Weapons. I told Captain Glassman if his men weren't out there by

1930, I would reorganize my position. Security was set up properly."

Ward speaks of Glassman in complimentary as well as unflattering terms. Glassman later became a lieutenant colonel, but was court-martialed for improper behavior. Ward says that he "was not unhappy to read that he had been court-martialed for improper operations. The only non-kosher Jewish Marine of my experience."

Lastly, "I remember Alpert, Greenberg, and Drucker fondly. Another good Marine, 1st Lieutenant Haskell Kivowitz, ran the Officers Club on the island of Kauai in 1944." At that time, the Marines had taken over what had been a children's hospital near the town of Kapaa. "Perhaps his background particularly qualified him for the job, but as a member of the auditing team and a frequent visitor to the club, I was most favorably impressed with his management skills . . . . Haskell Kivowitz impressed me with his professionalism, and if he survived WWII, probably opened his own night club."

Pete Santoro of Massachusetts recalls with affection his friend Ben Greenburg, a member of their boxing team. Ben was a good Marine with lots of guts: a flamethrower on Iwo Jima, Saipan, and Tinian. Although he has tried to locate him, he has been unsuccessful in doing so.

Mustang, Major, FBI agent (ret.), now engaged in private investigations and security consulting in Roswell, New Mexico, Earl G. Breeding was Company Commander of E Company, 2nd Battalion, 26th Marines, 3rd Marine Division at the siege of Khe Sanh, in Vietnam, in 1968. Before arriving at Khe Sanh, they were working south of Phu Bai (near Hue). Sometime in 1967, he had picked up an army flak jacket because he felt it was more comfortable than the Marine Corps issue. As it happened, it was virtually new. But what impressed him most was the fact that "some unknown soul had very artistically drawn a large Star of David on the back." Breeding thought this was not only unique, but he had never seen a Star so large: at times, small ones on helmets. What caught his attention most was the frequency that troops would "corner me and say things like, 'Skipper, I didn't know you were Jewish.' Well, I never said I was, and I never said I wasn't. I would tell them that there were a lot of things that they didn't know about me. On one occasion, a trooper came up to me and advised me how good it was that there were Jewish officers around."

Major Breeding related how Father Bob Brett, Catholic chaplain, "went from hole to hole and along the trench lines, talking to those who wanted to pray or just talk. I recall a young Jewish trooper saying how nice it was to talk with him and how good it was that Father Brett knew something about the Jewish faith."

The author was moved by a story in the November 2000 issue of *Leatherneck*. What follows is the essence of that story:

Ron Suciu served with L Company, 3rd Battalion, 4th Marines, in Vietnam, 1965–66, where he was wounded twice. After his service in Vietnam, Suciu attended the Citadel, the Military College of South Carolina, and is now (2001) on the history faculty of El Paso Community College. On the inside of his college ring, instead of his own name and degree, Suciu had engraved the following:

Sgt. J. A. Bateman, USMC
KIA May 1966
Vietnam

Sergeant James. A. Bateman served two tours of duty in Vietnam and was killed in action there. He was awarded two Purple Hearts and the Navy Commendation Medal.

Nora Cowan Bye (the 5th and youngest daughter of Fred James Cowan) wrote to convey the close relationship between her father and Joe (Red) Hecht. She wrote:

"It is both an honor and a privilege to share the one story my father told me about WWII, D-Day, himself and Joe (Red) Hecht. The love and the bond my father had for Red is still felt between my sisters and Red. It makes me proud to share this story with you.

"It was June 15, 1944, during D-Day, my father had not gotten far up the beach when he was hit. Laid out on his stomach, my father had seen Red running up the beach. After calling Red, he came for my father. My father was never considered a small man. At 6'3", about 240 pounds, my father was a bit larger than Red who was about 145 pounds. Red had a hard time trying to move my father. Both my father and Red knew they had to move quickly because the bombers were coming back to sweep the beach. Sweeping from left to right, they would kill as many of our men as they could. After two tries Red and my father staggered off the beach and near some trees. It was there that Red was able to pull the shrapnel out of my father's back. The shrapnel had gone through his pack and was pressing against his spine. My father said, 'I wore my pack like armor.' It would save his life more than once. My father made Red swear not to tell anyone how bad off he was. Knowing the officers had been either hurt or killed, and the mortars had to be moved, Red agreed. Davis was the only one Red told. During the next few days my father had to lean hard on Red. Red knew my father had to get through. The men never knew how bad off my father was. But after a few days, they began to see how strong he really was and they went on to do their job.

"Soon after Saipan, Joe got hurt and was sent home. My father only told me this story during his Marine reunions. My father would light up every time Red entered the room. Red would go running in the other direction screaming, 'That is the man who gave me my double hernia.' My father and Joe Hecht were both in the 2nd Battalion, 8th Regiment, 2nd Marine Division, 81st Mortars, Headquarters Company."

An interesting sidelight to this story is the following: Not only was Fred Cowan in the Marine Corps during the war, but his wife as well. They met on a blind date, and were married not long afterward.

Lastly, Joseph L. Murgida, DPM, Halifax, Massachusetts,

shared account of two Jewish comrades in 2nd Battalion, 25th Marines, 4th Marine Division. One was Pharmacist Mate William Friedman of Philadelphia who made all the landings in the Marshalls, Saipan, Tinian, and Iwo Jima. Friedman and his Indian friend "were in the thick of everything." He was finally killed on D-Day on Iwo Jima. Another Jewish friend with whom he served was 2nd Lieutenant Edward Eiland, Communications, who was wounded several times before being evacuated.

Chapter 9

It's Tough To Be the Only One

As he puts it, he was the only Jewish Marine officer in his outfit most of the time in the Corps. In fact, he was the only Jewish Marine in his outfit. This gave him reason to find some disappointment, and, at times, humor in that situation. While he never experienced any overt negative comments or actions directed at him because he was Jewish, if he was offended it was out of ignorance. For example, when his adjutants were Officers of the Day, Jacobs was always put on as OD on Christmas. On one occasion, the first time he was OD on Christmas, "I inspected the troops' mess hall and sampled the food. However, I did choose not to taste the Candied Ham Steaks. The senior cook present, a master sergeant, watched me and was quite insulted, as it was his special holiday treat. It was weeks later that I found out that the sergeant held a grudge against me. I found him and explained the value of ham in a Jewish diet."

Alan Henry Jacobs, USMC, retired from the Corps as a major in 1991. From 1975 to 1976, he was stationed at Quantico for Officers Candidate Course and COMMO School as second lieutenant. From 1976 to 84, he was at Jacksonville, NC, COMMO Radio Platoon Commander, 2nd Marine Division (1st Lt), and Assistant COMMO, 6th Marines (2nd Lt). From 1980–84, he was stationed in Okinawa, COMMO, MACG-18, 1st Marine Air Wing, as a captain, Jacksonville, NC, Sixth Marines (Captain), COMMO

2nd Tank Battalion (Captain). From 1984 to 1991, he had broken service as a reserve Marine as COMMO 2/25, Garden City, New York (Major).

Most of the time, he was the only Jew around. In 1977, he was appointed the "Acting Rabbi" on a peacetime operation named Display Determination. His Marine Amphibious Group was scheduled to attack Turkey. As it happened, they were approaching the Jewish High Holidays. The chief chaplain for the entire naval force found him after dining in the wardroom of the USS *Mt. Whitney*, the command and control headquarters for the operation. Jacobs was the only Jewish officer that could be found. The chief chaplain was sincerely concerned that the Jewish personnel be afforded the opportunity to observe Rosh Hashanah and Yom Kippur services. "He did this because he was sincerely concerned with the spiritual needs of his Jewish troops and he had a directive from his boss in Little Creek, Virginia, to hold Jewish services." As a result, the chaplain ordered a "Jewish Holiday Kit," with "a stock number, much the same as the number for ordering a machine gun. It had skullcaps, mini-Torah, and prayer books. The problem that the chaplain had was that I was the only Jew he could find to lead, much less attend the service. As the chaplain was a full captain, he had clout and put out a series of unclassified messages offering free pick-up/delivery by helo to any Jewish sailor or Marine who wanted to attend the services." However, only three Jews were collected to attend. "In a goodwill gesture, the chaplain and a few of his assistants participated in the Jewish service so we could approach a minyan. In any case, we tried, and I had a wonderful High Holiday experience."

In another incident, Jacobs was on a field exercise, and was one of a "stick" of Marines about to climb into a CH-53, a large Marine Corps helicopter. Suddenly, some dirt flew up in the rotorwash from the helo and scratched one of his corneas. He felt some pain, his left eye was red and tears flowed, his vision was blurry. The regimental doctor treated Jacobs with some ointment, a thick gauze eye bandage, and "a classic black eye patch. When

I returned to my unit, still in the field, my troops were startled with my new appearance. They didn't know what to say to me. Then one of my more worldly and brash corporals yelled out in an endearing way, 'here comes Lt. Moshe.' It was an obvious reference to Moshe Dayan, the Israeli general who wore an eye patch to cover up a combat-related eye injury. That nickname, Lt. Moshe, stuck with me for years."

While on Okinawa, he became the token Jewish Marine officer once again. There, the base chaplain organized monthly prayer breakfasts. Jacobs was volunteered once more by his boss to visit various locations on Okinawa and Korea to say a few Jewish prayers. Apparently, and once again, he seemed to be the only Jew at those functions. After he spoke, the guests would invariably ask questions about "being Jewish." "They wanted to know why we did not eat bacon or what 'Yiddish' was. The most popular question was asked after Passover. One young Pfc. wanted to know why a Jewish Navy doctor he saw was eating such large crackers all of a sudden. I explain the concept of *matzoh*. It was like the Pope talking heaven to Buddhists. Again, although I did not join the Marines to give rabbinical dissertations, I enjoyed it."

Chapter 10

In Peacetime as Well

My namesake, but no relation (as far as I know), Robert B. Leavitt, enlisted in the Marine Corps in June 1984, for a tour of duty of four years. He enlisted in Oakland, California, and did his boot camp at MCRD, San Diego. What he remembers most of boot camp are two things: one, the lack of sleep, and two, he was able to apply most of his time to the Corps. No sooner had he arrived at boot camp, however, than he wondered what the hell of a kind of mess he had gotten himself into and wanted to quit for the first two weeks. But he stuck it out and made it through. The chow hall at the camp was directly opposite the runway at San Diego International Airport which was a constant reminder three times a day, seven days a week, that he had "voluntarily signed up for hell and wouldn't be leaving on one of those planes any time soon."

Another aspect of boot camp which he recalls vividly is the number of recruits who tried to kill themselves. Bob watched one try to hang himself from a bathroom stall, and "we had to hold him up while the DI undid the belt around his neck. Another drank a bottle of rifle oil. And a third jumped from the third floor of our squad bay as we were going out to drill. He took a second too long though and a DI caught him by the back of his blouse as he passed the second story."

While Bob experienced no problems with anti-Semitic activity, what he did witness was a lot of racial tension between white and black Marines "which erupted into some fist fights and lots of name calling, but nothing more serious than that."

Volunteering for the Infantry, Leavitt was assigned to Camp Pendleton and trained as a 0351, antitank Dragon-weapon-system gunner. He "felt like a big target using a weapon which took eleven seconds to travel one thousand meters while a tank turret could traverse and fire in roughly five seconds. Thank God they don't use that any more. Off duty time was spent unsuccessfully trying "to pick up chicks. But Fate smiled on me when duty stations were handed out." He was sent to barracks duty in Bermuda.

Bermuda was a great place. "Not just for the climate, hordes of beautiful women tourists and natives, and lovely scenery, but because I fell in with a great group of Marines. Bob Moore, Kevin Feurst, and I became fast friends and had lots of good times, and more successful times, getting drunk and chasing women."

The good times came to an end with his transfer to Camp Lejeune. Here it was that he learned to be a "grunt." They "humped hundreds if not thousands of miles through the swamps of North Carolina, ate MREs by the pound and engaged in an endless cycle of field ops and police duty after field ops. I also fell in with a great group of guys here. But as with most 20–22 y/o our behaviors were much the same as other places. Woman (free and paid for) and booze."

Next on his itinerary was deployment to Okinawa and the Philippines. They found the same mode of operations both on and off duty, but the jungle was more lush than the pine swamps of North Carolina.

His most memorable event in the Marine Corps occurred in Olangapo in the Philippines. A friend and Bob had just "exited a bar in search of greener pastures and were standing on a corner, trying to decide what to do." At that moment, a Navy MP truck drove up. Bob had "the stupid idea that it would be fun to jump on the back and hold on as the MPs drove down the street." At first, it was fun. They felt as if they were on parade "as we drove down the street on top of the truck and waved to people on the street unknown to the MPs in the truck." As they continued on their way, waving happily to the crowds, a "short fat little red-faced MP ran up alongside the truck and started screaming at the driver to stop and for us to get down." They stopped, but Bob and his friend did not, and thus began a forty-five minute hide and seek chase through the streets of Olangapo. At the end, however, they got caught, and "had to get back on base to try and make roll call, only to find the short fat little red-faced MP watch commander waiting for us at the front gate to Subic Bay. Our commanding officer was not as amused as we were."

Leavitt rates his Marine Corps experience as good for the short run, but not something he would have made as his career. He found it very hard to take orders from people he considers unfit to give them. On the other hand, he is very proud to have served his country in the Marine Corps. As he notes, "I am proud to have defended freedom and democracy, as corny as that sounds. There is a lot wrong with this country, but it is still the best there has ever been on this planet." And, "The USMC provided me with a greater sense of self-discipline than I would have gotten anywhere else. It taught me the value of the moral qualities so severely lacking in our society today. Firstly, it taught me a great disdain for lack of moral fortitude. Secondly, it enlightened me as to the value of personal responsibility and accountability. And thirdly, it taught me that to lead one must make hard choices and be responsible for those choices."

Chapter 11

Letters from the Pacific

The letters of First Lieutenant Maurice Kranzberg of St. Louis were preserved by his family. In July 1944, he wrote to his mother from Saipan. It reads in part:

> "I also had a letter from Beverly Fisher, and one from cousin Rene Kranzberg, Harry's daughter, in which she told me she is engaged. Beverly told me about going to the Muny and the many pleasant nights spent there. Here we were sitting on boxes around a radio listening first to Tokyo Rose with its good American music. There were Gershwin selections, 'Showboat' music by Kern and some good Tommy Dorsey stuff. Then Tokyo Rose herself giving some news with no mention about Saipan. It was pretty hard to realize that there are people going to operas and shows back in St. Louis (Missouri) while there are millions all over the world like us who would be happy *just to be home*. It doesn't seem quite right. Here we were on the field where only a few weeks ago our buddies had fought bitterly to cross and take from the stubborn Japs. Men had gone bravely forward while millions at home could sit comfortably by their radios and remark smugly that those Marines had taken another island in the Pacific. It's an ugly, rotten, dirty business. When we get through covering this sector there is noth-

ing left. We really believe in utter destruction. 'Cause anything left standing is liable to hide a Jap. So we methodically wreck everything, and an American civilian has no conception of what a shelling or bombing can do. I hesitate to say it, but I sometimes believe that a light bombing of one of our cities might shorten this war by six months or a year.

"I guess I'm a little bitter today, but I'll be alright. Just wasn't busy and had time to reminisce too much. It's no fun to be away from family and home out on this godforsaken island living in filth, heat, mosquitoes, and flies. But I'm alright. I'm feeling good, and I guess won't even remember this a few years from now. Nothing else new. Regards to all."

Kranzberg writes about the combat in which he participates:

"The Second Division got into landing boats and raced toward shore, providing a diversionary appearance of a landing while the 4th Division landed on the narrow, less- protected beaches.

"By nightfall of July 24, nearly 16,000 Marines had been landed with a loss of only 15 killed and 225 wounded. A Japanese counterattack last night was launched, but our men held and piled up 476 dead enemy troops. By morning, 1,241 Japanese dead were piled up in front of the division line. By August 1st it was over. Tinian was taken in eight days instead of the projected two weeks.

"As for me, I was supposed to land with my men on D+1, and our landing was held up because of the fierce fighting that was still going on from the previous night. Anyway, when we landed around 10:30 A.M. and I reported to the regimental Headquarters, the assistant commander greeted me by pointed to a Japanese tank about 50 yards uproad from where we were standing and he said, 'Those Japs in that tank wanted to come up and

shake hands with the colonel last night, but we stopped
them just in time.'"

Kranzberg speaks of his first airplane ride. He had to get
socks for his men. He explained his mission to his colonel and
said that he had no transportation, whereupon the colonel said
that he would be taken to Saipan by the next observation plane
which came in.

"But the next plane that landed was a TBF, a torpedo bomber made by Grumman. As my mission was
urgent, I was given a seat in it. (It was my very *first airplane ride* in my life.)

"I was seated in the rear gunner's seat facing to the
rear of the plane, and when I stepped in I asked the pilot
what I could and what I couldn't touch. He pointed out a
lever which I shouldn't touch as it would propel me up
and out of the plane (to be used only to bail out). As I sat
in the rear gunner's turret, the first words I saw were
'Mfgd by Emerson Electric Company, St. Louis.' The ride
was quite a thrill and I thoroughly enjoyed it. It took
only eight minutes to get to the field on Saipan, but as
we circled in to land I saw Saipan from the air, a plane
which only a few weeks ago had been the site of much
fighting. It was a pleasant ride and there was no thrill to
it except the ride in the air."

In September 1944, Kranzberg attended Yom Kippur services, apparently in Hawaii. He wrote:

"Yesterday I went to our Yom Kippur services which
were very nice. I fasted, too, the first time in two years.
Last year I didn't and the year before I was in boot camp.
But yesterday I fasted and came through okay, except for
a slight headache which started around noon and lasted
until an hour after I ate.

"The services were well-attended and there were
soldiers, sailors, and Marines from all over the island.
We had a service from 10:00 A.M. to 2:30 P.M. with a 15-
minute break at about 12:30. Our cantor was a soldier

who sang beautifully and our chaplain spoke very well. I don't think I have ever paid so close attention to the service as I did yesterday."

"Later, they moved the service to the dining room of a hotel in the large town on the island. We were served after standing in line with a meal consisting of herring, rye bread, salami, and breaded veal chops, string beans, rice and gravy, and iced tea.

"After that we started back to camp, and there were about three small trucks in my convoy. The boys were all pretty happy after finishing fasting (and a surprisingly large number did fast) and we sang old *shul* songs and old Jewish songs all the way back to camp. It was a really pleasant evening."

Kranzberg concludes his letter with an "editor's note":

"The final session of the Yom Kippur services was held in the ballroom of the Maui Grand Hotel in Kahului which is in the port town of Maui and the town in which we always took liberty. The hotel was owned at that time by a Jewish man, a Mr. Boxer. It was good to have the final part of the service there so we could end the Yom Kippur service and have food awaiting at the same place. The Jewish Welfare Board and the division chaplain did a good job of coordinating things for all the servicemen."

In October, 1944, a good friend of First Lieutenant Kranzberg fixed him up with a date, and they double-dated; then described it in the following letter to his mother.

"A very good friend, Lt. Colonari, had a date with a girl, and she got her sister for me and we took the girls to the movies in town, after which we took them home and sat around and talked for the rest of the evening. They were intrigued by our description of the wonders of the States. Someday when I can wrote more fully or be able to tell you of our experiences here, you will hear some interesting stories. Incidentally, while I have been to places and danced and been to some affairs, last night was the first time I have had a date since I left the States. It was most interesting, and I'm sorry censorship regulation forbid me telling you some of the details. But taking a native girl out is somewhat different from taking out a girl in the States. However, when I say native girls, don't get worried."

Kranzberg explained a bit later that their dates were actually girls of Japanese descent, or *Nisei* –American girls born on the island of Maui to Japanese parents who were farmers living on the island. The girls had learned English attending the public schools of Hawaii. "How Lt. Colonari met these girls I do not know," wrote Kranzberg, "except that he was recreation officer of our regiment and he probably met them at some school event for which our regiment had supplied some entertainment."

In a letter from Iwo Jima, he wrote, "The bloody fierceness of the battle of Iwo Jima has been told many times. It was our bloodiest and toughest battle. For twenty-four grim days our men fought against a fanatic, determined, and intelligent enemy who was well-armed and prepared to fight from well-fortified and well-prepared positions."

In his first letter from Iwo, Kranzberg wrote to Jack and Mickey:

"First of all, I want to assure you that as of now I am perfectly okay, with not even a scratch to show for the terrible days and nights I have been through while on this island. So don't worry.

"Right now, I am sitting at the entrance of my foxhole here on this barren hunk of sand called Iwo Jima, only 750 miles from Tokyo. Every once in a while artillery shells whistle overhead, but that is becoming less frequent as our troops cover the remainder of the island and root out all the Japs, so only small arms can be used. We are so close to finishing the job here.

"Our supply dump and motor maintenance section is located in what was a scant week ago still one of the hottest spots on the island. We are inland about 500 yards from the beach, and about an equal or slightly longer distance from one of the three swell airfields on this island. There is nothing but coarse black sand all around. It is a volcanic, ashlike, heavy sand into which you sink to your ankles, making tough going. But the very nature of the sand probably makes it much easier to dig in, and although our men were pinned down on the beach, they at least had some protection from the terrific artillery and mortar barrage that was thrown at us.

"Now, as to my personal experience. As regimental motor transport and maintenance officer, my presence and my men's presence on the beach on D-Day at Saipan was considered foolish as we had nothing to do but dodge shells, so this time we were scheduled to come in on D + 2. However, the beach was so hot that we couldn't land many vehicles, so we weren't called in until D + 4. However, at that time, the Japs were still shelling all beaches and especially ours. The island is so small they could fire from almost anywhere to any other point on the island, and the terrain where we landed and pushed in initially offered no cover or concealment. So we had to stick close to our holes except when we had some delivering to do or when we had to work on some jeeps and trucks. Then there were snipers around for several days, and no one knew when we would be hit.

"Only four days ago, I dived into the captain's hole, near the one I occupy with one of the boys, as it was the closest, and shells started dropping around here. One landed only 15 feet from the hole I was in and in another hole. It killed two men and wounded two others. My ears rang all days from the crack of that shell, and I'll never forget it.

"If you could see the beach when I came in, the amount of our gear knocked out, the number of dead (we had no time to bury them for several days), the tired weary faces of the men, and if you could feel the terror of working and doing your job but never knowing when the whine of a shell and the sudden explosion that follows and ends everything in its path, you could get an idea of what we went through. Sometimes several hours would go by without a shell in our sector, and then suddenly the quick whine and crack of a shell, and dirt and dust everywhere, and there were dead and dying men around the spot where it hit."

"It's hard to tell you in words just what war is, and how it is, and what it does. It's hard to see your buddies get killed, young healthy men, with mothers, wives, sweethearts, families. One minute they're with you, and the next moment they're a piece of human flesh. All their hopes and plans and loves and laughs gone forever. A grim business, and I think I've aged ten years from this.

"One thing I've resolved, and I hope never to forget. Many a time during a shelling or close call of some kind I've resolved that when and if I ever get back I will not have completed my duty to my country and to my lost fellow Marines and soldiers and sailors unless I take a deep and personal interest in the future international affairs of my country. I believe I have gone through enough to prove my right to probe into everything that affects our country and to see to it that we have a strong country, a righteous country, and that future generations shall not have to go through what we are going through. War is hell! And it must never happen again. I don't pretend to know how we can prevent it, but at least I'll do my share to try and prevent it. (And not necessarily with our having the largest army and navy in the world.)"

Returning to Maui from Iwo Jima, Kranzberg wrote:

"Dear Mother (also a copy to Melvin).

"I am feeling fine and hope this finds you the same. First of all, how do you like the snazzy new stationery? Isn't it the nuts? It shows all the places we have taken, and it also shows the two ribbons that every man in the

division who came out with us rates. So I now have the
two ribbons shown above. The one on the left is the
Presidential Unit Citation given to this division for
Saipan and Tinian. The other one is the Asiatic-Pacific
Ribbon which every man is allowed to wear just for being out here. The stars represent a separate campaign.
As Saipan and Tinian were considered one operation,
we get only one star for that operation. However, as nice
as they are, I still regard the personal possession of my
'dog tags' as my important appendage. I hope and prefer
to bring them home.

"Now to tell you, without giving too many details so
it will pass the censor, about the reception when we
docked. We arrived early and as we pulled up to the
dock, a Seabee (U.S. naval construction battalion–C.B.)
band marched out and started playing 'The Marines'
Hymn.' They had a big sound truck with them, and the
men lined up at the rails really got a thrill out of that.
The girls started appearing on the docks and, as we tied
up, the girls started throwing flowers and packages of
candy up to the men on the ship. Then the master of
ceremonies introduced several of the girls who had a few
words to say about welcoming us back to the island. It
was really nice. People were shouting to old friends on
the docks, and the men were whistling to the girls and
yelling, and the band was playing, and altogether it was
almost like the receptions you have read about or dream
about except that it wasn't the good old USA, and, of
course, the number of people on the docks was not large.
Then after the troops debarked, USO and Salvation Army
people appeared and distributed candy and doughnuts
to the men as they came off the ship."

On March 10, 1944, Kranzberg wrote his mother of the Jewish religious services on Maui:

"Here is good news. I am located so that I can attend
the Jewish services which are held every Sunday morn-

ing here. Furthermore, I have talked with our Chaplain Rosenberg who told us that plans are completed for a Passover Seder to be held with a big prepared dinner in a suitable location. I am happy to hear about this and am looking forward to the occasion. Incidentally, that Dr. Weissman whom Jack wrote about is a nephew of Dr. Weintraub, is not in our division, but in another regiment. I don't know him but will look him up some time."

And,

"Tell the brothers and sisters all, thanks for the letters. I will write them all. I wrote Mel and Nancy today. I was happy to see Kenny's picture. I bet he's quite a big boy. I'm looking forward to getting some pictures of all of you, and I'll send some to you as soon as I take some."

In another letter, he comments:

"Meanwhile, I want to impress upon you that there is no need for worry. I am okay and feeling fine, and seeing the world at Uncle Sam's expense. I am getting a great education, and while at times I work pretty hard, most of the time this work isn't hard, and certainly hasn't the aggravation which I am sure the boys at the office are experiencing. Of course, at times there are certain hazards in this type of activity, but don't worry. With all those people at home praying for me, and with a few of the girls I left behind, asking God's blessing for me as they tell me in their letters, I am bound to come back in good shape."

Among Kranzberg's letters is a poem someone made up about the naval censor:

"We may have many marriages and many divorces.
Fierce battles and lengthy discourses,
Conflicts–with all the shot and shell,
Verifying Sherman that 'War is Hell.'

"But behind the scenes there is a guy

With a wearied and a red-rimmed eye,
I am the Censor, that peculiar fellow
Who spots the taboo, with a bellow.

"Sends for the culprit, that unfortunate guy
Who probably wouldn't harm a fly,
I threaten him with a deck court-martial,
I am the Censor, I must be impartial.

"I read all the letters to mothers and fathers,
To wives and sweethearts, sons and daughters,
Sometimes the paper almost smokes
With undying love or dirty jokes.

"I am kidded and cursed and berated,
For I am a Censor, to a skunk related,
I wonder when all this has passed
Whether I may perhaps be asked.

"The part I played in this damn war
And what I thought was fighting for,
I hope that no one will ever venture
To answer: 'Oh! He was a Censor.'"

Joseph Kohn

Joseph "Joe" Kohn, the son of Roy and Jeanette Kohn, was born in New Brunswick, New Jersey on December 13, 1924. While attending Metuchen High School in Metuchen, he played baseball and was captain of the football team. His family of father, mother, and sister, Rose, was very close-knit.

With the outbreak of the Second World War, Joe decided to enlist in the Marine Corps and, while attending Rider College, entered into the V-12 officer candidate program at Duke University. However, as that didn't work out as planned, it was not long before he found himself at boot camp in San Diego, in November 1943.

Having completed his training, Kohn arrived on Guadalcanal with the 54th Replacement Battalion in May 1944. As a member of the 15th Marines of the 6th Marine Division, he fought in the Okinawa campaign as an artillery forward observer. Later, he was transferred to Tsingtao, China, where he served as chaplain's assistant. He was discharged on March 7, 1946.

His wartime letters "reveal a compassion for the Marine Corps, America, and family and friends. Some of his thoughts and feelings, showing a mercurial, confident, and confused young man, so typical of other Marines of his age and time . . ."

"First impressions

Personal feelings are little thought of in any kind of a military organization. No one cares how you feel, what your thoughts are, or what becomes of you. This is what makes a man out of most boys because it makes them stand on their own and accept responsibility. I know I sound like I've been in for years, but it takes one but a few short weeks to realize that he is only a small cog in a very big machine–6 August 1943.

"On war

I guess that many changes have been made in many lives. Not many boys are around town or many young men. There have to be wars or people just don't appreciate the so many good little things we have . . . If only those people who aren't away from home and the ones they lives, would realize this . . . Sure guess the men who are overseas miss home one helluva lot more than those back home miss them . . . You betcha I'll win this war–5 October '43.

No kidding, the Marine Corps hasn't changed me too much. I'll be frank with you, the attitude around here is that we'll beat Germany in '44, but the Japs in '46 or so–6 December 1943.

"I have changed

Mom, Dad, Sis, if you should ever turn against me I know that life is just a prelude to something nothingness . . . I can't expect you to understand me at times but try to realize that under a normal cycle my trend of thought, would be considerably different. I feel very lonesome and my mood keyed to a pitch that to hold what I am thinking about within me would only burn like a fire longed to be cooled. I have changed, Mom and Dad, so please be patient with me when I am home–12 June 1945.

"Doing my duty

Mom, don't you be making a fool of yourself and yell about me in the service because there are so many in service and seeing action. I hope I'm in the occupation forces and get overseas a little while and see a bit of the world. Gosh, I hope you understand that I don't intend getting hurt . . . . 2 November 1943.

This was isn't over yet by any means. I've spoken to many men who have been over there and believe me the enemy is plenty smart and strong yet. Sure wish I could do more than I'm doing now. I wonder if all the people at home feel the same way–18 November 1943.

I didn't rock the frigging boat. I knew what to say and what to do–16 July 1994.

Know when the war is over that I've sure done my part . . . Remember there isn't a Jap alive that can keep me from coming home to you all–4 August 1944.

"In the Pacific Theater

(While working parties unloading ships on Guadalcanal in mid-1944 preparing for arrival of replacements) We were like the rear echelon, just sort of waiting. The 6th Marine Division was made up of different groups like the 1st Provisional Brigade. These old timers thought that no matter what we did we we're still the babies: so what the hell do you know? I used to have discussions with them–16 July 1944.

"Planning for post-war

It's time to talk about college when I come home. Well, you guessed it. Rutgers Aggies, if I do. You might even inquire what that department offers returning veterans. The government should pay my way but I wonder in the courses I need–13 March 1945.

When a person faces death and knows it, and has time to think about it, the more he wants to live. The longest night of my life was when I was on Sugar Loaf Hill. I stayed in that hole that night. I could hear some screaming and yelling. I knew men were being wounded and killed. I heard yelling for their God but most just for the mother. "Mommy, mommy," someone yelled. I'll never forget it. The stench of death was all around–Memoir ca 1988.

When I was on Sugar Loaf and some of the other places, and they (the wounded) were crying out, I said to whoever–if I can live through these days and nights I really will do good in my life, if I can just get out of this situation . . . It was like being in the movies. You knew death was all around you and it was a big dream. You did things automatically–16 July 1994.

"About letters home

(Had not been receiving much news) Is there anything you want to know? (Could not answer anyway) You must have a hard time trying to understand my letters. Write me about what is going on around town. When each of you has nothing to do just sit down and write me a long letter. Write anything that comes into your head. News of people I know, home stuff, business stuff, and people, movies, old times, new times, old things, new things. Hot and cold running anything. I know you could if you tried–22 January 1945.

A lot of the letters I wrote home were (to make) . . . them feel I was okay. I didn't tell them everything that was going on because if I did they wouldn't like it–16 July 1994.

"The war's over

What the hell. I've been pretty lucky, in a way, for though even life is cheap, it is very sweet. You know I have been with artillery forward observers all the time connected to the infantry. Now that's all over with. I can say I'd never done anything without the thought of my family and what they'd want me to do. I've done a lot of things that perhaps I shouldn't have done, but I hope also, that things that I have done that I didn't have to do will make up for it. It's a crazy world and life. Soon I'll be 21. Funny to celebrate it in China–17 August 1945."

(The above letters were reprinted from *Gyrene, The World War II United States Marine,* by Captain Wilbur D. Jones, Jr., USNR (ret.), White Mane Books, White Mane Publishing Co., POB 152, Shippensburg, Pa. 17257. Permission to use material requested from publisher).

After a long career in education, Joseph Kohn retired as principal of Ella G. Clarke Elementary School in Lakewood, New Jersey. He currently (2002) resides in Lake Worth, Florida.

Rabbi Roland Gittlesohn
Chaplain, 5th Marine Division
Delivered most famous sermon of World War II
"The Purest Democracy"

Raising the flag at Iwo Jima
Photo taken by Joe Rosenthal

HOWARD: —

OLD MARINES AS WELL AS GOOD FRIENDS ARE LIKE FAT THIGHS......

THEY ALWAYS MANAGE TO KEEP IN TOUCH!

SEMPER FI!

NAT M. BERMAN U.S.M.C
I-3-6 2ND MARINE DIVISIC
JUNE 1942 - SEPT. 1945

Reverse side says
This is not a Hallmark Card
Therefore I didn't care enough
to send the very best

Reverse side says
*"This is not a Hallmark Card
Therefore I didn't care enough
To send the very best*

Guadalcanal pilots,
Espíritu Santo, New
Hebrides, April 1943—
Al Clark (middle far right)

Guadalcanal pilots
Espirito Santo, New Hebrides,
April 1943
Al Clark (middle far right)

Captain W. J. Weinstein, USMCR
CO, 1st Bn, 23rd Marines, 4th
MarDiv
Saipan, 7/1944

Chaplain Sobel on ship en route to Korea
From "The Fighting Rabbis"

Bill Katz, Korea, 1952   *Sid Klein, 1944*

*◄ Irwin Howard,
Korea, 1952*

*Steve Judd
(second from
right) with shot-
gun, witnessing
his group's de-
struction of a
Japanese tank on
Saipan ►*

◄ Charles Jacobs, Wellington, NZ

Landing first day at Tokyo Bay (Norton Garfinkel)

Nat Berman, New Zealand, 1942 ➤

Rosabelle Cohen, 1944, 22 years of age ➤

President Bill Clinton on left, First Lady Hillary Rodham Clinton in center, and Marine Paul Maloff on right at the 50th Anniversary of the Battle of Iwo Jima, held February 19, 1995, at Arlington, Va.

Two Marines take a rare smoke break on Kunishi Ridge (Harold Dymond, l)

Major General Melvin Krulewitch at ceremonies in Trinity Churchyard, New York City, 1972, honoring Major Franklin Wharton, Commandant of the U.S. Marine in 1804 (from "Now That You Mention It")

David Ginsburg (100 years old)
Recipient of the French
Legion of Honor
Combat veteran of WWI
Oldest living former drill instructor
in the USMC

Colonel Norman Gertz, 1975   *(The Jewish Veteran, Summer 1999)*

Ben Greenburg (second from right) E/2/24

Sgt Jack Feinhor, USMC

William (Bill) Schaefer

The author, Korea, 1952

Original cartoon by Nat Berman

Col. Irving (Buck) Schecter, former CO. Ist Staff Group, Brooklyn, squints into weekend sun during training

Lt Colonel Arthur Friedman, USMC (with note to his daughter prior to his departure to Okinawa, 1973) ➤

◄ *Colonel Victor Bianchini, USMC*

Arthur Friedman, USMC (far left) Vietnam, from Newsweek *Magazine*

◄ *Major Marvin Schacher, NAS Pensacola, aboard Navy SNJ*

Captain Edward J. Leavitt, USMC, Soc Trang, Vietnam ➤

Original cartoons by Nat Berman, Rodeo, Camp Tarawa, 1942

PART IV

Profiles in Courage

Chapter 12

Profile in Courage–Robin R. Higgins

A true hero and a remarkable woman in America today, Lieutenant Colonel Robin Higgins, USMC (ret.), nee Ross, was born in the Bronx in 1950. She spent her early days on Long Island and obtained two degrees in English, a bachelor's from State University of New York at Oneonta and a master's from Long Island University.

After studying for a time at Hebrew University in Jerusalem, she returned to New York in May 1970 and completed college with a 4.0 average. Following her graduate studies, she taught high-school English on Long Island.

At her father's suggestion to go into the military, Higgins went to a local Marine Corps recruiting office and was accepted into OCS at Quantico. She was commissioned a second lieutenant and performed duties in communications and in military police at Quantico.

On December 23, 1977, she married Captain William R. (Rich) Higgins, USMC. The turning point and perhaps the most significant event of her life was the calamity that befell her husband, thrusting her name and image into national, if not international, attention. In 1988, while on duty as a lieutenant colonel and leader of a UN observer team in Lebanon, her husband was taken captive by Hezbollah terrorists and later murdered. Since "the Hezbollah were fanatically committed to the destruction of the Jewish state, during the period of his captivity, she "had to keep my Jewishness hidden. Ironically, it was that very Jewishness that helped me survive."[1]

She continued to perform her duties as a Marine officer during this period, all the while suffering the numbing terror and loneliness of a hostage's wife. She made diligent efforts to get information about her husband and to obtain his release, enduring extreme frustration and uncertainty. She learned of her husband's murder on July 29, 1989.

Rich Higgins was promoted to colonel while in captivity.

On October 4, 1997, Robin Higgins christened the guided-missile destroyer USS *Higgins* (DDG-76), named for her husband.

During 41st President George Bush's administration, she was appointed to the U.S. Department of Labor, where she served as deputy assistant secretary and then acting assistant secretary for Veterans' Employment and Training. While a senior executive at the Department of Labor, Lieutenant Colonel Higgins was an adviser to the Department of Veterans' Affairs Advisory Committee on Women Veterans and a commissioner on the Department of Defense's Defense Conversion Commission.

Moving to Florida after leaving the military, she served as director of public affairs for Florida's state comptroller, and then spent a year consulting, public speaking, and writing on a variety of topics, including media relations, public affairs, and veterans' advocacy.

In January, Governor Jeb Bush appointed Robin Higgins executive director of the Florida Department of Veterans' Affairs—the first Jew and the first woman to hold that job in Florida.

As the Governor's chief adviser on veterans' issues, she was responsible for advocacy programs for the state's 1.7 million veterans.

Then in early 2001, she was nominated by 43rd president George W. Bush to serve as the Under Secretary for Memorial Affairs at the U. S. Department of Veterans' Affairs. Confirmed by the U.S. Senate in May 2001, she is responsible for numer-

---

[1] Higgins, Robin, Lt. Col., USMC (ret.), *Patriot Dreams*, Marine Corps Association, Quantico, Va., p. XI.

ous burial benefits for the nation's veterans and oversees the National Cemetery Administration. She became the senior Jewish person ever to serve in the Department of Veterans' Affairs and the senior Jewish woman in the Administration.

Lieutenant Colonel Higgins is the recipient of numerous awards, including the Marine Corps League's Dickey Chapelle Award for outstanding service to Marines, the American Legion Auxiliary's Public Spirit Award for outstanding service to country, and the American Academy of Physician Assistants Veterans Caucus Award for outstanding service to veterans.

She is a member of the Disabled American Veterans, the Retired Officers' Association, the Jewish War Veterans, Gold Star Wives, AMVETS, and the Marine Corps League. Higgins has testified before Congress; appeared on numerous morning and evening news programs; and has had many letters, articles, and opinion pieces published in major publications, all in addition to her book, *PATRIOT DREAMS: The Murder of Colonel Rich Higgins*

Chapter 13

Diamonds in the Rough

Two diamonds of the Marine Corps were Leroy and Leland, better known as "Lou." They were not related. The former, along with his Guadalcanal buddies, Al Schmid and Johnny Rivers, were the subject of one of the first great war movies of the Second World War, *The Pride of the Marines*, and the latter was a legend in his own time, still referred to and admired for his exploits and influence on younger Marines who were destined to follow in his footsteps.

Corporal Leroy Diamond of Brooklyn led a three-man machine squad who, with Al Schmid and Johnny Rivers, achieved fame as a result of their exploits on Guadalcanal. In August 1942, they had their machine gun set up along the Tenaru River, waiting for the Japanese to begin a counter-attack. At the outbreak of firing, Rivers was killed almost instantly. While Schmid continued to fire, Diamond continued feverishly to feed ammunition. "The fighting was fierce; Japanese bodies kept falling from Schmid's gun. Diamond kept feeding the gun until he felt a burning sensation in his arm and he knew that he was wounded. He picked up Rivers' automatic weapon, firing it with his good arm."[1]

Schmid related the action as it happened: "Japs fell like flies. Diamond was furiously at work loading the gun when they

[1] Brody, Seymour, *Jewish Heroes &Heroines*, Lifetime Books, Hollywood, Fla., 1996, p. 202.

got him in the arm. He fell across my legs and could hardly move. He picked up his Reising automatic and tried to work it with his one good hand."[2]

A sniper in the trees behind them shot Schmid in the face, blinding him. But Diamond managed to keep talking to the now-blinded Schmid, shouting in what direction to continue to fire the machine gun and thus was able to exact a tremendous toll on the enemy.

When they were rescued by fellow Marines, they counted two hundred dead bodies of the enemy lying in front of their position. For his heroism, Leroy Diamond received the Navy Cross and Purple Heart, while Al Schmid, too, received the Navy Cross for the same action.

Master Gunnery Sergeant Leland Diamond, better known as "Lou," remains as a legend as one of the most famous of all "Old Breed Leathernecks."

Defying tradition of the time which dictated that all men would be smooth shaven, Lou's sun-bronzed face was adorned with a neatly trimmed goatee. Although his comrades addressed him as "Lou," he was also known affectionately as "Mr. Marine" and "Mr. Leatherneck."

He was born on May 30, 1890, in Bedford, Ohio. Enlisting in the Marine Corps at the advanced age of twenty-seven, "His salty, hard-driving personality soon expressed itself in both word and deed, and no Marine ever showed more devotion to the Corps," (Marine Corps Museum).

After boot camp, and now a corporal, he shipped out from Philadelphia in January 1918 aboard the USS *Von Steuben*. After landing at Brest, France, he saw action with the 6th Marines in the battles at Chateau-Thierry, Belleau Wood, the Aisne-Marne, St. Mihiel, and the Meuse-Argonne. As a sergeant, he entered Germany with the Army of Occupation. With the end of the war, Diamond received his honorable discharge from the Marine Corps on August 13, 1919.

2 Kaufman, I., *American Jews in World War II*, Dial Books, New York, 1948, p. 209.

However, as civilian life did not suit him, he re-enlisted on September 23, 1921. While serving as assistant armorer at Parris Island, South Carolina, he regained his sergeant's stripes.

Unsatisfied with stateside duty, he shipped out to Shanghai with M Company, 3rd Battalion, 4th Marines. As the conflict going on between Japan and China "was not much of a war, he returned to the States on June 10, 1933 aboard the USS *Henderson* at Mare Island, California: he was now a gunnery sergeant.

"Although he first enlisted at the age of twenty-seven—somewhat older than most recruits—the difference never was noticeable. His salty, hard-driving personality soon expressed itself in both word and deed, and no Marine ever showed more devotion to the Corps."

His salty, informal language did not exactly endear him to chaplains within earshot. However, his earthy manner of speech never appeared to detract from his role as a morale booster for his unit, nor from his ability as an instructor and leader.

One of Diamond's trademarks was his self-confidence, which bordered on cockiness. Anyone with less than ten years in the Corps was a "boot" to him. While he scolded recruits who saluted him, he frequently failed himself to salute officers with less than field grade. "Despite his peculiarities, and, in many ways, because of them, he was a 'Marine's Marine.'"

With the outbreak of hostilities in 1941, Lou Diamond shipped out to Guadalcanal with H Company, 2nd Battalion, 5th Marines, 1st Marine Division. Now fifty-two years old, they arrived at the beaches on August 7, 1942. "Among the many fables concerning his 'Canal' service is the tale that he lobbed a mortar shell down the smoke stack of an off-shore Japanese cruiser. It is considered a fact, however, that he drove the cruiser from the bay with his harassing 'near-misses.'"

Age and physical disabilities now forced his evacuation from Guadalcanal. Taken by air to the New Hebrides and then to a hospital in New Zealand, he inveigled orders to ship out to New Caledonia, where a friend "ordered" him to return to Guadalcanal, the supposed location of his old outfit. But, to his surprise, the division had already shipped out to Australia. He returned to his division by somewhat circuitous means–that is, hitching rides on planes, ships, and trains.

By now, however, his combat days were over. He returned to the States and was made an instructor at the Recruit Depot, Parris Island, later to transfer to Camp Lejeune on June 15, 1945, and joined the 5th Training Battalion, again as an instructor.

Although thoroughly military through and through, "Diamond lived informally, going hatless and wearing dungarees practically everywhere. He even accepted one of his decorations in dungarees. When receiving the citations awarded him in Australia by General A. A. Vandegrift, "Lou looked the general in the eye and said, 'I made my landing in dungarees–guess they're good enough to get my commendation in."

He rejected several opportunities to become an officer, explaining that "nobody can make a gentleman out of me." "Though not a 'spit and polish' Marine, Diamond proved himself an expert with both 60 and 81 mortars, his accurate fire being credited as the turning point of many an engagement in the Pacific during World War II."

He retired from the Marine Corps on November 23, 1945 and returned to Toledo, Ohio. He died on September 20, 1951, at the Great Lakes Naval Training Center Hospital, after which his funeral was attended by full military honors.

In an article of August 1944, in The *American Rifleman*, entitled *The Sniper*, Lou Diamond explains that Japanese snipers tie themselves in trees, using a contrivance like a boatswain's chair hauled up into the frond of a palm or into the crown of a conifer tree. They also work in pairs. Diamond relates that his mortar platoon on Guadalcanal got caught by a sniper team, the result being that several Marines had been killed during the day, and "we were all a bit jittery because we couldn't spot them."

In one case, a sniper located not far from Diamond's position, was "dropping his shots entirely too close to my mortar platoon for comfort." He was picking off Marines at the foot of the hill. Diamond called an officer to take care of the sniper. He approached the roof of the shack with a carbine, let off some rounds into the tree, and "he was dead enough when he stopped falling. After a man plunges and somersaults 400 feet there is no use to look for bullets wounds."

"'You asked for him, Diamond!' the officer yelled. 'There he comes.'"

On another occasion, an enemy soldier moved close to his position, and yelled, "Corporal of the guard! Post number 13." The idea of this was to make them disclose their position. However, "the Jap wasn't alive long enough to make any use of it. A Springfield cracked and the Jap dropped. One of my men, noting the moving shadow, had the man in his sights when he yelled.

"'How were you sure he was a Jap?' I asked."

"'I knew we didn't have any Post 13,' the Marine told me. 'Besides, he couldn't pronounce the 'l' in corporal. He said 'corporar.'"

As Diamond put it, "The Jap is tricky, but we learn tricks, too, to use against him. Maybe it was one of our billiard players who first figured out how to use ricochets against them . . . our ricochets were not all accidents. Some of our marksmen, having figured out just where a sniper had to be, figured out a spot where a steel-jacketed bullet could be banked off a rock wall against the sniper's otherwise vulnerable neck. It worked on many occasions, to the fatal embarrassment of many Japs."

Diamond spares nothing in his depiction of jungle warfare on Guadalcanal. He describes the fate of one Japanese sniper who was so unfortunate to have fallen into the hands of a more wary American Marine. As he says,

"I saw one, lying at the base of his tree, wearing his climbing irons and all tangled up in the wreckage of his boatswain's chair, who had been stabbed to death with a knife.

Some Marine must have spotted him, must have lain in wait for him, and caught him there as he came down out of his tree, probably to return to his unit.

"While he gives credit to his enemy, he describes his comrades-in-arms as more than their match. He said that our Marines became scouts overnight. How many of them had made Buffalo the Kid and plainsmen their boyhood heroes, I don't know, but I do know that they took to jungle fighting, hunting down their enemies from tree to tree like Indians. Danger sharpened their wits and eyes . . . I have seen Marine marksmen deliberately unmask a Jap sniper by calmly shooting away the leaves that hid him and then drilling him through the nose. If you remember Japanese noses, you will admit that that is good shooting! The *American Rifleman* describes Master Gunnery Sergeant Diamond as probably the best-known non-com in the armed forces: "His age is a strictly guarded military secret . . . It's a Marine Corps legend that 'Lou' wasn't born—he was issued."

Chapter 14

Once a Marine . . .

In December 1991, Nat Elliott returned to Pearl Harbor to commemorate the fifty-year anniversary of the bombing of Pearl Harbor. As he said, "the celebration had a special significance as he met with more than four hundred former Marines that form part of that exclusive group of eight thousand members known as the Pearl Harbor Survivors Association. "The Big One" was celebrated with such events as speeches by admirals and generals, parades, concerts, demonstrations of the latest military equipment, memorials to the fallen of that "Day of Infamy," and numerous meetings and banquets. "Old acquaintances were renewed and many a sea story was retold with new embellishments."

Elliott vividly remembers the Japanese planes flying over the parade grounds of the Pearl Harbor Navy Yard Marine Barracks en route to "Battleship Row." He was there, stationed with the 2nd Engineer Battalion, 2nd Marine Division, who were in the process of building a new camp, later named Camp Catlin, located about halfway between the Navy Yard and Honolulu. Thousands of wartime Marines passed through on their way to fight in the Pacific.

As battalion photographer, it was Elliott's job to take photos of the construction progress on a daily basis. He had to climb to the top of a tall tower and click away. He "had an assistant, Robert Wolber, from Peoria, Illinois. He and I built a complete darkroom inside our sleeping tent. At my disposal was a Harley-Davidson motorcycle with a side car and assigned driver." Elliott and the driver toured the island whenever they had the chance. The only excuse they needed was to claim they had to go to Honolulu to get film or other supplies.

However, with the attack by the Japanese planes, the paradise that they had found soon disappeared. Elliott and his assistant, Wolber, woke up to the sound of falling bombs. Grabbing their Speed Graphics, they ran to the parade ground to take pictures, and shrapnel shredded their tent and the darkroom within. Enemy pilots could easily be seen as they passed directly overhead. With Marines rushing out of their tents, they knew the war was on. "There was no mistaking the red meatball emblem on the sides of their aircraft." Soon, ammunition was distributed and the NCOs had the troops shooting at the attackers. With black smoke rising from the stricken ships, Elliott was unable to get many good pictures. After a short lull in the attack, a second wave of planes appeared. By now, the antiaircraft batteries were set and ready to be put into operation. But it was too late. The Japanese were on their way back to their carriers.

In the aftermath of the attack, Elliott, with other personnel took ammunition to the drydock. Upon their arrival at the dock area, he could appreciate the enormity of the damage and carnage the attack had caused. As he described the scene:

"Half naked men had swum ashore from some of the ships, many only with their skivvies on. I saw a first sergeant I had known—he was one of the lucky ones to get off his ship. We unloaded the ammunition and returned to our unit . . . Rumors were rife with supposed landings of enemy troops . . . The harbor was still ablaze and when a friendly plane came in to land, the trigger-happy guys from every ship and station might open up on it. When some ships were fired on, everybody started firing. This was much scarier than the bombing itself."

When people ask Elliott if he was afraid, he generally replies that there was not much time to be scared. And there was no place to hide. They were disciplined Marines used to carrying out orders.

A native of Chicago, Elliott enlisted in the Marine Corps on May 15, 1939, at 18. As he had attended summer camp for Reservists in 1939 and 1940, he did not go to recruit training.

In November 1940, even prior to the outbreak of World War II, he was called to active duty.

He, as the others, quit his job, packed his bags and equipment, kissed the family and girlfriend good-bye, and got on the train for San Diego. Transferred out of the band, he joined H Company, 2nd Marines, 2nd Marine Division—the company that was later to spearhead the invasion of Tulagi on August 7, 1942. As a member of a heavy-weapons company, "the days were filled with learning to take the weapons apart blindfolded, reciting the litany of how the damn thing operated, and how to fix stoppages." He was soon transferred to H & S Company, 2nd Engineer Battalion. Not long after, Elliott was sent stateside to Portland, Oregon, to spend six months with U.S. Army engineers at a mapmaking and printing facility.

Leaving Hawaii proved to be a sad experience. The troops were instructed not to discuss the damage to the fleet and its facilities. "It was heartbreaking to pass through the harbor and see the sunken and damaged vessels of the once great fleet."

Finishing his course with the Army engineers, Elliott was transferred to the newly formed 19th Marine Regiment, which proved to be a "wonderful assignment for me, as I was made chief of the reproduction section with the new rank of buck sergeant. Our equipment included two litho presses, each housed in its own mobile trailer. Another trailer contained a 24-inch copying camera complete with refrigerated trays to keep the developers cool in the expected warm climates to come. A fourth van housed the plate making facilities and storage for supplies."

The engineers shipped out on a former Dutch cruise liner built to hold three hundred passengers and crew. With more than three thousand Marines on board, the sixteen-day trip was no luxury cruise. Such overcrowding prevented the crew from celebrating the traditional ceremony of crossing the Equator. After sailing through a typhoon of ten days, they arrived in New Zealand.

In November, Elliott went ashore with the darkroom trailers in the invasion of Bougainville. "The Navy B-24s would fly reconnaissance missions and photograph the Japanese positions. They would drop the aerial films to us by parachute, and we would develop them and make mosaic maps showing where the enemy was concentrated. Major General Roy S. Geiger, USMC, the III Amphibious Corps commander, wrote us up with a letter of commendation for a job well done.

Around the end of 1943, Elliott was back at Guadalcanal, preparing for the landings on Guam. After the mop-up in July, his unit moved its equipment to Guam and started to prepare for the next battle which was to be Iwo Jima. On Guam they printed the maps that the Air Corps used to carry on bombing runs over Japan. Elliott was now a master technical sergeant.

With the end of the war, he took an early discharge on August 3, 1945.

Elliott, who, until recently resided in Denton, Texas, was quick to say, "Once a Marine, always a Marine. I feel that I owe my lifestyle and my career to the foundation instilled in me by having served those six years in the Marine Corps. I still get a lump in my throat when I see the American flag waving."

In the spring of 2001, Nat Elliott's wife wrote a letter in which she informed me that her husband has passed away.

Chapter 15

The Sagas of Bill Sager

The success, modesty, and personal satisfaction enjoyed by Bill Sager is due, at least in part to his experience, at times harrowing, other times exulting, in the South Pacific and China during World War II. Now counselor at law for the China Marine Association, he is well experienced in handling the legal affairs of national associations. In 1995, he retired from a staff position as attorney for the Society of Accountants. He has taught economics and law at the University of Virginia and the Georgetown University Law Center. "In addition to his outstanding professional career, Bill Sager is active in numerous civic and Marine organizations, and he is a life member of the China Marine Association."[1]

Bill and his wife of fifty-eight years are the parents of three children and grandparents of ten. In summing up his life, he paraphrases the late Admiral Arleigh Burke: "I have lived a good life. I wasn't killed in the war. I married the woman I loved. We've had a beautiful life together. I never had a job I didn't like. I am satisfied with my life and achievement, both military and civilian."

Sager didn't lose his life fighting on Guadalcanal. But he almost did—on more than one occasion.

Having survived the fighting on the "Canal," in October 1942, Bill volunteered for and was selected for duty (with five Marine

[1] *Scuttlebutt*, June, 1999, p. 8.

officers with South Pacific combat infantry experience) with the Sino-American Cooperation Organization (SACO), also known as Naval Group China.

After flying the "Hump" and reporting to SACO headquarters in Chungking, Bill was assigned to set up U.S. Naval Unit Ten in Kweichow Province, and to equip and train Chinese guerrillas and irregulars that operated against the Japanese in the Kweilin-Luchow corridor. Camp Ten equipped three battalions of guerrillas (known as Column Ten), each battalion consisting of approximately five hundred Chinese.

Bill Sager was so dedicated to the Marine Corps and the prestige of the Corps that he "would have preferred to stay in" after the war. But his wife "wouldn't hear of it after seeing me go off to war twice in two and a half years." His oldest daughter was born while he was in China. When he saw her for the first time when he returned from active duty, she was almost one-year old. Returning home, his "year old daughter wanted nothing to do with the strange man in the house."

Bill Sager joined the Marine Corps shortly after graduating from the University of Virginia in mid 1939. After graduating from the Platoon Leaders Class at Quantico in August 1940, he received his commission as a second lieutenant.

Before going overseas, he was assigned to Company K, 3rd Battalion, 1st Marines, at Tent City, New River, North Carolina, as a rifle platoon leader. While serving with K and I Companies, Bill quickly and modestly noted that both of his company commanders received the Silver Star, and the battalion commander, Lt. Colonel William "Spike" McKelvey won the Navy Cross.

Some of his most memorable experiences were combat patrols on Guadalcanal, and in China, "operating with excellent Chinese agents and troops (irregulars) against Japanese columns."

Bill Sager, Captain, U.S. Marine Corps, spent the last year of World War II with a unit known as the Sino-American Cooperation Organization, or SACO. In 1974, in a letter to the Torch, newsletter of the National Federation of Jewish Men's Clubs, Chicago, Illinois, he describes the functions of SACO:

"I spent the last year of World War II with a unit known as the Sino-American Cooperation Organization—SACO. In addition to coastal watching and river port watching, SACO also operated guerrilla troops behind the Japanese lines. One such unit of SACO (officially known as Naval Unit 13, but also known as the Yangtze Raiders or the River Unit) operated in the Hankow area. Immediately after the Japanese surrender on August 14, 1945, the Chinese and Americans operating with the River Unit moved into Hankow. They were the first Allied troops into the city, but since they were considered 'irregulars,' the Japanese refused to surrender to them. So, for a matter of weeks—almost a month— the armed Japanese and the armed members of SACO's River Unit managed to co-exist side by side until the American 14th Air Force airlifted some Chinese troops under Chinese command to the Hankow airport. These Chinese troops managed to collect the Japanese tanks, field guns, etc., and to impound the Japanese troops so that eventually the city was restored to Chinese military control.

"After the River Unit took it over, Hankow became the collection point for the other SACO units and teams operating in Central China. 'I was the commander of Naval Unit 10 in Kweichow Province and received orders from our headquarters in Chungking to join the River Unit at Hankow. It took us about six weeks and much hard traveling to make that rendezvous, but I recall that we arrived at Hankow on the evening of the "double-ten" (tenth day of the tenth month—October 10—which is a National Chinese holiday, like the Fourth of July.'"

It was precisely with this unit, Navy Group China, that he served as "CO Navy Unit Ten, operating with Chinese guerrillas and intelligence groups behind Japanese lines along the Kweilin-Luichow corridor, South Central China."

Sager affirms that the "rifle platoon leader is the hardest job in the world." But that "it prepares you to do anything in civilian life." His roommate at the University of Virginia was the best person he knew in the military. They joined up together, and "We served in the same company in the 1st Marine Division. He gave up his last leave in the U.S. so I could get married." He particularly admired Colonel William "Spike" McKelvey, Colonel (later Commandant) Clifton Cates, who was his CO at Officers Basic School, and later his 1st Marines commanding officer, and Admiral Milton "Mary" Miles, his CO for Navy Group, China. Seeing dead Marines was the most unpleasant experience for Sager, as well as "going through personal effects of Marines KIA, to send back to their parents." While he enjoyed visiting Melbourne, Australia, and Wellington, New Zealand, he described Calcutta, India, as the "absolute pits, when Navy Group, China, had its supply to gear you up for China."

In the middle of September 1942, K Company of the 1st Marines, commanded by Captain Robert J. Putnam, carried out a prodigious feat of arms that was described in an article by William H. Bartsch that "has been regarded as a sideshow to the main event at Bloody Ridge, but only a one-man deep Marine line blocked Major General Kiyotake Kawaguchi's Kuma Battalion from reaching Henderson Field."[2]

The 5,200 man force under Kawaguchi would mount "an attack from the south over a ridge to the south of Henderson Field which Kawaguchi himself lead himself."[3] Other Japanese officers would lead enemy formations from some other directions in order to cut off the defending Marine forces.

In this classic and epic action, 2nd Lieutenant Sager and his 1st platoon, and another Jewish-American Marine, Lieutenant Herman Abady (passed away March 4, 2001. Laid to rest at Richmond, Virginia's Beth El cemetery. Belatedly received the Silver Star Medal), commanding the 3rd platoon would play decisive roles. Lieutenants Sager and Abady were roommates at the University of Virginia for two years, went through Platoon Leaders Class and Basic School, and fought together in the same company. Abady received the Purple Heart and eventually retired from the Marine Corps as a lieutenant colonel.

Around midnight, a five-man listening post of Sager's pla-

[2] Bartsch, William, *Crucial Battle Ignored*, Marine Corps Gazette, September, 1997, p. 82.

[3] Op. cit.

toon had heard sounds like troop movements and was withdrawn as the company went on the alert. "K Company was as well prepared for a Japanese assault as it could be under the circumstances. Putnam had positioned Lt. Phil Wilheit's 2nd platoon on his left flank, Lt. Herman Abady's 3rd platoon in the center, and Lt. Bill Sager's 1st platoon on his right flank."[4] At about 0400, a period of deathly silence and darkness, "Harwood now began making out shapes around the barbed wire in front of him. Then, suddenly, a rifleman in Abady's platoon yelled 'Japs!' and ran toward the wire, joined by others rising out of their foxholes. Free swinging his machine-gun, Harwood continuously poured fire into the charging Japanese . . ."[5] Later, Sager was engaged as "Just before dawn, the stones in the ration cans attached to the barbed wire in front of Sager's platoon began to rattle. Then, "The assault on Sager's section proved to be the last of the night for the Japanese. None had managed to penetrate K Company's line."[6] Sager and Abady were instrumental in stopping an attack which would have menaced Henderson Field and thus seriously jeopardized the entire operation on Guadalcanal. As Bartsch said, "By holding their thin line, K Company had prevented a potentially disastrous breakthrough by the Japanese to Henderson Field and to the Marines' command on the island."[7]

But Bill Sager is not the only illustrious member of the family. His wife, talented writer Elizabeth Mopsik Sager, wrote her memoirs, entitled *The Sagas of a War Bride*. In it, she described Bill's work in China, and the fact that she had been unaware of his adventures in that part of the world. In her writing, she reveals that she had been led to believe that he was some—how out of danger: that he was posted in Ceylon, or perhaps India. She writes as follows:[8]

"The Japanese Emperor's rescript to his army and navy to

---

[4] Ibid., p. 85.

[5] Ibid., p. 87.

[6] Op. cit.

[7] Ibid., p. 89.

[8] Sager, Elizabeth, *The Saga of a War Bride*, Arlington, Va., 1998, p. 18.

lay down their arms and ceasecombat was issued on August 14, 1945. On September 2nd the Japanese surrender took place on the deck of the battleship *Missouri* in Tokyo Bay. About the third week of September I received a call from a reporter for the *Richmond Times Dispatch*. He asked if I were Elizabeth Sager, the wife of Marine Captain William Sager. I said I was. He said he had received an Associated Press wire from the Navy Department in Washington, stating that Captain William H. Sager, of Charlottesville, a University of Virginia graduate, was revealed to be a member of one of the most dramatic units playing a part in the war against Japan. The Navy Department had just released information that Marine Captain Sager was a member of a super-secret group known as SACO—the Sino-American Cooperation Organization, who acted as guerrilla troops, intelligence agents, and weather observers behind the Japanese lines in occupied China. The reporter continued to say that the wire release from the Navy Department described SACO as a dangerous fighting outfit, killing Japanese troops, blowing up trains and Japanese ships in the Chinese ports, and their operations extended from Indo-China to the Gobi Desert. He said the SACO Americans became adept at Chinese disguises and guided by SACO Chinese, slipped through the Japanese lines when they choose."

Bill Sager is extremely proud to have served in the Marine Corps. On the face of his personal stationery, on the envelope, is the inscription of a red bulldog with a World War I helmet stamped with the Marine Corps globe and anchor, and the bulldog encircled with, "United States Marines."

Bill Sager retired from the Marine Corps as a major.

Addendum to the *Sagas of Bill Sager*—his personal observations and remembrances:

"The holy days of Rosh Hashanah are referred to frequently as Days of Remembrance. In fact, one of the Rosh Hashanah prayers tells that God remembers our past, which also lives in our minds and in our hearts.

"As I sit in the synagogue, my mind cannot help but return to Rosh Hashanah of years ago. I seem to remember best the years of special anniversary numbers, such as 10, 25, and 30 years ago. As I sat through the Rosh Hashanah liturgy this year, my mind and memory kept returning to the Rosh Hashanah of 1942–41 years ago. 'Thou remembrest . . . our past which lives in our minds.'

"Rosh Hashanah in 1942 arrived early in September along with a renewed effort to recapture a worthless piece of real estate in the South Pacific called Guadalcanal.

"I observed Rosh Hashanah, 1942, on Guadalcanal. We gathered a dozen or so of our battalion's Jewish Marines from off the lines (plus a few Navy people) and hiked back to the edge of Henderson Field—the island's single airstrip bombed daily by the Japanese—to hold our Rosh Hashanah prayers under the palm trees. A young Pfc. from Washington, D.C., who, as an exhibition of faith had carried a small *tallit* and JWB prayer book in his pack, conducted this abbreviated service. When we came to the part in the service about who shall live and perish by the sword, we made jokes about meeting the business end of a samurai sword in a banzai charge, but a Navy doctor among us gave unequivocal assurance there was a loophole and the evil decree could be averted by giving generously to charity. This effort at humor was intended to break the tension of the siege mentality which affected us all.

"Our brief services were terminated at 12 noon when the Japanese bombers came over on their daily run to drop their string of bombs at Henderson Field. In fact, the Japanese were so prompt with their daily 12 appointment that you could set your watch and not be five minutes off either way. When the bombing was over, we shouldered our .03 Springfields and hiked back to our position on the Lunga River, which, because of the accuracy of our maps, was called the Ilu River. For the Marines on Guadalcanal, Rosh Hashanah, 1942, was over.

"Guadalcanal was a difficult campaign for the Navy, Marines, and the Jewish members of the forces who participated. We buried our Jewish dead in the Marines' cemetery without benefit of clergy and decorated the mounds of earth palm fronds.

We succored our Jewish wounded as best we could, and we watched as the most serious, those who probably would not make it, were evacuated to the Navy hospital in the Hebrides, whenever the Navy could fly out the seriously wounded. As the humorists among us stated (and only a sense of humor kept us going), Guadalcanal was not a place for a nice Jewish boy who didn't like Spam.

"After numerous sea engagements, Admiral Halsey and the U.S. Navy eventually cleared the Japanese from the sea lanes and held them clear. Our Navy and Marine flyers, although always outnumbered, kept Japanese bombers and transports off balance. Four months after the August 7 landing, the tired, weary, and malaria-infested Marines were told to stand by to leave Guadalcanal. General Patch of the U.S. Army had relieved General Vandegrift and his 1st Marine Division in early December 1942. My battalion combat team was assigned standby reserve position adjacent to an army field hospital which had arrived on the island only a week or so before. For the first time in over four months, I slept off the ground on a canvas cot in a pyramidal tent with duckboards for a floor.

"Early one Friday evening while enjoying the luxury of the canvas cot, I heard the bugle at the adjacent army field hospital sound church call. Now church call is not the most prevalent call in the bugler's handbook, and I doubt if many servicemen recognize it, and I doubt I would have recognized it had I not spent four years in a military with daily compulsory chapel attendance. I thought to myself that church call on Friday night could be for Jewish services, but not on Guadalcanal. Obviously, it's some Catholic holy day. I declined to answer church call and went to sleep.

"The following Sunday morning, I was again sacked out on my canvas cot when two army officers—one a major and the other a captain—entered my tent. Disregarding military courtesy, I remained stretched out on the cot—what Marine who had spent four and a half months as a mud-slosher on Guadalcanal was about to stand for a couple of army officers in freshly starched khaki. The major, who introduced himself as a medical officer at the army hospital, asked if I knew when my battalion was leaving.

"'Couldn't be too soon to suit me,' I replied. 'I've been on this God-stinkin' island since August. You can have it.'

"'I don't want the island,' he said, 'but I would like to have your cot and your duckboards when you leave.'

"'Take the g-d-m cot and duckboards when we leave,' I said, still prone on my cot. 'I sure as sh-t ain't taking them with me.'

"Apparently offended by my stream of profanity, the army captain turned to look down at me. The morning light coming through the entrance way reflected on his insignia. I pulled up to a sitting position. I just didn't believe what I was seeing.

"'Is that a Jewish chaplain's shield on your collar?' my voice trembled.

"He assured me that it was.

"'Then it was you who was having religious services Friday night? I heard the bugler sound church call.'

"He assured me that he did indeed hold religious services on Guadalcanal on the past Friday night.

"I sat on the edge of my cot and buried my head in my arms. For some reason which I shall never understand, I felt emotionally drained. My voice choked up. I didn't want these two army officers in fresh khaki to see that my eyes were moist. A hundred thoughts raced through my mind, but I could think of only one as I sat with my head buried in my arms. We who had existed through that terribly dangerous experience called Guadalcanal and were about to leave, would not be leaving our Jewish comrades alone and deserted in the military cemetery by the Lunga lagoon. A Jewish chaplain had come to Guadalcanal."

Chapter 16

He'd Rather Be a Marine

Chicago-born Seymour (Sy) Ivice, now a semi-retired business-man who resides (2002) in Wilmette, Illinois, offers readers some memories of his three years, eleven months, and two weeks in the Corps—having fought on Guadalcanal and Okinawa.

"On December 9, 1941, I went to the Navy enlistment office. While standing in line, a Marine sergeant in very impressive blues walked the line, like he was inspecting horses. I was a husky kid, and he asked me why I wanted to join the Navy—wouldn't I rather be a Marine? Before I could answer, I was one.

"At 16 years of age, I left for San Diego on December 15 and started an abbreviated boot camp of five weeks. Coming from Maxwell Street, I was used to taking care of myself.

"After recruit training, I was assigned to C Company, 1st Battalion, 2nd Marines. We left San Diego June 1, 1942, aboard the USS *President Jackson* and made a completely fouled-up practice landing on one of the Fiji Islands, in the South Pacific, north of New Zealand. Our lieutenant briefed us aboard ship for the landing. He said we'd take Tulagi and Guadalcanal, and, in seventy-two hours, the Army could come in and relieve us. The regiment lost some men in the surf. We landed on Florida Island (no Japs), and then went over to Tulagi (north of Guadalcanal). I believe it was F Company, 2nd Battalion, and suffered casualties on both Tanambogo and Gavuto.

"While garrisoning Tulagi, I was assigned to a cave. I hadn't realized that I suffered from claustrophobia. I went to my sergeant and volunteered for anything that would get me out of that cave.

"On Tulagi, we were eating tree roots and captured Jap rice with weevils, the daily water ration was about half a canteen cup. One day, when I went to get my food—picture a large, black pot such as you see in cartoons of cannibals—someone had found something that turned the rice and tree roots (and whatever else was in the pot) a chocolate color. As I was getting my rations, down this little trail comes a party of heavy brass, led by Admiral William Frederick 'Bull' Halsey (1882–1959). I remember he walked up to Captain Vasconcelos who was wearing a very dirty skivvy shirt and said, 'How's the chow?' The captain just held out his mess gear. Then I heard the admiral say a ship would be in on Thursday with food.

"I remember that working party I was on unloading. The first case of food was Spam. We broke it open and ate a can apiece like you would eat an apple. The next things that happened was a stroke of luck for me. The sergeant called me and told me to report to regular headquarters. They had called for volunteers and I was it. By this time, we were not in great shape. We had been on very short rations, and many of us were suffering form diarrhea, myself included, and had been taking bismuth and paregoric for some time. Most of us didn't take a pack, just our poncho, and I took two cans of heavy hash (cans of rations) and two cans of light biscuit (cans of rations)—plus one canteen of water. I knew that this landing had many snafus and this was one of them.

"I reported to regular headquarters. We ran the OP on top of the high point of the island, and manned the phones in General Rupertus' (Major General William H.) headquarters—the British Governor's old residence. The captain who was G-2 took a liking to me because, one night when a Jap destroyer was shelling us, I was manning the phones in the command post. It was like a scene in a movie—everyone was trying to get out and the captain saw me under a table with the phones. He said, 'What the hell are you doing there?' I said, 'I haven't been relieved, sir.' He told me to get the phones to the battle CP. I was slightly wounded on the way—just small scratches. The corpsman treated them. I still have the scars on my legs, but no Purple Heart for that one, probably because I was on detached duty. But the captain told me if I ever got to Parris Island, to see the major (whose name I forgot) in charge of Intelligence School and try for Intelligence because he saw that I liked the work. He also told me something I have never read. If we were ever given a Condition Black, we were to make our way to Florida as best we could and try to meet inland near a large hill or mountain that they pointed out to us, and take up the fight from there.

"Sometime in October, I think, I was sent back to C Company, and we went over to Guadalcanal to relieve the 1st Marines. About nine or ten of us were on patrol when we got a radio message that Japs attacked a small unit behind us. The lieutenant set up a sort of defensive line and put me in a spot that was about five feet from a very small bush. I moved over just to get a little cover. He came back and chewed me out for moving when he left. I moved back again. A minute or so later, a piece of shrapnel landed just about where the middle of my back would have been.

"When the lieutenant came back, he said, 'Ivice,' and I stopped him saying, 'He's dead. I'm his replacement.'

"Saw no Japs that day on another patrol. We had been in a minor firefight with a few Jap snipers. We were headed back to our lines and had to climb a rather steep hill, all the time being sniped at. When we got to the top, we found an Army outfit (I think the 132nd). In any case, we needed water, and believe it or not, I met a guy by the name of Marv Frank who had gone to Hebrew School with my brother. I warned Marv about the lousy security they had. I heard he was killed a few days later at that location.

"When the 164th Army came to relieve us, I was one of a few Marines who stayed with them for about a week as scouts. I was on a listening post with a sergeant by the name of Samuels or Samson. We would stay awake as long as we could and then wake the other man. The sergeant had just relieved me when a shot hit him. I couldn't see anything—it was a black night. He said he was hit in the head, so I felt his head which was wet, and, as it tasted salty, I assumed it was blood. I was helping him back to the command post (we were on top of a steep rise) when the Japs started a very heavy mortar barrage that lasted all night. One shell actually blew us off the edge of the hill. It turned out that the bullet had hit the sergeant's helmet and dented it so badly that the inner liner broke and a sharp edge made a small cut in his head. I spent the rest of the night in a foxhole shaking with a malaria attack. The next morning, a Catholic chaplain crawled around and gave us a shot of booze.

"In late November, we had been making good progress moving north when we were pulled all the way back to the beach near the airport to block an unexpected landing. There was no landing, but we took a whole night of Jap shelling from 15-inch naval gunfire. Another night of shaking like a leaf in a foxhole. We lost a couple of men to what must have been a direct hit. We never found the smallest piece of them.

"I think it was probably in January that we made a patrol every other day. Out of a company of 191 men, only about thirty at a time could make it. Man by man, we carried a BAR, and the ammunition for it as long as we could. Once in a while, when we had to carry a wounded man back, you almost wished he were dead, I'm ashamed to say. But we did bring them back.

"Most, if not all, of us, were weak and sick. I remember a dengue fever attack on Tulagi when a Jap plane flew over as if to strafe, or probably to photograph. Everyone ran for cover except myself and another guy with dengue (sometimes called 'bone-breaking' fever because of severe pains to the joints and muscles). We were afraid we *wouldn't* die.

"The 2nd Marines left the 'Canal for New Zealand in February after six months, the longest stretch any group was assigned. From New Zealand I was sent home with malaria, paratyphoid, a deformed duodenum, and hookworm. I spent about a year in and out of the hospital with malaria. I also did a few War Bond tours around Chicago, including a radio show at the Tribune Building. My brother and I still have a copy of the script.

"I was put on limited duty as a brig guard at nearby Great Lakes Naval Training Center.

After a run-in with a staff NCO, I got five days bread and water, better known in the Corps as 'piss and punk.' I figured that I had better get away from Great Lakes, and requested a transfer to Camp Lejeune so I could try for Intelligence School.

"I got to see the major and mentioned the captain from Tulagi. The major said I could pass the IQ test (called in the Corps GCT, which does not use the same numbers as the Stanford-Binet Intelligence Test), I would be in. William Manchester, who was my corporal later, said I passed with 140+. While attending the school, I met John Terrence, really the original 'Hawkeye,' who became my closest friend, who got me in all kinds of trouble, and whom I still miss today.

"Upon graduating, we were sent to the Intelligence Section, Headquarters, 2nd Battalion, 29th Marines, 6th Marine Division. I believe the Marines had the finest line officers in the world, but once in a while, a bad one falls through the cracks. Lieutenant G—from Birmingham, Alabama, I believe, was one of those. He was over his head. Almost all the others in our section were OCS washouts, which is what he should have been. We went to Guadalcanal to train.

"On the 'Canal, Terrence and I once left a working party to visit a CB (Construction Battalion, Seabees) camp for a good meal and refreshments. Lieutenant Smith, in charge of the work detail, took offense at our departure, so Captain Mabie gave us three days 'piss and punk.'

"The brig on the 'Canal was like a dog kennel made of barbed wire. The guards would lift the wire door a couple of times a day to allow us go to the head, which was about a 36-holer. Manchester and some of the other guys would meet us and supply John and me with whatever goodies they had.

"I think Lieutenant G— never forgave me for the following: on an exercise, I was to guide a platoon, of which G— was a member, in attacking a defended position. He told me to bring them up a certain trail. I asked the lieutenant leading the platoon if he would like to do it like a Jap would, and I took them through a bamboo forest. It was tough going, and but we came up from behind and surprised them. The colonel praised the lieutenant, but if looks could kill, G—'s would have.

"We landed on Okinawa on August 7. This was the first time G— put me at risk for no reason. Almost immediately after landing, we sent out a platoon patrol which our Sergeant Ford was part of. While pretty deep in, we found a small bridge that was partially set up to be blown. Ford and I disarmed the explosives, and I put a sizable sample in my pack. Later, while deeper in unknown territory, G— radios us to bring the explosive back to him. We suggested that the return trip by just the two of us might be hazardous to our health and that the damned explosive was not exactly a secret weapon. We had to make the trip back alone, which was uneventful, but stupid and dangerous.

"Another time, John and I, while on patrol with Captain Mabie, were called to try and talk some prisoners out of the bush. We did, my Japanese was fair. We brought these prisoners—two young, pretty girls, one young Okinawan home guard, and an older civilian—back to battalion headquarters. Although it was already getting dark, the captain insisted John and I take them to regiment. The most dangerous thing in the war was to walk around the rear echelon at night, let alone with prisoners. We offered to stay up and guard them, but the captain was insistent. We marched the prisoners down the trail (we were on the Motobu Peninsula then), singing the Marines' Hymn as loudly as we could.

"John finally hit a trip flare set up by our 37 mm antitank-guns boys. I pushed the two male prisoners down, and we used every curse word we knew to let the Marines know we were Marines. Finally, out of the darkness, a voice said, 'What in hell do you think you assholes are doing?' I said, 'Just what a bigger asshole with bars ordered us to do.' This captain got us a truck to drive us to regiment, but we still got fired on in the truck. To top it off, the major at G-2 wouldn't take the prisoners. When I asked what the hell we could do with them, his response was, 'You can guard them tonight, or shoot them,. but don't bring them back until daylight.' John and I guarded them, and turned them in at daylight.

"Another time, John and I were on a small mountain trail in the Motobu Mountains, when we heard the sounds of a firefight coming from the top of the hill. John, always the curious one, immediately said, 'Let's go look,' so, of course, I had to follow him. This wasn't bravado on John's part—it was his constant, damned curiosity. We found Fox Company taking fire from what appeared to be a 20 mm gun. John jumped into one hole and I into another. Mine had a Marine boondocker complete with a foot in it. Bill Peterson, a section member, had talked about his friend who lost a foot on the Motobu. I told him that I had found it.

"Captain Fowler drafted us, and we spent an uncomfortable night with Fox Company after setting up some security booby traps with grenades.

"I remember the time on the Motobu when we had a Marine photographer with us. He said he wanted to take some pictures, so John and I were delegated to take him around. We got lost in the hills, and the next thing we knew, we were looking down at a column of enemy troops. John called the photographer to the side of the hill and said, 'You want some pictures?' The photographer said, 'Where the hell are we?' John said, 'I don't know, but I think those are Japs, so we must be lost.' The photographer said, 'Get me the hell back!' among other assorted comments. There were no lines, we had just wandered a little too far. The photographer returned to the 2ⁿᵈ Battalion.

"One day, when it was raining hard, we were under heavy mortar fire. About four or five of us had to take shelter on the reverse slope of a small hill and were holding a piece of corrugated steel over us against the rain. Bill Manchester had a rather bad case of diarrhea and the slit trench was in the middle of the field, but the Japs would shell us for a few minutes, then stop for five or ten. Bill would run out to the slit trench whenever the shelling stopped. He had no pants on, just his poncho. One time they didn't give him the normal interval, and he came back soiled. He was sitting across from me, and I swear he wanted me to take my .45 and put him out of his misery. Funny, how you remember certain things.

"The day we got hit (June 5, 1945)—after having made an amphibious landing on the Oruku Peninsula a few days before—we were receiving constant fire from what we call a 'screaming meemie' rail-mounted eight-inch rocket gun which had been hitting a few hundred yards from the tomb where Bill Manchester, John Terrence, and I were taking cover (all of Okinawa has many caves and tombs dug into the limestone hillsides).

"I had just come in from an all-night OP watch and was heating some coffee with John when I heard one (shell) that I knew was had. I hollered to take cover, and I made it to the entrance of the tomb. I turned to call John, who never moved fast, when it hit in the courtyard just feet from us. I can confirm that light travels faster than sound or blast. All I saw was a big red flash—and in the millisecond it took for the shrapnel and blast to hit me, I remember saying very simply to myself, 'Aw, shit, I'm getting killed.' It was a very calm thing—I can't explain it any better than that. I was blown into the tomb, and when I came to, I was choking from the fumes of the shell. I couldn't see, I thought, because of the smoke. But, actually, I was blinded at that time. O'Neal helped me out because John was badly wounded right in front of the entrance to the tomb. In the ambulance (a jeep), someone said to me, 'How ya doin', kid?'

"I was feeling rather sorry for myself and didn't know at the time how badly wounded John was. He died at the aid station, I think, but they wouldn't tell me until the next day. (I only found out recently that John is buried in the Punchbowl National Cemetery in Honolulu.) Bill was severely wounded, hit in the upper back. He carries a piece of shrapnel near his heart to this day (2002).

"I wound up in an army hospital. I was sent there from the hospital ship, as it had an eye doctor. I recovered my sight within a week. The doc wanted to send me to New Hebrides, but I told him I would rather go back to my unit, as I didn't want to make the next landing with strangers.

"Shortly after, we went to Guam. I was in the hospital, having a little trouble with my eye, when The Bomb went off. The Marines sent people home, based on overseas and combat time. I was the only one in the section who had the points. I remember Captain Mabie asking me to be bartender at the officers' farewell party. I like to think it was his way of inviting me.

"I've been asked about the differences between Guadalcanal and Okinawa. To me, on the 'Canal you knew you could get killed, but at least for the first couple of months, when all we saw were Jap ships and planes, we couldn't be sure of winning. On Okinawa, where you *knew* you were going to get hurt or killed, you also knew that we *would* win.

"My final tale is when I was in the hospital at Great Lakes when it was over. My brother, a first lieutenant who flew a B-24, came to visit me. I couldn't get liberty, so I told him I would drive out with him. That went OK, but some Marine boot caught me climbing back in the next day. The doc was a nice guy and released me to the Marine barracks. He said I could come back to the hospital after it blew over. I found out I could be discharged immediately, and I was. End of story. The survivors of the section are still close, and we have been getting together every year or so with a mini-reunion.

Chapter 17

He Danced at Their Weddings

Fred Abel, Florida, was 19 when he was severely wounded during his second battle on Okinawa in 1945. His story of survival and determination to overcome daunting obstacles is told in his own words:

"I was born on August 11, 1925, in Yonkers, New York. My family moved around a lot because my father was a traveling salesman. When we came to live in California, I was 15 years old. I enlisted in the Marine Corps in Stockton, California, on March 16, 1943, at 17. After enlistment, I was sent to San Francisco where I was formally sworn in, then it was off to San Diego for boot camp.

"After training was over, I spent time at Hunters Point in San Francisco for guard duty. From Hunters Point, I was transferred to Camp Pendleton where the 5th Division was forming. I was taken out of that division and sent to Camp Elliott near San Diego to await overseas orders. My journey took me to many ports—first, Noumea, capital of New Caledonia; then to Guadalcanal for more training, and then to Guam, where we landed just off the beach and lost eighteen or nineteen LSTs (landing ship, tank). They were fully loaded and trying to make it to the beach. They were not attacked until around the eighteenth wave.

"I was sent back to Guadalcanal where the 29th Regiment

was awaiting our arrival to form the 6th Division which would consist of men from the 4th, 22nd, and 29th Regiments. (Prior to this time, we were the 1st Marine Brigade, consisting of men from the 4th and 22nd Regiments).

"As the 6th Marine Division, we were sent to Okinawa. I was part of K Company, 3rd Battalion, 22nd Regiment. We landed on Okinawa on Easter Sunday, April 1, 1945.

"We were on our line on Okinawa (on June 18, 1945) and General Buckner (Lieutenant

General Simon B. Buckner, Jr., USA, Commander of Army, Navy, and Marine units comprising the Expeditionary Troops for the Okinawa invasion) showed up in full dress uniform, swagger stick, polished boots, riding crop, Navy captains with all their gold showing, Marine Corps colonels. They were needed for planning. However, I felt that they need not to be fully dressed this way and on our lines. General Buckner came out to a point on a hill . . . The Japs commenced an artillery bombardment and he was killed. This attack lasted about half an hour. The men carried out about a dozen of the Marine, some killed and some wounded.

"I was assigned a Browning automatic (BAR) and sent into battle with an assistant, Arnold Raxton, a fellow Jewish Marine. We were in the rear echelon and supposed to be there three days. I got loaded on sick-bay alcohol. On the way to the lines, I was hoping some Japs would shoot me. That's how bad it was being drunk on sick-bay alcohol.

"The next day, it was decided that my squad was going to go out on patrol to pick up Japanese soldiers who were supposedly surrendering. When we arrived, we were caught in an ambush. They were not surrendering—they were fighting. We started back. We had to go through a clearing; while there, I saw another bullet graze the ground and penetrate his side. He lived long enough to get to the aid station and passed on to a better place soon after. During this, my second battle at war, my assistant was killed and I was left wounded.

"My wounds were quite severe. A bullet had entered my hip,

shattering everything in between upon its exit out the other side. I was told that I would never be able to walk, dance, have children, ride a horse, or anything that I loved doing. This news was devastating, especially when I loved to dance. At just 19, I had been named the 'Jitterbug King.' I would have to become accustomed to life as a paraplegic.

"I was hospitalized for twenty months. During my stay, I had the longest operation on record for that time. Afterward, I had a full body cast. One day I ripped off the cast, and, from that point on, it was sheer determination to overcome this tragedy that had been inflicted upon me. After months of rehab, I could walk with braces and crutches. The braces were initially short, but with age they increased in size up my legs, and today I am confined to a wheelchair.

"Before I left for overseas, I met the woman I would marry, and just two short years after my injury, I walked that woman down the aisle. It would be one year later, in 1948, that our oldest daughter would be born. By 1964, our youngest of six—three boys and three girls—would be born. They have all been married, and I have danced at every one of their weddings. As of today (2002), those six children have given me ten grandchildren.

"I went to school and retrained, and for many years, I owned and operated my own watch repair shop and stayed closely connected to the bases. Had I not been wounded in the war, I would have continued giving my life for my country in the Marine Corps."

Chapter 18

L'Audace, Toujours l'Audace

Born in Brooklyn, January 1, 1929, Richard P. Weinberg had finished his sophomore year at Hobart College, Geneva, New York, in June 1948. His draft notice came soon after, with a clear explanation that attending college was not a valid reason to be deferred. However, if the recipient enlisted in any one of the military Reserve components or the National Guard, he could remain in college through completion.

Weinberg decided to join the Naval Reserve and proceeded to the U.S. Navy/Marine Training Center on First Avenue and 51st Street, Brooklyn. Wrote Weinberg: "Some 3,000 (it seemed) were in line before me, stretching clear around the block. The rumor mill had it that the Navy quota was soon to be exhausted. What to do? Across the drill hall from the Navy recruiting desk was another, similar desk. This, however, was manned by a U.S. Marine Corps gunnery sergeant, four rows of ribbons loaded with battle stars on his chest, and not a single man in line. 'What the hell, I thought.' The 'Big War' ended three years ago. There's not going to be another for at least 20 years."

In July 1948, Weinberg took the oath to join the U.S. Marine Corps Reserve, and two weeks later, from that very same Navy/Marine Corps training center, he left for two weeks at Camp Lejeune where he was assigned to a 60 mm mortar platoon as a mortar gunner. "Because I was to return to Geneva to start my junior year at Hobart, I had to transfer to a Marine Reserve battalion in Rochester, New York, about forty miles from campus, to attend weekly night drills. This I did through my senior year, going to summer camp with the Rochester battalion in the summer of '49, proudly wearing my Pfc. stripes."

Weinberg graduated from Hobart College in late May 1950—the Korean War broke out a month later. His two-year enlistment ended about the same time. His draft board said he was eligible to be drafted since he was no longer a Reservist. "But," stated Weinberg, "I got married on Christmas Day, 1950. However, marriage as a deferment was soon phased out, and I considered my options before making too many commitments to a new wife and a budding career in journalism."

Rather than spend two years in the Army as a draftee, Weinberg decided to resume his Marine Corps career but with a new direction. His college degree qualified him for enlistment in the Marine Corps OCC program, and in September 1951, he reported in to Quantico. The enlistment contract held that if at any time in the concentrated OCC pre-offer recruit training a man failed to make the grade, he had to complete the remainder of the two-year enlistment with the rank of corporal.

"Those of us who did complete the course," said Weinberg, "were commissioned second lieutenants in the Marine Corps Reserve and assigned to the 13th Special Basic Class. In February 1952, I began five months of training in leadership and Marine Corps infantry skills. In July 1952, I was given the primary MOS 0301 (basic infantry officer)."

In August 1952, Weinberg was ordered to Camp Pendleton to join the 25th Replacement Draft to Korea. He arrived at Inchon in early September and was initially assigned to the 1st Marine Division's Combat Service Group stationed in Masan; his job, to set up base security. He then served for a short time as Marine liaison officer to the Air Force at an airfield designated K-10. His next—and final—assignment in Korea was I Company, 3rd Battalion, 5th Marines, as a rifle platoon commander. According to

Weinberg, 3/5 was—and is—one of the most decorated fighting units in the Marine Corps' entire 227-year history."

When Weinberg joined this unit, the distance separating UN forces and the Chinese/North Korean forces was virtually fixed at less than a mile. Both sides launched night and occasionally, day patrols from positions that resembled World War I trenches. "Both sides were dug in on their respective high ground and, in the area held by my company, the Chinese high ground was far superior to ours. Many of our casualties were the result of the sniper fire advantage this gave our enemies."

For the next few months, "Boredom was interrupted only by regular nighttime patrols and ambushes we attempted in the mile-wide no man's land between the two forces. Occasionally, our patrols would meet up with theirs and a brief firefight would erupt. Most of the time, each side was restricted to defined patrol routes because of the minefields and the fact that every square foot was preregistered by each side's mortars. More than once, we allowed opposing patrols to pass the interception point without incident. Sort of a gentleman's agreement based on the fact that truce talks (Panmunjon was only a few miles west of our position) were getting serious. No-one wanted to be the last casualty."

There were, according to Weinberg, times when the Chinese took limited offensive action in the Marines' area, and brief but intense fighting would ensue." Sadly, while this period of 'geographic inaction' was taking place, casualty rolls increased steadily, my own platoon included. During this period, I was cited by my company commander for an action that resulted in the rescue of a two-man listening post that was surrounded by a Chinese patrol. For this, I was awarded the Bronze Star Medal with Combat V."

In the first week of July 1953, Weinberg was assigned to a combat outpost some one thousand yards to the front of the Marines' MLR. The outpost was called Bunker Hill, and its total strength numbered twenty-seven Marines and one Navy corpsman. "The terrain was scary in that the nearest Chinese trench was about thirty yards from my position—an easy hand grenade toss. In addition, the entire area was dominated by what was designated on our maps as Hill 236, also called Taedok-san by the locals. Strategically, our position on Bunker Hill (122 meters high) was untenable."

When Weinberg's company commander (Captain Kenneth McLellan, who, when he retired many years later, did so as a four-star general and Assistant Commandant of the Marine Corps) told Weinberg that he would take over Bunker Hill, he was informed that he would be relieving an Army unit. "He (McLellan) suggested that I go out a night earlier than my troops so I could be briefed by the Army officer on the lay of the land, the enemy positions, and the location of the minefields. My platoon sergeant and I did so. We found the Army lieutenant in charge to be a West Pointer who referred us to his first sergeant to be briefed. All went well until I asked, 'Could you show us on your map overlay where the mines are that you laid around your outpost?' The Army sergeant replied, 'Sorry, Lieutenant. My lieutenant said it wasn't necessary to prepare an overlay.'"

On or about July 26, 1953, word was passed that a cease-fire agreement could go into effect at 2000 on July 27. Part of the agreement required that manned outposts such as Bunker Hill, situated within what was to become the new DMZ, would be abandoned as of the following day. In addition, both sides had to pull back their MLR an additional few miles to new defensive positions. "My Marines," reported Weinberg, "pointed out what was obvious to them and to every other commanding officer on both sides. 'Let's shoot every shell and bullet we have before the cease-fire goes into effect. That way, we don't have to carry them back to the new positions.'"

The night of the cease-fire was one of the costly in casualties for troops on the line as mortars and artillery units fired indiscriminately north and south. "It was both horrific and beautiful," Weinberg wrote, "star bursts, high-explosive air bursts, white phosphorus shells, while men literally died on the last night in the last minutes of a war. But miraculously, promptly at designated hour, it all stopped. Complete and eerie silence. I remember a war correspondent from the *New York World 'Telegram,* I think his last name was Johnson, interviewed a number of men in our company. I was quoted in his dispatch (my dad saved it) that you couldn't trust the Chinese. We had to stay awake."

Weinberg rotated home in September 1953, and was discharged on Treasure Island, San Francisco, as a first lieutenant. He flew home to New York, his wife, and a spare room in his mother-in-law's apartment in Rego Park, Queens. Fortunately, his wife had a good job and carried her husband for four months while he tried, with some difficulty, to readjust to civilian life only a month after ending a year in which his primary role was to kill the enemy while keeping as many of his own people alive as possible. Wrote Weinberg, "I was three months away from my 23rd birthday chronologically, but in many ways I felt older than Methuselah."

One of the first things Weinberg did was to report to the Marine Reserve Training Center in Brooklyn, where it all started in 1948, and join the unit (redesignated from the 19th Infantry Battalion that year to the 1st Infantry Battalion, 4th Marine Division). In 1953, he was given a rifle platoon and restarted an active career in the Marine Corps Reserve that was not to end until his promotion in 1972 to colonel and his eventual transfer to the Marine Corps Reserve Retired List in 1989 at age 60.

Weinberg's Reserve career (as distinguished from active-duty career, 1952–53) included billets as the aforementioned rifle platoon commander, rifle company commander, Battalion S-3 (Operations and Training Officer) Battalion S-2 (Intelligence Officer) battalion executive officer, and lastly, battalion commanding officer, 6th Communications Battalion, 4th Marine Division, headquartered in the Throgs Neck section of the Bronx.

After Weinberg's promotion to colonel, he was involved in forming the first Family Council unit in the Marine Corps situated at Freeport (Long Island), New York, and structured to Marines returning from Vietnam to readjust to civilian life and to find employment or continue in school. The success of this program was officially recognized in a commendation Weinberg received from Assistant Commandant of the Marine Corps, General Samuel Jaskilka in December 1976.

From 1954 to 1991, Weinberg was engaged in the publishing industry in New York, affiliated with Harcourt Brace Jovanovich for the last twenty years as an editor and publisher in its magazine division. He traveled throughout the world reporting on the development of the post-World War II automotive aftermarket industry following the patterns established in the American aftermarket.

He currently (2001) resides in Boynton Beach, Florida.

1-3-6 2ⁿᵈ Mar. Div. Weapons Platoon, Guadalcanal, 1943. (Berman, Back Row, Left of Flag). Photo supplied by Nat Berman.

1ˢᵗ Lt. Edward J. Leavitt, USMC
Platoon Commander, 1ˢᵗ Platoon, Camp Pendleton Honor
Guard

Krulewitch at Seagirt, New
Jersey, 1932
(from "Now That You
Mention It")

Sgt. Melvin "Acting Jack"
Krulewitch (from "Now That
You Mention It")

Pvt. Barney Ross, Parris Island, 1942

◄ *Arthur Friedman, USMC, in Vietnam. Hutton is getting his revenge.*

To Howard Leavitt

 We will remember the loss of those
Whom we knew and the lives they gave,
Of our Buddies who were close,
The Marines who were true and brave!
Memorial Day is every day, For those we have left behind,
Lt. Daniel Ginsberg, Iwo Jima! Always on my mind!
- Ed Miller

Colonel Mark Haiman,
Riverside National Cem-
etery, 9/92

Captain W. J. Weinstein, USMCR
Awarded Bronze Star with V for
heroism in battle at Iwo Jima 5/45

Colonel Melvin Krulewitch with Japanese prisoner
From "Now That you Mention It"

Leonard Pritikin, 1944,
Mare Island, Cal., Naval
Hospital

Colonel Edward J.
Leavitt, USMCR (ret.)

Mike Singer, (16 years of age)

Major General William J.
Weinstein, USMCR (official
USMC photo)

Ben Johnson, Vietnam, 1966–67

Colonel Jack Zimmermann

◄ *Lieutenant Colonel Robin Higgins salutes her husband for the final time, Andrews Air Force Base, Maryland, December 30, 1991*

Art Buchwald with Aunt Rose ➤

◄ *VMTB-131 Marine Torpedo Bomber A. J. Clark, pilot, Guadalcanal (Cactus) 1942*

Family of James A Bateman, Arlington National Cemetery ➤

Howard Blum, on tank, Vietnam 1967/68

Author on hill in Korea

Iwo Jima 3/45 after it was secured
Capt Sherman, Lt A Taylor, Lt M B Kranzberg

Iwo Jima 3/45 after it was secured

Lt. Edward Feldman, USN, receiving Silver Star Medal, Vietnam, 1966

VMF-311 "Hell's Belles" 1944
Max Halpin, eighth from left, top row

Sidney Goldberg, far left, standing, South Pacific

◄ *Neil Cohen, Mindoro, Philippine Islands*

Okinawa, 1945, remains of R5C flown into Yontan Airfield by Major Marvin Schacher (plane downed by suicide enemy plane) ➤

Irv Grossman on Yellow Beach I, Iwo Jima

◄ *In A-Test Marine Captain Benjamin Leffler of Jamaica is taking part in the series of atom test explosions at the Nevada desert proving grounds. A World War II veteran and winner of the Bronze Star, he is the son of Mr. and Mrs. Joseph Forgash of 89-26 168th Road, Jamaica*

Captain Yonel (Yogi) Dorelis, USAF, Afghanistan

Private Samuel Gross is on the right
Capture of Fort Riviere, Haiti, 1915
Painting by Colonel D. J. Neary, USMCR
Reproduction courtesy of the Marine Corps Art Collection

Major Marvin Schacher (right 1stLt. Tyrone Power (left)

Gunnery Sgt. Marco Meyer

Goldie Sockol Schwartz
(Henderson Hall, Virginia)

Sgt. Lou Diamond oversees one of his machine gun emplacements on guard at Soochow Creek, China, Refugees are crossing the bridge from the Chapel District to the International Settlement (Official Marine Corps photo, 1932)

PART V

In Which We Serve

Chapter 19

Art Buchwald, Ordnance Specialist

Having been awestruck by the Marines early on, Pulitzer-prize winner Art Buchwald "was completely inspired by U.S. Marine movies starring John Wayne and Victor McLaglen. I wanted to be a leatherneck more than anything else in the world and come back in Marine blues to Queens and show everyone what a real hero looked like."[1]

It even took a subterfuge to get him into the Corps. Because Buchwald was only 17, he was turned down for enlistment for being underage, his father having refused to sign the necessary papers. Undeterred by this temporary setback, Art left the recruiting office and headed for a street on Skid Row. A panhandler approached Buchwald pleading, "Would you give me a dime so I can get a drink?"[2] to which Art replied, "Ill do better than that—I'll give you a pint of whiskey."[3] The catch was that the bum had to pretend to be Buchwald's father and sign the papers as "Joseph Buchwald." Mission accomplished and now armed with the bogus papers duly signed, permission in hand, he raced back to the recruiting office five minutes before closing time and delivered them to the sergeant who, in turn, asked, "How long do you need to get things in order?"[4] Buchwald replied, "I'm ready to go this minute."[5]

[1] Buchwald, Art, *Leaving Home*, G. P. Putnam's Sons, New York, N.Y., 1993, p. 122.

[2] Ibid., p. 129.

[3] Op. cit.

[4] Ibid., p. 130.

"People are amazed when I tell them I was a Marine. For some reason, I don't look like one and I certainly don't act like one. But I was, and according to God or the traditions of the Marine Corps, I will always be a Marine."[6]

Buchwald's Marine Corps experience was, as with so many others, including mine, a turning point in his life. At 17, he was unhappy and undisciplined. A saying in the Marine Corps is, "Pain is temporary, pride is permanent." For Art Buchwald, "the Marine Corps was the right service in the right place at the right time."[7]

Although his father initially was not happy about his son having joined the Marines, he was proud that Art had enlisted. Once, when the senior Buchwald completed an order for black-out curtains, he delivered the goods to Governors Island, a U.S. military post off Manhattan. When the guard at the gate stopped him, Buchwald did not have his pass. However, "he produced my picture in uniform and said, 'My son is in the Marines. Do you think I'm going to blow up your fort?' They let him in."[8]

Art Buchwald's drill instructor was Peter Martin Bonardi. Buchwald's claim about his DI's personality was the same as most every Marine recruit. Buchwald's DI "was the toughest, meanest, son-of-a-bitch in the whole United States Marine Corps. It was no contest, mine was. Don't listen to other Marines. Trust me."[9]

His admiration for Bonardi was deep and lasting. In 1965, Buchwald received an assignment from *Life* Magazine to return to Parris Island to write an article about the training there, and requested permission from Editor George Hunt to have Bonardi accompany him. During this time, Buchwald realized that "the Marine Corps was the first father figure I had ever known. From early morning to late at night they took care of my needs. It was a love-hate relationship, as many father-son relationships are. I mentioned this to a master sergeant who was escorting us, and

[6] Ibid., p. 132.

[7] Ibid., p. 139.

[8] Op. cit.

[9] Ibid., p. 136.

he said, "Fifty percent of all recruits coming through here feel the same way."[10]

In 1991, Buchwald received a call from a man who said, "'Your pal Bonardi is dying from cancer. He is at the hospital in Southampton, Long Island.'

"I called the hospital and spoke to him. He told me . . . he didn't think that he was going to make the obstacle course. After I hung up, I remembered the photos taken by *Life* . . . I took out one of the two of us, nose to nose. I wrote on it, 'To Pete Bonardi, who made a man out of me. I'll never forget you.' And signed it.

"His wife wrote to me and said that Pete put it up in his hospital room so that everyone could read it. The clincher was that just before he died, Bonardi requested that the photo be buried with him.

"It was."[11]

In a story on Art Buchwald and Pete Bonardi in *The Greatest Generation*, Tom Brokaw writes: "I confess that I weep almost every time I read that account, for it so encapsulates the bonds within that generation that last a lifetime. For all their differences Art Buchwald and Pete Bonardi were joined in a noble cause and an elite corps, each in his own way enriching the life of the other. Their common ground went well beyond the obstacle course at Parris Island."

Buchwald recounts the day he and the other recruits of Platoon 911 marched together for the last time at Parris Island. The DIs had accomplished an impossible task in just eight weeks. Although the recruits were far from seasoned and tested Marines, they looked as though they were. And, for the first time, Buchwald noticed a smile on the face of Bonardi. "We knew he was pleased, because he had won money on our performance from the drill instructor training the platoon in the next barracks. I vowed that I would never see him again. It turned out that I did."[12]

[10] Ibid., p. 140.

[11] Ibid., p. 142.

[12] Ibid., p. 139.

In a way, his duty in the Corps after graduation from recruit training was a letdown. Buchwald and others had "joined the Corps with one purpose—to kill Japs."[13] But he, with others, was assigned to an air wing. "This was depriving us of this privilege. We would never hit the beaches as we had seen in our favorite films."[14]

When Buchwald's group arrived at MCAS, Cherry Point, it "looked as beautiful as Tahiti. We were free men. We could go to the PX, the slop chute (for beer), and the movies without permission. We didn't have to say 'sir' to noncommissioned officers. For a few days until I got bored, I couldn't believe I had so many choices."[15]

It was not long before Buchwald began to indulge himself in his favorite and lifelong passion, smoking cigars. "I averaged eight cigars a day in my prime and maintained the habit until I was 59 years old."[16] In the Marines, he started with cheap ones, finally upgrading his choice until "he was puffing on Davidoffs from Cuba and Dunhills from the Dominican Republic."[17]

At Cherry Point, Buchwald was assigned to ordnance and, despite his aversion to weaponry, learned about guns, bombs, and torpedoes. "A year later, I was in the Central Pacific, loading a five-hundred pound bomb on a Corsair fighter plane. I pushed the wrong thingamajig and released the bomb from the rack. It plummeted to the ground, just missing my foot. Everyone along the flight line either headed for bomb shelters or hit the deck."[18]

At Naval Air Facility, Memphis, Tennessee, he received more weapons schooling. Upon graduation, he received his advanced diploma in ordnance, which entitled him to load ammunition onto anything that could fly.

Buchwald was then assigned to VMF-113, a fighter squadron that flew F4U Corsairs. It was made up of seasoned veterans

---

[13] Ibid., p. 143.

[14] Ibid., p. 144.

[15] Ibid., p. 145.

[16] Op. cit.

[17] Op. cit.

[18] Ibid., p. 148.

of Guadalcanal, both pilots and ground personnel, plus assorted "greenhorns like myself." The ace of the unit was Major Loren D. "Doc" Everton who had shot down ten Japanese fighters; the assignment was to get the squadron back into shape so the men could return to combat in the Pacific.

Buchwald's duties involved loading and cleaning the .50-caliber machine guns, not a difficult job for most people. But it was for Buchwald who admitted that "when it came to cleaning anything, I had a very short attention span."[19] He soon received a promotion to corporal, "which was the equivalent—the Marines maintained—of making major in the Army."[20]

Buchwald left California in early 1943. The squadron and the planes were loaded aboard a brand-new aircraft carrier, the USS *Bunker Hill.* The ocean voyages proved to be uneventful. The only thing worthy of note was his assignment to brig duty, which taught Buchwald "how easy it was to be inhumane to someone. I hate cruelty. But like most people, I can be influenced to behave cruelly in a bad situation."[21]

After disembarking at Oahu, his squadron was transferred by bus to the Marine Air Base at Ewa. The men stayed a short time before being ordered to join up with a task force leaving for the Central Pacific. Boarding the USS *President Wilson,* they sailed for Eniwetok Atoll in the Marshall Islands. They "entered the lagoon, bombed the hell out of the defenders, and on February 19, 1944, landed on its shores." Where Buchwald and others received orders for burial duty.

He said, "I got the willies when I put one on a stretcher. I wore a handkerchief over my nose because the smell was awful. As I struggled with the stretchers, I said to myself, "I wish I had sprays of flowers to put on each."[22]

Buchwald's unit's mission was to keep watch on islands that the Navy had bypassed and neutralize the Japanese by bombing them every time they were sticking their noses out of the ground.

[19] Ibid., p. 152.

[20] Op. cit.

[21] Ibid., p. 159.

[22] Ibid., p. 166.

Their main target was Ponape. Buchwald's job was to clean guns and planes and edit his unit's newsletter, *The U-Man Comedy.*

When the Japanese bombed Engebi on March 8, 1944, an ammunition dump was hit, causing particularly anxious moments for Art and his buddies. "Everything from rockets to gasoline went flying, causing a fire 100 feet in the air. We had dug foxholes and that's where I was hunched over.

"I had my first real taste of fear that night, and it remained with me for months. After that incident, every time there was an air-raid drill, I shook with fright and crouched in a fetal position and said things like, 'I don't want to die.' For the enlisted men of VMF-113, this was as rough as it could get."[23]

After a transfer to Okinawa and a brief stay there, "where the new men saw far too much action from *kamikaze* planes," Buchwald got the news that he was going home. It took thirty days to reach San Francisco.

When he finally arrived in New York, Buchwald was both excited and scared. He did not know what to expect upon going home. Though Forest Hills was the same, he was not. He had changed greatly. "For one thing, all my growing up had taken place in the Marines. I was very sure of myself. I had been tested (not as much as I pretended) by my stay in the Pacific and all my other adventures in the service . . . Everyone at home was excited by my homecoming. There was a lot of screaming, shouting, and hugging."[24] Returning to Cherry Point, he was assigned to Torpedo School at Jacksonville, Florida, where he graduated with honors and given leave to go home.

On November 12, 1945, Sergeant Art Buchwald was honorably discharged from the Marine Corps. "I owe the Corps. When I meet another Marine, we share a bond. It's like belonging to the same lodge."[25] In expressing his appreciation of the Marine Corps, he said: "The importance of those three years of service was that

---

[23] Ibid., p. 169.

[24] Ibid., p. 182.

[25] Ibid., p. 195.

they were the ones which could have caused me the most trouble if I had remained in civilian life."[26]

Once when Buchwald arrived on a college campus for a speaking engagement, he was assigned as his guide a pretty girl whose father happened to be a Marine colonel serving on the staff of the retired President Nixon.' She called her father, "who was very embittered at the media, and said, "Dad, guess who I am escorting around campus?' When she told him, he said 'That SOB.'" Then she add, 'But, Dad, he was a Marine.' Her father responded, 'That's the only good thing about him."[27]

In reflecting on the past, Buchwald stated, "I can say now without hesitation that the Marine Corps was the best foster home I ever had."[28]

---

[26] Ibid., p. 196.

[27] Op. cit.

[28] Op. cit.

Chapter 20

From the Halls of Parris Island to the Shores of Galilee

Ernie Brydon's resume reads like something out of *Soldier of Fortune*. Not only does he wear the paratrooper wings of the U.S. Marine Corps, but of a half-dozen other countries as well. He has spent almost enough time observing and participating in the exercises of the armed forces of Israel to qualify him as at least an honorary *Sabra*.

Brydon first enlisted in the Marine Corps as a private in 1942 and completed boot camp at Parris Island. His first assignment was that of scout sniper, serving in the Pacific in the campaigns on Guam and Bougainville. Leaving active duty after the war, he joined the Marine Corps Reserve with the 6th Infantry Battalion in Philadelphia, winning a meritorious promotion from platoon sergeant to 2nd lieutenant. In 1951, he did a tour of duty in Korea as Platoon and Company, Dog Company, 2nd Battalion, 1st Marines, where he was wounded twice.

He left the Marine Corps with the rank of colonel. While modesty (and security) forbids details of his prowess and experience, he served on staff and command groups in the Corps, and in 1988 was awarded the coveted accolade as the Outstanding Battalion Commander in the Marine Corps Reserve by the Commandant of the Marine Corps.

Colonel Brydon has attended and has qualified at the following military schools and courses:

Airborne, Ft. Benning, Georgia; Special Forces, Ft. Bragg, N.C., Amphibious Warfare School, Quantico, Va., Command 7 Staff College, Quantico; Jumpmaster Course, Ft. Campbell, with the 101st Airborne Division; Landing Forces Planning Courses, Virginia and California; Survival, Escape, and Evasion Training, Jungle and Mountain Warfare, Trained with the 11th Special Forces, U.S. Army Green Berets; Expert on Small Arms and Tactics in a Modern Battlefield Environment; and a member of the Small Arms Conference Board.

In 1984, Colonel Brydon received the Meritorious Service Medal from the Commandant of the Marine Corps for his work in preparing Marines for desert operations.

It was in a number of countries where Brydon has also jumped and trained. He spent considerable time in Israel in all battle areas and with a number of Israeli units, especially the Airborne Corps.

A chronological list of his achievements and experience follows:

1965   Guest of Israel's Airborne School. Completed course and was awarded Parachutist Wings

1967   Observed the Six-Day War in all battle areas

1973   Observed the Yom Kippur War in all battle areas
       Observed Operation "Bright Star" in Egypt. American and Egyptian troop training. Later, participated in parachute operations with Israeli paratroops in Israel

1981   September: observed heavy fighting in Beirut, met with Lebanese dignitaries and observed results of the massacre at the Sabra-Shatilla camp

1982   Observed fighting between Druse and Shiites in Lebanon

1994   Received Master Paratrooper Wings on his 50th jump with the Israeli Airborne Forces.

During the intervening years, Colonel Brydon was a frequent guest of the Israel Defense Forces. He jumped with the airborne forces, observed security measures, and patrolled all borders of Israel with the IDF and Border Police. In 1989, he visited and patrolled with the Army of South Africa. He was awarded jump wings of the South African forces after jumping with their paratroops. In 1991, he jumped with the Chinese Army in Beijing, and was awarded paratrooper wings of China. In Hong Kong, he observed and trained with British and Ghurka troops.

Nineteen ninety-two saw Brydon observing Kurdish settlements along the Turkey/Iraq border, observed joint operations of the U.S. 6th Fleet and Israeli Navy missile boats, and trained and jumped with Russian Army paratroops and commandos, participating in live fire exercises with various Russian Army weapons.

Two years later, he was once again in Israel with night paratroop operations, and the following year he participated in a parachute operation in North Vietnam. He jumped on the fortieth anniversary of Dien Bien Phu with the French Foreign Legion and was awarded North Vietnamese and French paratroop wings.

During the following year of 1995, he participated in an airborne operation with British paratroopers on the fiftieth anniversary of the Battle of Arnhem, Netherlands, at the bridge and battle made famous in the movie, *A Bridge Too Far.* Following the exercise, he received British and Dutch paratrooper wings.

In 1997, he trained and parachuted with Polish airborne forces, and was the guest of German Special Forces/Counter Terrorist groups. In 1998, he jumped with Israeli paratroops in night operations and in 1999, he jumped with Turkish Army paratroopers and a final exercise in Israel with their paratroops.

Ralph C. Finkel joined the Marine Corps in 1946. With the termination of his enlistment the following year, he went to Israel as a volunteer with the fledgling army of Israel, and remained there as a citizen of that country with his Hebraized name of Raphael Ben-Yosef. In the succeeding years of 1956, 1967, and 1972, he saw further combat as a soldier in the Army of Israel. In fact, it was his Marine buddies and his gunnery sergeant who saw his future in Israel. In 1947, they told him, 'You're going to Israel. It's your duty."

His experiences in the Marine Corps were invaluable. "It made me feel wanted and if I trained myself, I could get over the barrier. The Marines are no better soldiers than the Army. But they think they are and train to be good. This attitude helped me in business, too." And, he was "Proud to have served in an outfit with a justifiably heroic tradition."

To Ralph Finkel, four months of boot camp "seemed like a year." There, he learned individual and group discipline, learned how to shoot and how to guard. He was nicknamed "Patrick" because of his friendship with Tom Quinn, a New York Irishman.

During boot camp ,he was particularly proud of having survived an all night march in the rain in the Parris Island swampland, and returning to the Parris Island parade ground with the band playing, "All of us marching sharp as though in dress blues."

They had a difficult boot camp. One of his four DIs was sentenced to two years at Portsmouth for maltreatment of boots, a sentence "which he didn't deserve. He wanted to teach us to stay alive."

Raphael particularly admired the colonel in charge of Camp Mathews. He "not only tasted the food before the troops were allowed to eat, but inspected the scissors of the camp barber for cleanliness."

One of his principal gems of advice is to "wear clean skivvy shorts and socks." Raphael Ben-Yosef, ex-Ralph C. Finkel, most favorable experience was "getting the Marine Corps emblem after finishing boot camp."

One of the "Chosen" or "Choosing Few" is Joseph Lowit. And he isn't even American by birth. He was probably impressed by the well-publicized ad, "The Proud, The Few, the Marines." He is still perfecting his English. Joseph Lowit, unbeknownst to most of his fellow co-religionists, is a very fortunate young man. He travels a lot, finds meaning in his work, is making a difference in the world, has nice clothes, the best medical and dental care for free, and enjoys good company. When he departs the Corps, presumably in several years, he will be a better person, physically, socially, emotionally, vocationally,and more confident than the tyro who joined in 1997. He will find that he will be far better prepared to face the vicissitudes of life with the advantages of four years of Marine experience to draw upon.

Corporal Joseph F. Lowit was featured in an article of *Leatherneck* Magazine in February 1999. On shore leave with his unit, the 24th Marine Expeditionary Unit (Special Operations Capable), in Israel, Joseph, born in Israel, had "a once-in-a-lifetime opportunity to do MEU training and visit some of the tourist attractions of the Holy Land."

However, for Joseph, it proved to be far more than that. He had the "the opportunity to reunite with his father, Dr. David Ben-Menachem."

Joseph's mother and father had separated when he was eighteen months old. The story of Joseph's visit to Israel made the newspapers, Dr. Ben-Menachem saw Joseph's picture in the paper, and contacted the editor. Whereupon, Dr. Ben-Menachem traveled to the Shivta training area and requested permission to see his son. "The father and son embraced and in an emotional meeting discussed the past, the frustration and pain of separation, and hopes for the future."

Corporal Lowit is a triplet, one boy and two girls. Moving to the States, he joined the Marine Corps on July 2, 1997, and completed recruit training on October 31 with Bravo Company, 1094 lead series. As he had a little difficulty with marksmanship, he had to stay longer at Parris Island. Following boot camp, he trained at the School of Infantry and was sent to his duty station at Camp Lejeune, North Carolina.

He is currently (2001) on deployment with the 24th MEU somewhere in the Mediterranean, the exact location he is not at liberty to reveal. He has trained at Twentynine Palms, California, and at Ft. Bragg, and is having the opportunity to travel a lot and see many places. "My job is 0311, Infantry, and am a lance corporal, and enjoy the Marines very much, although it is very disturbing to find I am the only Jew aboard ship and in the whole company."

Corporal Lowit is a very fortunate young man: a committed Marine and a committed Jew. He notes that "it was very difficult being the only Jew for the holidays and away from home. I had no-one to pray with. Back in Miami, Florida, I go to synagogue as much as possible and I am a single Marine who loves everything."

Bob Smallman is not new to literature any more than he is new to the military. He is a writer and has written four novels on science fiction and fantasy which were on the Internet. Not only did he serve in the American Armed Forces, but has also served in the Israeli Army as a driver until he was released as being overage.

Smallman enlisted in the Marine Corps at the age of seventeen in 1945, and completed boot camp at Parris Island. He found the training to be very rough, but, on the other side of the coin, it probably saved his life. Prior to going overseas as 1011 Aviation Intelligence, he pulled guard at Norfolk Navy Yard as an MP, then he trained at Camp Pendleton, where he found some anti-Semitism, mostly covert.

Near the close of the Second World War, he was stationed in China, at Taku, Tientsen, and Tsingtao. He found himself under attack at the North China ammo dump at Taku.

Smallman felt that he was denied the opportunity to be assigned to an aviation unit. His interest had always been in aviation: he was a member of the Civil Air Patrol, with student pilot license, prior to his enlistment in the Marine Corps. He had also worked for Pan-American. Instead, he was sent to a guard company.

He was, however, somewhat vindicated, when he was recalled to active duty for the Korean War. He was re-activated and assigned to fighter squadron VMF-232, MAG 15, at El Toro, California, attached to S-2 Intelligence, after completing Intelligence School.

Originally, he had been accepted for Platoon Leaders Senior Class, but was ultimately refused permission to attend. When he was promoted to corporal, he was again invited to attend Platoon Leaders Class, but, this time, he declined the invitation.

Bob Smallman, now living in Israel, regrets the fact that he did not get his commission. If he had, he would have remained in the Corps, and would have retired with thirty years of service, at the age of forty-seven.

Also currently living in Israel, Sam York (now Samuel Yankelowitz) joined the Marine Corps at the age of twenty-four. For him, the military was a necessary experience during World War II. In particular, however, he disliked his loss of identity, but felt that all of his problems could be classified under one heading—staying alive.

Despite his wound at Iwo Jima, he did manage to stay alive and returned home to the States. He depicts boot camp as a "good place to get into shape and learn discipline and to lose one's individuality. He was just as unsuccessful at making friends as making enemies." After completing boot camp, and firing sharpshooter, he was ready for combat training.

That took place at Camp Pendleton, where he qualified with the 60 mm mortar, learned defensive tactics, and, as usual, made neither friends nor enemies.

His most difficult and distasteful task in the military was burying the dead.

Sam York served in Hawaii, Saipan, Iwo Jima, Guam, Pearl Harbor, and San Diego. It was in San Diego that he experienced his most unusual incident: right after receiving his discharge from the Marine Corps, he "was standing by the freeway waiting for my ride home. Along came a little red coupe with a very beautiful young woman with a very short skirt. She asked me, 'Where is Broadway?' I answered, 'I'm looking at it.'"

Sam York admired the doctors and corpsmen very much. An experience in which he felt disappointed was the time his "sergeant borrowed $10 from the men in his platoon including me and absconded with the funds. One month later he was killed at Iwo Jima."

In March 1944, York wrote the following letter to his parents after being wounded during the battle for Iwo Jima.

I am perfectly all right, notwithstanding the long period you have not heard from me. You probably will already have received a form telegram from the NavyDepartment stating that I have been wounded in action. I was nicked by a Japanese sniper bullet which luckily hit no bones and merely ripped out three small pieces of flesh on my back.

Now I am comfortably resting in a hospital area far from the scene of battle and am able to walk around, eat, sleep, go to movies, and enjoy life just like a civilian. I still am a little battle weary and hope they won't shove me into action so soon.

So don't worry. You will hear from me very soon. I know you and my prayers are the same—for the return soon of all of us. With all my love. You are constantly in my mind. Your loving son, Sam.

Lastly, now a member of Kibbutz Sasa (Israel), Yaakov (Jacob) Matek served in the Pacific as a rear gunner on a SBD dive bomber. In the one case of anti-Semitism he faced, he was matched with his tormentor in a boxing match, "forced to fight each other till one of us quit. He gave up, and I had no problems with anti-Semitism after that."

After training at Miramar, California, he was assigned to a dive bomber squadron which operated mostly against Japanese shipping and other small military targets at sea and on land. The plane was very slow, and had to dive very low in order to deliver its bombs and fire its machine guns. It was extremely vulnerable to attacks from enemy planes and antiaircraft fire.

He was badly injured while a member of Marine Fighter Squadron 212. One of its fighters, an F4U crashed on landing after being hit by enemy fire. When the Marines tried to extricate the pilot, the plane blew up and only seven of the twenty-seven who participated in the rescue survived, one of whom was Jacob. Matek was subsequently treated on the hospital ship, ultimately returned to the United States for discharge, and received the Purple Heart Medal.

Chapter 21

Have Camera and Gun, Well Traveled

Harrold A. Weinberger was called "The Marine Behind the Camera." His epic of patriotism, guts, and pride spans more than fifty years—starting long before World War II.

The noted cameraman, at times known as the original "Hollywood Marine," started his career in 1923 after his service in World War I. With a hand-cranked camera, he filmed the 1925 World Series between the Washington Senators and the Pittsburgh Pirates. Ten years later, he was the drama director at George Washington University, Washington, D.C. With the advent of television and the huge increase in its popularity, he became assistant director or production manager of numerous productions in both media. His TV credits include such series as *Gomer Pyle, The Green Hornet,* and *Death Valley Days;* his feature film credits include such classics as *The Wizard of Oz, Northwest Passage, Twelve O'Clock,High, Tora! Tora! Tora!,* and *Night Must Fall.* But the road to filming real-life stories of the Marines at the age of 43 is even more remarkable than his Hollywood career.

Weinberger, commonly known as Hal, joined the Navy at the age of 17 during World War. He lied to get in, as the minimum age for enlistment was 18. His first duty was aboard the wooden ship-of-the-line *Granite State*, moored at the 96th Street Pier in New York City. Built shortly after the War of 1812, the ship saw action in the Union Navy during the Civil War. "On board that ship we learned the ropes of seamanship. We mastered small boat handling by rowing the *Granite State's* four whaleboats up and down the Hudson River in races. At night we slept below in hammocks. Learning to get inside is an art. You grab the overhead beam and pull yourself up, lower your buttocks inside is an art. You grab the overhead beam and pull yourself up, lower your buttocks inside, then swing your feet in."[1]

After transferring to the cruiser USS *Birmingham* on convoy duty up to Halifax, Nova Scotia, Weinberger's enlistment ended when his real age was discovered. Still not content with sitting out the war on the sidelines, he took a train to Toronto and enlisted in the Canadian Army under the assumed name of Harrold Wynants. He was told to fill out an application and wait. So, "I filled out an application and waited. A corporal called out 'Harold Wynants!' That's the name I used in my paper work to hide my real identity; I borrowed the last name from an old shipmate. It didn't occur to me to answer."[2] Finally, after three calls, Weinberger did answer, whereupon the sergeant major looked at Weinberger, who had listed his age as 18, took him aside, and informed him that the minimum age for enlistment in the Canadian Army was 19. "The sergeant major must have seen the disappointed look in my eyes because he said:

"'Are you Harold Wynants?'

"'Yes, sir, I replied.'

"'You were born in Toronto?'

"'Yes, sir.' I had marked down Toronto as my birthplace.

"'I knew your father well,' he led on. 'I remember when you were born. It was 4 November 1898, not 4 December. Here, let me correct that mistake on your application.'"

Private "Wynants" was now hopeful about getting to Europe before World War I was over. Finally assigned to the Canadian Field Artillery, Weinberger practiced a variety of drills on horseback, including mounting and dismounting at a gallop and lance spearing. After only several weeks of training, he embarked for

[1] Vergun, David, GySgt., USMC, *Fortitudine*, Washington, D.C., Fall, 1993, p. 21.

[2] Op. cit.

Scotland on a transport department from Halifax. En route, the convoy was attacked by German U-boats.

"I watched as one of our destroyers rolled barrel-shaped depth bombs off an angled rack attached to the stern and into the water. At the same time I saw an enemy torpedo pass close by, just missing us. I later learned that our destroyers had sunk a U-boat. None of our ships was hit."

Landing at the Firth of Clyde, at anchor in Glasgow, he disembarked at Whitley, about thirty miles south of London. For the next six months, his unit practiced and drilled so much that they began to believe they would be there until the end of the war.

However, with the Germans advancing on Paris, Weinberger and his unit shipped to the front to participate in the Second Battle of the Marne. Hal was now with the 8th Army Brigade of the Canadian Field Artillery. His battery consisted of four 18-pounders. (An 18-pounder is a light artillery piece which lobs an 18-pound projective up to four miles.)

Although wounded by shell fragments during the ensuing engagement, Hal returned to duty almost immediately. He was also gassed. As he related it:

"The attack came one foggy morning. It was the perfect weather for a gas attack because there was no wind to disperse it away from us. When the gas alarm sounded, I hurried to put on my mask, but, before I could, the phosgene (suffocating gas) had engulfed me and I was inhaling lethal fumes. I managed to put it on anyway, but for a long time I fought for air. Treatment was to move you to a place where there was plenty of fresh air and then wait, hopefully, for the body to clear itself. I was back at the front the following day, but years later I could still feel the effects."[3]

One day, while observing from a small bluff, his commanding officer stood up. At that moment, "a German machine gunner sawed him in half with eight rounds. Perhaps the next day or week that machine gunner would also make a mistake—or just be unlucky—and he'd be at the receiving end of a bullet. Such are the vicissitudes of war."[4]

---

[3] Ibid., p. 22.

[4] Ibid., p. 23.

At 0500 on November 11, 1918, his unit was ordered to cease fire, and an hour later they were given the command to "stand down." At 0900, they were notified that an armistice would take effect at 1100: No-one cheered. They were too tired. That day, they crossed into Belgium where they were given a warm welcome by the townspeople. "The town's brewery was opened and there was dancing all day and night in the town square. That afternoon, the realization finally sunk in that the war was finally over."[5]

With his discharge from the Canadian Army in hand and now back in the United States, Weinberger joined the U.S. Merchant Marine. "The effects of the gas attack lingered, so I sought a job where I would get lots of fresh air," he said. On board ships crossing the Atlantic between New York, Europe, and South America, Weinberger got plenty of fresh air. His ship was the first to pass through Germany's Kiel Canal (61-mile canal linking the North Sea with the Baltic) after World War I.

With the outbreak of World War II, Weinberger joined the California State Guard as a lieutenant. But it was soon apparent that his services in the Guard would not be needed: California was not going to be invaded by the enemy. "Although I was 43 years old, far above the age limit for enlistment in the Marine Corps, they needed cinematographers," so he was permitted to enlist. "I may have been the oldest private in the Marine Corps," he said.

Following recruit training, Weinberger received training at several camera schools and then joined the 4th Marine Division—landing with it at Roi-Namur in the Kwajalein Atoll, Saipan, Tinian, and Iwo Jima. During those campaigns, he was the staff NCO of the G-2 photo section. Weinberger described the unit:

"There were twenty men in my section, ten still photographers and ten motion picture photographers. We operated in teams of two, a still photographer and a motion-picture photographer, one man working the camera and the other covering him with a rifle. I shot motion pictures using a Bell and Howell Automaster Camera loaded with 16-mm Kodachrome film. We were the first

[5] Op. cit.

combat photographers to carry color film in our motion-picture camera. It had an ASA (film speed) of only eight so we could shoot only during the day. While Europe was seen by viewers in black and white, we brought the war in the Pacific to you in living color."[6]

Preparing to leave Hawaii to attack Saipan, Weinberger was witness to what became known as the West Loch disaster. On May 21, 1944, on board a transport at Pearl Harbor, he heard explosions and saw huge fireballs in nearby West Loch. He and some of his cameramen raced to the scene in one of the landing craft of the transport, where they photographed the disaster and assisted with the rescue work. "The accident killed 163 sailors and Marines, injured 396, and destroyed six fully loaded LSTs. The accident happened during the loading of 4.2-inch high-explosive mortar shells on board the LST, but the cause has never been determined."[7]

Weinberger hit the beach at Iwo Jima on February 19, 1945. He was in either the second or third wave, and landed at 0805. "The Japanese fired at us with their machine guns, mortars, and artillery which were hidden in caves on the slopes. From these well-concealed vantage points they commanded a full sweep of the island and no place was safe from their fire."[8]

Ashore, Weinberger shared a foxhole fashioned from a deep hole with Mark Kaufman who was later to become a fashion photographer with *Life* Magazine. Horrendous artillery and other weapons fire made sleep next to impossible that night. Also, their ammunition dump blew up. "In the morning, Mark said to me, 'I'll never sleep with you again, you again. You SOB. How could I get any rest with your loud snoring?"

According to one account of Weinberger's combat action, "he had an easy assignment on Iwo Jima. With his outfit of the 4th Marine Division, all he had to do was take interesting pictures." He was doing just that "when a couple of Jap fragments . . . slammed him in the groin and elbow." After a while, "when his

[6] Ibid., p. 24.

[7] Op. cit.

[8] Op.cit.

brain cleared and the bells stopped ringing in his ears, he realized that he had become a casualty because he forgot to duck in time, and the camera was still grinding away."

During his hospital confinement, Staff Sergeant Weinberger wrote: "Now I know what Hell is like. We were bracketed by artillery, mortar, and rocket fire from the cliffs. The Japs' artillery fire was deadly in its accuracy. It didn't matter where a shell fell, the beach was so densely populated that any missile was bound to cause a half-dozen casualties or more. Not one of these men (the Marines) underestimated the enemy and not one did not know his statistical expectancy of life. Too many of these men became statistics. Friends of mine—husbands, brothers, and sons—now lie in the loose gravel and sand of Iwo. So forgive us please, if in the years to come, we grow morose and pensive as we speak of Iwo."

Weinberger relates seeing some of the first blacks on Iwo Jima. He says, "To his credit, Major General Clifton Cates, our division commanding general who is a Southerner, addressed the division exhorting us to 'treat them as one of your own buddies.' I admired Major General Cates for that. During the campaign, I heard not one instance of racial discrimination."[9]

One of Weinberger's crewmen, Sergeant William Genaust, filmed the second flag-raising on Mount Suribachi, on Iwo Jima. Both he and Joe Rosenthal shot that scene, Rosenthal with the still camera and Genaust with the motion-picture camera. They both captured identical views of the scene. However, one importance of the filming of the raising was that it proved that Rosenthal's picture was not staged.

General Cates summoned Weinberger to his command post on Iwo—a shell hole about 10–15 feet deep, covered with tarps and timber. There were three people in the hole: General Cates, Colonel McCormick, the G-2; and Weinberger. As Weinberger was asked,

"Sergeant, if tendered a commission, would you accept?" Hal responded with, "Yes, sir." The general replied, "Thank you, that is all. Dismissed."

<hr>

[9] Ibid., p. 25.

Weinberger continues, "I didn't hear any more about the subject for a few months, but, just before the war ended, I was commissioned a second lieutenant. Imagine that, I was now the oldest second lieutenant in the Marine Corps at age 45."[10] Weinberger thus became a mustang (an officer who received his or her commission while still an enlisted man or woman).

In addition to being commissioned in the field, Weinberger earned a Purple Heart. His citation for the Bronze Star Medal reads as follows:

"For meritorious service on Iwo Jima. Much of his work was performed under conditions of extraordinary danger which he encountered in a cool, aggressive manner, not allowing danger to interfere with the accomplishments of his mission."

He also received a National Headlines Club Award in 1945 which read:

"For his personal part in the motion-picture coverage of the Iwo Jima operation that provided the American public, through the newsreel, the outstanding footage of he war and added vital tactical, training, and intelligence information to the military records."[11]

If covering the war and its combat with camera were not enough, Weinberger had more than ample opportunities to engage the enemy with weapons other than still and movie camera. On Tinian and elsewhere, he was forced to confront the enemy at close range with personal weapons. On the fourth day of the Tinian campaign, he was attached to an infantry unit advancing along the west-central coastline. In his autobiography, *Up the Cargo Net,* he describes the ensuing action:

"We were getting a lot of mortar and machine-gun fire. This area was flat and open country. The Marines were well deployed, irregular intervals of fifteen to thirty feet between men. I was nearest the cliff edge when a grenade, coming from the right and from below, arced over my head, landing to my left and wounding the Marine nearest me. I had hit the deck when I first saw the grenade. Now I crawled to the cliff edge ten feet away and looked

[10] Op. cit.

[11] Op. cit.

over. On a ledge some three feet wide and eight feet long and only ten feet below, I saw a crouched enemy soldier. He had another grenade in his right hand. He was looking upward, his face half-turned away from me. As if by instinct, he turned his head and we were eyeball to eyeball. It was almost point-blank range. I fired before he could react further. He died instantly with a bullet in his face and toppled over the ledge edge to jagged rocks sixty feet below."[1 2]

As Weinberger approached a Marine machine-gun emplacement, a mortar burst raked the position. He dove headfirst into a small hole and fortunately was unhurt. Three others were not as lucky. In describing his reactions regarding one of the men who was killed, Weinberger wrote:

"He lay in an awkward position. His right arm was tucked in a cramped position beside him with the wrist bent backward showing the palm face up. I knelt by him, straightened the arm so it rested gracefully and comfortably by his side. He was wearing a plain gold band on his fourth finger, left hand—a married man, like me. This was my brother, my brother man, my brother Marine, and, there, but for the grace of God, lay I. Looking upon him, I saw myself. My eyes teared, his body had become mine, and I was crying for myself, crying for the anguish that the news of his death would bring to his wife and family.

"I didn't know his religion. I did not care—I would recite the *Kaddish* for him. It is read and recited several times in every Jewish religious service and has also become part of the ritual of a mourner's prayers.

"I stood up and recited the *Kaddish* for him. Then bending over him, I pressed his right hand as in a farewell handshake, released his hand, straightened up, and walked away."[1 3]

After the war, he produced training films and other programs for the Marine Corps. On September 1, 1962, Harrold Weinberger, now a major, retired from the Marine Corps Reserve.

Until he died in Los Angeles on February 6, 1997, at the age

---

[12] Weinberger, Harrold, *Up the Cargo Net*, The Autobiography of Harrold Weinberger, vol. II, 1981, p. 314.

[13] Ibid., p. 346.

of 97, he remained an active member of the Marine Corps Combat Correspondents Association, the Marine Corps Reserve Officers Association, the Marine Mustang Association, and the 4th Marine Division Association.

"Although Hal became well-known for his Hollywood achievement, up to his death he continued to have a special place in his heart for the Corps. 'I can honestly tell you, I never had an unhappy in the Marine Corps.'"[14]

---

[14] Vergun, op. cit., p. 25

Chapter 22

Vignettes of Sid Klein's Boot Camp

He said it himself, his service was not distinguished. But, then, most of us who served, did so *sans* distinction. Most of us didn't have the chance to be distinguished. In the case of Sid Klein, he didn't even go overseas. Nevertheless, we still do what we are told, especially in the Marine Corps.

Sid Klein's experience consisted of a year of service just after World War II. He was assigned to the machine shop of a Motor Transport Battalion, composed mostly of survivors of Iwo, Okinawa, Guadalcanal, Tulagi, and other campaigns. There were a number of highlights, however, of his short-lived career in the Marine Corps, including saving a fellow Marine's life, a non-Jew. As Sid put, "Well, I saved a gentile's life—not in combat—none of us made a big deal of it. To me, the best part is that all my buddies knew that it was Jew who did it."

Klein's family is not a stranger to the military: His father served in the Hungarian Army in World War I. He was taken prisoner in Siberia and escaped after four years. His brother was a corporal in the 3rd Army, and his son is a lieutenant colonel in the Army Reserve with three years of active duty.

Sid thinks very highly of his service in the Marine Corps. Short-lived as it was, it has been very meaningful in his private and professional life.

He provides a number of vignettes of his service which are

more than deserving of relating, and without changing a word. These are some stories of Sidney Klein:

"We've lined up at the rifle range. Gunnysarge Tatum quietly looks over his new charges for a moment then roars. 'Anybody here a Jew?' Everyone knew I was the only one and, though they weren't especially crazy about me, they were as startled as I. No-one spoke or even looked my way. I yelled, 'Here, sir!' He came over. 'Yew a Jew?' 'Yessir!' 'Meet me behind that target there!' I could see some of the guys move their heads as I ran. I'll be damned, they actually looked worried about me. Not as worried as I was.

"Soon it was just the gunnysarge and me. 'Yew really a Jew?' he asked again, quietly, in an Alabama drawl. 'Yessir!' 'Why the hell don't I ever see you at Friday night services?' 'It's a training day, sir.' Though I probably could get permission to go, it'd be misinterpreted by the other guys. Specially skuzzy duties were generally scheduled then. 'Sir, I've never seen you on Sunday morning.' That's when I did go. 'Hell, that's my sack time,' he grinned. We talked more, and he told me he's a self-converted Jew. After Protestant services one Sunday morning, he told the chaplain he'd enjoy his sermon. The chaplain replied pompously, 'Well, I'm glad you liked it.' Tatum said, 'Go f—k yourself'[and next week thought he'd try out the Jewish services]. He hit it off with Chaplain Barnston and declared himself a Jew from then on. He'd already been circumcised in the field in Guadalcanal with others, for sanitary reasons, and figured he was fully qualified. Was I going to tell him otherwise? He had nothing but questions about Judaism, but he'd hold them for a future visit to my boot barracks. When I returned to the guys, waiting in formation, they looked me over and decided that everything was OK, though they hadn't a clue as to what went on. That was probably the only time I detected a sincere concern for me on the part of those guys."

"Tatum strode into our barracks on Sunday. The first boot who saw him was so shocked to see someone with five stripes on his sleeve that it took a second for him to remember to yell, 'Ten

HUH!' and jumped up. All 74 of us snapped to attention as he continued in, and said, 'Carry on,' and came straight to me. It's hard to describe this scene without explaining Marine hierarchy. A boot is lower than whale shit. A Pfc. is highly respected. Our lives were in the hands of our DIs, who were corporals and we rarely saw anyone with three stripes up close. In addition, a gunny is respected more than anyone and by everyone, including generals. He's a line NCO who's always in the thick of battle and has such a high casualty rate that he's held in awe just seeing one walking around alive. And here's a gunny with a friendly smile, asking to see my *tephilin*. With utmost respect he rewrapped the straps, determined to do it just so. It was the first of many chats we had, including after boot camp. We corresponded a bit between Cullman, Alabama, and Yonkers after we were both discharged, but I never saw him again."

"I didn't know it at the time, but while I was in boot camp, he wrote to Mom and Pop more than once, telling them I was safe and sound and doing well in training, and how great it was to meet a real Jew. He'll never know what a *mitzvah* he did. Actually as a parent and grandparent, I now fully appreciate it myself. Mom and Pop cherished those letters beyond description. It was enough that they got independent confirmation that I was really alive. The compliments were a bonus."

"On day three of boot camp, our platoon was herded into a large building to hear someone with brass on his shoulders tell us that war is hell or some such message. Iwo Jima and Okinawa had happened just months ago, the assault on Japan was imminent and so we were warned to take our training seriously. Two quotes from this officer have stayed in my mind: 'Some of you will not return.' That was amusing, because he was talking about everyone else. The other was, 'Whatever religion you have, follow it. If you don't have a religion . . . (here he looked at us intently) . . . GET ONE!'

"The 74 of us were then instructed to fall out to the side of the buildings and meet the chaplains. A benign-looking Navy officer with crosses on his collar showed up, waved his hand to the right, and yelled, 'Protestants over here!' A similar-looking officer waved to the left at the 30 of us who hadn't moved and yelled, 'Catholics over here!' I was getting lonely, standing by myself, when another officer appeared. Reading from a 3 x 5 card, he said, 'Klein?'

"It was Chaplain Barnston (ne Bernstein) from Dallas and his first question was whether I was orthodox, conservative, or reform. His eyes bugged out at my response and he shouted, 'Orthodox? What the hell are you doing in the Marines?' His next question was, 'Where are you from?' and when I answered, 'Pennsylvania,' his eyes bugged out further. 'You're NOT from NEW YORK?' We became instant friends.

"Some of the 'salts' in my outfit had souvenirs from exotic places like Iwo and Okinawa. A samurai sword was amongst the most prized. There was an article in *Leatherneck* Magazine about them and how to remove the handle to see possible inscriptions on the tang (That's not an orange drink. It's the metal end of the sword that is buried into the handle.) A buddy brought two swords to me for help in following the directions. To my surprise, it worked. The handle came off the first one and there was some official Japanese inscription on the tang. We made a rubbing of it in case he'd find anyone who could read it.

"The handle of the second one came off nicely, too, and it had a similar inscription. But, in addition, there were two crude X's scratched on the hard metal. We looked at it and at each other and were completely silent as I put the handle back on and returned it to him. We both felt sick. I must have washed my hands for about five minutes. And we never, ever mentioned that incident to each other afterwards."

"Before you graduate to the rifle range, you practice on 22s fitted with sights that are identical to those on the carbine and the M-1. Thirty guys side by side fire on the '1,000 inch' range (30 meters) at 5 x 7 inch targets with bulls eyes about an inch in diameter. For a short while the shooting is ferocious, then we all check our targets. Then the coaches look at them and scream and call us awful, terrible names because we're shooting so badly. Then we shoot again. (No wonder I can't hear so good.)

"Sometimes the rifle jams. This can mean a $10,000 reward. But the coaches are quick to point out that it's your beneficiary who gets it. That's why you must clean and care and coddle your rifle, because it's your very best friend. And that's why, when my rifle jammed and I hit it and said, 'Come on, you SOB,' my coach blanched in mock horror. His next order to me was explicit.

"All activity stopped as the entire platoon sat in a circle around me to hear as I nuzzled my rifle to my cheek. 'I'm really sorry I called you a SOB, sweetheart. You know I love you more than anything in the whole world, that you're the only one who might save my scrawny undeserving ass some day. I promise never to call you a SOB again. Please forgive me, darlin'.'"

"We're on the 30 meter range. Thirty guys, each with rifles that fire 20 rounds of .22 ammunition, are about to be given the order to fire. A seagull with a death wish and a wing spread of a B-17 comes out of nowhere and proceeds to fly from right to left, directly in front of the 30 targets. The coach goes insane with joy. 'Kill that SOB!' he screams. The Battle of Bull Run could not have been louder. That seagull did not fly fast. He actually sauntered across the targets, flapping only as if in contempt. He must have been deaf because the noise should have given him a heart attack.

"That's what our coach had, as that enormous bird gently wheeled about and flew out to sea, dropped not so much as a feather."

"In the center of the barracks, just outside the heads and showers are the firehoses. Two men are preassigned to stand by them in case of a fire or a drill, while everyone runs out. If a drill, an officer often enters to inspect.

"Every time an alarm went off, it caught several guys in the shower. They'd have to grab a blanket, run outside and look like Sitting Bull, shivering. This happened to me more often than lots of others, perhaps because a shower was one of my favorite forms of recreation. I didn't play cards or shoot craps. I'd rather lather up and sing my little heart out. One day, between requests for 'I Saw A Crash On The Hiway' and 'Lady Be Good,' a great idea came to me. As I toweled off, I explained it to my buddies who agreed it was pure genius. Instead of rational firehouse duty, the first four guys running out of the shower would man the hoses while everyone else ran out. This could prevent some nasty colds.

"The plan was activated immediately, and, of course, I profited more than most. But I had neglected to think the plan completely through. Seconds after the alarm would sound, I and three other stark naked guys would be standing at attention by the hoses. What a remarkable contrast as the Colonel walked by with his entourage of lesser officers. The Colonel in his dress greens, polished eagles, campaign ribbons from his shoulder to his *pupik* (navel), and we with residual lather making its way down our shoulders to our pupiks and beyond.

"After a few such experiences, the Colonel finally exploded. He stopped and screamed in my face, 'Boy, is this your assigned duty?' 'YesSIR.' His eyes narrowed. 'Is this your officially designated station?' 'YesSir.' Pause.

"Heavy breathing. 'Why the F don't you EVER WEAR ANY F CLOTHES?' 'I was caught in the shower, sir' and (thinking, 'why are you ignoring the other three naked guys?') 'Do you F LIVE in that F shower?' 'NoSIR.' 'The next F time I'm here I want to see some F CLOTHES on you. Is that F clear?' 'YesSIR.'

"We returned to rotational firehouse duty.

"I love milk, but I was served only in the morning, a little in a bowl to go with cereal. Once on garbage detail, I devised a way to steal milk. Every time I thought I wasn't watched, I'd hide a full quart carton of milk in with a case of empties and cart them off to the dump, about 100 yards behind the mess hall. Standing knee deep in garbage, I was alone except for bugs the size of silver dollars scurrying all over. Looking around furtively, I'd chug the whole quart. Then I'd waddle back to work."

"Marine *shalashudis* consists of, well, I'll call it baloney and cheese. So my instruction that Saturday afternoon was to flop three slices of each on every tray. No serving instruments slow us down. After a while, the mess sergeant comes along: "'Are your hands clean, boy?' 'They are now, sir.' The sarge strolls by."

"Breakfast is ready and a thousand hungry Marines are at the still-locked mess hall doors, waiting to pour in. We've been slaving since 0400 for this moment. There's the usual SOS, bacon and other *chazerei*, and today, huge pans of 'scrambled (reconstituted powdered) eggs' are ready to be carried out to the chow lines to be ladled onto each moving tray. A couple of guys have enough energy left to do a little grabassing. This is loosely defined as slapping each other around, wrestling, no harm intended. One pushes the other against a soda-acid fire extinguisher on the bulkhead. It falls to the deck and activates. Wow, the hose comes alive, writhing and spinning out a yellowish foam, much of it getting on the eggs. The sergeant looks at his watch. Two minutes to go. With a shrug, he grabs a ladle and stirs the foam into the eggs. Breakfast is served."

Stay tuned. We all get subtle messages.

But the message of Sidney Klein is not so subtle. It is loud and clear. Service in the Marine Corps affected his overall outlook on life: it empowered him to acquire a certain self-reliance, a can-do attitude that he can accomplish anything he sets out to do. Finish the job. No patience with whining—be they kids, adults, male or female. He says unambiguously that one, he made a lot of friends in the Corps; two, he always made it scrupulously clear that he was a practicing and observant Jew; and, three, recounting his pride in having served in the military, he says, "Better believe it. Especially love when no-one can believe that a Jew would join the Marines."

Chapter 23

Master Sergeant Abe Rubinstein's Tour of Duty

Abe Rubinstein's log of military experience is a record of achievement, worldwide activity, pride, modesty, and example. It encompasses thirty-two years of service to country, Corps, and family.

It began in 1938 when he enlisted in the U.S. Army before the entry of the country into the Second World War. While he was stationed at Fort Jackson, South Carolina, he began to take flying lessons. He loved flying. One day, after having completed ten hours of instruction, the instructor told him, "Okay, Abe, you're ready to solo, take 'er up." "It was a very thrilling moment for me as I gunned the throttle and the Piper Cub roared down the runway . . . It was a feeling that I will never forget."

However, once he attained his student pilot's license, all civilian licenses were revoked, and he never renewed it. He never flew since then as a pilot—only as a co-pilot.

Abe chose discharge upon completion of his enlistment in 1941. He had completed a three-year Army hitch, he had been corporal and leader of a machine-gun crew, and "the experience of the kind of life that I could never find anywhere else."

Right after the outbreak of World War II, Abe Rubinstein went down to the Marine Corps recruiting office which was, "already jam-packed with young men waiting to enlist. Everyone, it seemed, was flocking to the colors and frankly, it gave me a feeling of pride and patriotism." After being sworn in, he was posted at Brooklyn Navy Yard as a security guard where he would never forget those very cold and windy nights.

After months at the Yard, he was transferred to Quantico, Virginia, for training in radar, which was, at the time, a new device, and introduced to the military under utmost secret conditions. Training completed, he was transferred to VMO-251, a Marine observation Squadron, in San Diego, California. The entire unit, with its Grumman Wildcats, shipped out in June 1942, aboard the USS *Heywood*. After several days at sea, they saw the pirate flag of skull and crossbones raised to the masthead signifying that they were nearing the Equator. It also signified that all personnel who had never crossed the Equator had to be initiated and "washed clean before they can be permitted to enter the 'Domain of King Neptunas Rex—the Ruler of the Raging Main.'"

During that hazing, all the "Shellbacks" (those who had previously crossed the Equator) had to round up all the "Pollywogs" and take them to the "Royal Court of King Neptune" to be judged and sentenced. Some men were sentenced and subsequently punished: one, getting jabbed in the groin by a poker with an electric charge by the "Royal Executioner;" two, having all one's hair shaved; three, kissing the "Royal Baby's Tummy (the fattest sailor on board; or four, scrubbing the deck of the ship with a toothbrush while being hosed down with salt water.

Another ordeal was to crawl through a long, wet canvas bag filled with garbage, while a hose on the other end sprays the culprit with water at full blast. Abe Rubinstein underwent this ordeal, "and had a real tough time of it, too." Although the decks were awash with garbage, "everyone had a real good time—even those being initiated. In the end, we were all 'shellbacks,' and with it a certain feeling of pride, especially when you think about all the sailors, soldiers, and Marines who had been through the same initiation for almost the last 200 years."

Arriving at American Samoa, they remained at anchor for several days. To those who went ashore, the island looked like a tropical paradise, "with beautiful white sandy beaches, lined with all sorts of coconut and palm trees." Later, they proceeded to British Samoa, which was equally beautiful. It was here that Robert Louis Stevenson lived for the last several years of his life, and was buried there on a hill overlooking the Pacific.

Arriving at the main harbor of Espiritu Santo, they went ashore and set up camp including their SCR-270 radar unit. Their mission was to provide for the early warning detection of enemy ships or aircraft approaching their sector. Abe Rubinstein describes the assistance provided by Melanesian native in digging air raid shelters, garbage dumps, and latrines:

"As they worked, they kept us entertained by singing songs in their native tongue, and some of us even learned the melodies to them after a while. We found these people very fascinating, and learned quite a bit about their culture. Some spoke a language called 'Pidgin English,' which is a form of the English language with a native dialect. We got along with them very well, and they openly voiced their dislike for the Japanese."

On the island, they were constantly overflown and harassed by a lone Japanese bomber. It caused little damage because "Washing Machine Charlie" generally dropped its bombs in the harbor or on land out of danger. One day, however, one of the American pilots shot it down, effectively ending the incursions of "Washing Machine Charlie." With the consolidation of the southern Solomons, and limited action on Guadalcanal, Abe Rubinstein contracted malaria, and was shipped back to the States.

Back at Coney Island, he joined his brother, Hy, who was also home on leave from the 8th Air Force in England. Leave completed, he reported to his new unit at Goleta, California, an airfield which was later to be the site of the University of California, Santa Barbara.

After additional training in new radar techniques, Abe departed the States in March 1945, and arrived at Oahu, Hawaii. There, he was shocked to learn of the death of President Roosevelt.

He was disappointed that he couldn't have lived one more month to witness the surrender of Germany.

From Hawaii, Rubinstein sailed for Okinawa and Kuma Shima, stopping at Guam, Saipan, and Eniwetok. They went ashore at Kuma Shima, a short distance from Okinawa, and set up their radar station. Their mission was to provide early warning detection of enemy aircraft approaching the Okinawa area. With a few Japanese soldiers still remaining on the island, a platoon of Reconnaissance Marines was placed around the perimeter. Not content with simply waiting out the Japanese, they began search and destroy operations. They were successful in locating the enemy and disposing of them. However, in one of the skirmishes, Platoon Sergeant Ludlow was seriously wounded in the abdomen, evacuated to the Medical Evacuation Station, and died en route. "It was ironic for him to lose his life in a small and almost insignificant skirmish such as that, especially when he survived such large-scale campaigns as Tarawa and Saipan. His death was a real loss for the Recon Platoon, and to the Marine Corps as well."

With the surrender of the Japanese, Abe Rubinstein and his group went to Tsingtao, China, where they participated in the disarmament of the Japanese troops. In 1945, after two months, he was on his way home aboard the cruiser USS *San Francisco*, returning to his wife and daughter in Brooklyn.

But with the outbreak of the war in Korea, Rubinstein's stint as a civilian was to be short-lived. He was one of the first reservists to be recalled. First assigned to Camp Lejeune, shortly thereafter he was transferred to Cherry Point and assigned to Marine Ground Control Intercept Squadron 5 (MGCIS-5), and assumed his duties as Operations Chief. Several months later, he re-enlisted in the regular Marine Corps, with the intention of remaining in the service.

In February 1953, he received orders, boarded a DC-3 airplane, and with twenty-five others, flew to Pohang, Korea, after a rough trip with stops at Hawaii and Wake Island. In the freezing weather of Korea, they managed to be warm and comfortable in their huts at K-3 airfield. Abe Rubinstein became Operations Chief of the Tactical Air Control Center (TACC), whose main duties were to present an up-to-date picture of all friendly and enemy aircraft flying in air spaces within the Korean combat area, "with information provided to us by our strategically-placed radar sites, and further plotted on our plotting board. Whenever any of our friendly zones were penetrated by an enemy aircraft, a CAP (Combat Air Patrol fighter planes) would be 'scrambled' to intercept."

With the end of the war in Korea, Abe Rubinstein returned to New York on a thirty-day leave. Subsequently, he, with his wife, Lil, daughter Marsha, and son Gary returned to California where Abe was assigned to Marine Air Support Squadron 3 as Operations Chief. They stayed at Wherry Park Housing, near El Toro Marine Air Base for three years.

In 1955, he participated in the atomic exercise known as "Operation Teapot" held at Camp Desert Rock, near Las Vegas, Nevada. The purpose of the exercise was to test troops, weapons, and supplies under Atomic Tactical Conditions. In the morning of the exercise, the troops closest to ground zero (two miles) "were huddled in their well-prepared trenches, while the rest of us crouched down with our backs toward the detonation point." After the countdown,

"Followed by the biggest flash that I had ever seen in my life. It was easily more than 100 times brighter than the sun itself. My eyes were tightly shut and buried well in my arms and yet, I could still see the flash. We immediately turned around to face in the direction of ground zero, and were absolutely awe-struck at the sights in front of us. A large, white mushroom cloud rapidly rising to thousands of feet in altitude. Seconds later, we felt the initial blast which just about knocked all of us down. The sound effect of that blast was absolutely deafening and was at least hundreds of times louder than thunder. After a few seconds had passed by, we heard and felt the rebounding shock wave that was just about as strong. At this moment, I couldn't help but think of those troops in the trenches so close to ground zero."

Abe Rubinstein describes the damage caused by the blast:

"The war tanks within a few hundred yards of ground zero were melted outright, including the tower that held the bomb . . . Most of the troops in the trenches suffered some heat and blast effects. For the most part, the whole area for a couple of miles around resembled a dead, silent world, completely devastated by the effects of the bomb. It was an awesome and eerie sight."

In March 1957, Abe Rubinstein found himself back in the Pacific. His assignment was at Atsugi Air Base, Japan, as part of Marine Air Control Squadron–(MACS-1) as Operations Chief. Later, they shipped out for maneuvers in the Philippines where they landed on the island of Luzon. At Corregidor, he visited gun emplacement and bombed out buildings, relics of the early campaigns of World War II. There were still a number of live artillery shells and bombs lying around, but an Explosive Ordnance Disposal Team was at work clearing the area. In 1958, when Abe received the news that his father had passed away, he returned home with a permanent change of orders.

They remained at New River, North Carolina, for a year. At that time, he received orders once again for Atsugi, Japan. Flying from San Francisco, with stops at Hawaii and Wake Island, he arrived at Atsugi for a year of duty. His tour completed, he returned to the States and reported to El Toro and Marine Air Support Squadron-3, Operations Section.

Before his last assignment of three years at El Toro, the Cuban Missile Crisis loomed and Abe Rubinstein was again engaged in the defense of his country. Among the first of American troops to be deployed, Abe headed toward Cuba by ship, via the Panama Canal. Arriving in the area, his task force began sailing around the island as a quarantine measure to keep all other shipping from either coming in or going out. His ship was at sea for over two weeks, with occasional stops at Vieques Island and Port-au-Prince, Haiti. They returned to the United States via the Panama Canal in late December 1962.

After three years at El Toro, California, and with a total of over twenty-one years of active military service, Abe Rubinstein retired from the Marine Corps on April 30, 1965, with the rank of master sergeant.

Reflecting on the years in the service of his country, Abe Rubinstein says, "How many people can make claim to having had two careers? I saw a lot of the world and met different people from all walks of live, including those of foreign countries . . . the latter experience has made me appreciate the good old USA that much more . . . I feel very sorry for those that might try to destroy it. Our form of government may not be a perfect one, but it certainly is the very best of all of them."

Chapter 24

Banzai!

Ralph Most, Philadelphia, had a lot of Jewish buddies in the 4th Marine Division. But most of them are gone now. His story is told in terse, right to the point narrative, describing the many twists and turns, the good and the bad, and the unforgettable moments in the Marine Corps.

Joining the Marine Corps as a seventeen-year old in February 1943, he was in pretty good physical shape as a result of his working with his dad on the Philadelphia waterfront from the time he was eight years old. Being tough and resolute, he was of no mind to take any guff from anybody. His father, a veteran of the First World War, however, had advised him to keep his mouth shut.

While he found some difficulty in accepting discipline and the BS of some of the orders, he was never intimidated by the DIs. What was difficult was the inability to hit back.

He found it humorous that "H" for Hebrew had been imprinted on his dog tags. He felt it should have been "J." Other than that, he recalls a number of incidents that he relates:

"Never being able to go hunting for rabbit and going on extended order because the DI liked rabbit.

"Being the only Jew in my platoon and going to Friday night services alone, then being given different details so I missed a few services.

"I had a problem with a Polack, who, after we were through with mess and before leaving PI and he had busted my balls about being a Jew. I had kept quiet till we were through, then put the gloves on and he a different view about the Jews when he was able to talk.

"Firing my first weapon, the M-1, then later on the Reising, carbine, BAR, Thompson, and the .45. A knife was never a problem such as the Kbar. As a kid, I always carried one for protection.

"Burial at sea. When the tractors broke loose in the hold of the LST and killed one of the men in my comm. station.

"The awesome beauty of Hawaii, especially Kauai and Maui.

"My first landing D-1 on Ivan and Jacob in Roi-Namur in the Marshalls.

"The explosion on Namur of a pillbox by a platoon of F Co., 2nd Battalion, 24th Marines. Led by Lt. Steiner and Sergeant Sol Jaslow. It was a big one.

"D-Day and Saipan. Transferred for one week to the 2nd Marines, 2nd Marine Division for their assault on Mt. Topochuki.

"Traveling zig and the shell going in a zag on the beach on Saipan and getting shook up bad.

"The flies on Saipan, coming down with dysentery, dehydration, dengue—but not getting wounded.

"The taking out of the first Jap—the close calls.

"The front assault on Tinian, but never going ashore, spending the night on an LST in the rain with my best buddy, Tony Avocato, singing the music of our time to our Marines on the hood of a radio jeep.

"The camp on Maui. Setting fire to the officers' outhouses, the march to the mess hall, the ball busting, the toughness of the 4th four landings in thirteen months.

"Turning eighteen at Lejeune, nineteen on Saipan, coming off the line and pulling guard duty on my birthday there. Coming home.

"Surviving Iwo from D-Day till March 15 without a scratch and not even a cold. The '45 typhoon, a Merchant Marine ship where the only meat were the mice that fell into the soup coming back from Saipan.

"The preparation for Operation Olympic.

"The base camp at Maui between the landings.

"The ceremony of turning in regimental colors in Camp Pendleton in November, 1945.

"Telephone School. Field telephone. Part of a five-man team, F O team. Four combat stars, two Presidential Unit Citations, recommended for the Bronze Star, but did not get it.

"My training and time in the Corps and the 4th Marine Division. Till this day remains the most memorable time of my life. Being married, children, and grandchildren, almost a tie, but two different experiences.

"Looking up and seeing the flag on Mt. Suribachi, while laying wire to 3rd Battalion, 25th Marines.

"My religious life. I attended service—but to this day am only comfortable in an orthodox or Lubavitch *shul.*

"The military, or Marine Corps, taught me many things. One of the most important things, as long as you can get up in the morning, you got it made. I thought every day since I came home is a bonus. It also taught me respect.

Father – U.S. Navy, World War I

Uncle – Army, France, World War I

Brother – Regular Army, three years World War II

Uncle – Tank battalion, World War II

Cousin – Medical doctor, Captain, World War II

"I was proud to serve my country, my Corps. The Marines that remained my friends, always there when you need them. To be part of history. To have survived.

"I admired two sergeants, one in my outfit, and the other in the 24th. My friends and Marines in our comm. section.

"The Colonel, 'Slaughterhouse' Johnson of the 2nd Marines, upon Topochuki, wounded in the leg, refusing evacuation and directing his regiment, limping on a cane, his leg and thigh bleeding badly.

"A platoon of Marines, moving out in a blink of an eyelash at the first crack of machine-gun fire.

"My friend, Tony Avocato, diving off an LST, trying to save the life of an officer. I was alone when I was told.

"One that bothered me was a Marine sitting on the tailgate of a 6 By pulling up in front of our tent area. After the Iwo landing, the truck stopped and he went over the tailgate and landed on his head. He died the next day—fate—five months later, the war was over. Many instances like that.

"Why the LST blew up in Pearl Harbor. The flies not bothering the Catholic chaplain during the services on Saipan.

"Watching the Japanese women and children and elders jumping off the cliffs on Saipan and not being able to stop it.

"I never had an easy assignment.

"The experiences in boot camp, especially the dietary part. I had never eaten pork, ham, hominy grits, ketchup on eggs for breakfast, fish for lunch.

"The burial of a member of our comm. section at sea.

"D+1 in the Marshalls. The Japanese counterattack or banzai charge on Saipan. A machine-gun opening up on us as we were leaving foxholes on the line on Saipan. Not being able to swim and the hole in my rubber tube.

"The love and affection of my family was marvelous. I didn't party too much upon my return.

"The awakening at three in the morning by one of the sergeants, telling us that the war was over.

As for the rest of the story, Ralph Most has been very reticent about his experiences in the Marine Corps. Up to now, he "has never written or discussed any experience as a Marine with anyone except the guys in my outfit." However, recently, he has opened up a bit, and "What is interesting, my grandsons want to know more. I gave them both a Division history."

In 1973, Ralph Most was invited to go to Japan to give a lecture on business management in the beauty industry. At first, he was reluctant to go. But his wife and partner prevailed upon him—so he went.

Upon his arrival in Tokyo, his hosts took him to a restaurant.

Their tables were set up as a square horseshoe. His host leans over, and begins to speak in English. He addresses himself to Ralph, and says, "Most, you American Marine." At first, this rather infuriated Most. He had known him for four years and never knew he spoke English. Nor had Ralph ever mentioned that he had served in the Marine Corps. His host asked Ralph where he was during the war. His answer was that he was in the 4ᵗʰ Marine Division on Iwo Jima. Fortunately, he had already consumed two sakes. He also said that he had been in the Marshalls, Saipan, and Tinian. At the moment his host hears "Iwo," "he stands up and calls something in Japanese. The room quiets down, and he says to me, 'The man on the end of table, he on Iwo Jima.' Meanwhile the man is standing, holding a glass, and says something in Japanese, translated to me.

"'He drinking to the U.S. Marines, to the 4ᵗʰ Marine Division, and the U.S.A.,' and all the time I'm saying to myself, how did this f—r get away? And accolades continue." Then, Most was told that he had to stand up and make a toast. The Japanese man ends his toast with a "Kempai."

Then, Most says,

"I stand up. I hold a glass of sake and the words just flowed. I drink to the Imperial Army, Navy, and the Imperial Marines, the world's finest fighting force. There is silence in the room. I continue on, and I say, 'Banzai,' and if we ever fight again, let us be on the same side. The room is in an uproar. They are all up with the glasses. They are waiting for me to raise my glass to drink. I first shout, 'Banzai!' Once, twice, and three times. Drink the sake.

"The room is still in an uproar. My friend, Tanaka, then tells me, 'The man he called on said he was very lucky to be alive. He was evacuated three days before the landing.'"

"Because of my speech and I meant what I said, I had two of the greatest weeks of my life in Japan and Hong Kong as a special gift from them.

"Fate is a strange bedfellow."

As a footnote, Ralph Most was the first private to be elected as President of the 4ᵗʰ Marine Division Association.

He had the honor of asking General Clifton Cates if they could present an award to the best company, battery, battalion, and regiment. This was done and is still in effect. It is called the General C.B. Cates Award. As the 4ᵗʰ Marine Division is a reserve unit, they make the award each year.

On the back of Ralph's envelope containing his story was the inscription, "PS. The best of the book."

Chapter 25

Here Comes the Judge

Victor Bianchini, Colonel, USMCR (ret.) is a remarkable man: a remarkable man as so many others herein depicted. On the one hand, his story is typical of many, yet the facts portray a unique individual set apart by the incredible pieces that form the checkerboard life of Victor E. Bianchini, Judge of the Superior Court of California.

There are some similarities between Judge Bianchini and Judge Marovitz. They are both first generation Americans, their fathers having been born in Europe. With an overwhelming fervor to join not only the military, but the Marine Corps, they both faced obstacles to which lesser types would have succumbed, but which had to be overcome before they would be admitted to the only service to which they aspired. Their experience in the Marine Corps proved to be an important, if not defining, influence, personal and professional, in their lives. And, lastly, their pride in being part of the Marine Corps is obvious and genuine, and their severing of official ties with the Corps is touching, wrenching, and sincere.

Vic Bianchini's life, military and professional, is a fascinating study in determination, guts, will power, pride, and achievement. There are many among the dozens of people depicted in this book whose life story provides material for exciting autobiographical study. Some might even match that of Vic

Bianchini.. But it is questionable that any other could eclipse it. It would be difficult to do justice in a few pages to the life of Vic Bianchini. His list of accomplishments, awards, honors, publications, continuing education, and law-related teaching is far too long to be listed herein. Suffice it to say that it would take the resume of a Supreme Court Justice to come even close to it.

Judge Bianchini takes particular pride in his role as a mediator. As such, he says that,

"I have successfully mediated many hundreds of complex civil litigation cases including construction defect, employment, personal injury, contract disputes and miscellaneous matters. I successfully mediated the Rancho San Diego construction defect litigation judge for all purposes and settled that case for approximately five million dollars. I have many other mediations in excess of one million dollars, in a variety of causes of action. Recognized by the Superior Court as an effective mediator, I have a dedicated calendar for the conduct of mediation, taking them from all parts of the county."

Readers, in particular, those not of the flock of Abraham, might have cause to muse on any connection between the name Bianchini and that which is Jewish. How, they might ask, and with considerable reason, can a Bianchini be a personage in a book about Jewish-Americans in the Marine Corps?

In simple terms, he who is born of a Jewish mother (and other means as well) is Jewish by birth. His family background, at least on his mother's side, is fascinating. As he describes "My Jewish roots,"

"I am a Sephardic Jew. My understanding of my background is that my ancestors of long ago migrated from Spain during the Inquisition to Morocco. Much later, my great-grandfather immigrated to Palestine in the 1800s.

"I am the great-grandson of the Chief Rabbi of Tiberias, Israel, Shmuel Ben Kiki, who was a specialist and widely published in his time in the area of family law. His writings are considered historical and are honored by being on display and preserved in the Town Center of Tiberias. I am the grandson of another notable Tiberias rabbi, Chaim Ben Kiki, who died of cholera while on a mission to Yemen. My mother, Judith, was born in Tiberias and spoke a number of languages, and was particularly fluent in Arabic. With the exceptions of a few cousins, I have a very large and extensive family on my mother's side. My Israeli family is very involved in the law. For example, my deceased cousin, Joseph Bahlul, was a District Court Judge and President of the Court in Nazareth. My Uncle David Tavron was a municipal judge, my aunt and man cousins are lawyers in Israel.

Difficult as it may appear, Bianchini's military achievements may very well be as impressive as his personal or legal. His long and distinguished military record can be summed up with his comments: "Having served in the U.S. Marine Corps for approximately thirty-one and a half years is the very best professional thing I have ever done. I have such favorable feelings about the military in general and the Marine Corps in particular, it pains me that I can no longer be an active part of the military. I truly miss the Marine Corps."

Colonel Bianchini's Marine Corps career began as an officer candidate in the Platoon Leaders Class, Camp Upshur and Mainside, Quantico, Virginia. He completed training in the summer of 1960 and was commissioned as second lieutenant in September of that year.

His initial training was "uneventful." He was "highly motivated because I wished to emulate my father, who was a chief warrant officer in the United States Navy." He served with distinction at the tail end of the First World War, after committing the very pardonable transgression of lying about his age in order to enlist. He also served during World War II, and at the beginning of the war in Korea. During Vic's time in the military, he experienced no anti-Semitism that he can recall, which was a departure from that which he experienced "as a college student in my personal relationships and from a college fraternity, but none in the military." He ascribes great permanent values in civilian life to the training and experience in the military. He says, "I received tank amphibious training and tank training, firearms training, leadership training, parachute training, reconnaissance training, amphibious landing training, military law training, NATO officer orientation, and training in other miscellaneous disciplines. All of this training was challenging and interesting.

His duties were:

1. Inspector-General investigator at Headquarters, Marine Corps during Desert Shield/Desert Storm, Colonel, 1991
2. Deputy Inspector-General, U.S. European Command, Stuttgart, Germany, Colonel, 1988–91
3. Special Staff Officer, Mobilization Training Unit Project, Marine Corps Reserve Support Center, Overland Park, Kansas, Colonel, 1987–88
4. Senior reserve general/special courts-martial Judge, Military Reserve Judge Unit, Camp Pendleton, California, Colonel, 1984–87
5. Commanding Officer, Executive Officer, Member, Mobilization Training Unit (LAW), Lt. Colonel, 1972–73
6. Trial /Defense Counsel, Acting Staff Judge, Judge Advocate, Marine Corps Recruit Depot, San Diego, Captain, 1966–67
7. Vietnam Service, 1st Marine Aircraft Wing, DaNang, South Vietnam, Wing Civil Affairs Officer, Photographics Officer, Public Affairs Officer, Trial/Defense Counsel, Captain, 1965–66
8. Commanding Officer, Executive Officer, Operations Officer, Platoon Commander, 4th Force Reconnaissance Company (parachute, scuba, surreptitious entry unit), 1st Lieutenant/Major, 1961–64, 1968–71
9. Tank Platoon Commander, 4th Tank Battalion, Camp Eliot, California, 2nd Lieutenant–1st Lieutenant
10. Navy/Marine Corps Parachute qualified, Fort Benning, 1963
11. Combat Aircrew designation, 1965
12. Vietnamese Parachute Qualification, 1965

His overseas and combat experiences include Vietnam for thirteen months and Deputy Inspector-General, U.S. European Command, Stuttgart, Germany. In Vietnam 1961, he participated in sixty-one flight-strike missions against the enemy in helicopters, several combat ground patrols, and numerous forays into villages for civil action missions.

His experiences in Vietnam are even more remarkable considering the hardship he had to overcome to be accepted into the Marine Corps. He had a difficult time even trying to get into the Navy. "I had congenital severe flat feet and I had also suffered a catastrophic injury to my left hand as a seven-year old. My middle finger almost had to be amputated, and to this day is a disabling injury. The Navy put me through a battery of tests, and officials were reluctant to sign me up. The Marine Corps, on the other hand, confirmed a verifiable temperature and didn't ask me to take off my socks. I passed with flying colors and joined the Platoon Leaders Class Law Program, whereby I was commissioned after completion of the initial training and released to attend law school."

After clerking for a year for Chief U.S. District Court Judge James M. Carter, he entered active duty. His first assignment was as Trial/Defense Counsel in Iwakuni, Japan, but "Just before I arrived there in June 1965, Vietnam broke out and I really wanted to be a part of it, so I volunteered. About three weeks later, I was in Da Nang, Vietnam, defending Marines accused of violations of the Uniform Code of Military Justice."

While in Vietnam, he handled a number of cases involving all aspects of military law, but the most interesting was one "involving charges of theft of government property, violation of orders, absent without leave, and other assorted charges against three Marines, two of whom were my clients. Later, after my clients were acquitted, the commander agree to vacate his conviction and thereafter dismissed the charges."

Bianchini was later assigned as the Wing Photographic Officer, the Wing Informational Services Officer, and the Wing Civil

Affairs Officer. "This was a fascinating job that put me on flight orders with hazardous duty pay. I became a photo journalist and wrote many stories and had a number of pictures published, mostly in the *Stars and Stripes*, including a 'double truck' of one of the most significant Viet Cong attacks on the Marble Mountain helicopter facility in late 1965. I also had a photo on the cover of *Leatherneck* Magazine. I am a Life Member of the U.S. Marine Corps Combat Correspondents Association."

One of his best assignments in the Corps was as the Deputy Inspector General of the U.S. European Command, Stuttgart, Germany, from 1988 to 1991. "This job required inspections of the military arm of the U.S. embassies in the NATO theater." As such, he traveled to "London, Paris, Athens, the Hague, Tunis, Rabat, Trondheim (Norway), and several other places. As duty in a joint command, I worked with very fine officers and enlisted personnel from all the other services, and it was a simply wonderful experience. Also, I served in Washington, D.C., Camp Smith, Hawaii, Iwakuni, Japan, DaNang, Vietnam, and many other training centers."

Judge Bianchini's list of decorations and awards is as impressive as his assignments and accomplishments. They include the Legion of Merit, Bronze Star with Combat V, three Air Medals, Joint Services Commendation Medal, Combat Action Ribbon, Presidential Unit Citation, Joint Meritorious Unit Award, Navy Unit Commendation, Navy Meritorious Unit Commendation, Marine Corps Organized Reserve Medal, National Defense Medal (with bronze star), Armed Forces Reserve Medal with two hourglass awards and a Mobilization M, Republic of Vietnam Gallantry Citation, Republic Civic Actions Unit Citation, and the Republic of Vietnam Service Medal.

His list of professional, legal, and educational achievements is no less impressive. He is presently the Honorable Victor E. Bianchini, San Diego Superior Court, in El Cajon, California. A few of the organizations in which he has membership include, California Judges Association, San Diego Judges Association, American Academy of Forensic Sciences, Marine Corps Reserve

Officers Association, National Judge Advocate General, Counselor at Large, Director, Life Member, U.S. Marine Corps Reconnaissance Association, United States Marine Corps Combat Correspondents Association, U.S. Marine Corps Vietnam Helicopter Pilots and Aircrew Association, Veterans of Foreign Wars, and U.S. Coast Guard Auxiliary.

Colonel Bianchini's modesty forbids detailing of his military exploits. However, he speaks of his most memorable incident in the following terms:

"When serving as the commanding officer of the 4th Reconnaissance Company, I was the only qualified jumpmaster for the unit. We had not had a parachute practice mission in about six months. Thus, nerves were a little raw. In parachuting, one of the main concerns is the landing and the potential for injury if the placement of the jumpers is not accurate.

I managed to place all 'sticks' dead center in the drop zone. I was the last jumper out and off the drop zone. As we approached the trucks containing the troops waiting for convoy back to the reserve center, they all stood up and cheered. It was one of the great moments of my career. Nevertheless, there are so many enjoyable moments, it would take up too much space to recount them here."

And,

"I also had very positive experiences as an Inspector General investigator at Head- quarters, Marine Corps, during Desert Shield/Desert Storm. I was assigned to do a number of sensitive investigations including several investigations involving allegations of racial prejudice. I was very proud of the Marine Corps for its conduct exhibited in the case I investigated. There was some unfortunate fallout from these investigations, but, on balance, and in the long run, the Marine Corps stood tall. It was for this duty and my overall career that I received the Legion of Merit."

In one sense, Colonel Bianchini is typical of virtually all of the Jewish-Americans highlighted in this project: their pride in being members of the Marine Corps. He says that "The U.S.

Marine Corps is the most elite and the most respected fighting force in the world. I cannot express adequately the pride and sense of accomplishment I feel for having belonged to such a magnificent organization, with its proud history of accomplishment in the service of our country. The Marine Corps is a brotherhood, as has been said, a 'band of brothers' (and sisters), who have served with such distinction, in which its members can be seen to have contributed to society in many distinguished ways. Many of our country's leaders in business, industry, politics, and the humanities, have served in the Corps and their service in the Corps, they will tell you, has, in no small, measure, contributed to their success."

He describes his military service as follows: "Words cannot express how grateful I am for having experienced military service. Of course, it goes without saying that the world would be a much better place if there was no need for a military, and wars and conflicts were unknown to us. Regrettably, the human race has not found a way to avoid this. Thus, my military career I see as service to my country in a difficult world where, regrettably, the military is necessary. I believe that the leadership principles I learned have enhanced my life and my civilian career as a Superior Judge."

Chapter 26

Noble, Resolute, Proud

If the concept of *noblesse oblige* has any significance today, it would be embodied in the lives of two exemplary Marines by names of Green and Friedman: officers, Jewish, proud, professional, decorated, gung ho, faithful and devoted husbands and fathers, superb role models for Marines and would-be Marines of any race, creed, or social caste.

Frederic Alvin Green is typical of the first generation born in the United States. His father, originally from Russia, arrived in the U.S. from England, where the family name was changed to Green. As a boy, Frederic Green played the violin, had a decent Jewish education, and knew the prayers in Hebrew for all the festivals. In his Bar Mitzvah picture, he looks chunky and cheerful.

Prior to his enlistment in the Marine Corps at the age of seventeen, he had been a member of the Civil Air Patrol. In the Marines, he trained as an infantryman being readied for the invasion of Japan. As his daughter, Judith, explained, "Fortunately, the atomic bomb brought the war to an end before invasion became necessary. Otherwise, as my mother said, we children would not be here, since the casualty rate from an amphibious attack would have been terribly high."

Frederic Green received a presidential appointment to the U.S. Naval Academy and graduated with the class of 1950. He and his wife were cousins by marriage and were introduced by a matchmaking aunt when Green was in his second year at the Academy. Five children were produced from this union, the last, Leslie, born in 1948, in Baltimore, Maryland.

Frederic Green's military career began in earnest after officer training at Quantico. He was sent to Korea as a second lieutenant in command of a rifle company. Following Korea, he taught English at the Navy Preparatory School in Bainbridge, Maryland, a tour of duty at Camp Lejeune, and, in 1956, as a captain, was sent to Japan as part of the last contingent of American occupying forces before the country was returned to the control of the Japanese civil government. During this tour, he spent time at Camp Fuji and on Okinawa. Upon returning from Japan, he was assigned to Fort Holabird, where he taught at the Army Counter-Intelligence School for three years. He received promotion to major at the termination of that tour of duty.

A three-year tour of duty followed at Marine Corps Schools, Quantico, where he attended Junior School, and a two-year tour as Executive Officer of the 2nd Battalion, 2nd Marines, at Camp Lejeune, at which time he was promoted to lieutenant colonel. In 1966, Green was sent to Vietnam for a fourteen-month tour, where he served as battalion commander, and then as G-2 of the 1st Marine Division. Subsequently assigned to the Pentagon for three years, he did "whatever one does at the Pentagon," and then went to Camp Pendleton for his last tour before retirement. He was very disappointed for having been passed over for full colonel. In addition, he " . . . had become disillusioned with American foreign policy and the American attitude toward the military as the Vietnam War dragged on to its conclusion. He retired from the Marine Corps in 1971."

As his daughter described his situation, "In 1991, he developed lymphatic tumors and was diagnosed with non-Hodgin's lymphoma, probably caused by exposure to Agent Orange in Vietnam a quarter of a century before. The government accepted responsibility, and Daddy was granted a disability pension. He was told he had about two years left. Because of his overall good health and physical fitness, he was able to hold his own for more than three years, though the radiation and chemotherapy treatments took more and more of its toll. He died December 4, 1994, at the age of sixty-seven."

Military life, especially that of the Marine Corps, was not easy for a Jewish family. With few Jewish families, religious life, though pleasant and often inspirational, was marginal. They rarely lived near centers of Jewish community life or synagogues. As his daughter, Judith, describes it, "With five children and two parents, we were almost a *minyan*. We enjoyed this; so did he." When the congregation formed at Quantico, we loved going to Friday night services and looked forward to them all week."

Unfortunately, the ugly side of religious animus showed its face when . . . "There were also instances of intolerance, insensitivity, and outright anti-Semitism that happened both to my father and to us."

Lieutenant Colonel Green was the recipient of many awards. They include the Bronze Star Medal with Gold Star and Combat V, Vietnam Cross of Gallantry with Palm, Victory Medal WWII, National Defense Service Medal, Vietnam Service Medal with 3 Stars, United Nations Service Medal, Asiatic Campaign Medal, Korean Service Medal with 3 stars, Korean Presidential Unit Citation, Vietnam Campaign Medal, Presidential Unit Citation with Star, Combat Action Ribbon, Letter of Commendation with Combat V, Meritorious Service Medal, American Theater Medal, and Navy Unit Commendation.

Disillusionment over a number of things, some caused by their religious isolation, others by the insensitivity of neighbors and friends, set in among the Green family. This caused them to reconsider their place in religion in general, and in Judaism in particular. As Frederic Green's daughter, Judith, relates it, "It took nearly twenty years for me to reassemble some feelings for the religious rituals of Judaism. I rejoined a synagogue in 1990. I think my father would be glad to know that."

If the message is not clear, if there are those who still do not recognize the role that Jewish-Americans have played and continue to play in their country's armed forces, especially in the Marine Corps, the role of Arthur D. Friedman, USMC (ret.) should resolve the issue. His friend, Lieutenant Colonel Thomas Jones, USMC (ret.) Green Bay, Wisconsin (deceased 2002) was right when he said: "I saw in the last CALTRAP that you are writing a book on Marines of the Jewish faith. None would be complete without the biography of Colonel Arthur Friedman, USMC (deceased). I served with him as an enlisted and as a Mustang and there was none better."

In an address in the Jewish chapel at Camp Lejeune on November 9, 1979, Colonel Friedman said these words:

"What's a smart Jewish boy like you doing in the Marine Corps?" That question, whether asked through idle curiosity, or in an attempt to criticize, has been following me for over thirty-two years.

"The answers that I have to it have been subject to constant change through the years, dependent upon my mood at the moment, increased knowledge, and experience, and in my own changing values.

"Tonight, I'll try to tell you what it has been like, as a Jew, to have served thirty-two years as a Marine.

"My answer to the 'Jew vs Marine' question, when I first enlisted as a private in 1947, was 'To try to get away from people like you who want to impose artificial and undesirable life-styles on me. And, incidentally, to serve my country in a way that you all are unwilling to.'

"This, of course, was the highly defensive retort of an eighteen-year old Jew who was trying to rationalize, to himself as well as his inquisitors, a very large decision he'd just made. And a very large decision it was to leave a small town in New Jersey; to leave an upper middle-class environment; to leave a father's offer of four years of college and a merchandising job as the prize at the end. Home was security. Marine Corps was the unknown.

"Culture shock was never so intense as that encountered at Parris Island, South Carolina. Although from a small town in New Jersey, I found myself stereotyped as a wise, New York 'Jewboy' who was, in some mysterious way, out to subvert the authority of my drill instructor, and, heaven forbid, 'get away with something.' The 'French' system of jurisprudence, guilty until proven innocent, is applied quite liberally in boot camp. I had to prove to my DI that I wasn't what he said I was, that I really wanted, with all my heart and soul, to be a good Marine, that I was willing to conform to all regulations, follow all orders, submit to very rigorous tests in order to prove myself worthy of the name 'Marine.' By constantly reminding myself of the purposes of boot camp and my personal goal of 'proving myself,' I made it through. When my DI granted permission to wear the Marine Corps emblem on my hat, for the first time, in my twelfth week of boot camp, he said, 'You've earned the privilege to wear the emblem of our Corps. Do was well in your assignment as you've done here and we may have another Lou Diamond comin' up through the ranks.'

"This DI who had ridden my back for twelve weeks wasn't really anti-Semitic! He knew Lou Diamond personally. He knew Barney Ross and other famous and colorful Marines who had proudly carried the twin heritages of Judaism and the Marine Corps. Through my enlisted years, 1947 through 1953, during which I rose from private to sergeant, surprisingly few examples of overt anti-Semitism were encountered. And those few examples were based upon ignorance, committed by persons in my own rank, handled, in most cases by a quick fist fight following by respect and friendship. Under no circumstances did I encounter overt anti-Semitism in my senior non-coms or officers. I worked, did my job, plus a little bit more, and I was looked upon as a Marine who happened to be Jewish. I never concealed my Judaism, making quite sure that everyone knew that I was Jewish and that I respected my faith as well as the faith of others.

"I met some fine Jewish Marines along the way. Jacob Goldberg (retired as a colonel), Len Fribourg, (retired as a Brigadier General), Merrit Adelman (retired as a colonel), 'Ike Eisenberg (a retired sergeant-major), Irv Schecter (retired as a colonel). The list is much longer, but these few will serve to demonstrate that Judaism and the Marine Corps are compatible.

"And now, what about that 'question' again? I have had it asked of me as recently as a month ago. And what an answer I gave that time? Last October, while visiting in Philadelphia where my son, a first lieutenant in the Marine Corps, was spending some time with wife and in-laws, the question arose during a cocktail party. This time, I was able to answer from a perspective of thirty-two years experience.

"First of all, I'm serving my country to the best of my ability. The Marine Corps has enabled me to accomplish all of my life's goals. They gave me:

1. Positions of increasing responsibility.
2. The opportunity to acquire two college degrees.
3. More than adequate pay with which to support a loving wife and two beautiful children.
4. Extensive travels all over the world.
5. The privilege of being a member of a true 'Band of brothers,' who constitute the finest fighting force in the world today.
6. The satisfaction, as a Jew, of participating in one of the few 'aristocracies of merit' available in our country.
7. And, finally, the ultimate satisfaction of knowing that my efforts have contributed to the continuation of the history of our faith, our country, and my Corps.

It's difficult to discern which personal trait or characteristic of Colonel Friedman is most obvious: it has to be modesty, dedication, familial affection and devotion, or patriotism. Jews do not take too kindly to the description of patriot: we feel uncomfortable with it, and are loath to demonstrate it. Colonel Friedman, thus, flies in the face of this perception. He must be an exception. His writings clearly demonstrate his love of country. It is equally difficult to decide which of his passions—family, country, Corps—are the most important. Perhaps he wouldn't want to prioritize them anyway.

His dedication and steadfast determination to complete a

task is clearly demonstrated in his writings. "During July of 1947, when I reported to Parris Island, a fresh-caught enlistee, my drill instructor told me that:

1. I wasn't good enough to be a Marine.
2. The Marine Corps Recruiting Service was perpetuating the ultimate outrage by shipping me in as a recruit.
3. Only a few Americans were privileged to serve as Marines, and, looking at me, I wasn't one of them.
4. Finally, that I had a couple of weeks (of the thirteen weeks recruit training session) to shape up or ship out.

"Being suitably impressed with the warm welcome, I proceeded to prove to him that he was dead wrong on all counts." The gauntlet that the DI threw down to challenge Friedman was more than welcomed and overcome. His dedication and patriotism gleams when he said:

"Throughout the age, when dissidents, demonstrators, and yes, even relations and other Marines questioned the value of a career spent in the profession of arms, I remember the glow that warmed my heart that day in Parris Island when I was told that Marines are honorable men, strong men armed with the weapons, moral certainty, and professional abilities that enable them to fight, if necessary, to keep our country free or to help others to be free. I never argued with these people. I simply told them that what I was doing with my life was honorable and necessary. I then asked them to evaluate their own ways of living in relation to those two criteria."

His military career spanned thirty-two years of active duty, during which time he advanced form private to colonel. He entered the Marine Corps as a private in 1947, was a Mustang as a second lieutenant, and proceeded through the ranks till reaching the rank of colonel. Clearly, his tenure in the enlisted ranks contributed to his humanity and his effectiveness as an officer.

His devotion to duty, if not patriotism, led him to volunteer for duty in Vietnam. Not unlike my status during the Korean War in which I had pangs of guilt in seeing other Marines go off to war from my perch of comfort and safety. Major Friedman was ensconced in a secure position of student in Command and Staff School at Quantico. He, as so many others, agonized with the options at hand. It was a painful decision, especially given his position as husband and father of two children. As he said, "I went through the usual soul-searching that a married Marine does before volunteering for a combat assignment. After all, I had a beautiful and loving wife, a fine son twelve years old and a lively, pretty seven-year-old daughter. My wife, ever the strong and loyal person that she was, gave me the ability to volunteer without the guilt associated with leaving the family." Friedman had learned that there was a critical shortage of majors in the Marine units in Vietnam. It was not in Major Friedman's psyche to ignore this call.

Colonel Friedman served honorably and well in Vietnam, no less than in all of his assignments. He was always resolute, driven to success, and always a model of deportment and ability. In Vietnam, he served in combat assignments in small, fast riverboats, and supported Special Forces in various projects. As a result of his success working with Army Special Forces, he was appointed as the First Marine Division Special Forces Liaison Officer.

As Team Leader, he reported to camp at Khan Duc. His responsibility lay in training civil irregular defense groups (CIDG) who defended their own villages only, training LLDB (Lluk Long Dac Biet), the Vietnamese equivalent of Special Forces, training PF (Popular Forces), who could be used throughout the province of Quan Ngai, and hosting the "Studies and Observation Group," later known as Special Operations Group, commonly referred as "black pajama spooks."

Colonel Friedman's son, Mark, followed his dad into the Marine Corps. Graduating from the University of Colorado in 1976, he was commissioned as a second lieutenant after completing OCS. He became a communications officer, "just like my dad and was fortunate to graduate first in my class. My dad was the guest speaker and also handed me the certificate for being Number One. It was a great day for me and my family, and I'll never forget it."

Mark Friedman was stationed at El Toro and assigned to the Marine Air Wing Communications Squadron 38 and later to Marine Air Support Squadron 3. He was released to inactive duty in August 1980 as a first lieutenant. "I enjoyed my time in the Marine Corps and look back fondly on most of my experience."

On the day of Mark's commissioning, Mark leaned over to his dad, "who was the senior Marine commissioned officer at the time and me being the junior Marine officer, and saying, 'We've got them surrounded.'"

On August 8, 1996, Colonel Arthur Friedman was diagnosed with terminal cancer. His daughter, Rose, quotes from the movie *Don Juan de Marco:*

"There are only four questions of value in life, Don Octavio . . . What is sacred?

Of what is the spirit made?

What is worth living for?

What is worth dying for?

"The answer to each is the same . . . only love."

His grandson, Ben Cooper Grier, will forever be endeared to his beloved grandfather. On the wall of his small room at home in Florida is permanently displayed the sword of this remarkable man.

In November 1996, Uncle Jerry Kustin wrote:

"Along the way, you have touched many people, family, friends, children, a wife. You have touched them in many kind and loving ways. If there is any solace in Death, you must know, my dear, that you have won the war of life. And though this is your last battle, you may rest in peace with the knowledge that you leave behind a legacy of love and friendship and admiration by those you touched. So go in Peace, my friend, we will remember and hope for the day when we may join in the peace and bliss which should be your reward.

At 7:00 A.M., November 21, 1996, his daughter, Rose Ellen

Friedman Grier, wrote: "We just heard Dad's last breath. He's FREE!!!"

Chapter 27

The Leavitts, A Study in Contrast

My own military service can be characterized by one word—undistinguished. Not that I planned it that way: you still do what you are told—especially in the Marine Corps. Frankly, I am embarrassed: my experience pales in comparison to those of any Marine or other hero or heroine described in this book. But failing to make some personal observations would be tantamount to dereliction of duty. And I've never been accused of that.

Actually, it started off pretty well. I joined the Marine Corps Reserve before turning eighteen while still in high school. We drilled at the Boston Navy Yard. I felt real good in my ill-fitting greens. One day another member of my platoon, Private Violet, and I went to NAS, Squantum, Massachusetts (near Boston). There, we hitched a ride on a C-47 and bounced up and down in the air until we got to NAS, Quonset Point, Rhode Island, only about a half-hour flight. It turned out that we were delivering a cargo of rockets. We were glad to disembark.

Called to active duty in April 1951, I applied to and was accepted into OCC, a ten-week program at Parris Island for college grads to train as platoon leaders. I enjoyed most of it, and actually did well in close-order drill, overall appearance, weapons, and physical activities. I was surprisingly adept with the M-1 rifle, barely missing out on Expert. However, I was not among those who graduated. I didn't exactly wash out—I finished the course. I just didn't graduate. I was rated unqualified. It took many years to come to grips with this failure. I conjured up all sorts of reasons or excuses, refusing to accept the realities of the situation: I was not officer material; I failed to complete too many of the basic assignments; and my performance was unacceptable and substandard.

However, I did some things right. Soon after arriving at Parris Island, I left everyone behind when we dove into the pool for our swimming qualification. But my performance in a few small details—such as leadership, command appearance, officer potential, and field navigation—left a lot to be desired. Around the middle of the program, a rumor persisted that was later confirmed: candidates lacking officer appearance or potential would not graduate, irrespective of scores. I knew right then that I was doomed. I had low evaluations, both from peers and from DIs. Ultimately, to my credit, I did not wash out (many of the candidates were forced to leave the course before its end: I finished it out)—I just didn't graduate. Sometime during the last week, after having been informed of my failure, languishing in my bunk and feeling sorry for myself, I last saw my platoon returning from a field exercise singing and doing monkey drill with their rifles.

Still in the Reserve, I was kept on active duty as an enlisted man and sent to Camp Lejeune the summer of 1951. Because of my typing ability, I was assigned as clerk-typist at 2nd Marine Division Headquarters where I performed well and received excellent evaluations. From time to time, I actually considered applying to OCS at Quantico.

In late November, we went to the rifle range to requalify. One of our company sergeants, Blemel, a short, overweight loudmouth who had served on the cruiser USS *St. Paul*, and never ceased reminding everyone about it, also bragged endlessly about being a good shot. When I tired of hearing about it, I bet him ten bucks I would beat him on the range. He greedily took up the challenge. Despite a cold and blustery wind on qualification day, I beat him by a couple of points, and even managed to collect my ten dollars.

After about seven months of boredom and pangs of guilt from cutting orders for others to go to Korea, Frank Bitterman and I requested transfers to the 1st Marine Division in Korea, which were promptly approved. We were on our way, and I looked forward to it eagerly. The thought of being in combat did not faze me at all. Despite my MOS (0143, clerk-typist), I thought that was where I should be and would be—on the front lines.

My request for overseas assignment now approved, I reported to Camp Pendleton for three months of infantry training. However, another unpleasant surprise awaited me: I was assigned another month of mess duty. I thought this must have been a mistake—it was a violation of a standing rule that prohibited an individual from being assigned more than thirty days of mess duty within a calendar year. Nevertheless, a Marine does what he or she is told. Semper Fi.

I was assigned to pots and pans-pot walloper which, in the Marine Corps—as I suspect they do in the Navy, Merchant Marine, and Joe's Diner—has the same curious and disgusting habit of becoming encrusted with black, obsidian-like gunk that resists all efforts to remove it, becoming impervious to scrubbing, rubbing, scouring, hammering, chipping, polishing, or any other futile attempts to eradicate it from its host utensil.

The inspecting officers would not be impressed with excuses or explanations, so I did not offer any. I knew what their reaction would be, so why waste words and risk embarrassment? Verdict: crappy job. Sentence: three hours in the grease pit—the punishment would fit the crime.

Those unfamiliar with the term "grease pit" will better understand the term "septic tank." Get into the grease pit about twelve feet down, stand knee-high in excrement, swill, and the ghoulish gray-white, filthy, oozing spongy mass of metamorphosed residue that stinks to high heaven, and begin to shovel it into buckets that are handed down from the rim. Three hours on assignment to the "grease pit" or a week on dishes at Camp Lejeune in summer are both hell on earth. And I still don't know which is worse.

Mess duty at Camp Lejeune, right after reporting there, was arguably the lowest part of my military career. I know that everyone pulls it—enlisted personnel, that is—so I am not beefing about the obligation. However, it was so fatiguing and degrading that, to me, nothing could compare with it. The hot and humid weather made mess duty at the Staff NCO School even more unbearable.

Our quarters were not too bad. I liked living in tents. And the food was good—all you could eat. The students, that is, the staff NCOs in training, ate family-style—no trays or mess kits for them—like eating in one's own family dining room. They had their training and their classes under no less oppressive conditions, but at least they could relax and eat like human beings.

My first assignment was peeling potatoes. That this had been even more of a drudgery in the "Old Corps" was no consolation—that was *their* problem. We all have to bear our own crosses. They managed to cope with it; I had to cope with mine. We still had to pick up each spud individually, scoop out the eyes, and then press it into the machine which made a half-assed attempt to peel it—arguably an improvement over the earlier peel-it-by-hand method.

My next one, however, *was* the worst—I was tapped to wash dishes. As serving was done family-style, individual plates, cutlery, cups, saucers, and bowls were used. Maybe the Corps thought the staff NCOs were entitled to humane treatment, or maybe it wanted to retain as much of a homey atmosphere as possible. But that was no consolation to the messmen. It was on me and the other messmen charged with washing their dinnerware that the torment was inflicted. As each NCO finished his meal, he would bring his plates and silverware to us at the dishwasher and lay them on the mountain of dirty dishes already piled up in front of us, whereupon we would have to scrape the leftovers of the food, rinse, and douse them in hot, steamy water—laced with cheap, strong detergent—that was rapidly becoming more pungent and irritating, not to mention dirtier.

My hands became red, swollen, sore, and irritated—and my

temperament did not fare much better. Supposedly no-one had ever lasted more than three days washing dishes. I think I broke the record—I lasted a week.

Following mess duty, I was assigned to an infantry training company preparing for service in Korea. I enjoyed the training very much and received excellent evaluations. Maybe I was cut out to be a Marine after all. As a bonus, I was promoted to corporal and became a fire-team leader.

The nineteen-day journey on the USS *Meigs* proved to be a welcome change. Despite a storm at sea, I enjoyed the trip and found the storm fascinating. I enjoyed standing at the rail of the promenade deck, watching the huge waves crashing on and around the ship, pitching and rolling, and seeing the small sea birds, unaffected and unconcerned with the elements, soaring and swooping at the sides and stern of the ship.

In a sense, it was unreal—a carefree sea voyage unfettered by duties of discipline. It was also surreal—especially at night, the boat alone, the waves lightly striking its sides—not the cinematographic vision of warships and grand fleets, transported by ships large and small. In a way, it was a letdown—hardly the panoramic exaltation of naval might strutting on the post-World War II movie screen.

Arriving at Inchon and standing offshore, we offloaded onto landing craft, walked the short course of the beach to board train boxcars, and loaded our rifles in anticipation of guerrilla activity. Shortly before dusk, we stopped and loaded into trucks—destination the reserve battalion area. En route, it was like the Fourth of July. To the right and to the front erupted a gigantic fireworks display of tracers and artillery fire. Could it have been *just* for us? And why were we headed in that direction?

The question was answered soon enough when the convoy stopped. Amid loud and seemingly confused argument, the vehicles turned around and went to the rear. We had been heading in the wrong direction. The lead driver had taken a wrong turn.

In the morning at the reserve battalion area, we saw some

incoming shells burst not far from our bivouac, a few of which detonated within our perimeter. A bedraggled, unkempt, forlorn, and unenthusiastic platoon straggled back into camp after combat at the front. Welcome to Korea. And my real war was over.

We did not have to wait long for our assignments. I don't remember if I greeted mine with relief or with trepidation. While most of the guys were assigned to front-line companies, I got orders for a rear-echelon administrative unit of the 7th Marines.

There, for seven months, I handled personnel records, safely ensconced in a tent and behind a makeshift desk with a manual typewriter, and an old one at that, completely out of harm's way. We were not far from some friendly artillery units, however, and could see and hear their fire every night—a reminder that war was close at hand. One of our clerks, Michel Winkeleer, with whom I had worked at Lejeune, had a dispute with his top sergeant, was shipped out to a front-line unit as a machine gunner, was wounded, and received a Bronze Star Medal. More than once, I considered volunteering to go to the front. After all, I had volunteered for Korea from security, warm bed, hot chow, and liberty in Washington, D.C., but I was neither insane nor suicidal. There they knew where I was. If they needed me, they could find me.

In fact, there was a rumor going around in early February of 1953 that we were going up to the front lines. There had been a lot of casualties, and replacements were not due for a long time. We were available. Nothing came of it, however, and we remained safe and sound ten miles or so behind the lines.

Otherwise, things were uneventful. We came under fire one clear, winter night about ten o'clock. Hearing the unmistakable sound of rifle fire, we rushed out of our tents in white T-shirts in full moonlight—lined up in a prone firing line and watched tracers laze over our heads. Later, we learned that some drunken South Koreans had fired in our direction. No-one got hurt, but we made great targets.

Returning home on the USS *General Walker* after seven months, I was stationed at Treasure Island to await release from active duty. The officer in charge, a captain, tried to convince me to ship over—they would even keep me at Treasure Island. Tempting as it was, I had other plans. Sometimes I wonder if I made the right decision.

For the most part, I enjoyed my short military career. In retrospect, I would never have been part of any other service. It was in the Marine Corps that I became a man. The lessons I learned and the benefits I derived, such as pride, self-discipline, punctuality, attention to detail and appearance, teamwork, physical and mental health, and hard work carried over into my succeeding professional and personal life. They were invaluable; there was no other way I could have learned such lessons. My service was important to me—I felt a part of a real team, accomplished a lot, and would at least be able to tell my children that their dad served his country and was indeed a part of a great effort.

My military career was revived somewhat in May 1997. A notice appeared in the local newspaper requesting former Marines to join a Marine honor detail at Riverside National Cemetery for the purpose of rendering military honors to deceased veterans. Now (2002) we are the only civilian group in the country authorized to wear Marine dress blues. I consider it an honor and a privilege to be part of such a dedicated and modest group of men and women, still performing a valuable service to their country, fellow veterans, and families of veterans.

My younger brother, Edward Leavitt, had a much longer and certainly more distinguished military career than I.

Born November 20, 1931, in Brookline, he was graduated from the Naval Academy and he resigned his commission in 1963 to complete law school in San Diego.

Ed retained a Reserve commission and, after twenty years of Reserve service as a tank officer—and a total of thirty years' service as a Regular and Reserve Marine—he retired as a colonel, USMCR, in 1983. His awards and decorations include the Meritorious Service Medal with two gold stars in lieu of second and third awards, the Organized Marine Corps Reserve Medal, the National Defense Service Medal with bronze star in lieu of a second award, Navy Commendation Medal, the Korean Service Medal, the Vietnam Service Medal with bronze star, the Armed Forces Reserve Medal, the U.S. Navy Expert Rifle Medal, the Republic of Vietnam Gallantry Cross with Palm Unit Citation, the United Nations Service Medal, eight awards of the Marine Corps Expert Rifle Badge, and seven awards of the Marine Corps Expert Pistol Badge.

While stationed in Japan from 1961 to 1963, Colonel Leavitt was the shooting captain of the 1st Marine Air Wing Rifle and Pistol Team. He personally won a championship in one event and placed second in another with the M-1 service rifle at the 8th U.S. Army Interservice Invitational High-Power Rifle Tournament in Korea. His 1st Marine Air Wing team came in second in a competition with more than forty teams from all U.S. services and numerous foreign countries.

Extremely proud of the role played by his family members in five of our country's wars and all of our armed forces, he wished to relate the following:

"My father served in the U.S. Navy during World War I. He raised my brother (the author of this book) and me to believe in the greatness of this country and told us, over and over, that it was our duty to serve in its armed forces, especially in wartime. I am proud of Howard for going on active duty with the Marines in 1951 during the Korean War. I signed up for the Marine Corps while at the Naval Academy in 1952, still a time of war, and when I graduated in June 1953, went into the Corps. I later heard from a number of relatives and my father's friends that when my brother and I were both on wartime active duty in the Marine Corps, Howard already in Korea and me on my way there, my father was a most frightened man. But I also heard that he was the proudest."

Colonel Leavitt practiced law in San Diego for over twenty years before retiring from that profession in 1985. During that time, he also served as Judge of the State Bar Court, a Master, a Mediator, and an Arbitrator of the Superior Court of the County of San Diego, and a Judge Pro Tem of the Superior Court for ten years.

Since that time, he has pursued his hobby of International (Olympic) trap and American trap shooting, winning numerous awards and trophies, including National Senior Champion and California State Class Champion, both in 1995; and California State Senior Champion, 1998—all in International (Olympic) trap shooting.

Other International (Olympic) trap shooting awards are USA Shooting Maple Leaf Tournament Senior Champion in 1994 and 1998 and Class Champion in 1993 and 1995. He took the USA Shooting Southwest Regional Championship Tournament (California, Nevada, Utah, Colorado, New Mexico, Wyoming) Runner-Up Class Championship in 1995.

"My older brother, Howard, the author, feels that our careers are characterized by contrast. I believe we are brothers, however, united in deep and abiding feeling for the Marine Corps and all it stands for. We both feel acute loyalty to the tenets of the Corps as eloquently and simply expressed in the motto of the Corps, *Semper Fidelis*—and beyond. We both cherish and feel proud of our strongly held beliefs in total commitment to our duty and honor, whether in uniform or not, as Marines.

"To have earned the privilege of being a Marine is to always have the duty and the right to be a Marine forever, and to take exquisite pride in being a Marine and an American. To be a Marine is not only a Jewish thing, it is much more. It is a bright, shining, beautiful American ideal."

Howard Leavitt is proud to present one of his brother Edward's numerous citations:

"The President of the United States takes pleasure in presenting the MERITORIOUS SERVICE MEDAL (Gold Star in lieu of the Third Award) to
COLONEL EDWARD J. LEAVITT
UNITED STATES MARINE CORPS RESERVE
For service set forth in the following CITATION:
For outstanding meritorious service as the Commanding Officer of MTU (Law) CA-12 and Senior Advi-

sor, Appropriate Duty Membership, MTU (Law), Fallbrook, California, from May 1981 through June 1983. During these assignments, Colonel Leavitt demonstrated superior leadership in command of his Reserve unit and superior legal abilities in support of the active duty Naval and Marine Corps establishment in the California area. His creation and implementation of Reserve legal programs to support legal readiness of Navy destroyer squadrons, submarine groups, and Marine Corps installations contributed significantly to enhanced troop morale and greater combat readiness. Colonel Leavitt's single-handed establishment of instructional seminars designed for continued training of active duty Naval attorneys was an exceptional accomplishment which resulted from his untiring efforts and unselfish devotion. His personal leadership qualities and skills as a practicing military Reserve attorney were recognized as superior throughout the Naval Service and the community. Colonel Leavitt's judicial ability, keen judgment, and unflagging dedication to duty reflected great credit upon himself and were in keeping with the highest traditions of the Marine Corps and the United States Naval Service. For the President,
[signed] William Ball
Secretary of the Navy"

Chapter 28

Marathon Man at Ground Zero and in the Desert

David Ashe is not only a competitor in marathon, he is a Renaissance Man: scholar, athlete, professional soldier, or more precisely, Marine, lawyer, patriot, and humanitarian. At an early age, he has already earned accolades by way of his accomplishments, his virtues, and his humanitarianism. He has no problem about relating his exploits and his desire and plans for the present and the future. While he is still in the throes of trying to figure out his mission, both personal and professional, he has already made his mark in the eyes of his friends, family, and fellow Marines.

He chooses to tell his story in his own words, a task which he does with passion, professionalism, and with pride. But this is hardly surprising. He is an aspiring author in his own right, having already written one novel, and, like most of us, experiencing the sting of rejection from publishers. But, as he says, "I'll keep plugging away."

The following is the David Ashe story:

"I'm from Virginia Beach, Virginia. For as long as I can remember, I always had a fascination with military history and hardware. I read C. B. Colby books all the time and built nearly every Estes scale model warplane that came out.

My family is from France and Germany, and so 20th century military had personal importance; my aunts and uncles remember fondly and sadly the many members of my family killed in the Holocaust.

Also, my grandfather was quite an inspiration. Master Chief Henry Goldberg, USN, served 30 years. He liked to talk about how he worked with a new invention called 'radar,' mostly in regard to fire control on surface ships. However, anti-Semitism was a little more prevalent; my grandfather mentioned that he wanted to serve so that people would notice and say, 'Hey, that guy's a Jew and he serves.'

To be honest, that was part of my motivation. By and by, people find out that I'm Jewish. I get the standard response that most of us get: 'Wow, you're Jewish? There aren't many Jewish people in the military, are there?' At that point, I always enjoy giving them a quick, friendly thirty seconds worth about how 8,000 Jews served in the Union Army in the Civil War; Jews earned 1,100 citations for valor in WWI, including three Medals of Honor; over fifty Jewish families lost two or more children in combat in WWII.

So, how did I get here? I graduated from Virginia Tech in 1991, then I was a ski-bum in Breckenridge, Colorado, for a year. Then, in 1992, I worked on Capitol Hill for a senator from Michigan. Mostly, I wrote speeches and did research. After that, I worked for a large lobby group with a focus on health care and NAFT until 1994.

After that amount of time working in macro law, I wanted to focus on law as it affects individuals. I started law school in 1994. After my second year of school, I went to OCS (Officers Candidate School) in summer, 1996, with the PLC (Platoon Leaders Course) Bravo Company. Then I returned to law school to finish my third year.

I took the Virginia bar exam in August '97, and was sworn in in November '97.

From there, I checked into the Basic School's Bravo Company in 1998 and graduated in July 1998. I always liked the fact that regardless of whether you fly a plane, drive a tank or practice law, we're all Infantry Marines first and last.

After TBS (The Basic School), I went to Newport, Rhode Island, for ten weeks at the Naval Justice School where I graduated and re-accepted the fact that I was a lawyer and not a grunt. From there, I was assigned to Camp Pendleton.

As you know, there are two main kingdoms of military law: courts-martial and legal assistance. I've been at the Legal Assistance office for about seventeen months, but I'm about to move to a trial billet as a defense counsel at Legal Team Echo. But I enjoyed legal assistance and its broad scope of law. We do it all there—tax, wills, divorce, auto contracts, landlord-tenant disputes, etc. I really do love this job. And, I feel like I've gained enough experience to place me past the apprenticeship sages of lawyering. But I'm excited to go to trial billet.

On my off time, I've been exploring quite a bit of the desert and mountains as I train for triathlons. In fact, the Marine Corps has a triathlon team which I squeaked onto. I'm glacial-speed compared to most of the team. Can you believe we actually have local sponsors who pay for our entry fees to races as long as we wear their gear? Hey, I would have worn it anyway.

Somehow, I decided to compete in the Ironman California triathlon on May 20. I actually felt a little queasy when I saw my name on the official participants list.

Thing is, Tri training has an insidious way of making one think you're never training enough. Even if I swim and lift one day, I still need to bike and run the next, and then over and over, etc. I've done about twelve or so regular triathlons, but this Iron Man is 2.4 mile Swim, 112 mile Bike, and then 26.2 Run. It starts at 7:00 am, and I have until 11:00 pm to finish. Yes, masochism rears its head.

I was so glad to find the Jewish Marines website. I'm proud of my Jewish heritage and I'm very proud to be a U.S. Marine. As a 30-year old single captain, I feel very accomplished being a Marine. Unlike some of the fundamentalist religious, I don't shove my religion at everyone. But–and this may sound off–I'm motivated to be a good Marine on the off-chance someone thinks, 'Oh, yeah, Ashe, he's good-to-go. He's Jewish, too.'

After five and a half years of active duty, I felt ready for something new. I was due to hit my EAS on 15 September 2001. But the world was different by the time I became a civilian.

I really don't know New York. But by Thursday morning, I couldn't sit on the couch any more. I was on terminal leave and unable to return to base in California. So, about 0500 on September 13, I rented a car and drove from my parents' house in Virginia Beach, Virginia, to Manhattan. A note on the kitchen counter read, 'Drove to New York. Will be in touch.'

Flying blind? I was flying dumb. I had absolutely no expectation that I would be used as a volunteer much less go to ground zero. I expected to shop up, offer my held, accept rejection, and then drive the 400 miles back home frustrated by glad I tried.

Surprisingly, there was no traffic. A little standard slowness around DC, but no other traffic at all even as I drove into New York City. I made a brief stop at a hardware store to purchase a hardhat, gloves, and goggles. As I drove, I stumbled onto a report that a volunteer center was at 37th St. at the Jacob Javits Convention Center. Good. That made it easy since my directions plopped me off at 42nd at the end of the Lincoln Tunnel. I really didn't know New York.

My skepticism was justified: thousands of people were wrapped around the convention center. I momentarily considered trying to bluff: 'Yes, I'm a fireman, or a steel worker, etc.' But, a full two seconds of contemplation reminded me that a lot of people would depend on any promise of expertise and could be hurt if any of us was a bluffing jackass. So, I went for the truthful approach and it worked. Somehow, I went to the head of the line to ask one of the uniformed National Guard soldiers how the line worked. He asked if I was a fireman or ironworker. I told him, no, but I was in the Marine Corps for five and a half years. I left out the part about how I was a Judge Advocate and how I was still on terminal leave which was probably for the best because the next thing I knew, he was lifting the yellow tape and waving me in.

I walked to one of the staging areas on the side of the huge convention center and introduced myself to a disinterested fire chief who told me 'sit tight and wait, crackerjack.' I was sure I had no chance of getting down there to do my part.

A group of construction workers and police officers arrived on the scene replete with workboots, gloves, hats, tools, loaded for bear. They reported to the fire chief and I was then to go around the corner of the building. 'What are we doing?' I asked as I joined them. 'Bus is pickin' us up here,' someone replied.

Yeah. Right. I could barely conceal my skepticism. I was positive that we'd been snubbed. Then gear began to arrive. Who needs a flashlight? Here's more food. Everyone take water! There is no water downtown! Hmmm, maybe this was for real. I gotta be honest, even when the bus appeared and we were loaded on, I still thought they were going to ship us to Jersey and dump us off.

On the bus at the outer perimeter, we passed a group of smiling volunteers and waved out the windows as they cheered and passed coffee and food to us through the windows. They pumped signs in the air that read, 'Bless you, Heroes.' Hero? I felt like I was simply lucky at best and a fraud at worst. I wasn't a hero, just lucky—and grateful—to be on the bus with a chance to do something. When we passed that group, things felt real. When the bus turned south onto Church St. with the rubble area lit six blocks away, it became completely real.

Stadiums are not as well lit as this section of Manhattan was. It was after 5:00 P.M. and the generator-powered lighting had already beaten the sun by a few billion candlepower. Dust, steam, and smoke rolled thick stumbling and searching for an escape from the littered streets. Debris rolled in the gutters and past vehicles. We approached a fire truck and were glad for the familiar sight of it. However, we gaped in awe as we walked by and saw that it was a burned hulk leftover from the events of Tuesday. 'Getting close now, boys,' I heard someone say.

What did the area look like? I'd like to take a paragraph to describe it. I stood under the upright remains of the north tower. I'd seen the image on TV. Heard it stood like a work of modern art. That sounded about right. The rubble pile was anywhere from street-level to seventy-five feet high. The steel beams that make the basic framework were a foot square thick of solid steel but bent like copper wire. The entire area smelled like someone lit a stack of newspapers and doused it with formaldehyde. Various trucks and the upright remains channeled everyone to enter the rubble from the south. From the south side of the WTC plaza, the main debris pile stretched one block north to the upright remains I'd first seen, to about two blocks west up to the edge of the still standing Battery Park buildings. At some points, we could still see glowing red steel deep in the pile and even a few flames in nearby buildings or on parts of the rubble that we could not access. I stood on Church St. twenty-five feet from the base of the building . . . and the street was clear. The buildings fell cleanly and eerily on top of themselves.

As I stepped into the main rubble pile, I was eager to hear a voice through a bullhorn telling me to do this, do that. But, there was no identifiable chain of command. No matter, well formed lines–the bucket brigades–snaked into the rubble.

One line passed the buckets out, another passed them back in. I climbed to a point where a new line was forming about thirty feet into the rubble about ten feet high. I took my place and passed buckets for about two hours. The search and rescue method was simple: we dug into the side of the pile as if to dig a cave. We'd dig and bucket as much silt and cement as we would and then ironworkers would follow and cut metal away so that we could go farther. When it was too tight for shovels we used our hands.

There was a high motivation at ground zero. Lots of urgency. No one lost sight of the fact that this was search and rescue, not just cleanup. There was a pervading sense of how the next bucket, the next turn of a shovel might yield a person, a body, a piece of evidence. When a person took a break, it was just long enough to grab fresh gear. When we stopped for food, there was new vigor as if now we must earn that meal or bottle of water. I was about to walk up to the front of the line and take a turn shoveling when the first collapse came.

One Liberty Plaza was a bombed out wreck. Nearly half the windows on his west side facing the debris area were shattered. The others were caked with ash and some lower parts of its face were completely gone to grant intrusive intimate views into private offices. Supposedly, engineers determined the building had begun to list. The collapse came when new glass popped out and tumbled down on us. With adrenalin and haste, we scrambled south past what I think was the American Express building and held our hardhats on our heads when we tilted our heads back far enough to see the top of the sixty stories of One Liberty. I recall that this was the first time I'd noticed that a piece of the WTC was hanging on the scarred face of the Amex building. No collapse, no immediate danger. The all clear was given and we went back to the rubble.

A little after midnight, I was shoveling when the next warning came. This time, I saw some of the elements of the concern: a few of us were waiting for an ironworker to cut a girder as we felt the forceful wind of the predicted thunderstorm front. Newly flung dust and glass pegged our backs and helmets from the west as we looked east at One Liberty. Several of us saw more glass pop and tumble. Before we could comment to ourselves, a warning sounded and the crowd of SAR workers again scrambled south. I think we moved slower off the pile this time, it was slow going to move over the debris; if that building wanted us, it was going to get us. The wind whipped along with us as rain entered the scene.

No collapse, just nervous watchers when the wind stirred the area. But rain was not a part of the operation. It poured. It started light, but soon it was absolutely torrential. We waited for the all clear as some anguished over speculation that the rain might drown survivors. When the all clear was sounded, we returned to the debris which was now matted with our footprints and the rain.

Ash drifts had now become mud layers. We covered our dusty short sleeve shirts with Red Cross dispensed raincoats and the rain seeped into the ground, the dust and our boots. We restarted at 1 A.M. or so and I was on a shovel this time aiming my digs into the waiting buckets. I stayed on that shovel for a long time; it was an outstanding shovel, long, narrow, and I could get to places that others could not. As we cleared debris from the immovable metal we started to use our hands again. I'm not sure if it was a shovel or hand that touched the body first.

Most of his clothes were torn away, but some of his sport coat was still on him and his wallet was in the breast pocket. Morgue and medical staff ran to the spot instantly and took control of his recovery. He was mostly lying on his back and he was flattened from the waist up. Even his face was pressed flat. As we looked into the dent we'd dug, he was about ten feet to my left. Around 0400, I heard some workers near us found a hand and a piece of aircraft. Evidence techs were on the scene but I never heard further confirmation about that.

By 0500, I was starting to stumble and I was soaked from the pouring rain. I walked north on Church Street hoping to find a van or a bus that would let me on for a nap. I found a large doorway with a few other sleeping figures in it. A Red Cross van across the street gave me a few blankets and I stopped in that dry doorway for a luxurious three-hour nap. I woke feeling very fresh and walked the three blocks back to the site.

I was soaked and shivering a little in the steady rain, so I walked into the bombed-out Burger King that was marked NYPD HQ. The top level was used as a great station and I eagerly refreshed my attire. They had everything. The shattered and burned Brooks Brothers store in One Liberty donated their unburnt clothing. I put on a smelly, but dry, eighty-dollar sweater. Then, I found serviceable raingear, fresh gloves, and dry socks. The socks soaked up the water of my sodden boots quickly, but it still felt good to change out of the dirty shreds I'd had on my feet all night.

Back in the rubble, I passed buckets for about three hours then went with a group to clear debris below the American Express building with that awesome shovel that I had found. We weren't really anything SAR related. I realized later that we were clearing the space so that an enormous crane could be assembled on the site. It required a second crane just to put it together; the mass it could clutch and carry in its grip was worth one thousand of our buckets.

Around noon, all personnel except for those operating the cranes were cleared back. The cranes chewed through the massive girders that we had been digging around. Since we were to stand idly by, I took the time to walk out of the area to buy a disposable camera. I walked north about ten blocks on Broadway before finding any stores open. I would have looked around elsewhere but I really don't know New York very well. I chatted with each police officer and National Guardsman on my path: 'Staying dry? 'Hanging in there?' What I was really saying was, 'Remember my face so that you'll let me back in.'

When I returned to the Plaza it was still cranes only on the rubble for another hour. Approximately twenty feet of the rubble we'd hollowed the night before was gone and a fresh wall of ash and cement was attacked once again by our hands and shovels.

Around 4 P.M., I'm not sure because I wasn't wearing a watch, someone near me had been talking on a cell phone and heard that the President's helicopter had landed about a mile away. When the President arrived later, I was by One Liberty Plaza with a few hundred others who were pressed back by security while the President looked at the debris. Though we couldn't make out the words, we could hear his voice on a bullhorn. His exact words were drowned out by engine noises and the chant of USA, USA, from the workers. I've been watching the news because I'm still curious exactly what he said.

When he left, I rejoined a bucket line for several house, and by dark, I began shoveling again. It was now Friday evening and still, the material we turned with the shovel spades was mostly cement and muddy ash. When I thought of the buildings, I thought of the steel and cement, and I also thought of the glass, the chairs, tables, computers, carpets, and people. However, it seemed a pile of nothing but cement and metal.

By midnight, I had new blisters from shoveling despite an outstanding set of new gloves I'd received at the police station. I took a place in the bucket line until I started getting tired around 0400. I went back to the doorway from the night before and even found some Red Cross blankets along the way. However, I woke up two hours later, cold and shivering. I was freezing and it probably wasn't even below 50 degrees. I got up and walked back to the WTC Plaza with the intent to work up a sweat. However, it was cranes only again for about an hour. We waited around on the edge, shivering away body heat until we were let back on the pile. The sun returned later that day but still gave us a freezing cold night in the doorways again.

When I finally did leave New York, it was partly because I wanted to get back to my family and in particular, as we volunteers were under the misconception that when we left, new volunteers would be brought in to have their chance to contribute. Later, I would find out that no further civilian volunteers were to be brought in. The overwhelming supply of firemen, police, and union workers were determined to be the best to continue the job.

I walked north until I passed the disaster perimeter and the tireless military personnel who secured them. On my way out, I spotted a few Marine chevrons on some of the personnel and chatted with a tired motivated devil dog who chuckled at the beard I'd grown on terminal leave. When they saw my sooted clothes and face, many asked about the scene. A few showed me pictures of missing loved ones and asked if I'd seen any of the faces. The answer was always 'no.'

As I walked the remaining blocks to the parking garage, I passed a few candle vigils still in progress at various street corners. I am eternally grateful and honored to have had a chance to contribute. Those workers on the site need no lessons from anyone about honor, courage, and commitment. It was an extraordinarily proud way for me to spend my last days before my EAS from the Marine Corps . . . even thought I was recalled two weeks later. I exited the garage and checked with the parking attendant for directions back to the Lincoln Tunnel. I really don't know New York.

After six years of shaving every single day, I couldn't wait to grow a beard. I loved being a JAG in the Marine Corps, but I was ready to try some other things. By Labor Day weekend of 2001, I was feeling quite settled into civilian life. I was home in Virginia Beach to run the rock 'n' roll half-marathon, and, by the way, my beard was going great. Ten days later, I was in New York picking up pieces of the World Trade Center and putting them in a bucket.

I was fortunate enough to be one of the search and rescue workers at Ground Zero, arriving in New York two days after the World Trade Center attacks on September 11. However, even after that experience, I had the feeling that my part in the 'bucket brigades' was not the last of my public service.

I was right. Two weeks later, back on my couch in San Diego, California, the phone rang. 'Good morning, may I speak to Captain Ashe?' 'Um, this is Captain Ashe.'

'Right. Anyway, *Captain,* you've been recalled. I'll fax you your involuntary reactivation orders. You'll report in five days.'

Reactivation. Report. My job. My beard. I had only been a civilian for about two weeks before being swept back into the arms of Mother Marine Corps.

My new billet was deputy staff judge advocate (SJA) with the First Marine Expeditionary Force (I MEF). I MEF is a large command that owns three Marine Expeditionary Units (MEU). A MEU is a floating regiment of about 2,500 Marines floating around on three ships carrying a sign that says, 'In case of war, break glass.' In recent times, it was a combined force of two MEUs that kicked down the door in Kandahar and established a foothold for us in Afghanistan.

The SJA is the legal adviser to the commanding general (CG) as his counsel for all matters whether we break laws or break windows plus a very large range of operational law. OpLaw is everything from targeting to rules of engagement (ROE), to force protection, to UN Charter articles and resolutions.

I attended Yom Kippur services attired in my khaki-green

Alpha uniform and noticed a few other uniforms at the La Jolla synagogue. I wondered if anyone else was a recalled reservist. I'm not sure about recalled reservists, but I know that there were plenty of veterans in the congregation.

Several people, including the rabbi, came by to personally welcome those of us in uniform and tell a bit about their own military service. Most people, even Jews, aren't aware of our contribution to the U. S. military. Numbers tell all: We've always been about 1.5 per cent of the population (actually, it's been between two and three per cent—writer's note), but we've accounted for over three percent of the U.S. military (during wartime—possibly. But substantially less during peacetime—writer's note); 8,000 Jews served in the Union Army during the Civil War, Jewish veterans earned 1,100 citations for valor in WWI including three Medals of Honor; in WWII, over fifty Jewish families lost two or more family members killed in action.

The uniform of the day at the base was the dark green camouflaged uniform. However, more and more Marines wearing the light-colored desert cammies appeared each day . . . and disappeared just as quickly. A few months before, I was part of search and rescue in New York. Now, I was advising on search and destroy. After all, the three-star general I worked for owned the task force that was on the ground in Kandahar.

Marines were being put on ships and planes headed for harm's way. Those of us working on the general's staff wondered, 'Who of us would get a turn?' When the question of deployment did come to me, I hoped I would have the right answer.

'Please have your ID and a copy of your orders ready. Ensure all weapons are checked,' announced a tired but friendly looking lady who was in charge of herding us to the proper gate at an airport in DC a few weeks later.

DOD had chartered a DC-10 and its crew to bring service members to various locations outside the continental U.S. (OCONUS). The plane was full when we departed, but we deplaned a few in the Azores, a few at Aviano, and by the time we left

Italian air space, the enormous contained only about thirty of us, all military, bound for the Middle East.

At 0200 local time, I reached my destination. The plane rolled to a stop and I watched ground crew wheel large stadium lights into place around our plane; a squad of army soldiers jogged to a circle around the aircraft. A soldier in desert fatigues, flak vest, and Kevlar helmet stepped on and welcomed us.

'Good morning, ladies and gentlemen. I'm Staff Sergeant Smith. My job is to take you from this plane to the bus that will transport you to the base.' A few security details followed and then we walked briskly down to the tarmac and to the bus. My last waking sight before a quick nap was the escorting pair of hardback Humvees that led and trailed us, soldiers manning the mounted machine guns.

'Plan sounds alright so far,' said our commanding general. The general continued, 'The ops guys are sure standing SOP is appropriate for the entire mission?'

'Situation dependent, yes, sir,' said the chief of staff. The general sat at the head of a long table while we principal staff members tried to read his body language for the final decision.

'Okay, let's make it happen. And, Judge, give me a legal chop on the rules of engagement issues.'

Judge? That's me. The Staff Judge Advocate. I've yet to hear SJA, JAG, lawyer, or even my name very often. I'm just 'Judge.' I always thought it was army slang, but I'm happy to answer it.

And since I've been here since March, I'm used to it. The base here is mostly Army and mostly comfortable. Berthing is a large flimsy warehouse with twin-size mattresses and wall lockers. Our office space is a letter better. A double-wide trailer fitted with air conditioners to keep the staff, and more importantly, our computers, cool. Our conference room is a large tent that actually feels more sturdy than the trailer.

Work space is so-so. Privacy is nonexistent and the heat is like a punch in the face. However, two things here are state of the art–the chow and the gym. Every place has a center of gravity. Here, it's the gym. Huge, smelly, dirty, well-equipped, crowded, in a word–spectacular. It's no secret of medical science that people acclimate to harsh conditions better when they get plenty of exercise. Luckily, our commanding general is very on-board with that and supports our attempts to get in as much PT as possible.

So, special purpose joint task force, what the heck is that? Actually, we're a C/JTF. Task force just means we're not a typical unit. We're assembled from other commands to do a particular mission. Joint task force means we have members from all services, not just Marines. The C is for coalition. We have three different nations in our CJTF. And believe you me, it definitely keeps the legal guy jumping.

As with all things, the missions we initially receive are drastically different by the time we reach our destination. Many times, I'd hear a description of a new turn of events and think, 'Gee, that sounds really doggone cool.' Then, I'd think 'Wait a minute, that's us, that's our mission. Golly.'

However, I assure you, I'm not exactly fast-roping into Tora Bora. For certain, my assignment out here is supercool and I'm lucky to have it. However, things that are exciting for me might be a snooze-fest for other troops. It's just a thrill to be part of actual operations.

Despite of austerity of desert living, I was actually able to participate in a small Seder during Passover. An Army colonel, who is a rabbi, visited the base and led services and a Seder at the base chapel. It was not the feast and story-telling I would have enjoyed with my family in Virginia Beach or the services I would have enjoyed at Temple Israel in Norfolk. But in the middle of a Muslim region that doesn't even recognize the State of Israel on a map, I'll take what I can get.

PART VI

Chaplains and Medics

Chapter 29

Introduction (Chaplains)

Like doctors and corpsmen in any war, chaplains are also with the troops when they are needed. As in the case of medical personnel, services are performed for the Marine Corps by naval chaplains, at times in Marine Corps uniforms. These chaplains minister to the spiritual needs of all ranks and faiths under all conditions.

Subject to the same rigors and discomforts in combat as Marine assault troops, these unarmed Navy chaplains often landed with the assault waves in World War II. One Navy chaplain was awarded the Medal of Honor (posthumously) while serving with the 5th Marines in Vietnam in 1967.

In the Preface to Dov Peretz Elkins' book, *God's Warriors*, the Chief of Chaplains, U.S. Army, Major General Francis L. Sampson (a non-Jew) writes:

"Jewish chaplains have played an exciting and dramatic role in the Armed Forces of the United States, particularly during and subsequent to the Civil War. Wherever they have served, in peace or in conflict, they have carried the message of the Almighty to their Jewish brethren with unswerving devotion, and extended the comfort of their faith in times of stress."

From *The History of the Chaplain Corps, United States Navy, 1939–1949*, by Captain Clifford M. Drury (ChC), USN, comes the following account of a Yom Kippur service held during combat on Peleliu in World War II:

"As soon as the combat situation permitted, chaplains held divine services, very often within the range of enemy guns. Several times during the war, a major religious holiday occurred after a combat operation had begun. Such was the case at Peleliu, where the Jewish New Year, Rosh Hashanah, fell when the fighting was heaviest. But by Yom Kippur, the Day of Atonement, which is the holiest of all Jewish religious observances, conditions were fairly secure at the beach area. Of this holiday on Peleliu, Rabbi Edgar E. Siskin, the Jewish chaplain of the 1st Marine Division, wrote afterwards:

"We held services in the morning in the Division CP area. Word had got around somehow and the boys drifted in from all parts of the island. Some had come from lines where fighting was still going on. They straggled in—bearded, dirty, carrying their weapons. The altar rigged by Chaplain Murphy, Division Chaplain, was improvised out of ammunition boxes, and was covered over by a length of captured Japanese silk. Over this we draped our Ten Commandment Banner. The symbolism of this act was not lost to our small congregation.

"And there we were—72 men—praying, chanting the old Yom Kippur mode, summoned by a call heard above the tumult of battle. There we were not 200 yards from a ridge still held by the Japs, within range of sniper and mortar fire. And throughout the service the artillery kept up a shattering fire overhead . . . This Yom Kippur no service anywhere, I dare say, surpassed in the significance ours, for all its makeshift appointments, and bedraggled worshippers."

Chaplains

Jon E. Cutler

Inducted at Wyndmoor, Pennsylvania, as a Jewish chaplain, U.S. Navy, John E. Cutler served at Camp Butler, Okinawa, as rabbi from 1991 to 1992 for all the armed forces on the island, planned and conducted worship services and educational programs (for adults and children), and acted as Jewish liaison representative to non-Jewish organizations. In addition, he supervised chaplains' assistants, administered the Religious Offering Fund, led pastoral counseling at the naval Hospital and Marine Corps Base brig, planned and taught the World Religions course under the auspices of the University of Maryland, Asia, and planned and led spiritual-growth-retreat weekends.

In 1991, he participated in Operation Desert Storm in Saudi Arabia and Kuwait as a member of the 1st MEF. In that capacity, he served as the only rabbi for the U.S. Marine Corps and the U.S. Navy, and as the Jewish liaison on the general's staff. He also administered pastoral counseling at the Naval Field Hospital during combat operations.

From 1989 to 1991, he was the sole rabbi for Camp Lejeune and the entire Jacksonville, North Carolina area—conducting worship services, leading congregational involvement in social-action projects, and serving as Jewish liaison representative through speaking engagement before non-Jewish organizations. He was also battalion chaplain for the School of Infantry and counselor for Marines and their families.

In December 1989, the Commander of the U.S. Pacific Fleet awarded Cutler the Navy Commendation Medal for religious and community service. In April 1992, the Commandant of the Marine Corps awarded him another Navy Commendation Medal for his service during Desert Storm.

Like other Marines of his faith, Rabbi Cutler found that military service had a profound effect on his life. "I learned how to deal and appreciate so many different types of people."

His tour of duty took him to such far-reaching places as Subic Bay and Clark Air Force Base in the Philippines, the island of Diego Garcia in the Indian Ocean, Iwakuni and Tokyo, Kuwait and Saudi Arabia.

His Naval and Marine Corps experience was "excellent," he

wrote, "because I was able to meet and work with so many people. In addition, I was able to do good ministry to all people."

In 1998, Rabbi Cutler was named adjunct professor in religious studies at St. Joseph's University, Philadelphia. As of 2001, he resides in Flourtown, Pennsylvania.

Roland B. Gittelsohn

One of the most famous chaplains serving with the U.S. Marine Corps was Rabbi Roland B. Gittelsohn of Rockville Center, New York, who wrote the sermon, or eulogy to be delivered at the dedication of the Marine cemetery on Iwo Jima. It would be appropriate to quote some of his words written during the still on-going battle for the island in March 1945:

"The worst hell was the first two days. By the time we landed, the front lines were far up enough so that we had no trouble at all. We were living at 14 Gut-Ache Lane. The street was so-named by me on discovering that digging a foxhole big enough for two is a little strenuous on the belly muscles. I started writing this letter this afternoon while visiting the wounded. I can look down on the ground where we made our landings and see more ships of more different kinds that you would ever believe possible.

"I spent most of the day visiting one of the hospital ships offshore. Besides doing what I went for, I met several Jewish boys from the crew who had not seen a Jewish chaplain before, and I promised to write their folks when I got a chance.

"Yesterday I spent the whole afternoon at the division cemetery. It is a gruesome business. I have seen and smelled human bodies in a way they should never be seen or smelled. It is impossible to believe how even a softy like me could build up so carefully a wall of detachment under these circumstances.

"There was a group of twelve Christian boys to be buried yesterday afternoon, and Chaplain Cuthriell invited me to participate in the service along with himself and two Protestant chaplains. I read a Psalm for the scriptural portion of the service. Later in the afternoon, I had two Jewish burials, two of the first in our cemetery.

"I could write reams on how wonderful most of our kids are in combat. I haven't heard one whimper yet, no matter how badly hurt the boy is. I have seen a kid whose hand I held while the doctor was digging hunks of shrapnel from a hole in the back of his knee big enough for two fists, and I felt his hand trembling in miner but he wouldn't admit it hurts.

"I have seen another tell the medics to take care of everyone else, saying that there was nothing wrong with him but a scratch, and then discovering an hour later that he had a bullet clear through his leg. The only time those kids break down is when they tell about buddies who were killed beside them. Their behavior is encouraging and wonderful and terribly, terribly pathetic.

"Last night I held what was probably the first service held on Iwo Jima . . . Eighteen men gathered for a most impressive service just before dark. We stood high on a cliff . . . [1]

Mass burial ceremonies were conducted on an interreligious basis because "so many of the bodies were simply pieces of bone shreds of flesh in sacks."

Marine Jacob Marks, the only draftsman on Iwo Jima doing map work for the engineers of the 5th Amphibious Corps, recounts an experience with Chaplain Gittelsohn, who was preparing to board ship leaving Iwo Jima. Marks requested assistance from the chaplain to put together a Passover *Seder*. Chaplain Gittelsohn obliged by getting Passover supplies such as matzoh, gefilte fish, and wine. Marks reported that "the ship's mess crew offered to serve us a separate dinner both evenings, but I didn't want to take advantage."

The next day, everyone chipped in—the chaplains, the ship's cooks, and Marks—and they succeeded in putting together the traditional *Seder* of hard-boiled eggs in salt, roasted beef bone, *charoses* made of honey and nuts, and lettuce—accompanied by the only jar of horseradish on board. Thus, during the evenings

[1] Kaufman, L., *American Jews in World War II*, Dial Press, New York, N.Y., p. 316–17.

of April 14 and 15, with the ship's chaplain assisting, Marine and Navy personnel participated in the Seder on a ship traveling from Iwo to Maui.

Chaplain Gittelsohn estimated that there were approximately fifteen hundred Jewish Marines on the island, of whom at least one hundred fifty were killed and four hundred wounded. The number of Jewish casualties may have been proportionately higher than that of non-Jews because of the large number of corpsmen who suffered especially heavy losses as they administered first aid under battle fire.

With the termination of the Battle of Iwo Jima, Senior Division Chaplain Warren F. Cuthriell selected Gittelsohn to deliver the principal address at the dedication ceremony of the 5th Marine Division. However, the day before he was scheduled to present the eulogy, all the division's chaplains and most of its Catholic chaplains threatened to boycott the ceremony if the Jewish chaplain gave the sermon, asserting that since most of the deceased men were Christian, one of that faith should preside over the ceremony.

Chaplain Cuthriell , who had chosen Rabbi Gittelsohn precisely for the reason that he represented the smallest American religious minority, was unable to convince the other chaplains to change their minds.

Gittelsohn, upon learning of the threat, immediately asked to be relieved of the assignment to avoid a controversy that might endanger the senior chaplain's military career, and proceeded to deliver his sermon to Jewish Marines.

Two Protestant chaplains were so incensed at the threatened boycott by their colleagues' behavior that they attended the Jewish ceremony. "They refused to attend their own denominational service because they insisted on listening to their colleague, the Jewish chaplain."[2] One of the Protestant chaplains asked for Gittelsohn's onionskin copy which he secretly mimeographed and distributed to thousands of Marines, who subsequently mailed them to their families throughout the United States.

Roland Gittelsohn's eulogy, "The Purest Democracy," delivered on March 21, 1945, follows in part:

"This is perhaps the grimmest, and surely the holiest, task we have faced since D-Day. Here, before us, lie the bodies of comrades and friends—men who, until yesterday or last week, laughed with us, joked with us, and went over the sides with us as we prepared to hit the beaches of this island. Here lie officers and men, Negroes and whites, rich and poor, together. Here are Protestants, Catholics, and Jews, together. Here no man prefers another because of his faith or despises him because of his color. Among these men there is no discrimination, no prejudice, no hatred. Theirs is the highest and purest democracy. Any man among us, the living, who fails to understand that will thereby betray those who lie here dead. Whoever of us lifts his hand in hate against a brother, or thinks himself superior to those who happen to be in the minority, makes of this ceremony and of the bloody sacrifice it commemorates, an empty hollow mockery . . ."[3]

Thus, just when Rabbi Gittelsohn thought he might lose his faith in brotherhood, he realized that for every man whose heart is poisoned with prejudice and hatred, there are many more who are filled with love of all men, and respect and understanding for men of all faiths."[4]

Joel D. Newman

As Americans of the Jewish faith continue to serve our country in the armed forces, Jewish chaplains are also on active duty throughout the world—approximately eleven at any given time, a number that increases when there is an armed conflict. During holidays, the number is expanded when Reserve Jewish chaplains come aboard for temporary duty. One such rabbis serving in the Navy is Joel D. Newman. Rabbi Newman, like others, is

[2] Elkins, Dov Peretz, Jonathan David, *God's Warriors*, Middle Village Pubs., Middle Village, NY., 1974, p. 31.

[3] Ibid., p. 29.

[4] Ibid., p. 31.

quite busy traveling from place to place throughout the world, offering the guidance and solace that chaplains are pledged to provide and many servicemen and women crave. As Rabbi Newman said, "You get around a bit."[5]

Born in Cleveland and raised in Dallas, Lieutenant Commander Joel D. Newman (ChC). USN, commissioned in 1990 and served as chaplain with a Reserve unit in Denver, Colorado. In 1991, he received the prestigious Pluralism Award from the Naval Affairs Committee of the State of Rhode Island for exemplifying the Chaplain Corps motto, "Cooperation Without Compromise." This honor is awarded to the chaplain who not only provides for members of his own denomination, but facilitates for members of other faiths as well—caring for all.

After serving in the Reserve for two years, he chose to go on active duty in 1992, assigned to 1st FSSG (Force Service Support Group) with the Marines at Camp Pendleton. He says, "I have had only positive experiences. I was afforded the opportunity to conduct High Holy Days services in Japan (Tokyo Bay), Hanukkah in Ecuador and Somalia, and High Holy Days and Pesach in the Gulf. With each year I find the military more enjoyable. It takes time to adjust to the system and methods they follow, but one having done so, it is a great career."[6]

In 1998, for example, Rabbi Newman led Yom Kippur for about thirty men aboard the aircraft carrier USS *Abraham Lincoln* while stationed in the Persian Gulf. "With *yarmulkes*, candles, wine, a miniature Torah with camouflage, and an Ark provided by the Jewish Welfare Board"—Newman describes as an open briefcase—"it looked like a nice little *shul*."

In 1999, on a ship somewhere in the Persian Gulf, Chaplain Newman conducted the Passover Seder, in addition to leading services in Bahrain, Kuwait, and Saudi Arabia.

He is encouraged by what he perceives as a spiritual awakening among the younger Jewish members of the armed forces, especially those who have not had much of a religious background. He says that "members of the military, particularly

---

[5] The Jewish Bulletin of Northern California, March 26, 1999, p. 26.

[6] Th. I...:.l V... W.... D. C. ....

younger personnel away from home for the first time, often become more interested in religion during their time of service."

In San Diego, for example, where, like other military chaplains, he attended to the needs of personnel of all faiths. Rabbi Newman led a Hebrew class for Jewish members of the Marines. "It's like bringing a little piece of home to them. When you bring out that first bite of matzoh, there's no substitute for that."

In a letter memorandum of April 29, 1999, Lieutenant Commander Joel D. Newman, Chaplain, U.S. Navy, writes, in conclusion of a recapitulation of duties in the Persian Gulf: "Now feeling a little like Peter O'Toole, or 'Joel of Arabia,' I got more hugs from fellow servicemen and women in the Gulf than in a year of synagogue work. Their gratitude to the Jewish Welfare Board for its tireless work making their Jewish lives better overseas could be seen in their smiles. But, most of all, in their hearts they knew that the United States military generously gave them a Passover to remember as they continue to stand watch over all who love and seek freedom."

As of the year 2000, Chaplain Newman remains on active duty.

Milton Rosenbaum

Thirteen men in a slit trench were very close to the Japanese lines on Saipan. Japanese machine guns raked their positions, and mortar shells came raining down on them. Fighter bombers strafed their position. Snipers attempted to catch unwary Marines in their sights.

Only the chaplain, Rabbi Milton Rosenbaum of Cleveland, was Jewish. Though all did not profess a particular religion, most were nominally Protestant or Catholic. Yet, it was fitting that they turn to him, a rabbi, for divine intervention and support. "Amid the pounding of guns, he recited, and they intoned after him [Psalm 23], 'The Lord is my Shepherd, I shall not want. He maketh me to lie down in green pastures. He leadeth me beside the still waters . . . Yea, though I walk through the valley of the shadow of death, I will fear no evil . . . "[7]

Then men "faced their fate together, stronger now for what they had heard." Though of diverse creeds, they were able to withstand the rigors and dangers that continued. "They say that in the foxholes there was no discrimination by man against man because of creed or race or color."

Leon Rosenberg

Chaplains minister to servicemen and women of all faiths. Thus, it is not unusual for a Protestant or Catholic chaplain to minister the *Shma* to the Jewish soldier, sailor, or Marine in his or her last throes of life. So it is that a Jewish chaplain may be called upon to lead individuals of other faiths to worship. A case in point was that of Chaplain Leon Rosenberg of Philadelphia, on board ship with Marines en route to the Marshall Islands in World War II, who called "all hands on deck on the eve of the invasion and conducted a common service for them.

He read from the Jewish prayer book and from the Presbyterian Book of Common Prayer."[8] They all sang hymns from *The Army and Navy Song and Service Book for Ship and Field*. "Chaplain Rosenberg spoke of the common origin of all faiths. He then closed the service with a silent prayer."[9]

Hillel E. Silverman

Rabbi Hillel E. Silverman chose to relate a story rather than go into details of his military service.

Inducted into the Navy in the early 1950s from New York

[7] Kaufman, L., *American Jews in World War II*, Dial Press, New York, N.Y., 1946, p. 314.

[8] Blumenthal, L. Roy, et al, *Fighting for America*, compiled by the Bureau of War Records, National Jewish Welfare Board, 1944, p. 19.

[9] Op. cit.

City, he trained as a chaplain at the Chaplains School, Newport, after which he was assigned as Jewish chaplain, Marine Corps Recruit Depot, Parris Island. His next duty station was at Sixth Fleet, Headquarters, Naples, Italy.

He related the Passover saga of Private Brody.

"In 1952, I conducted a Passover Seder at the Marine Recruit Depot, Parris Island, South Carolina. At that time, the Marines were drafting young men for service during the Korean War. With the help of the Jewish Welfare Board and the Protestant and Catholic chaplains, we arranged a large Passover Seder in the main mess hall and accommodated over seven hundred recruits undergoing basic training.

"I conducted the Seder from a table in the center. At the head table behind me sat the Commanding General, his Chief of Staff, and Catholic and Protestant chaplains assigned to the base.

"When we reached the point of the *afikomen* [a piece of matzoh broken off from the center one of three matzohs set before the leader of the seder, hidden by the leader and later searched for by the children, with the finder, usually the youngest, receiving a reward], I asked, 'Who stole the *afikomen?*' A young recruit raised his hand and said, 'I stole the *afikomen.*'

"Suddenly from the head table at another microphone resounded the voice of the Commanding General, who had been imbibing from the red kosher Manischewitz wine.

"What do you mean someone stole this here *afikomen?* I will place him in the brig for seven days on bread and water!'

"Someone whispered to the general, 'No bread on Passover.'

"I asked the young man, 'What is your name and where are you from?'

"My name is Private Brody, and I'm from the Bronx.

"I replied to him, 'I would like to give you a present for the *afikomen.* What would you like?'

"I want a ten-day leave.'

"Private Brody, you know that no-one at boot camp can ever go on any type of leave until training is over. Please ask me for something else!'

"But Private Brody insisted that this is what he demanded, that he would take nothing less.

"'Private Brody,' I explained, 'you understand we cannot finish this Passover Seder unless we all partake of the *afikomen*.'

"Suddenly, there was a raucous voice on the microphone at the head table. It was the Commanding General who was not on the way to inebriation.

"He shouted, 'Corporal Brody (a spot promotion), you understand that I am the Father of this household. And I say to you, Corporal Brody, ten-day leave granted!'

"Seven hundred battered Marines in Marine uniform all stood on their feet and applauded."

Rabbi Silverman, who attained the rank of commander, USNR, wrote, "I was very proud of my service. Enjoyed the opportunity to serve. Flirted with the idea of joining the regular service. Remained in the Naval Reserve for twenty years."

Samuel Sobel

Over the course of the Korean War, rabbis provided hands-on ministry. Twelve received Bronze Star Medals for heroic action and one, Samuel Sobel, was also awarded the Purple Heart for having been wounded in battle. His citation for the Bronze Star Medal reads as follows:

"Carrying out frequent trips to the front lines, he imparted strength and peace of mind to the troops throughout many days and nights while under heavy artillery and mortar fire. He ministered to the spiritual needs of the wounded and dying at the front lines, forward aid stations, and medical companies of the division."[10]

Rabbi Sobel, as a chaplain assigned to the 1st Marine Division, recounted that all the chaplains used the same jeep when visiting the troops. They painted a sign reading "Marine Padres

Incorporated," with a cross and a Star of David on either side of the sign.

I remember the 1st Marine Division chapel was quite similar. Over the front door of the chapel was displayed a cross and a Star of David right under it.

---

[10] Slomovitz, Albert I., *The Fighting Rabbis*, New York University Press, New York, N.Y., 1999, p. 112.

Chapter 30

Medics (Introduction)

All U.S. armed forces have their own medical and dental personnel with the exception of the Marine Corps, whose needs in this area are met by the U.S. Navy. Those who serve in the Fleet Marine Force are fully integrated into the Marine Corps while retaining their status as U.S. Navy personnel—including officers, such as doctors and dentists, and enlisted men and women.

A *corpsman* in the U.S. Navy and serving with the U.S. Marine Corps and a *medic* in the Army perform the same duties—they accompany combat troops into battle to give first aid and perform a variety of other medical duties.

Every bit as gung-ho, courageous, and dedicated as their combatant partners, corpsmen do not usually carry weapons unless under dire circumstances in which they are required to defend themselves. As essential in carrying out their mission as any grunt in the field, they are as daring and take as many risks as those to which care they are committed. Often more exposed to enemy fire than their armed comrades, corpsmen cannot seek the cover that fighting Marines must and are expected to do under perilous conditions.

Unless someone has been wounded in combat, treated where he has fallen, and evacuated under fire, it is almost impossible to convey the feeling of relief experienced by a casualty who knows he will soon receive tender care and expert medical assistance. All Marines have a special respect for corpsmen serving with them. All Marines give them the extraordinary honor of regarding them in all senses of the word, as Marines.

Too much cannot be said about the dedication and courage of corpsmen serving with Marine units in combat. The heroism of combat medical personnel was well chronicled during the combat in the Pacific. In World War II, and, in fact, from the early twentieth century, corpsmen won twenty-one Medals of Honor. The courage and professionalism of Navy medics can be shown by the extraordinary number of lives they have saved, the high proportion of casualties they suffered, and the number of decorations they received.

The gallant efforts of the medics resulted in a high casualty rate among hospital corpsmen. On Iwo Jima, no less than among the combat ground troops, the corpsmen suffered a high casualty rate. In the 4th Marine Division, their casualty rate was thirty-eight percent. During World War II, 108 corpsmen, organic to U.S. Marine units, were killed in action, and another nine died of wounds. The number of wounded in action was 430.

Murray Bromberg

Born in Brooklyn in October 1924, Murray Bromberg had been a first-aid instructor at the age of 16 prior to entering the Navy in 1942. Following recruit training, he trained as a medical corpsman at a naval hospital and then attended field medical school at Camp Elliott where "we practiced and qualified at the range with the M-1, Springfield .03 and the carbine," even training in the use of the flamethrower, hand-to-hand combat, live-ammunition obstacle course, and chemical warfare.

Bromberg participated in the invasion landings with assault forces of the 1st Marine Division in the Solomon Islands and in Luzon and Mindanao in the Philippines. At the meeting of President Franklin Delano Roosevelt, Admiral Chester Nimitz, and

General Douglas MacArthur in Hawaii to plan strategy of the war in the Pacific, Bromberg was among the troops who passed in review. His tours of duty also included Hawaii, Emirau, New Guinea, Mindoro in the Philippines, Los Negros, Manus—and El Toro, Camp Miramar, San Francisco, and Long Beach, California.

He was fortunate to have known Rabbi Roland B. Gittelsohn whom he met at Camp Elliott before the invasion of Iwo Jima. Bromberg reminds us that Rabbi Gittelsohn "became famous with his speech at the dedication of the 5th Marine Division cemetery and his experience with the other chaplains in the division."

Bromberg appreciates the assistance Gittelsohn gave him and others prior to their returning home after their military service. The rabbi was particularly anxious that they not shock their parents, relatives, and friends with the all-too-familiar Navy and Marine language they had acquired. Instead of using the common, "That's T.S." in response to a question or a statement, Gittelsohn suggested *Takkeh shlecht* (meaning, roughly, "really bad") or a similar innocuous expression. To Bromberg and others, "He was very supportive."

Bromberg came home to a memorable reception from family and friends, including a block party thrown by neighbors. Many returning veterans had not been home for years, but, unfortunately, "many of us came home with nightmares which we had for many years, or with malaria or hepatitis, etc."

He is the recipient of the Navy Commendation Medal with one gold star in lieu of a second award, the American Campaign Medal, the Asiatic-Pacific Campaign Medal with four bronze stars, the World War II Victory Medal, the Philippine Liberation Medal with one bronze star, and the Philippine Republic Presidential Unit Citation. He was discharged in April 1946, as a pharmacist's mate third class.

After the war, Bromberg attended Brooklyn College and had podiatric education and an internship in Chicago. A diplomate of the American Board of Podiatric Orthopedics and a fellow and past president of the American College of Foot and Ankle Orthopedics and Medicine, he has had offices in Bloomfield, New Jersey, since 1952.

His brother served in the infantry in the European Theater of Operations shortly after the invasion of Germany, including the Battle of the Bulge.

From 1946 to 1971, Dr. Bromberg was a scout leader and district commissioner of the Boy Scouts of America. An author and lecturer, he currently serves on the Bloomfield Joint Veterans Memorial Committee and is in charge of providing military units for parades. In

1999, as the Grand Marshal of the Memorial Parade delivered the principal address.

Bruce A. Cohen

Battalion surgeon Bruce A. Cohen's citation for the Navy Commendation Medal with Combat V for valor reads as follows:

"For heroic achievement while serving as battalion surgeon, Headquarters and Service Company, 1st Battalion, 25th Marines, 1st Marine Division, during Operation DESERT STORM. On February 24, 1991, 1st Battalion, 25th Marines forward command post advanced two Iraqi obstacle belts in trace of the assaulting task forces for the purpose of establishing a temporary holding area for an unexpected large number of Iraqi prisoners of war. This location was situated in an area that was still under enemy direct and indirect fire. Lieutenant Commander Cohen was immediately confronted with the dilemma of dealing with large numbers of wounded Iraqi soldiers and some wounded Marines. Undaunted by the indirect fire going on around him, Lieutenant Commander Cohen worked feverishly through the next four days, during which he directed the medical evacuation of three hundred wounded Iraqi soldiers and treated over six hundred others for various types of ailments. His professional yet compassionate spirit and style inspired all who observed him and contributed significantly to the accomplishment of the unit's mission. Lieutenant Commander Cohen's courage, initiative, and selfless devotion to duty reflected great credit upon himself and were in keeping with the highest traditions of the United States Naval Service."

Now Commander Bruce A. Cohen, Medical Corps, U.S. Navy, he entered the Navy from his hometown of Reading, Pennsylvania. His initial training and assignments were at NAS, Pensacola, and Camp Lejeune.

He was, in his words, "a DCO (direct commissioned officer) in the Reserves. My class was composed of physicians, nurses, and merchant marines. We were already professionals and looking for the camaraderie the Navy would bring us. We were a wild bunch of sailors."

Commander Cohen completed tours of duty at the Philadelphia Naval Hospital; 4th FUSS (Detachment D), Reading, Pennsylvania, Submarine Group 9, U.S. Naval Submarine Base, Bangor, Washington, Duke University, Durham, North Carolina, U.S. Naval Submarine Base, New London, Connecticut, and overseas tours at Rota, Spain, and the Persian Gulf during the Desert Storm conflict. As of 1999, he achieved the rank of commander, Medical Corps, U.S. Navy.

A Navy doctor, he is also qualified as a Navy diver. During his tour as battalion surgeon, 1st Battalion, 25th Marines, he not only handled various weapons—including the M-16, 9mm pistol, and grenades—but also came under fire while in the Persian Gulf. He is indeed a career sailor/doctor and Marine. He "will not leave until thrown out, asked to leave, or can't function anymore."

Dr. Cohen currently resides in Norfolk, Virginia.

Larry Diamond

Brooklyn native Larry Diamond attended recruit training at Sampson Naval Training Center on Lake Geneva in upstate New York before becoming a corpsman. He not only participated in the D-Day invasion of Normandy, but also fought with the 8th Marines, 2nd Marine Division, who went ashore on D-Day in Iwo Jima.

Following the cessation of hostilities, Diamond joined the 8th Marines on occupation duty in Japan. In early 1946, he volunteered his time to promote a successful campaign to combat venereal disease. He held classes on venereal disease, and had the support of Marine MPs to get the Marines back to the base for preventive protection. "Even inspected Japanese girls and gave a Japanese doctor some of our sulfa pills to treat the infected women."

Diamond describes two incidents during combat in the Pacific:

"February 19, 1944, D-Day, Iwo Jima:

"As the Navy coxswain brought the LCM (landing craft, mechanized) close to shore, he told us to keep our heads down. As he opened the ramp for us to depart, I could see the Marines motionless on the beach. I thought they were all dead and asked God to let me go down fighting. Moments after landing and crawling on my tummy through the soft sand, I was relieved to notice most of the motionless Marines were alive and, like myself, were just crawling through the soft sand. I will always be grateful for the wounded Marine sergeant I cared for in Hawaii for telling me to get off the beach as quickly as possible.

"One day, a Marine I knew asked me if I would accompany him 'up front' where his wounded buddy was, he thought, dying. He asked me to wait about 50 feet before a labyrinth; he was going to bring his buddy out. Moments after he entered the labyrinth, he came out crying, 'I'm hit, I'm hit!' I pulled him down to the ground and treated his wound and called for the Marines who were in a foxhole to bring a stretcher. Note: Japanese used wounded to lure other Marines to go in and get their buddies."

Diamond currently (2000) resides in Hendersonville, North Carolina.

Edward Feldman

Heroics beyond the call of duty would succinctly, and inadequately, describe the action of Navy surgeon Edward Feldman (then 26) in a spectacular operation performed on the Vietnamese field of battle in January 1968.

On Wednesday, January 24, 1968, the *New York Times* reported in an article entitled, "Surgeon Removes Live Mortar Fuse From Marine," how the Queens resident removed an explosive portion of an enemy mortar shell from the stomach of an American Marine the previous Sunday.

As the article related, "Working under the dim glow of flashlights, a young Navy doctor removed an explosive portion of a North Vietnamese mortar shell from the abdomen of an American Marine Sunday.

"Lieut. Edward Feldman, 26 years old, of 108–39 65th Avenue, Forest Hills, Queens, was assisted in the operation by a medical corpsman and a Marine demolition expert.

"'He told me I might as well take off my steel helmet and flak jacket for the operation,' Lieutenant Feldman said, 'because if the thing blew they wouldn't do me any good.'

"The operation began minutes after North Vietnamese forces surrounding the Marine post at Khesanh began an artillery, rocket, and mortar attack at 5 A.M. Sunday.

"Shells set fire to a tent that Lieutenant Feldman had set up as a medical station for Marines of the 26th Marine Regiment. Lieutenant Feldman had just moved into an underground bunker when his first patient arrived.

"The Marine, Pfc. Robert J. Mussari, of Scranton, Pa., had a gaping wound in his abdomen.

"'We weren't quite sure what it was,' said Lieutenant Feldman in an interview. 'When I removed the battle dressing I could see the end of this large metallic object with screw thread. I said, "Hold everything."'

"A crude barrier of sandbags was constructed in a corner of the bunker and Private Mussari was placed on a litter behind the sandbags. He was given morphine and fluids intravenously while the doctor sent for a combat engineer familiar with explosives.

"When the engineer, Staff Sgt. Ronald Sniegowski, 30, of San Clemente, Calif., arrived, he said that he feared that an 82-mm mortar shell—or its fuse assembly—had struck Private Mussari, Sergeant Sniegowski suspected that it was a delayed-action fuse that might explode 2-1/2 hours after firing.

"By the time Sergeant Sniegowski gave this opinion to Lieutenant Feldman, 45 minutes of the 2-1/2 hours period remained.

"Lieutenant Feldman lay on top of one wall of sandbags as he worked on the private. Sergeant Sniegowski stood behind him and two corpsmen volunteered to hold flashlights. The rest of the bunker was evacuated.

"Private Mussari, who was fully conscious throughout the operation, was unaware of the nature of the object lodged in his body. The mortar fuse—three to four inches long and about the size of a half-dollar in diameter—had burned blood vessels and suppressed bleeding.

"'I lifted it out as gently as I could,' Lieutenant Feldman said, 'and the sergeant got his hands under it and carefully carried it out of the bunker.'

There are a few things in the background of Edward Feldman that might be clues to the heroics that he performed in the face of imminent risk to his own life. One was the fact that even during his days at Forest Hills High School, Forest Hills, New York, he had notions of joining the Marine Corps. In addition, he admired two uncles who served in the U.S. Army infantry, and a cousin in the Air Corps. One uncle, Bill Newman, earned two Bronze Stars, and his cousin, Ed Rothkrug, was the recipient of two Distinguished Flying Crosses. Cousin Ed Rothkrug remained in the service as a career Air Force officer, finally attaining the rank of lieutenant colonel. They all served with distinction and with pride. In addition, he admired a number of movie idols who portrayed soldiers and sailors in various films.

Edward Michael Feldman was born on February 26, 1941, in New York City, the son of Sidney Saul Feldman and Anna Newman Feldman. He attended PS 93 and PS 75, both on Manhattan, New York, and graduated from Forest Hills High School. His summers were spent in New Jersey, where he worked as a camp counselor and a waterfront instructor. After graduating from high school in 1958, he attended Columbia University, where he received his B.S. in 1952.

Having graduated from medical school, he entered the U.S. Navy Reserve and was assigned as a doctor with the Marines at Camp Pendleton, California. Indeed, one of the prime reasons he enlisted was precisely to serve with the infantry of the Marine Corps. There, with "moderate intensity," he trained with the Marines, undergoing orientation with weapons, field exercises, physical fitness, field medicine, and orientation as to combat medical situations in Vietnam. He was given his chance to realize his wish, "To serve with the Marine infantry."

It was there, in combat, that he found his most dangerous assignments—active combat with the North Vietnamese Army. And it was there that he rose to the occasion in performing this heroic operation which earned him the Silver Star Medal.

And it was there, at the siege of Khesanh, the Marine Corps combat base in the northwest corridor of South Vietnam, for three months, surrounded by an estimated 40,000 North Vietnamese regulars.

Dr. Feldman says, "Flown into a major battle involving a reinforced advanced infantry battalion of NVA regulars with artillery support that had ambushed an American column of armored personnel carriers. It was a bitter fight during typhoon conditions, with heavy casualties on both sides. I assumed command of our forces due to attrition of command elements." It is for the valor displayed during this battle that Dr. Feldman is currently being considered for the Congressional Medal of Honor.

When the APCs (armored personnel carriers) began climbing the hill, they received what Lt. Feldman thought was heavy mortar fire. Once atop the hill, Lt. Feldman guided the men in forming a perimeter until all the APCs were in position.

The following account is taken from the official dispatch of the action: "Some time after getting position, a lieutenant informed Army A Company 1/61 that, to prepare night defenses, only a small amount of concertina wire and about thirty-two claymore mines were available. Feldman was further informed that because of the poor weather they would not be getting any close air or artillery support and that it was unlikely that there would be any evacuation of casualties. Undaunted, Lt. Feldman directed the men in establishing a defense perimeter, and then, with enemy activity in the area slackening somewhat with the fall of darkness, Lt. Feldman busied himself reevaluating the existing casualties and checking to make sure that any new casualties received medical attention.

"Until Lt. Feldman arrived, A Company 1/61 had been caring for its wounded as best it could. Once the company had been assembled by Lt. Feldman atop the hill, he ordered all non-ambulatory men placed in a tight perimeter within the main defense position so that he (Lt. Feldman), while being assisted by one or two A Company men, could work on them. There, the wounded were in a relatively safe position. A dozen or more such wounded were administered by Lt. Feldman there. Many of these wounded men had gone into shock because of their loss of blood. Dr. Feldman separated those casualties that could be saved from those for which there was no hope. Lt. Feldman gave the mortally wounded morphine and made them as comfortable as possible.

"At 1930 hours, C Company 1/61 arrived to reinforce A company thus relieving Lt. Feldman of responsibility for A Company's defense. However, Lt. Feldman retained command over the evacuation of the wounded. Once the wounded were stabilized, Lt.

Feldman placed a call on the radio for a CH-47 Chinook for the evacuation of the wounded. Lt. Feldman knew that, due to the fact A Company's position on the hill was still being subject to enemy fire, the wounded would stand a better chance if all were evacuated at one time, thus necessitating the Chinook. Lt. Feldman then directed the men in establishing a landing zone for the medevac. All the while, A Company 1/61 was still taking sporadic small arms fire.

"At 2245 hours, a U.S. Army Chinook helicopter landed on the hill. Lt. Feldman ordered all the wounded of A Company 1/61 to be placed on board. The dead were also evacuated and their bodies were placed on the floor of the Chinook. Lt. Feldman refused evacuation himself, choosing instead to stay with the men whom he had placed in his care. He remained with A Company 1/61 until 6 September 1968 at which time he was flown to C2.

"Lt. Feldman's demonstrated aggressiveness in taking command and reorganizing the separated elements of A Company 1/61, placed the company in a strong position on high ground one from which it would have a reasonable chance of withstanding a determined enemy assault if one came. Moreover, Lt. Feldman's presence had a profound impact on the survival of A Company 1/61's wounded."

In regard of the recognition of Jewish-Americans for consideration to receive the Medal of Honor, Dr. Feldman says, "My recent readings, and other sources of information suggest strong possibilities that there is need to probe further and assess acts of gallantry on a case by case basis. There should be a mechanism that can be invoked that would provide an element of objectivity that can be utilized." As to whether being Jewish had any influence on his performance in the military, he states that "My Jewish heritage on a day to day basis did not impact me. I think that like many Jews, we wanted to be well thought of as American warriors and thus acted accordingly." However, he did not feel that he, as a Jew, was treated somewhat differently.

In commenting about the actions of her husband to the Long

Island Post, on February 1, 1968, Mrs. Feldman said, "I always knew he was a good doctor." When the metal piece embedded in Private Mussari's body was identified as a mortar fuse, Dr. Feldman quickly ordered everyone present to the front end of the bunker, placed Mussari in one corner and ordered a sandbag barrier built around him.

"Then, with light provided by flashlight, he calmly operated to remove the deadly object. The potentially deadly fuse was gingerly carried outside and buried beneath sandbags.

"Immediately afterward, without pausing to relax, the dark-haired, soft-spoken doctor turned his attention to the sixty other wounded men awaiting his attention.

"Later, he calmly and modestly analyzed his life-saving surgery on Pfc. Mussari, who was reported as 'doing surprisingly well.'

"'It was about as crude a surgery as I've done,' he said. 'It was not really difficult and it didn't take long.'

"He didn't mention that during the nerve-wracking operation any metal-to-metal contact between his instruments and the fuse might have set it off."

Besides that crowning glory and achievement of his military career, Dr. Feldman was honored to have provided medical support to Richard Nixon and his family at the inaugural events in January 1960. Also, while assigned as a staff doctor in the Department of Obstetrics at St. Albans Naval Hospital, St. Albans, New York, he delivered the baby of Army Captain Connors. The Department Chairman, a career officer, assigned Feldman that task despite the fact that he was not a trained obstetrician at the time. His superior officer made a point about rank: "Don't be concerned. The father is of the same rank as yourself."

However, "He was beyond shock when the father-in-law (presumably a civilian by his dress the day of the delivery) was sipping coffee the next day with me in full regalia: that of an active duty lieutenant general (Lt. General Connors, Commander of the Third Army, General Patton's old command)."

Of the men in the military he looked up to, the ones he admired the most were James B. Wilkinson, Lt. Col., UCMC (ret.), General Raymond Davis, USMC (ret.), and James Finnegan, M.D.

Dr. Edward Michael Feldman attained the rank of lieutenant commander in the Navy Medical Corps. Married to Patricia Feldman, he is the father of Stuart Jay, David Scott, and Jessica Feldman, and grandfather of Carly Beth and Allison Ray Feldman. He continues to practice Obstetrics and Gynecologic Surgery in private practice. In addition, he has been Professor of Gynecologic Surgery at the New Jersey Medical School and Western University, Pomona, California.

Dr. Feldman has been appointed as Board Member to the California Veterans' Affairs Board by Governor Gray Davis, and assumed those duties as of September 15, 2001.

Dr. Feldman is a gifted, modest, and successful man, proud of the service he has rendered to humanity in general and to his country in particular. If he had to do it again, he would without question. "I consider myself a proud American. I would do all that I can to serve my country."

Lieutenant Commander Ed Feldman is the possessor of the following awards and decorations: Silver Star Medal, Bronze Star Medal with combat V, Vietnamese Cross of Gallantry, Marine Corps Combat Action Ribbon, Presidential Unit Citation, Vietnamese Campaign Ribbon with three battle stars, Vietnamese Service Ribbon, and the Navy Unit Citation.

He is currently (5/2002) under consideration to receive the Congressional Medal of Honor for his feat of taking command of a U.S. Army infantry unit in the heat of battle and successfully beating back the attacking enemy force.

Albert J. Finkelstein

On April 29, 1945, Samuel Finkelstein of Brooklyn, received a letter from Captain T. B. Tighe, Headquarters, 31st Replacement Draft, FMF, 5th Marine Division, Fleet Post Office, San Francisco. It read as follows:

"My dear Mr. Finkelstein: It is with deep regret and sympathy that I write to you concerning the death of your son during the battle for Iwo Jima, Volcano Islands. His devotion to duty in rendering aid to wounded Marines in the face of enemy fire during the operation at Iwo Jima earned him the deepest respect of all who came to know him. Your son made the supreme sacrifice with great courage."

Another letter was received by the Finkelstein family from the Secretary of the Navy. It read:

"The President of the United States takes pride in presenting the SILVER STAR MEDAL posthumously to ALBERT JACOB FINKELSTEIN, HOSPITAL APPRENTICE FIRST CLASS UNITED STATES NAVAL RESERVE for service as set forth in the following CITATION;

For conspicuous gallantry and intrepidity as a Hospital Corpsman attached to a Marine rifle company, 2nd Battalion, 26th Marines, 5th Marine Division, during action against enemy Japanese forces at Iwo Jima, Volcano Islands, from February 19 to March 15. Moving forward beyond the front lines on repeated occasions, exposed continually to murderous enemy fire, FINKELSTEIN administered vital first aid and brought many wounded men back to safety and additional medical attention in an area under knee-high mortar and rifle concentration. On March 15, he heroically answered the cries of a helpless Marine and, although he himself suffered a mortal wound, he treated the casualty so skillfully that the man survived, to be removed later in satisfactory condition for further treatment. His courageous, inspiring, and undaunted devotion to duty, in utter disregard of imminent peril to own life, was in keeping with the highest traditions of the United States Naval Service. He gallantly gave his life for his country.

For the President,

(signed) James Forrestal, Secretary of the Navy"

Irving Grossman

In 1998, while watching television's History Channel, Irving Grossman of Livingston, New Jersey, saw a number of Japanese veterans being interviewed with the assistance of a translator. One Japanese veteran said that whenever his "comrades were dying or severely wounded, they invariably called out for their mother."

This revelation was of particular significance for Grossman after more than a half a century. "I don't have to tell you my relief and the expelling of all the tensions that I had been building up through the years." As he explained, "While advancing toward our objective on Iwo Jima in the early hours, I was severely wounded by machine-gun fire. As I was falling to the ground, I involuntarily called out to my mother. I was conscious all the time, and, in spite of the thought that I may be dying, my main concern was that I hope my comrades did not hear my short cry." He thought of this incident at times throughout the intervening years, and kept it to himself. Now confronted with the same image, and by enemy soldiers at that, he could finally come to terms with a feeling of uncertainty and distress which he had harbored for so long.

After his training at Camps Lejeune and Pendleton, Grossman participated in the invasions of Roi-Namur, Saipan, Tinian, and Iwo Jima. On Saipan, he received slight facial wounds from hand grenades; on Iwo Jima, he was severely wounded.

He writes poignantly and descriptively of "My Longest Day":

"The date is February 19, 1945. Reveille is 0300 in the morning. We have been on board our LST for a number of weeks approaching our rendezvous point after leaving Pearl Harbor. The target is a place I never heard of before: a two-by-five-mile volcanic island called Iwo Jima, a scant 700 miles from Tokyo, Japan.

After the traditional breakfast of steak and eggs, we retire to check our equipment and clean our weapons.

This operation would be my fourth major battle. Somehow before this, I never doubted that I would survive. However, this time there was an air of apprehension hovering over me. I knew that I had to relieve myself of this feeling quickly, and I did. I found time to write a V-mail letter to my mother and father. I told them I missed them and looked forward to seeing them soon. But if that was not to be, they could find solace in living in a new and better world.

We go on deck to watch the heavy barrages of battleships, cruiser, destroyers, and carrier planes blast the island incessantly. It seems impossible to believe that anyone or anything could survive that pounding.

It is time to board the Amtracs and prepare for the 0900 landing which we do, and proceed to circle the area. We are scheduled for the third wave, but we have to wait for the point blank shelling to end.

Then, the moment of truth has arrived and we head on full speed for Yellow Beach One.

There is no way to describe the feeling we all have after we lock and load and lower our heads waiting for that familiar thump when the ramp dropped and we hit the beach.

Out we go running for protective cover. What I saw was a clogged beach of men and damaged equipment. What greeted us was a constant barrage of Japanese mortars and artillery and gunfire which was zeroed in on our positions from the high ground to our right and from the towering Mount Suribachi to our left.

What struck me immediately were the sights, the sounds, and the smells. The sights of almost total confusion and the carnage all around me. The sounds of the whirring incoming mortar shells, and the sounds of the dying. The smells of the cordite in the air and the smells of fear itself.

Finally, we rise up and advance toward our main objective which was Motoyama Airfield #1. We ran from one shell hole to another until we were three quarters toward our goal.

Just prior to reaching the next shell hole, I heard the chatter of light machine-gun fire, and then it felt as if someone hit me with a sledge hammer. Just before I hit the ground, my weapon went one way and my helmet went the other. I then realized that I was badly wounded. At first, I thought that my right arm was shot off, and I waited for the end as the Japanese gunner kept shooting at me and splashing black sand all over me.

After what seemed like an eternity, Lt. Britson called out to me. I told him that I couldn't move, so he crawled out and pulled me into the shell hole where first aid was administered. We then waited for assistance to evacuate me as soon as possible.

Finally, two stretcher bearers came and picked me up and we started off to the beach. That Japanese gunner started up again and I was dumped to the ground as the corpsmen ran for cover. After a while, they picked me up and we reached the evacuation area at around 1300.

All the wounded and I were laid down in a line on the beach waiting for an available landing craft to take us off the island. At around 1800, we were loaded on the craft and we took off for the hospital ship. But as luck would have it, reports came in that Kamikaze planes were approaching. So the ships had to pull up anchor and zig zag the area. That meant that the landing craft had to follow suit.

Around 0600 the next morning, I was hoisted up the ship and laid down on the wooden deck as a doctor and assistants came to administer aid. Suddenly, I felt that I was going into shock and told that to the doctor. He immediately gave me blood transfusions and then right into the operating room for final treatment.

Eleven months later, after a number of naval hospitals and rehabilitation centers it was over.

Over six thousand men died for a two-by-five-mile island of ugly black sand which quickly turned red. I often wonder why I was able to come back while so many young men died there. I still haven't found the answer. Some day I hope to do so.

In conclusion, this day was the beginning of the end of the

war in the Pacific. For me, it was the Day That Changed My Life Forever.

This was my longest day."

Bernie Kauffman

After recruit training and Hospital Corps School at Bainbridge, Bernie Kauffman joined the 1st Marine Division at Camp Pendleton. He later became a member of C Company, 4th Medical Battalion, 4th Marine Division, and participated in landings at Roi-Namur, Saipan, Tinian, and Iwo Jima. He was awarded the Purple Heart for wounds received at Iwo Jima.

One of Kauffman's cousins, a soldier in the 1st Infantry Division who fought in North Africa, Italy, and on D-Day in France, was wounded three times and received the Silver Star Medal. Another cousin served in the Navy, engaged in combat in the Pacific, and was wounded during the invasion of the Philippines.

There were six Jews in Kauffman's company, two of whom were killed—Larry Cohn on Iwo Jima and Jerry Sander on Tinian. Kauffman made many friends during his military service and still keeps up with at least two of them.

"I'm very proud to have served with the Marines," wrote Kauffman, who is currently (2001) in St. Petersburg, Florida. "Consider myself a Marine."

In February 1948, Bernie's father received the following letter from the Commandant of the Marine Corps, General Clifton B. Cates:

"My dear Mr. Kauffman:

"I have recently found a file, which has been lost for a long time, containing your letter of April 21, 1945. Even at this late date, I want you to know that I appreciated it.

"Please give my regards to your son, and I trust that

all is well with him. He certainly did his part in the war and deserves much credit.

"With very best wishes and thanking you for your nice letter, I am
Very sincerely
C. B. Cates"

Sol M. Kozol

The physicians and dentists, too, work under extreme conditions. They are often exposed to hostile fire, making it impossible for them to seek cover. They continue to perform their surgery and treatment in disregard for their own safety. Their only concern is the care of their patients.

Lieutenant Sol M. Kozol of Boston, serving with the Marines as a dentist in the Pacific, worked on the teeth of some twenty-five hundred Marines in such places as a beachhead on a South Pacific island, a native thatched hut, and wobbling landing craft off Tarawa.

Dr. Kozol invented a few phrases to "calm down the terror-struck Marines" faced with the prospect of having dental work. He would say, invitingly, "Open your kisser, chum," or "Am I hurting you, dear?" Dr. Kozol would have you believe that those niceties would put his patients at ease.

Herman Rabeck

Even before his assignment to Marine units, Herman Rabeck of San Diego served as a medical corpsman at sea. He joined the Navy at 17—the fastest way he was going to be able to get back at the Nazis—and was sent to medical corpsman school, finishing the six-month course in eight weeks. (A shortage of corpsmen necessitated shortening the training period drastically.) A few months later, he was helping Patton's men land at Fedella Bay, eighteen miles north of Casablanca.

Not long after it had landed the troops and some equipment, his convoy was caught by a U-boat "wolf pack" (German submarines) and only three of the eight ships survived. We picked up many survivors then zig zagged at sea all night while caring for all the burn survivors and headed into Casablanca harbor, docking near the *Jean Bart,* France's largest battleship that had been sunk the night before with a secret "Fido" magnetic bomb. One of the subs was sunk by a Coast Guard seaplane just a few feet from the entrance to the docks of Casablanca as the flagship, USS *Leonard Wood* (APA12), lurched away from the wake of a torpedo.

After that campaign, Rabeck was sent to Norfolk and assigned to FMF, Camp Lejeune. Originally, there were forty-two corpsmen in his group—Rabeck was the only one to make it to Iwo Jima, his fifth invasion.

He was with the 3rd Marine Division when it left Camp Lejeune for Camp Pendleton. The 23rd Marines stayed behind to form the 4th Division. In February, 1944, he participated in the invasion and capture of Roi-Namur in the Marshall Islands, then in the invasions of Saipan, Tinian, and, in February 1945, Iwo Jima. Four days into the battle of Iwo Jima, he was wounded and shipped to Guam for treatment.

Rabeck's entire career with the Marine Corps was as a frontline company aid man, never serving in a hospital area while in action. He retains a close relationship to this day with the men of the 4th Marine Division, especially those of Headquarters and K Companies, as well as L Company, 3rd Battalion, 23rd Marines.

In his outfit, three Jewish corpsmen were killed on Iwo and several more were wounded on various islands. Herman Rabeck is the recipient of the Navy and Marine Corps Medal, Bronze Star with V for valor, awarded for uncommon heroism in saving Marine lives, two Purple Hearts, four Navy commendations, and four Presidential Unit Citations.

Richard Ruben

Dr. Richard Ruben is a staff physician at the Veterans Home of California in Yountville, a position he turned to after a successful practice in San Francisco from 1960 to 1993.

His father was an Army veteran of World War I. Dr. Ruben graduated from Washington and Jefferson College, Washington, Pennsylvania, magna cum laude and Phi Beta Kappa, after which he attended and graduated from the Chicago Medical School in 1954. He entered the Navy in July 1956, and completed two weeks of indoctrination at Philadelphia Naval Hospital. After a year at the Naval Air Technical Training Center, Norman, Oklahoma, he was assigned to the USS *John C. Fremont*, APA-44, based at Norfolk. The ship embarked for a Mediterranean cruise on a NATO exercise, landing at ports throughout Europe. The 2nd Battalion, 6th Marines, from Camp Lejeune, was put ashore at Gallipoli, Turkey. Prior to returning to Norfolk, his ship stopped at the amphibious base at Little Creek for troop basic training with the amphibious forces, which consisted of landing craft familiarization, loading equipment, and salt-water indoctrination. From there, the ship returned to Norfolk, and in early 1958 sailed to the Mediterranean for its regular six-month tour as part of the Sixth Fleet.

Dr. Ruben made many landings in the Mediterranean, and, in addition to serving as the ship's doctor, spent many hours in landing craft with the Marines. His ship sailed into Gibraltar to meet the relief squadron in June, then sailed east again to patrol the coast of Lebanon. After a short trip to Antalya, Turkey, near the coast of Syria, it put the 1st Battalion, 8th Marines, from Camp Lejeune ashore in Lebanon.

Dr. Ruben enjoyed various ports of call in the Mediterranean—Gibraltar; Barcelona; Villefranche; Livorno, Naples, and other ports in Italy; Crete, Piraeus, and Salonica, Greece; Majorca; and Antalya, Turkey.

During the summer of 1957, he sailed as medical officer on a weekend midshipman cruise from Norfolk to Baltimore aboard the *Spiegel Grove*, LDG-32

Dr. Ruben left active duty in 1958. He maintains his rank as lieutenant commander in the Reserve.

Harold Schainberg

Harold Schainberg enlisted in the Navy on April 17, 1951, in New York City at the age of 19. It was just before Passover, and he found himself in Newport, Rhode Island, at a Seder held at the Recruit Training Center there. Also, at Newport, he had the opportunity of attending services at Touro Synagogue which had a servicemen's center.

Schainberg had tried to enlist in the Marines but was turned down because of poor eyesight. When he knew he would be rejected by the Navy, he memorized the eye chart and was accepted. He volunteered for the Field Medical School, was accepted, and was sent to Camp Pendleton, where he spent the four longest weeks of his life. Although Schainberg was scheduled to depart for service in Korea, the war ended in July, 1953, and he was reassigned to the 3rd Marine Division currently being formed at Camp Pendleton. He was quartered in Tent Camp #3 and assigned to E Company, 3rd Medical Battalion, 3rd Marine Division.

Japan was like a vacation. The ship's personnel had occasional time for visits to Mount Fuji, Iwo Jima, Okinawa, and Korea. In Korea, Harold assisted in the repatriation of twenty-two thousand Chinese who did not want to return to Red China. One day, "while loading one of the Marine guard unit, an LST collided with an LCU (landing craft, utility) in Inchon Harbor. The LCU capsized and fifty enlisted Marines, three Marine officers, three corpsmen, and two doctors drowned. Their packs pulled them under."

Before return to the States, Schainberg was stationed at Gifu,

Japan. Upon arriving back in the States, he was sent to Pensacola Naval Hospital until 1955, when he was discharged from the Navy.

Three months after his discharge, he joined the Air Force Reserve. After nine months he was transferred into a Navy Reserve unit. He then joined the Marine Corps Reserve and became a member of the 4th ANGLICO, Miami. After fifteen years in the 4th ANGLICO, he had a disagreement with his CO who wanted Harold to shave off his mustache. When he refused to do so, Schainberg was transferred to a naval air unit until his retirement in 1980.

One of the best days of Schainberg's life was the one on which he made Staff NCO. "It was like being promoted to royalty.

"Am I proud to have served in the Marine Corps? Well, every time they start to play 'The Marines' Hymn, I stand a little straighter and my chest goes out with pride to think that at some time in past history I was part of the Corps."

Jacob Sheiker

Jacob Sheiker enlisted in the Navy on May 6, 1952. After completing recruit training, he was schooled as a pharmacist's mate and assigned to the Fleet Marine Force. After training with the Marines at Camp Pendleton, he was attached to D Company, 2nd Battalion, 28th Marines, 5th Marine Division.

Sheiker was then shipped to Hilo, where he was trained for the assault on Iwo Jima.

On D-Day, February 19, 1945, his company was in the first wave to hit the island. The sand on the beach was black ash. When the men were finally able to get off the beach, they moved out in the direction of Mount Suribachi. A mortar shell landed right among his group of eight men. It did not harm them because the earth was so soft—it only managed to billow a cloud of smoke. The men thought it was gas. As everyone had discarded their masks upon landing on the beach, they all scattered quickly out of the hole they were dug in.

The second day, fire from the top of the mount was intense. Sheiker wrote, "I really don't remember if I volunteered or was asked to go down toward the beach to bring back a tank. I brought back a tank and it directed fire on Suribachi. The Japanese stopped firing from that particular target on Suribachi and the tank also stopped. It then took some of the wounded Marines to the beach where their wounds could be treated."

Sometime later, he and his best friend were lying side by side when a shell landed right between them. His friend took most of the blast and was killed instantly. Sheiker was wounded in the face, hand, and arm. He was taken off the island and put aboard ship were he was operated on.

One officer and two enlisted men were wounded badly when the ship was attacked by kamikazes. The ship was badly damaged, sustaining a large hole on one side.

"I was a 17-year-old baby when I left home, and returned a man. My time in service was a good thing for me because I knew I had to fight for my country and for me to understand what life was all about."

Jacob Sheiker, PHM2C, was awarded the Purple Heart, the Presidential Unit Citation, the American Campaign Medal, the Asiatic-Pacific Medal with one bronze star, and the World War II Victory Medal.

As of the year 2000, he resides in Bayside, New York.

David Swerdlow

David Swerdlow joined the Navy in August 1942. After serving seven months with the Navy, he was transferred to the Corps' 4th Marine Division which was being formed at Camp Lejeune and described the transition: "long training hours, strenuous marches, weapons training, and everything else to prepare for the combat to come."

Swerdlow noted, like so many others, that Navy medics with the Marines are highly respected. "I appreciated that, since the Navy could care less about the corpsmen."

He completed training at Camp Pendleton and became permanently attached to the 4th Marine Division. He enjoyed being with the Marines, and was physically and mentally prepared for the battles that were soon to come. The first was in the Marshall Islands, where he learned what war was really about. It prepared him for the next engagements fought on Saipan and Tinian, which he described as "really tough." He wrote, "You have really not seen battle action until you are a corpsman giving aid to the wounded at the battlefront." He was kept busy day and night.

On his third day on Iwo Jima, he was wounded straight through the right ankle. Evacuated to Saipan, he was then sent back to Hawaii where he spent four months in a hospital before returning in June 1944 to the States where he was medically discharged two months later.

Service with the Marines was a lifetime experience. He has forgotten very little of it. He feels that "many times being a Jew made it harder as you never can interact with the other men and feel secure and comfortable with your conversations and actions." He recounts that "some of the southerners could not believe I was a Jew and I had to assure them I had no horns on my head, and that I would not harm them."

Swerdlow relates an anti-Semitic incident with a drunken Marine in his company. "We had some fights and I held my own and after that, you could not believe the attitude of them who saw the fight and praised me afterward as my opponent was much bigger than I and most men did not care for him and his big mouth. No-one ever bothered me again and what a relief that was!"

Swerdlow said, "I feel good about myself for serving and how proud I was with the Marines and as a medic. We were issued carbines and no medical insignia on our uniforms as we were more vulnerable to the enemy when we were carrying wounded in open territory.

General Cates, the division commander, and the doctors were his heroes. He could not write enough in praise of them.

Pharmacist's Mate Third Class Herman (Steve) Trevor received the following citation in April 1945:

From: The Commanding Officer

To: (1) The Commanding General, 24th Marines

(2) The Commanding General, 4th Marine Division, Fleet Marine Force

Subject: SILVER STAR MEDAL, recommendation for, case of Pharmacist's Mate, Third Class Herman TREVOR, (878-18-31), U. S. Naval Reserve

1. It is recommended that Pharmacists' Mate Third Class Herman S. TREVOR be awarded the SILVER STAR MEDAL for conspicuous gallantry and intrepidity in action against enemy Japanese forces while serving as a company aid man attached to Headquarters Company, 2nd Battalion, 24th Marines, 4th Marine Division, FMF, from 19 February to 16 March, 1945, on IWO JIMA, VOLCANO ISLANDS

2. Pharmacist's Mate Third Class TREVOR landed on Iwo Jima on D Day with the 81 mm mortar platoon to which he was attached. On the day that TREVOR performed the action described in reference (a) the mortar platoon was operating on a wide flat beach. Every man could be seen by the enemy from a mountain on the left, an airstrip straight ahead and a hill on the right. Enemy mortar artillery and flat trajectory fire came from all three directions almost continuously. In the course of a six-hour period, on 20

February 1945, four members of the mortar platoon were killed and ten seriously wounded. TREVOR exposed himself completely to render first aid to each of these casualties. Even when enemy fire was so intense that the mortar platoon had to cease firing and displace to new positions, TREVOR was seen running from foxhole to foxhole dressing the wounded and encouraging the others. His coolness under fire and his tireless devotion to duty without regard to his personal safety were a constant inspiration to his entire platoon.

3. Pharmacist's Mate Third Class TREVOR participated in the battles of Saipan and Tinian, Marianas Islands. He received a Letter of Commendation from the Commanding General, 4th Marine Division, Fleet Marine Force, for company aid work performed on Saipan.

Steve Trevor received the Silver Star Medal for his extraordinary heroism in the Pacific. He had been recommended for the Navy Cross but as it was not "official," it came down eventually as the Silver Star.

Steve recalls that during the landing on the island of Saipan, as he started to disembark from the landing craft, he was held back by his buddy, who chided him with, "Pharmacist Mates go last, so you can pick us up!" And with that, his buddy was struck down as he stepped out of the craft, just where Steve would have been. Steve was very hurt by this, and it played on his conscience for a very long time. This episode was just one, "there by the grace of God" incidents that were very heart rending.

Steve remained in the Naval Reserve and was called back to duty for Korea—the very first man in Los Angeles to be called. Because of his WWII experiences, he was placed in a recruiting capacity, rather than sending him back into further combat.

Chaplain Gittlesohn delivers Dedication Address to Jewish Marines. Ed Miller's face is partially hidden by lectern

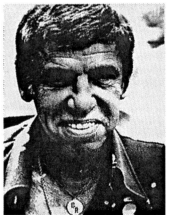

Cpl. Buddy Rich

Captain David Rosenthal, Guam, 1944/45

Captain Max Halpin (in front of his F4U Corsair)

Ralph Most (extreme lower right), Tinian 10/44

Gerry Newhouse, Vietnam, 1966

Mike Nechin with Marilyn Monroe, Korea, 1952

The Zimmermann Family
(l to r) David, Ilene (she served, too), Jack, Terri Jacobs

Cpl. Jack Groskin (far left) with dead Japanese on Iwo Jima

Jacob Sheiker, Iwo Jima, 1945

Murray Moskowitz, Korea, 1952

⋀ *Gunnery Sergeant Sam Winer (in middle, bottom), before leaving for Iwo Jima*

Cpl. Leon Uris ➤

*Brigadier General Martin
Rockmore*

*James Austin Bateman, KIA,
Vietnam, 1966*

Major Bill Sager, USMCR

*2nd Lt. Yonel (Yogi) Dorelis,
USMC*

Sgt. Major Abe Marovitz (with two brothers)

Captain Max Halpin, USMCR, 1945

Berl (Bo) Olswanger, Vietnam

Col. Marvin Schacher (far right
Reception at 21 Club, Commandant USMC Gen. Wallace Greene
(far left)

Retirement ceremony Major General William J Weinstein

Marv Goodman, Camp Tarawa,
Hawaii, 1945

Erwin Small

Summer of 1968 at Camp
Pendleton, Calif, 36-year old
Major Edward J. Leavitt (on
right), giving instructions to
some of his company com-
manders while directing the
firing of tanks of the 4th Tank
Battalion, Force Troops, Fleet
Marine Force, at the tank
firing range

Al Clark with author's cousin
Merrill (1942)

A Co., 1ˢᵗ Battalion, 24ᵗʰ Marines, 4ᵗʰ Marine Division (survivors). They left the States with 234 men. Survivors after Roi-Namur, Saipan, and Tinian. Company. Commander Capt. Irving Schecter standing in middle, wearing jacket and trousers ([with grenade in left pocket], left behind flag)

(Photo courtesy of Roger Trimble, one of the survivors)

Brig. Gen. William Weinstein (far right) with Brig. Gen. S. L. A. Marshall (military historian), and George Jessel

1st Lt. William Weinstein (OP on Iwo Jima)

Gunnery Sergeant Leland ([Lou] Diamond, 53), congratulated by Major General A. A. Vandegrift, CG 1st Marine Division, for commendation for heroic action on Guadalcanal. It was also farewell to Lou, departing for the U.S. (Official Marine Corps photo, May, 1943)

Lieutenant General Robert Magnus, USMC

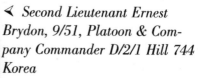

◄ *Second Lieutenant Ernest Brydon, 9/51, Platoon & Company Commander D/2/1 Hill 744 Korea*

Ernest Brydon, Guest Speaker, Marine Corps Birthday Ball Philadelphia, Pa. 11/92 ➤

◄ *Private Ernest Brydon, USMC, Parris Island, SC, 10/42*

"Bo" Olswanger in middle, Col. Paul X Kelley (future comman-dant of the USMC, left, Maj. Ed Looney, right, Vietnam)

Steve Judd (kneeling, bottom right) on liberty

PART VII

The Coldest War

Chapter 31

Korea (Introduction)

The Korean War was the first real test of the military unity of the United Nations. It was a challenge to the Free World to stand up against Communist aggression. It was an obscenity in its production of human suffering.

Japan completed annexation of Korea by the end of the Russo-Japanese War in 1905. During World War II in 1943, the United States, Great Britain, and later (and later, Russia) signed the Cairo Declaration which stated the conditions for the liberation of Korea from the Japanese after the war ended. The terms of the Japanese capitulation on August 11, 1945, set out that the Russians would accept the surrender of the Japanese north of the 38th Parallel, and the United States south of that line. The Russians immediately occupied the territory north of the 38th Parallel. Communist leader Kim Il Sung, with the aid of the Soviets, set up a Communist government in the north.

On June 25, 1950, the North, in an attempt to unite what had become the two Koreas, invaded the South with seven infantry divisions, heavily supported by artillery and tanks. (Later, in November, 1950, nine divisions of the People's Republic of China joined in the battle with the avowed purpose of destroying the 1st Marine Division). The UN quickly resolved that its member countries would come to the aid of South Korea, with General of the Army Douglas

MacArthur, U.S. Army, commanding all UN forces. While the United States furnished most of the fighting forces, other countries contributed troops as well. They included Great Britain, Australia, Colombia, Canada, France, Thailand, Turkey, Greece, New Zealand, and the Union of South Africa.

This was the first valid, but tragic, opportunity for the Free World to demonstrate its unity against Communist aggression.

Within weeks of the June 1950 invasion, the first Marine units to be deployed to the war—6,534-man 1st Provisional Marine Brigade—was sent to Korea. Ultimately, the 1st Marine Division (Reinf) and the 1st MAW would become part of the UN fighting forces.

On June 23, 1951, the Soviet UN representative proposed the commencement of cease-fire negotiations. Truce talks between the two warring sides began. After two years and 158 meetings (during which talks an additional 56,000 Americans had been killed or wounded), an armistice was signed on July 27, 1953. The new border between the North and South remained essentially the same as the pre-war border—the 38th Parallel.

Total U.S. combat losses were 33,629 battle deaths and 103,308 wounded. Of those, 4,262 Marines died in battle and 26,038 were wounded. The Republic of South Korea armed forces had approximately 850,000 casualties. The Communist losses were estimated at 1,420,000, with the CCF suffering 900,000 casualties and the NKPA, 520,000.

Leonard C. Brody

Born on October 20, 1935, in Providence, Leonard Brody joined the Marine Corps Reserve while a senior at Hope High School there. Upon graduation, he entered the Marine Corps and served five years of active duty, followed by three years in the Reserve. He was a peacetime Marine, joining up after the termination of the Korean War. Called to active duty in November, 1954, he did his recruit training at Parris Island, followed by infantry training at Camp Lejeune. He attended and was graduated from the Sea School at Portsmouth, Virginia, and assigned to the Marine detachment aboard the USS *Des Moines*. His first enlistment terminated with his honorable discharge in November 1956.

One month later, Brody reenlisted and was assigned to school at Great Lakes Naval Training Center, after which he returned to Camp Lejeune. He went on two Mediterranean cruises with the 3rd Battalion, 6th Marines, participated in the Lebanon landing in 1958. Upon his return from Lebanon, he was transferred to the 2nd Marine Air Wing at Cherry Point, where he was in charge of a squadron armory.

Between 1954 and 1958, he attended a number of Marine Corps schools—including NCO Leadership School, Camp Lejeune, and Weapons Repair Machinist School Quantico—and took various Marine Corps Institute correspondence courses. He also completed training as an infantry weapons armorer. In December 1959, he received his discharge as Sergeant E-4.

His military awards included the Marine Corps Good Conduct Medal, the National Defense Service Medal, the Navy Occupation Service Medal, the Armed Forces Expeditionary Medal (for service in Lebanon, 1958).

Jack Feinhor

All three Feinhor boys enlisted in the Marine Corps. Marvin Feinhor served during World War II and was wounded on Iwo Jima. Jack and Joe both served during the war in Korea.

The Feinhors' parents, both immigrants, worked very hard to support their family. But Jack and Joe were constantly getting in trouble. Marvin, on the other hand, was a fine boy who kept out of trouble. With World War II, he enlisted in the Marine Corps, went to Iwo Jima, fought there for nine days till he was wounded.

Brother Joe joined the Marine Corps prior to the Korean War. When Jack got into trouble with the law, the judge gave him thirty days to leave Cincinnati, join the service, or go to jail. Seeking to join the Marines, they turned him down for being underage. At first, his parents refused to sign the papers due to the fact that Marvin had been wounded on Iwo. When Jack threatened to have some other parents sign for him, they gave in and finally consented.

As Jack admits to being somewhat of a juvenile delinquent, he credits the Marine Corps for straightening him out and saving him from a life of crime.

Parris Island was "thirteen tough ass training (May, 1948) weeks." He got along with all his platoon mates, although he hated the DIs. However, when he got to Korea, he "thanks God for the great training. My DIs had brainwashed me as I feel this helped me in Korea."

His duty stations included Camp Lejeune, with the 2nd Marine Division and more training, Guard Company and Engineering, then to Headquarters, Marine Corps. Henderson Hall Guard Company. At Camp Pendleton, he was an assistant BARman.

A very unpleasant incident was the occasion when, upon taking a hill in Korea, "one of the new Marines stepped in front of me and took a bullet in his head. This has always bothered me." Service in the military made him "feel very proud to be an American. Also very guilty for surviving Korea and my Marine brothers did not."

As a member of H/3/7, 3rd Battalion, 7th Marines, he went ashore at Inchon in September1950. He participated in the Inchon/Seoul campaign as an assistant BARman and rifleman. He was wounded by shrapnel at Suicide Saddle Hill on September 27, taken to the aid station, and returned to duty not long after.

Advancing to the 38th Parallel, they went to Wonson, then to Hungnam. During the trek to the Chosin Reservoir, they were engaged in many fire fights, and a number of his company were killed, wounded, or suffered frostbite. Jack captured two Chinese soldiers at Hagaru-ri and delivered them to the Division MPs.

Feinhor vividly recalls the early morning of December 8, when

> "In thick fog, with no air support, the Chinese bugles were blasting, flares lighted up the sky, and they knew the Gooks were coming. They had put on their bayonets and he was so scared and cold that he couldn't move. This big ox of a Marine came up to him and said, 'Let's move.' Feinhor heard him but he just stayed there. The Marine saw that Feinhor was in trouble and picked him up and started running with him to get him motivated.
>
> "They then came down off the mountain, regrouped at Kotori, and marched out singing the Marine Corps Hymn. The men of the Chosin are a special group. They boarded ship and departed for the rest area, soon to depart to fight in other areas."

Jack thanked God that he was one of the survivors of the Chosin campaign. Fifteen thousand Marines were trapped there by 120,000 Chinese. During Operation Killer and Ripper and the Spring offensive, one of the platoon commanders, Lt. Walter Kennedy was pinned down and wounded, remaining on top of the mountain, exposed to the line of fire. Platoon runner Jack Feinhor went to his rescue and dragged him out of danger.

After several fire fights, he was relieved of duty, then returned to the States for guard duty at Norfolk Naval Base until his discharge in 1952.

Jack Feinhor's medals and decorations include the Purple Heart, Presidential Unit Citation with two bronze stars, Good Conduct Medal, National Defense Service Medal, Korean Service Medal with four bronze stars, Korean Presidential Unit Citation, United Nations Service Medal, and Expert Rifle Badge.

Although Jack Feinhor almost lost his life in Korea, he says that "This has made me a better person. I would certainly go back in if at all possible. I am very much involved with many military organizations. Once a Marine, always a Marine."

Abraham Geller

Those who find fasting on Yom Kippur an annoyance, or an inconvenience, should find the saga of Abraham Geller to be a downright revelation, a relief, or a vindication.

Corporal Abraham Geller, of the New York East Side, son of a rabbi, lived near Delancey Street. An Orthodox Jew, he got up a half-hour earlier than his comrades so that he could perform morning prayers.

In Korea, the Marines had crossed the Han River and cut the Seoul-Kaesong Road.

Hunkered down in foxholes for the night, they would soon be fighting near the Korean capital. There, in October 1950, on Yom Kippur, Abraham Geller commenced his fast.

Shortly before dawn, Geller finished his prayers. Captain George O'Connor suggested he get a cup of coffee. Declining the offer, Geller said he had to wait until sundown. O'Connor was amazed that Geller wouldn't eat until the day was over.

When Geller's company moved forward the next day, they encountered stiff resistance. A badly wounded North Korean was playing dead among the bodies strewn on the field as the

Company moved through the area. Geller suddenly saw him move close to O'Connor. Pulling out his bayonet, Geller dove for the enemy and killed him. But he also stopped three bullets intended for the captain.

Geller did not receive medical treatment until three hours later. His wounds required an hour of surgery. Later, O'Connor, who had waited, inquired about the results of the operation. The doctor said Geller was doing well. "The bullets went through his abdomen and penicillin prevented peritonitis. In a sense, Geller owes life to the fact that there was hardly any food in his stomach. Then, "O'Connor shook his head as he started to understand a little bit more about the meaning of fasting on Yom Kippur."[1]

Irwin Howard

Irwin Howard was 21 when he reported to the draft board on Whitehall Street, New York City, in 1951. Picked for the Marines, he was sent to recruit training at Parris Island. He then went to Camp Lejeune, Camp Pendleton, and finally to Pickle Meadows, California, for cold-weather training before shipped to Korea as a radar operator, MOS 0711.

As Inchon Harbor was too shallow for big ships, it took about two hours to get ashore on landing craft. Halfway to shore, the air-raid alarm sounded and a blackout was ordered. It was said to be "Hot-Shot Charlie," a North Korean pilot making the rounds in a small plane and dropping a few bombs.

Howard arrived at Inchon just as the fighting intensified above Seoul. After spending several hours at the staging center, Ascom City, his unit boarded trucks and headed for the railroad station where shelling could be heard in the distance. The men were issued ammunition against any possible guerrilla attacks on their train.

Eleven hours later, they arrived at Pusan where Howard was attached to Battery D, 1st 90mm AAA Battalion, to work the command post phones, plot grids on the radar screens, and call in bogies (unidentified planes). He spent most of the time observing the small, yellow screen on a radar set in a tent with an antenna whirling on top. His duty was four hours on and four off. He noted, "It was easy to let yourself drift off to sleep watching the radar beam circling endlessly picking up the blips." Images of Pearl Harbor were always present, and he "was not going to fail

---

1 Brody, Seymour, *Jewish Heroes & Heroines of America*, Lifetime Books, Hollywood, Fla., 1996, p.256.

my job by not catching an air attack. This thought helped keep me awake."

Howard, who started his apprenticeship as a dental technician at age 15, returned to his calling after being discharged from the Marine Corps in 1953 and owns his own dental laboratory in Tuckahoe. He currently (2001) resides in Chappaqua, New York. Presently, he is a proud life member and officer of Westchester County Detachment , Marine Corps League.

William Katz

Bill Katz enlisted in the Marine Corps in January 1931, and graduated from boot training around the end of March. He admits he "wasn't a poster Marine. I barely qualified with the rifle and had more Maggie's drawers (a red flag waved in the butts—where the targets are—by the personnel manning the targets to indicate a complete miss or a second zero) than bull's-eyes.

But he fared better with other weapons when he got the MOS of 1811, tank crewman. Following Parris Island, he underwent his tank training at Camp Pendleton.

Arriving in Korea on March 12, 1953, with the 30th Replacement Draft, Katz was assigned to A Company, 1st Tank Battalion, 1st Marine Division.

During the last month of the war as each side was trying to gain ground before the truce, the war heated up a bit. Katz, as the result of a hearing loss from tank gunfire, suffered a 40 percent disability.

On the last day of the war, July 27, 1953, Johnny Olsen and Katz were performing preventive maintenance on their tank during the early hours of that sunny day. "Suddenly two shots rang out from a sniper. Johnny and I jumped off the tank. A bullet had knocked the ring off the little finger of my right hand," whereupon Katz "went into a bunker and stayed there until 10:00 P.M. At that time, the Chinese released three green flares and we shot up three white ones signifying recognition of the truce. The Chinese played Bing Crosby's recording of 'White Christmas on their loudspeakers, which was a nice change of page from 'Marine, tonight you die!'"

Bill Katz loved the Marine Corps and the men he served with.

Today, he maintains contact with the service and the men with whom he served, including the men who failed to return home as he did. His organization, the Bureau of Wholesale Sales Representatives sponsors a project to build an amphitheater at the Visitors Center at Arlington National Cemetery. The five million school-age children who visit the cemetery each year can't see beyond the rows of white crosses and Stars of David. And, "They don't know the meaning of sacrifice. This film will give them a brief outline of what they're about to see. The 1st Marine Division has made a generous contribution to this project. The Bureau in town is working with the Marines' Toys for Tots. They hope to get ten thousand reps and the million buyers to come to shows with one unwrapped toy for an indigent child."

Currently (2001), he resides in his hometown of Huntingdon Valley, Pennsylvania. He is Vice-President of the Liberty Bell Chapter of the 1st Marine Division Association.

Myron (Mike) Nechin

Born February 25, 1930, in the Bronx, Mike Nechin enlisted in the Marine Corps April 21, 1952. After graduating from recruit training at Parris Island on June 26, he was assigned to 1st Battalion, 10th Marines, 2nd Marine Division, FMF, at Camp Lejeune, after which he returned to working in administrative duties at Parris Island. There he attended Personnel Administration School and graduated first in his class in October.

Nechin was assigned to 1st Battalion, 10th Marines, as a clerk-typist and then ordered to Korea. The trip on board the USS

Walker was pleasant and uneventful—a sojourn during which Nechin served as news editor on the staff of the *Jarhead*.

Upon arrival in Korea, he was assigned to an antitank company. Later, one Sunday morning Nechin awakened at dawn and observed a farmer "harvesting rice with his ox in the valley below. I was taken by surprise when the rice planter removed his straw hat and withdrew pencil and paper. He began writing while observing our position. I immediately went next-door and awakened our first sergeant and company commander. We grabbed our weapons and raced down to the valley below. The farmer saw us coming and began to run while trying to swallow the notes he had written. We grabbed him and the notes and brought him back to our encampment. Intelligence was notified while I stood guard over our prisoner. Through letters and papers he carried on him, he was identified as a major in the North Korean Army."

On July 1, 1953, Nechin was promoted to corporal.

In mid-July, North Korean troops overran a nearby hill sending the U.S. Army occupying force into retreat. Antitank Company was ordered to move out and defend another hill in the same area. "We arrived by truck with extra armaments. Pup tents were set on the side of a hill. We were fearful of infiltrators with knives who could slip into our camp and slit our throats while we slept. Sleeping that night was impossible."

"The next morning was spent digging in. Tanks were in place around the hill. That night, flares lit up the sky. Navy planes were dive-bombing and caused masses of earth to be covered with fire. The bombings and fire continued until we were relieved. We could see tracers being poured unforgivably into this pile of dirt. At assembly that morning, the first sergeant addressed us: 'Good news! We took the hill. The enemy has backed off. Our orders are to return to reserve. Be ready to ship out at 1500.'"

The next day, Corporal Nechin was back to his typewriter. His time as an infantryman was over. By October, Mike was transferred to HQ Company. His new duties would be as disbursing clerk. His assignment on Officers' Payroll helped him get a part-time job as bartender in the Officers' Club. In January 1954,

Nechin welcomed legendary film star Marilyn Monroe and hosted her show at the Marine Corps Command Post in South Korea.

Mike Nechin is the recipient of the Korea Service Medal with one battle star, the United Nations Service Medal, the National Defense Service Medal, and, just recently, after fifty years, received the Korean War Service Medal from the Republic of Korea. He was discharged form the Marine Corps Reserve on April 20, 1960.

Wrote Nechin, "I served with special men—dedicated, tough, and kind. I have the highest respect for our USMC 'Brotherhood.'"

Past President and Treasurer of Air Engineering, Inc., he is retired and currently (2001) resides with his wife, Selvia in Delray Beach, Florida.

Meyer Rossum

There have always been Jewish career Marines, those who have served during peacetime as well as war. One of those was Meyer Rossum, was born in Buffalo, New York, shortly after the end of the First World War on June 19, 1919. At the time of his enlistment, on November 14, 1939, he was living in Los Angeles, California.

He completed boot camp at MCRD, San Diego. On February 16, 1940, he shipped out to Pearl Harbor, and served at Marine Barracks, NAD, Lluolualo, from April, 1940 to December, 1942. During the attack on Hawaii on December 7, 1941, he participated in the defense of Pearl Harbor. In September, 1943, he joined the 1st Marine Battalion, first at Headquarters Battalion, then to 1st Motor Transport Battalion during the New Guinea and Okinawa campaigns.

Remaining in the Marine Corps at the end of World War II, Rossum was stationed stateside from November 1945 to August 1950, at Marine Barracks, Great Lakes, Illinois; San Francisco, and at Camp Pendleton. With the outbreak of the Korean War,

Rossum rejoined the 1ˢᵗ Marine Division, Headquarters Battalion, participated in the Inchon landing, then further action at Seoul, Wonsan, and Hungnam.

The battles at Hagaru-Ri in November, 1950, saw Rossum as first sergeant of forward echelon of Headquarters Company, Headquarters Battalion, commanded by Major "Fearless" Freddie Simpson. In the withdrawal from Hagaru to Koto-ri, he was wounded in the head from shrapnel, and received the Purple Heart in addition to his Bronze Star. He was evacuated by plane to the offshore hospital ship and then to Yokosuka Naval Hospital where he remained for two months. Hospitalization completed, he was transferred to C Company, then to Camp Otsu, then back to Division in August 1951. He was returned to the States in October 1951, because Commanding General G. C. Thomas didn't want anyone who went through the winter of 1950 to stay for another.

He received his promotion to master sergeant on June 1, 1952.

His next duty stations included MC DepSup SF (Motor Pool), SupCo, and 3ʳᵈ MC Recruit Training Battalion, MCRD, San Diego, then to MB NS, Long Beach, and VMIT, El Toro. His next overseas assignment was to Camp Smedley, Okinawa, from December 1957 to May 1959.

He completed his active service with the 1ˢᵗ Pioneer Battalion, 1ˢᵗ Marine Division, Camp Pendleton, then to SOES MCAS, El Toro, where he transferred to the Fleet Reserve on June 1, 1962.

In addition to his personal decorations and campaign medals, other awards include Marksman for pistol and rifle.

Master Sergeant Rossum found his military experience very much to his liking. He says, "I spent twenty-three years in the Corps. The Marine Corps was good to me. I lost my first wife in 1954, and the Marine Corps transferred me close to my daughter (age 7) and I was able to rehabilitate her by close to her."

For Meyer Rossum, the military, that of the Marine Corps, was a lifestyle in which he found meaning, importance, and pride.

Jack Sands

Jack Sands of New Orleans is the recipient of numerous awards and citations granted for his work on behalf of men and women on active and Reserve duty with the armed forces, as well as his charitable works benefiting his community.

The following citation was presented by the: Commandant of the Marine Corps

"The Commandant of the Marine Corps takes pleasure in presenting the Meritorious Public Service Award to Mr. Jack Sands for service set forward in the following CITATION:

"For selflessly giving of himself to advance the good of the Marine Corps. Mr. Sands is extremely supportive of a strong national defense and takes great pains to highlight the contributions of the armed forces. He is a strong supporter of national defense policies and initiatives. His hosting of numerous Marine Reserve Force functions and events that include a Marine Corps luncheon and his support of the young Marines have been particularly noteworthy. Mr. Sands's selfless devotion to our country reflects great credit upon himself and the United States Marine Corps and in keeping with the highest traditions of the United States Naval Service."

Prior to graduating from Alcee Fortier High School, New Orleans, Sands entered the Marine Corps Reserve's 10th Battalion, B Company. He enlisted in the Marine Corps upon graduation in May 1950, and completed recruit training at Parris Island where he was stationed with the Military Police Detachment. Remaining in military police, he was transferred to Marine Barracks, Pearl Harbor, later to be promoted to corporal, He was sent on TAD (Temporary Additional Duty) to Midway Island, returned to Pearl Harbor on TAC to CinCPac (Commander in Chief, Pacific Fleet), later to be assigned to a special detail to Kaesong, Korea, as orderly to Admiral Arthur H. Radford. Promoted to sergeant, he completed his tour at Pearl Harbor. He was then transferred to NAS, Pensacola, Military Police Detachment, finally receiving his honorable discharge in January 1954.

He opened the Tavern on the Park Restaurant in New Orleans in February 1967 and has on display there an extensive collection of Marine Corps memorabilia.

Sands held his first Tavern on the Park Marine Corps Birthday luncheon in 1966, attended by approximately fifteen former Marines. This luncheon has become an annual event and has become an annual event and has grown in attendance to over one hundred active and former Marines.

Burton "Bud" Schwartz

.Burton "Bud" Schwartz enlisted in the Marine Corps for the Korean War in January 1951 at the age of nineteen. Boot camp at San Diego was not easy: "It was what you made of it, training was hard, not too much so."

Completing boot camp, he was offered the chance to join the base swimming team. But he turned it down; he didn't want to be stuck at MCRD, San Diego.

Arriving next at Camp Pendleton for infantry training, he felt that the combat training was intense, good, and he learned a great deal. Most of the instructors were combat veterans. Schwartz's first MOS was 0300, basic infantry, then 0311.

He arrived in Korea in August 1951, and was assigned to H Company, 3rd Battalion, 1st Marines of the 1st Marine Division. At the time, there were in reserve. Joining the unit, he was designated as the BAR man. When it was noticed that he had the bipods, one of the men who had seen some action told him that when they entered into combat, to get rid of their bipods. "The reason was that the enemy always knew to look for automatic weapons to knock out."

Schwartz was wounded on September 9, 1951 in the area of the Punchbowl and sent to Charlie Med station. His company had taken some high ground from the North Koreans. "After a bit, the ROKs came to relieve us. Before we got off the hill, the ROKs fell back to different positions. We had to go back up and retake the hill, all over again. It was Hill 854. We had forty-seven men in our platoon. When I left for the med station, there were thirteen men left who were standing on their own feet. The rest were wounded or dead. Our regiment was awarded the PUC and the Korean PUC and three battle stars." Schwartz received the Purple Heart, the Conduct Medal, Korean Service Medal, National Defense Service, and the United Nations Service Medal.

After leaving Charlie Med, he was transferred to Special Service. When his younger sister passed away, he returned home on emergency leave. Returning to Korea, he became the Jewish Chaplain's assistant, where he helped with services when the chaplain could not make it with certain units.

One incident that stands out in his mind was the rumor which persisted prior to shipping out to Korea. Schwartz and three buddies started a rumor that they were going to Korea in PT boats, six men to a boat. "At a dress parade, the CO of the battalion didn't think it was too funny."

Bud Schwartz came out of the Corps a very proud sergeant. He considered staying in the Corps, but "when I was going to be discharged, they switched to a peacetime schedule. It was all spit and polish."

He was also proud of the fact that two of his cousins had served in the Marine Corps during World War II. That was one important consideration in joining the Corps himself. He respected most of the officers, especially those who had been Mustangs. "They knew what the enlisted men were going through."

His worst time in the Corps took place in Korea. "We were moving up north in the Punchbowl and we were between three mountain ranges. We were marching through this valley when suddenly bugles began playing all around us. They saw us coming, but we couldn't see them. My heart slowly sank to my toes. That is the worst feeling I ever had."

Oscar Sherman

Oscar Sherman of Brooklyn enlisted in the Marine Corps for a three-year hitch upon graduation from DeWitt Clinton High School in 1951.

After recruit training at Parris Island, he was sent to Korea on November 15, 1951, with the 15th Replacement Draft and the 1st Marine Division, participating in operations against enemy forces in South and Central Korea as a member of the 1st Combat Service Group and MAG-33, 1st MAW. When his unit was under a night attack, one of the men in his squad was unable to get out of his sleeping bag because the zipper had frozen up. He was dragged away by the Chinese and found later—hanging in the bag.

Returning to the States, Sherman served with the 2nd Marine Division at Camp Lejeune.

Discharged with the rank of sergeant, he is the recipient of the Presidential Unit Citation, the Good Conduct Medal, National Defense Service Medal, the Korean Service Medal, with four battle stars, the United Nations Service Medal, and the Republic of Korea Presidential Unit Citation, the Navy Unit Commendation, the New York Conspicuous Service Star and Cross.

Ted Sklaver

The military career of Ted Sklaver with its vagaries of fortune took many twists and turns. He could have been an officer had he so chosen.

Even his induction was somewhat bizarre. After receiving his draft notice, he was inducted on December 11, 1951. When he passed his physical at the old Army Base in South Boston, he, with forty other draftees, were ushered into a large room. Each of them was shown a 4 x 5 card listing the branches of the armed services. A Marine sergeant in dress blues told them that it made no difference what service they checked off, they were going into the Marines anyway. Further complicating the issue, they were also told that the card would accompany them to boot camp at Parris Island, and "if we checked off anything other than the USMC, our asses would be shit." It was only later than he learned that what they had been told was not exactly correct. They would have gone into whatever service they had chosen.

At Parris Island, he found that he had a real talent with Morse code which enabled him to attend radio school in San Diego. In addition, he fired Expert with the rifle and was promoted to Pfc. right after boot camp.

From radio school, he trained at Camp Pendleton, which included cold weather training for Korea. Before leaving for overseas, he received a wire saying that his father was very ill. He tried to get emergency leave, but was told that it was impossible at that time because his records had already been located aboard ship. When he was told that nothing could be done without the records, "a smart ass master sergeant" said he could get him the leave if he re-enlisted. He did so and was granted the leave to go home. It turned out that his dad was fine.

Returning to Camp Pendleton, he was put on the next ship to Korea. During the period prior to departure, he received his promotion to corporal. He served with the 1st Marine Division in Korea from January 1953 to May 1954, as a radio operator in a radio van. He also commanded five radio jeeps. When offered the chance to go to Quantico, for officer candidate school, he turned it down because it would have meant returning to Korea. Before departing Korea, he participated in the Freedom Exchange of prisoners between North Korea and the United Nations.

Returning from Korea, he spent the rest of his enlistment at Cherry Point, North Carolina.

An interesting occasion was conducting Passover services in 1953 and 1954 on an aircraft carrier with Marines and naval personnel. "The Jewish Welfare Board gave us everything we needed for the services."

While at Cherry Point, he was one of four sergeants who ran the control tower radio station keeping in touch with all aircraft on the eastern seaboard with naval and Marine aviators.

Anti-Semitism raised its ugly head during his time in the Marine Corps. He found quite a bit of it, mostly from southerners, with such statements as, "Where's your horns?" Though he does not attribute the following to anti-Semitic behavior, he had a rather chilling incident in Puerto Rico: "I was attacked by four drunken Marines while I was on guard duty. I was carrying a club rather than any weapons. I knocked out two and the others ran away. I was sent to the brig, where once I explained what happened, I didn't receive any punishment. But the ones I knocked out were given time."

His best friend was Corporal Arthur Goodman, Chicago, "I have tried for all these years to locate him, but have been unable."

Ted had a number of relatives who served in the armed forces: a cousin, Arthur Seronick, was killed on the USS *Whole* while at Pearl Harbor. His uncle, Sidney Seronick, served in the Army Air Corps in World War II; cousin, Richard Seronick, was in the Air Force during the Korean War, and another cousin, Doris Seronick, served in the WAVES from 1953 to 1956.

Ted Sklaver is a product of a very religious family. His father "knew the Torah backwards and forward and could leave his seat in *shul* and come back and know just where they were reading. I never got that good. I was bar mitzvahed on April 1, 1943, at the Fesseden Street Synagogue, Dorchester, Mass."

On one occasion he was placed in charge of two radio jeeps traveling from Cherry Point to Morehead City, N.C. with a convoy of trucks taking troops to ships. He caught pneumonia and spent several months in hospital at Camp Lejeune. Weakened lungs resulted from which he never fully recovered. However, he did not complain about it. As a result, his medical records showed that he was fine at the time of his release from active duty.

Confusion reigned one day in Korea when his records were misplaced. Instead of going to battalion radio telegraph, he was sent to 4.2 Mortar Company as radio man. One of his tasks was to carry a roll of wire on his back, plus a telephone to replace broken lines to the outposts.

One day, he had to walk several miles checking wire for breaks. While he was walking north to the observation post, he heard a creaking noise to his rear and saw a tank coming towards him. He had to turn down their offer of a ride because he would not be able to see the wire on the ground. Often, it was covered with dirt. Just after they passed, the North Koreans opened up with the 78 howitzers at the tank. One round overshot the tank and blew Ted into the air. It knocked him out. When he came to, he found neither a wound nor any type of injury: just a terrific headache which soon passed. His watch was broken and the tank was gone. He finally found the break in the wire, repaired it, and then returned to base.

Another time in 1953, he was at Freedom Bridge with a colonel. When they arrived at the DMZ, they found all kinds of American weapons which had been sent to China. Ted took a number of photographs, but when he got back to his base, the film was confiscated and never returned.

Another incident, this time somewhat gruesome, took place shortly before the truce. While patrolling near the outpost, Ted saw and took pictures of three Marines—crucified on crosses. There were a number of Russian officers near them. Sklaver took pictures of the scene and the Russians. Somehow, however, G-2 learned of what had occurred and confiscated the film. Subsequently, he heard nothing of the film nor of the Russians.

His Marine Corps career concluded in 1954. His enjoyed his entire career in the Corps, and "would have stayed in for twenty years, but my wife was against it. She won."

Murray Moskowitz

The fact that Murray Moskowitz was drafted did not reflect at all on his bearing and his pride in his service in the Marine Corps.

Born in 1930 in Canarsie, Brooklyn, New York, he graduated from Tilden High School in June 1948, worked for a couple of years, then was drafted in October 1951.

Boot camp at Parris Island was "pretty tough. Highly disciplined. Most of the men from New York drafted from my hometown, Brooklyn. Two of my DIs were from New York. Good training."

Following boot camp, Murray was sent to Camp Pendleton and attached to a machine-gun section, with I Company, 2nd Battalion, 1st Infantry Training Regiment. The training lasted approximately three and a half months.

As with most of us, Moskowitz was then shipped to Korea to join the 1st Marine Division. He was attached to the 1st Marines, where his unit was heavily engaged in combat action near the 38th Parallel. As a result of his participation, he was severely wounded in both legs, and nearly lost his life.

The people whom he most admired in the Marine Corps were the corpsmen. "They were the best. If not for them, matters could've been worse."

PART VIII

The Longest War

Chapter 32

Vietnam (Introduction)

While the origins of the Vietnam War, and, in particular, the American involvement in Southeast Asia go much further, we can articulate that it commences with the division of that country into two entities: the North and the South.

That division, at least in terms of modern times, had its beginnings in the Japanese surrender agreement signed aboard the USS *Missouri* in Tokyo Harbor on September 2, 1945, thus effectively bringing that world conflagration to its conclusion. This agreement called for the Chinese Nationalists to receive the surrender of Japanese forces north of the 16ᵗʰ Parallel, and British forces, south of that line.

Some French units were allowed in the South as a courtesy. The French built up their forces until they regained control of the South, and, by agreement with the Chinese Nationalists, replaced them in the North. Control of the entire country, which the French accomplished, was resisted by the Communist North Vietnamese. The French Indochinese War began (Ho Chi Minh [1890?–1969], president of North Vietnam 1954–1969, had already proclaimed the Communist Republic of Vietnam in the North on September 2, 1945.

The eight-year French Indochinese War started with French forces of 20,000 men, gradually increasing to 150,000 by 1949, along with about 100,000 loyal Vietnamese troops. The North

Vietnamese Communists entered the war with 50,000 troops, a number which increased to 250,000 by war's end—all under the command of General Vo Nguyen Giap (who also commanded all North Vietnamese armed forces throughout the Vietnam War).

The French Indochinese War ended in 1954 when Dien Bien Phu, a village in North Vietnam near the Laotian border, defended initially by 16,000 French troops, surrendered to Giap's 50,000 guerrillas after a 56-day battle. A cease-fire agreement was signed in Geneva, Switzerland, on July 21, 1954. This agreement gave North Vietnam (the Democratic Republic of Vietnam), under Communist Ho Chi Minh, all of Vietnam north of the Ben Hai River (roughly at the 17 Parallel) and superimposed a demilitarized zone (DMZ) over the partition line.

By the end of the following year, South Vietnam (the Republic of Vietnam) was controlled by a dictator, President Ngo Dinh Diem, who came to power by means of a rigged plebiscite held in 1955.

Thus, the stage was set for war as the North exhibited warlike intentions of conquest of the entire country. The United States believed that its interests would be best served if the South were supported militarily to discourage the Communist expansion southward.

To that end, President Harry S. Truman (1884–1972) ordered the establishment in South Vietnam of the U.S. Military Assistance Advisory Group (USMAAG, also known as MAAG), in mid-1950. Thus began the U.S. involvement in Vietnam that escalated into the Vietnam War, our Longest War.

With a constant building of forces came the incident known as The Gulf of Tonkin Incident. Amid the ominous building of forces among both sides, two U.S. destroyers, the USS *Maddox* and USS *C. Turner Joy*, cruising off the coast of North Vietnam in the Gulf of Tonkin on August 4, 1964, were reportedly attacked by North Vietnamese gunboats. President Lyndon B. Johnson (1908–73) and Congress used the incident to pass the Gulf of Tonkin Resolution which was tantamount to a declaration of war.

It has never been established conclusively whether the attack on the U.S. warships occurred at all. It has always been regarded with suspicion. *New York Times* correspondent David Halbertstam reported that when President was asked months later what had actually happened in the Gulf of Tonkin on August 4, 1964, Johnson replied with a grin: "For all I know, our Navy was shooting at whales out there."

Large-scale American involvement soon followed with a gradual increase in the number of American troops. Serious Marine participation commenced with the landing of two reinforced battalions from the 9th Marine Expeditionary Brigade, under Brigadier General Raymond G. Davis, USMC, commanding, at DaNang, near the coast of the South China Sea, about one hundred miles south of the North-South dividing line. This was the first U.S. ground combat unit in Vietnam. There had been some 23,500 servicemen (mostly U.S. Army troops) in Vietnam, but only in an advisory capacity.

The war continued into early 1972, with the forces of the North gradually pushing the opposition more and more to the south. Peace negotiations were afoot.

On December 30, 1972, it was announced that peace talks would resume between U.S. statesman Henry Kissinger (who would later become Secretary of State 1973–77 and win a Nobel Peace Prize in 1973) and his counterpart, Le Duc Tho. The bombing halted. After twenty-four rounds of talks in forty-two months, the formal end of the war was proclaimed by both sides, and a cease-fire agreement was signed in January 1973.

On April 30, 1975, South Vietnamese General Guong Van Minh surrendered Saigon to the Northern Communist armed forces. The war was finally over. American forces had reached a half-million men in the mid-1960s; they had suffered over 58,000 dead and over 300,000 wounded.

Howard Blum

When Howard Blum approached the base gates to MCRD, Parris Island, there was already excitement in the air. "Several of us even started to sing 'The Marines' Hymn and we were thrilled being there." However, "that feeling immediately ceased when the bus came to a stop and three drill instructors rushed on board to welcome us in the traditional fashion: yelling orders to shut up, get off the bus, stand on the yellow foot marks, and don't move. We were no longer free to choose what to do—we were told what to do and how to do it. For ten weeks we were trained, pushed to our physical limits, harassed, screamed at, poked, hit, and molded into Marines. It was during the Vietnam War, and our training was certainly appropriate for the times."

At graduation from recruit training, Blum was in his best physical condition, after losing four inches from his waist and about thirty-five pounds. His graduation was attended by his parents, brother, and sister.

Following three weeks of leave, he was assigned to Camp Lejeune, only to depart for Camp Pendleton for additional training. As Blum had always worked in retail sales, printing, and advertising, he was, "of course, given MOS 1811, as a tank crewman."

After completing tank training, he received orders for WestPac (Western Pacific theater of operations), which meant Vietnam. Then, for another month, he received additional training in jungle warfare.

Arriving in Okinawa, he was assigned to A Company, 5th Tank Battalion, a small unit with about three officers, five NCOs, and six enlisted ranks private first class or below. He quickly learned that "the unit was formed to teach flame tank operations because there were numerous flame tanks in Vietnam" and not many tankers had been trained to operate them. By the end of May 1967, the unit was increased to over 130 men. As they prepared to go to Japan for additional training, another group of about fifteen, including Blum, was chosen for Vietnam.

Upon his arrival there, Blum was assigned to the Flame section, A Company, 3rd Tank Battalion, at Dong Ha in I Corps. His unit operated in Quang Tri Province (Dong Ha, Cam Lo, and Con Thien area). Blum was a driver and gunner. He was soon assigned as a tank commander of a flame tank and had to train a new crew. During Operation BUFFALO, his tank was fired upon by antitank rockets. It returned fire with their main gun and wiped out the attackers, whereupon the crew named their tank "'The Cremator' . . . and it received appropriate recognition," said Blum. "As I approached the end of my tour, I was training others in flame operation." Blum was wounded in action at Con Thien on July 7, 1967.

Upon his return to the States on February 17, 1968, he was assigned to the Track Vehicle School at Quantico. When riots broke out that month in Washington, D.C., he was assigned to riot-control activities there.

Following his military service, he attended and was graduated from American University, Washington, D.C., with a certificate, associate, and a bachelor of science degree. He also completed all course work for a master of science degree.

As a member of the Metropolitan Police Department of Washington, D.C, Blum graduated number one in his cadet class and received a college scholarship. His assignments have included patrol functions, tactical operations, and vice and criminal investigations. He was a detective for eighteen years, after which he retired as a sergeant in 1991 after twenty-one years of service. In addition to over sixty commendations, he was honored as Officer of the Month and Outstanding Veteran 1978.

After retirement from the police department, Blum stayed in the security and law enforcement field. He is currently (2001) Chief of the Security Services Division for the Smithsonian Institution and responsible for their criminal investigations, security escort services, and personnel security.

Stewart Burr

Private First Class Stewart S. Burr of Passaic, New Jersey, was a member of the high-school track and cross-country team at Passaic High School. He had attended college for two years when he decided to enlist in the U.S. Marine Corps. He was killed in action in Vietnam on April 23, 1969, while his company was attempting to reinforce a nearby unit that had become heavily engaged with the enemy near Cam Lo.

Burr was serving as a rifleman with E Company, 2nd Battalion, 9th Marines, when his squad came under fire from automatic weapons and mortars in a well-entrenched bunker complex. Burr and his squad engaged the enemy by firing into the bunkers until the Marines' supply of ammunition was nearly exhausted.

Burr volunteered to gather more ammunition from an adjacent Marine squad which was in place in an open field between them and the enemy troops. Fearlessly, Burr, using his skill of high-school track and cross-country, dashed across the fire-swept terrain and succeeded in obtaining the ammunition that his unit so desperately needed. Returning with the supply of machine-gun ammunition, he was wounded by enemy fire. Despite the pain of his wounds, he reached his unit and, as he arrived with the ammunition, was mortally wounded by grenade fragments.

He was awarded the Silver Star Medal posthumously. The citation summed up Burr's intrepid deeds that day:

"His heroic and timely actions inspired all who observed him and contributed significantly to the accomplishment of the unit's mission. By his courage, bold initiative, and unwavering devotion to duty, Private First Class Burr maintained the highest traditions of the United States Naval Service. He gallantly gave his life for his country."

At a ceremony held at Passaic City Hall, his family received the Silver Star Medal. Burr was also the recipient of the Purple

Heart, the National Defense Service Medal, the Vietnam Service Medal, and the Republic of Vietnam Campaign Medal.

Neil M. Cohen

New York native Neil Cohen joined the Marine Corps in late 1960 and went to recruit training at Parris Island. "After a while," Cohen said, "I saw what the Corps was trying to do. We went in as individuals and came out as a team, and for that it was a good thing." Following recruit training, he went to Camp Lejeune for advanced infantry training and eventually wound up with several MOSs in communications and motor transport. He then joined the 3rd Marine Division at Camp Pendleton.

While he was stationed on Okinawa around the end of 1960, there were rumors going around the possibility of being sent to Vietnam. They became a reality in 1963. "In the Mekong Delta, every insect and bug and snake and croc were there. If it wasn't very hot, then it was raining. We were there for three months."

Following Vietnam, he returned to Okinawa and then got shipped back to Camp Lejeune. Between those times, he went on operations in the Philippines, Laos, Taiwan, Thailand, and Japan. In 1963, his unit was sent to the waters off Cuba.

Cohen stayed in the Marine Corps until February 1964, when he was honorably discharged as a corporal and received two Good Conduct Medals and a campaign ribbon for Vietnam.

He added, "By the way, I was born on November 10, 1960, and used to cut the cake for the Marine Corps birthday. I believe I will always be a Marine."

Allen E. Falk

Allen Falk of Glen Rock, New Jersey, expressed the sentiments that the military "gave me maturity, discipline, pride, and self-confidence." He was proud to have served in the military. "It made me a much wiser and better person." It also gave him a sense of meaningful service. Having joined the Marine Corps as an enlisted man with the rank of Pfc., Falk became a second lieutenant and finally a member of the Marine Corps Judge Advocate Division after graduation from Rutgers Law School (New Jersey).

Captain Falk was a Staff Legal Officer with the 1st Marine Division in the I Corps area of Vietnam from 1969 to 1970. As a new military lawyer, he was given three first-degree murder cases to handle. All his combat, however, was not in the courtroom— he was occasionally under mortar, sniper, and rocket fire. One of his most unnerving experiences was during a rocket attack in which he was forced to dive into a ditch containing black water and dead rats. His most difficult, or distasteful, assignment was that of President of Special Courts-Martial involving desertion cases at Camp Pendleton.

Among his most memorable times was an occasion after Basic School: Answering the call for "All Jews," he was sent to High Holy Days services at Fort Belvoir. Out of this led to his acquiring the nickname of "Moishe" and became the butt of a few slightly off-color remarks. Other than these innocuous comments, he experienced little anti-Semitism.

His principal assignment while in Vietnam in the 1st Marine Division, I Corps, 1969–70, was as Captain, JAG officer, 3/27/ 9th Marines. He also served as Battalion OD checking positions and manning the battalion headquarters, during which time he was the occasional target of enemy shelling, rocket, mortar, and sniper fire.

His service to his country did not cease with the expiration of his military obligations. Returning to civilian life, he served for eight years at Chairman of the New Jersey Orange Commission, and as consultant to the Veterans Administration Advisory Committee on the effects of herbicides.

Ben J. Johnson

Upon his return from Vietnam, Ben Johnson of Waco, Texas, felt that "the way I was treated was if I had done a terrible wrong instead of serving my country." He was proud to have served his country and community.

Johnson volunteered for the draft in Osceola, Iowa, and reported to MCRD, San Diego, for recruit training. He completed advanced infantry training at Camp Pendleton, after which he was assigned to mechanics school. Although then qualified as a mechanic, he never held a job in the Marine Corps in that field; he was always assigned as a rifleman. He completed two tours of duty in Vietnam, the first from September 1966 to October 1967; the second, for ten months in 1970." "Vietnam was a bitch. Would have stayed in, and yes, I would do it again."

In 1966, Johnson helped building the fortification of Khe Sahn, and in 1970, he was there once again to turn it over to the South Vietnamese Army (SVA). In September 1966, he performed security duty on convoys as an automatic rifleman, radioman, and, on various vehicles, riding shotgun. In April 1967, he was injured by a box mine and suffered wounds to his right knee. In April and May 1967, on Hill 881, at Khe Sahn, he was under constant mortar, rocket, and artillery fire from the North Vietnamese Army (NVA). At Marble Mountain Air Facility, he was wounded by shrapnel in the right forearm. On August 28, 1967, six men in his squad were killed in a heavy mortar and rocket attack. He was promoted to lance corporal in September 1967, went on R & R (rest and recreation) to Japan the same month, and was rotated back to the States the following months. While in Vietnam, he was assigned to Phu Bai, Heu, Quang Tri, Monkey Mountain, Hill 881, Dong Ha, Khe Sanh, Ky Ha, and "other places I cannot remember."

In 1970, Johnson transferred to the 9th Engineer Battalion, Chu Lai, as a reactionary platoon sergeant; then to the 7th Engineer Battalion, Da Nang; 3rd Battalion, 7th Marines, Security NCOIC for Subsection C, Da Nang; and duty as an Embarkation NCO.

His studies included Marine Corps NCO School, 1968, and Military Functions in Civil Disaster Disturbance School. Johnson received the Purple Heart, the Combat Action Ribbon, the Good Conduct Medal, the Vietnamese Service Medal with three bronze stars, and the Republic of Vietnam Campaign Medal. He was also awarded a meritorious mast.

After leaving the Marine Corps, Johnson served in the Texas National Guard from 1974 to 1976 with the rank of E-4. He was a tank commander with the 12th Cavalry.

Gerry Newhouse

In 1964, when Gerry Newhouse of Dayton, Ohio, told his parents, Orthodox Jews, that he had enlisted in the Marine Corps, they "were understandably upset." However, their disappointment was somewhat assuaged when he promised he "will go to college when I get out of the service . . ."

Near the end of recruit training at MCRD, San Diego, Newhouse was able to attend services at the nearby Naval Training Center. There were sailors and other Marine recruits from MCRD at the services. Attending Jewish services was a real treat, as the Jewish chaplain let those of us who smoked light up as much as we wanted. In addition, we had great food and a glass of wine. When I told the other guys in my platoon, they all wanted to convert."

Newhouse left San Diego for infantry training at Camp

Pendleton.

Sent to Okinawa after training as field radio operator/forward observer for 81mm mortars, he soon underwent jungle training. Six weeks into training, the war heated up in Vietnam. As he was close to that area, he was soon on his way to "Nam." He made the landing on Red Beach, near Da Nang, with the 2nd Battalion, 9th Marine Expeditionary Brigade, 3rd Marine Division. As it happened, there was a Catholic chaplain aboard Newhouse's landing craft who led a prayer for the gentiles. When Newhouse told the chaplain he was Jewish, "he looked surprised, then smiled, and recited the *Shma*. I felt much better."

Newhouse continued to run into that chaplain while in combat in Vietnam. "He always made a point of telling me something encouraging. On one occasion, I was coming off a night ambush that had gone terribly wrong. Several of our guys were severely wounded. I returned to camp covered in blood from one of the guys I helped carry to the medivac chopper. The chaplain came running over and said, "Newhouse, get cleaned up, you're going to Da Nang Air Base for Passover services." Newhouse had not realized it was Passover. His two days at Da Nang "were wonderful, hot showers, great food, and I was able to call my parents at the MARS (a telephone-radio link for overseas calls) relay station. Sometime later, I learned the chaplain was killed. He was a good guy. I wish I could remember his name." Newhouse remained in Vietnam for eleven-and-a-half months, was promoted to lance corporal, and left for home on Friday the 13th of May 1966. It was ironic that the man who replaced him was another Jewish-American Marine named Levine.

Returning home on a thirty-day leave, he met his future wife at the Dayton Jewish Community Center swimming pool. He spent his last year in the Corps as a training NCO at Camp Lejeune, North Carolina. Following his honorable discharge in August 1967, he went to college-as he had promised his parents—earning two degrees from Ohio State University in Columbus.

Recalling his times in the Marine Corps, Newhouse summed it all up with, "Thinking back on both the good times and bad, I believe my Marine years made me a better person. Once a Marine, always a Marine."

Berl (Bo) Olswanger, Jr.

"Upon completion of OCS when they pinned the gold bars on my collars, that was the proudest moment of my life. It was something I earned," stated Bo Olswanger.

OCS was the most difficult challenge of his life. While "hell week" for the fraternity in college was rough, "OCS was a real shocker. Almost fifty percent of the candidates washed out," he said. In praise of the Marine Corps, he wrote: "I don't think any training, especially officer training, is as good or tough as the Marines. I can say this because I've seen the Army's best and the Marines' best."

He encountered only one incident of anti-Semitism—and even that was a contradiction.

During Basic School, a friend whom he had known for several months "discovered" that he was a Jew. "He was from Texas and for some reason hated Jews. He constantly made smart remarks, like sitting in class and hollering 'Jew,' etc. After a month or so, I could see ignoring him wouldn't work, so I knocked the dog shit out of him. No more problems after.that."

Bo was sent to Vietnam as a second lieutenant platoon leader and civil affairs officer. He found Da Nang and Hue City to be interesting, but the "worst were the villages that had been devastated." His last six months in Vietnam were spent as Civil Affairs Officer, which enabled him to have a pass to anywhere, anytime, no questions asked.

He was wounded in combat, for which he received the Purple Heart Medal. He also received the combat action ribbon, Vietnamese Staff Service Honor Medal, "and all the others that came with deployment."

One aspect of the military that he enjoyed was making new

friends and seeing other cultures and countries, and making a positive difference in the lives of other people. While he had little or no respect for many of his superior officers, one exception was his regimental commander, P. X. Kelley, later to become the 28th Commandant of the Marine Corps. "He knew I was a green lieutenant and took care of me (and others like me). He was brilliant, caring, innovative, and knew how to handle all situations."

Fifteen years after leaving active duty with the Marine Corps as a captain, Bo joined the Army Reserve, and is now (2001) a lieutenant colonel, Civil Affairs Officer. His unit was deployed to Bosnia, where he spent nine months on active duty.

Barry A. Rice

Despite being misled into signing up for the Marine Corps under a guaranteed assignment of an aviation certificate, Barry Rice of Buena Park, California, completed two of a four-year hitch and volunteered for Vietnam as a member of the 11th Engineer Battalion, 3rd Marine Division, in the Northern I Corps sector.

On the way to recruit training at MCRD, San Diego, as a 17-year-old, he came in for a surprise—he learned that basic training time had changed from sixteen weeks to eight. Going into the Corps at 125 pounds, he completed recruit training at 165 pounds, a "lean, green, fighting machine."

During recruit training, the DIs were unusually hard on the members of his platoon because they insisted that theirs was going to be the best platoon and would not settle for anything else.

Rice was assigned the MOS of 1345, heavy equipment operator, with a secondary MOS of 0351, machine gunner, after completion of recruit training. He then shipped to Camp Lejeune for schooling, where he was stationed for several months in a maintenance company, 2nd Marine Division. Before long, he became dissatisfied with the constant harassments and inspections. Shortly after turning 18, Rice—along with his buddy John Kepler—decided to get out of there by volunteering for Vietnam.

Assigned to the 11th Engineer Battalion, 3rd Marine Division, they were given the tasks of digging bunkers, clearing and constructing roads, going out with the infantry to clear paths, cutting mass graves, deploying in base defense, or acting as infantry with units that were shorthanded. In addition, Rice was dropped on hilltops by helicopter to cut landing zones and fire-support bases. He belonged to an elite unit of five men who took on various kinds of what he termed "suicide missions." He felt that he did not have much to return to and preferred to take on those hazardous missions in place of those with wives and children.

During his time in Vietnam, Rice participated in about sixteen firefights, most of the time employing his M60 machine gun. In one such fight, he was on a forward command and logistics base called Vandegrift or LZ Stud when the fire-support base was targeted by the NVA. The personnel consisted of one officer, four NCOs, equipment operators, truck drivers, welders, and mechanics. With orders to hold the position "at all costs," they held the base against an elite sapper regiment with supporting Vietcong (VC) companies. "During the all-night fight we lost one officer, NCOs, and communications in the first few minutes, and only five of us walked out the next morning when a mechanized unit came in to relieve us." Rice remembers that the day was May 9, 1969.

On another occasion, Rice was dropped onto a ridge that had been sprayed with Agent Orange. As a result, today he is in constant pain from peripheral neuropathy.

On Memorial Day 1999 and 2000, he participated in the Run for the Wall, when veterans make a yearly pilgrimage from California to Washington, D.C., to memorialize the KIAs, POWs and MIAs still unaccounted for.

Sidney S. Rubinstein

Both parents of Sidney Rubinstein were in the Army during World War II—his mother, a nurse, was stationed at Camp Blanding, Florida, for the duration of the war; his father served on Guadalcanal and in the Philippines. Rubinstein's brother was in the Air Force; his brother-in-law, in the Army. Almost of all his uncles and cousins have served in every branch of service except the Marine Corps.

Born November 2, 1946, in Dania, Florida, Rubinstein enlisted in the Marine Corps in August 1966. "After talking to all the other military recruiters, I realized the Marine was the only one who did not lie (exaggerated) to get me to sign up. He said he could only guarantee me one meal and two hours of sleep a day. And we learned later he wasn't too far off."

Sidney Rubinstein found another Rubinstein at recruit training at Parris Island—a DI gunnery sergeant who hailed from West Virginia. "He was a career Marine, having served in World War II, Korea, and Vietnam . . . he said to me as he was screaming at me, going up and down the other, 'This Marine Corps is not big enough for two Rubinsteins.'"

Sidney Rubinstein continued on to infantry training at Camp Lejeune. He was then transferred to Camp Pendleton for a three-month course as a mechanic on LVTP-5 amphibian tractors, after which he shipped out to Vietnam, with a stop in Okinawa.

He was then transferred to the 3rd Amphibian Tractor Battalion, 1st Marine Division. At first, he was sent to 2nd Battalion, 5th Marines, in a combat zone and later assigned to the 1st Amphibian Tractor Battalion near the DMZ. Things were rather quiet and uneventful until he was assigned to a platoon. The battalion moved from Hill 34 to Marble Mountain on the South China Sea. Then came the Tet offensive.

Rubinstein was on a lead vehicle carrying men and supplies when "we ran over a command-detonated land mine. Luckily, no one was hurt. On the second amtrac in the column was my buddy Ralph. He ran over a mine and wasn't as lucky. All the guys on his amtrac died from the explosion or from burns." Following Tet, except for occasional incoming mortars or rockets, things were pretty quiet. Rubinstein took R & R in Hong Kong and went to Australia "when no one else wanted to go there."

On the occasion of the *Pueblo* incident, his unit was alerted to the possibility of intervening in that operation. Later, upon termination of his tour of duty in Vietnam, he went to Okinawa and then was transferred to MCAS, El Toro. At Okinawa, "Whom do you believe I bump into? Master Sergeant Rubinstein on his way back to Vietnam for another tour. We had lunch together and talked. He asked me if I was going to stay in, and I told him I remembered words of wisdom someone told me once: 'This Marine Corps is not big enough for two Rubinsteins.' We had a good laugh after that. We stayed in touch for many years until his death after retirement."

Sidney Rubinstein was awarded the Combat Action Ribbon, the Presidential Unit Citation, Navy Unit Citation, National Defense Service Medal, the Vietnam Service Medal, and the Vietnam Presidential Unit Citation.

He left the Marine Corps as a lance corporal, and currently (2001) resides in Hollywood, Florida.

Aaron Zeff

Aaron Zeff's first mistake was striking a captain during the first week of recruit training; his punishment, thirty days at hard labor. That incident, as he puts it, changed his life, and from then on, "I walked the straight and narrow."

Zeff was appointed platoon guide. Knowing that he liked Hershey's chocolate bars, his mother began sending them enclosed in letters. His DIs had some fun with him on that. Zeff was allowed to keep the chocolate bars, provided he would share them with the other recruits. "There were eighty of us and making that chocolate stretch wasn't easy. One wasn't too bad. But my mother kept sending this stuff until she received my letters pleading for the supply of chocolate to stop. For me and most of us, graduation and really becoming a Marine was the Good."

After Parris Island, Zeff was transferred to Camp Geiger, a part of Camp Lejeune, where he was assigned MOS 0351 machine gunner, rockets, flame thrower, plus 106 recoilless rifle.

Now with the 1st Battalion, 6th Marines, at Camp Lejeune, he was assigned to a weapons platoon. He was aboard ship for a Caribbean and a Mediterranean cruise. His numerous requests for transfer to Vietnam were turned down. In disgust, Zeff went AWOL (absent without leave) for ten days. Returning to camp, his captain told him, "Turn in your gear, pack, you are going to Vietnam." He continued with, "You better be off this base by noon" or he would court-martial him. With that, Zeff said, "I got my wish and was very happy."

Next stop, 1st Battalion, 4th Marines, Vietnam, where he was assigned to Weapons Platoon, D Company. His platoon was located below the DMZ in a number of places-Con Thien, the Rockpile, Camp Carroll, and the A Shau Valley. Zeff's principal weapon was the M-16 rifle, and later he crewed on the 106mm recoilless rifle. He was still a private after two and a half years in the Marines. However, the squad leader kept breaking his own glasses deliberately and failed to take patrols out. As a result, Zeff's platoon sergeant asked him if he wanted to take a patrol out, which was exactly what Zeff wanted. After all, "This is why I wanted to be a Marine. I was a Pfc. thirty days later and, by the time I left Vietnam thirteen months later, I was an E-5 sergeant. I had finally found my place in the Marines, a place that would never go away."

Zeff remembers when he and his unit were on a hill when the CO sent a patrol to get water at a stream at the bottom of the hill. The patrol came under attack and called for help. Zeff, now the platoon sergeant, the platoon commander, and a number of others moved the 106s to more effective locations. Once, under fire, they spotted for them and drew incoming fire. They employed every round of ammunition, including .50-caliber spotting ammo. After the attack on the patrol ended, each member stopped and hugged Zeff for helping them.

On the occasion of a week-long patrol in Vietnam, Zeff and his comrades ran out of food. After a while, they saw several helicopters approaching with nets strung underneath and they knew that food was on the way. It was food all right—raw onions. They had a feast.

In Vietnam, particularly when troops were in the rear, they had to "burn the shitters"—field toilets called "heads," and other names—cut from 55-gallon drums that would ignite when someone threw in kerosene, lit them, and stirred. "I was asked to send a work party of two Marines to burn the battalion commander's 'shitter.' No problem. I send the two guys and get on with my business. A few minutes later, someone comes running up to me and says I better get down to the battalion commander's 'shitter.' My work party burned the 'shitters' without taking them out of the outhouse. They burned it down. I got to fill sandbags for two days as punishment."

Zeff returned to the States to the 6th Marines and was ultimately discharged from active duty. Upon graduating from the University of Pittsburgh, he reenlisted in the Marine Corps, attended OCS at Quantico, and graduated as a second lieutenant, returned to the 6th Marines, Headquarters Company, stayed a year, and was then discharged.

Paul Zonderman

Paul Zonderman's father was a World War II Army veteran, and his grandfather served during the Spanish-American War.

Zonderman served as a legal officer in the Marines. He completed the Platoon Leaders Program-Law in 1962 and was commissioned a second lieutenant, following which his request to enter and complete law school was granted. With that, he entered the Reserve and received his law degree in June 1964. Now married, he started his three years of active duty commencing in January 1965 as a first lieutenant. After six months at The Basic School in Quantico, he received the MOS of 4405, Trial/ Defense Counsel. Following a brief orientation at the Naval Justice School at Newport, Rhode Island, he reported to Marine Corps Base, Twentynine Palms where he was promoted to captain.

Duties as legal officer in Vietnam provided no immunity to enemy fire. Assigned to I Corps, first in Da Nang, then in Phu Bai, Zonderman served with the Division Legal Office, 3rd Marine Division. There were occasions "when I was lying on my face in the mud of our bunker and incoming mortar rounds were exploding all around us."

Zonderman's awards and citations include the Presidential Unit Citation, the National Defense Service Medal, the Vietnam Service Medal with two bronze stars, the Republic of Vietnam Gallantry Cross with Palm Unit Citation, and the Republic of Vietnam Campaign Medal.

Having completed his tour of duty in Vietnam and his active duty service obligation simultaneously, he spent a few days in a California hospital while being checked out. In December, 1967, he returned home to Boston, his wife, and his 6-month daughter whom he had never seen.

PART IX

Eagles

Chapter 33

Avenger

Prior to graduating from Boston University, Alvin Clark enlisted as a seaman second class at NAS, Squantum. As such, he was allowed to skip final exams and graduated shortly thereafter. Upon completing ten hours of flight time without a mishap, he qualified as a Naval Aviation cadet and was transferred to NAS, Jacksonville, Florida, where he combined his seven months of flight training with athletics. He had been on the varsity football team at Boston University and continued playing football for the air station team. He became a Naval Aviator in January 1942, was commissioned a second lieutenant in the Marine Corps Reserve, and spent six months at El Toro.

Once, during an interview with a squadron flight surgeon, the doctor apologized to Clark "for having Semitic features and that my name could be Jewish (Brenner), but *I* certainly am *not*." Al clasped his hand *firmly* and told him in no uncertain terms that "*I* was despite the looks and the name. I thought he would drop dead! I then threatened him with a court-martial for any future remarks."

After carrier landing training at Miami, Florida, Clark received orders to an active-duty squadron of dive bombers, VMSB-131, San Diego, then off to MAB, Ewa, ten miles west of Pearl Harbor, where he picked up the new torpedo bomber,

Grumman TBF Avenger. Once trained in the new Avenger, he was shipped to the South Pacific with rank of first lieutenant.

His first station was Espiritu Santo, then back and forth to Guadalcanal, back to the States for a few months, became captain, then again to the Marshall Islands, Eniwetok, and Guam for antisubmarine patrol. From the end of 1944, now with the rank of major, through the middle of 1945, he was a member of VMTB-242 on Tinian and Saipan in the Marianas, and on Iwo Jima. During this time, he was engaged almost continually in combat flying, bombing Japanese positions and on antisubmarine patrols. Once, while flying antisub patrol south of Guam, he aided in capturing six Japanese aviation specialists on board a raft. He summoned a Navy minesweeper in the area and had the opportunity of witnessing the capture. Later, at Naval Intelligence, he met the senior Japanese being interrogated. "He didn't enjoy meeting me."

Clark related: "During a Jap air attack on Guadalcanal in 1942, the siren sounded, Condition Red, hit your foxhole! Someone yelled from Headquarters that it was only 'friendly aircraft,' whereupon (someone) yelled back to the former to ask 'if those friendly planes were dropping friendly bombs' (as they detonated on Henderson Field). This sort of humor kept one's mind stable."

Later, one dark night half-asleep in bivouac area, I saw a form sneaking from tent to tent. Thinking it was a Jap, I pulled my .45 from under my pillow (two weeks before, Japs blew up a nearby tent and killed several pilots). 'Who goes there?' The very scared voice said, 'It's me, Tom Reese' (a fellow pilot with dysentery). He was headed for the latrine. Obviously, he didn't make it.

Although released from active duty in 1946, Clark remained in the Reserve as a pilot, giving him the opportunity to right a wrong that had been in force all the previous years—the Reservists must spend a minimum of thirty days on active duty to be eligible for compensation or hospital care in a U.S. government facility. While on his annual two-week Reserve duty flying Corsairs at Cherry Point, he and his pilots were making routine landings after bombing practice. One of the pilots, George Finnegan, from Jamaica Plain, Massachusetts, flipped over, the cockpit cover pinning his arm to the runway. Arriving at the scene, the doctor determined that unless the mangled forearm was amputated, gangrene would set in and cause his death. Finnegan told the doctor to get permission from Major Clark, CO of Squadron 235. As he says, "I need not tell you this was the toughest decision of my life, considering the fact that Finnegan was a commercial pilot with Eastern Airlines." The doctor, Finnegan, and Clark agreed upon the amputation. "The ordeal was further magnified when we were told that because it happened in a time period less than the required thirty days, Finnegan would have to be hospitalized and treated in the Merchant Marine Hospital in Brighton, Massachusetts."

Clark was appalled to learn that Finnegan would be ineligible for treatment in a U.S. government hospital and that the government would not be responsible for medical costs. Al continued, "I immediately got on the podium at Cherry Point and told every man just what to expect if they got injured. I got all present to write pronto to John W. McCormack, then Speaker of the House, and, finally, a bill was enacted retroactively covering all branches of the Reserve, full coverage in the event of death or injury while on active or Reserve duty. This was a campaign well worth fighting for."

According to Clark, "I met Jack Kennedy when we were both aspiring politicians—he was running for Congress and I for Massachusetts state senator. Later, I wound up as executor and joint owner of his birthplace with my mother. After my Dad's death, she married Louis Pollock who owned the house at 83 Beale Street, Brookline (designated in 1965 the John Fitzgerald Kennedy National Historic Site), just around the corner from where you (the author) lived."

Major Clark remained in the Active Reserve as Commanding Officer of Squadron 235 based at NAS Squantum, Quincy,

Mass. He was appointed Military Aide serving two governors, Paul Dever and Foster Furcolo. In 1949, he married Evelyn Kravit with whom they had four children, Roseanne, Deborah, Russel, and Peter.

Major Clark is the recipient of four Air Medals.

Chapter 34

Down The Stack

It's hard to imagine a more unlikely place as the origin of a great Jewish-American hero than a small town in Maine, like Caribou, for example. Yet, Abraham "Dan" Daniels was indeed born there in 1917, which, as of the year of our Lord 2002, makes him eighty-five years old, and getting famously and well, thank you. He came from a typical Jewish family of the times, two parents and seven siblings.

Life was simple for the Daniels, even for Caribou. They received water through a piping system, which was a great improvement over the previous well located outside the house. Before they put in a real inside toilet, they used an outhouse. As Abe said, "What a break it was to have a toilet inside. It didn't mean a hell of a lot to me. I was young. I didn't know really what it was all about, but for the older people, everybody, my brothers and sisters, my father and mother, it was a lot of talk, a lot of happiness about it."

They had a small farm on which they raised potatoes and a small market in which they carried almost everything imaginable, at least for rural Maine. Their fortune was in the children, certainly not in the income that his father didn't earn. If they made any money at harvest season, his dad would split it with the married couple who cared for the farm. As Abe recalls, there wasn't a lot of money made either from the farm or from the store.

Abe hated school. Due to a speech impediment, the kids would make fun of him. While he participated in sports and other activities, he didn't do much talking. "When I'd get excited, no-one could understand me and they made fun of me."

He, with his mother and two sisters, moved to Montreal when he was six. And he hated Montreal. He couldn't even speak English well, and they were trying to teach him French. But when his father came up to Montreal, sized up the situation, he decided that Montreal was not exactly the right place, they returned right back to Caribou.

Abe liked Caribou very much. Playing with friends, hockey in the winter, ice and horse racing on the river, too. Sulky racing. To Abe, northern Marine was beautiful. "No pollution, your streams and your lakes were as clear as could be. Lots of times when we went fishing, you could see lots of fish. It was beautiful. Very clear."

Later, when things were not turning out too well in Caribou, his dad went to the Dorchester section of Boston and found quite a good-size home. Abe doesn't remember whether he bought it or rented it. Two sisters opened a beauty parlor in the house.

Abe hated the city. He returned to Caribou after his Bar Mitzvah. After graduating from Caribou High School, Abe learned the meat cutting business and butchering. He became an expert in curing and smoking meats. He "could make you ham and bacon as good as any place you could buy it." He also learned how to hunt and trap all sorts of animals. There were many varieties of wild animals, and he was able to trap and skin almost every animal they hunted.

In 1939, Daniels knew that a war was on the horizon, and the United States would soon be involved. He wanted to go into the Marines—bad. He wasn't interested in the Army or the Navy. But, "If I couldn't make the Marines, I would have gone in any one of those. In those days, of all the military forces in the world, the United States Marines were tops. In 1939, there were more policemen in New York City than all the Marines put together, only 16,000, and they were elite men."

After enlisting in Bangor, he went by train to New Bern, North Carolina. Last stop before Parris Island. They were met by a Marine sergeant, who was a veteran of about twenty years of service. "He acted tough and spoke tough. He was built like any male person would want to be built, terrific physique."

Most of his boot camp experience was positive. Although he was smaller in stature than most of the others, it didn't mean that much. He had to compete with the others and he was able to do just that on very good terms.

"The parade grounds or drill grounds was a hell hole. Coming from the North, I had never experienced 105–110 degrees and the humidity was terrible. If one passed out three different times, they didn't want him. They sent him back home. I remember two or three times when I thought I had had it. But I had no place to go. Anyway, boot camp those days was almost four months.

"When I graduated boot camp, a lot of my buddies came over to shake my hand. They didn't think I could make it because of my stature and being a little bit on the frail side. I think I must have weighed about hundred thirty pounds. Many times on our drill, or our march, we had to carry full pack and sometimes I carried anywhere from forty to sixty pounds. Those days we had two blankets, a little tiny pickaxe and shovel, a shelter half, and all the rest of the gear went with it. So sometimes it weighed about fifty pounds. And me being short and not very muscular, it was a laugh to some of the fellows."

Daniels was assigned to Marine Aviation after graduating from boot camp. Despite his pleadings otherwise, and due to the fact that he knew typing and shorthand, he was assigned as company clerk.

Once, while at Quantico, the commanding officer was requested to submit a list of eighteen enlisted men to be selected for pilot training. While typing the list, Daniels wondered why he wasn't there. When Daniels went to the CO and requested to be placed on the list, "He looked at me and laughed and said, 'You're too small, you wouldn't make the grade.'" With that, Daniels told him about boot camp and how he showed everyone who thought he wouldn't make the grade there, either.

Accepted for flight training in May or June of 1941, he was sent to Pensacola, where the enlisted pilots took the same course as the cadets. There, he was in the company of young men who had had at least two years of college. In addition, being cadets, if they didn't make the grade, they could return to civilian life. On the other hand, if Daniels and the other enlisted men washed out, they had to return to their old outfits, "probably hang our heads in shame and our promotions would be stopped for a certain time."

"You could imagine what I went through. Here I was out of high school six years and I had to take aerodynamics, meteorology, engineering, and the whole works, and after six years of not having any schooling it was rough. Whereas these cadets, they all had at least two years of college, some college graduates. Can you imagine me rubbing elbows with a Dartmouth man, a Harvard man, a Yale man, even MIT men?" Abe contrasted his status with those of the Ivy League. He knew that they were smart as hell. Whereas he and the other enlisted candidates worked day and night, they couldn't seem to make the grade at all.

With the outbreak of the war in late 1941, Abe heard the news and was "a little leery like the rest of us. We didn't know just exactly what was going to happen. It was almost a mass confusion right there."

However, Abe did graduate and received his wings in early 1942. After flying and qualifying for many types of planes, he was transferred to San Diego in order to put more time training on the SBD dive-bomber. It was while he was there that he got orders to fly a plane from San Diego to Seattle.

"The plane I had to fly to Seattle was a torpedo bomber. It's a three-place job with a torpedo. It was comparably new in those days to get into the cockpit. They had regular slots like you put the left toe in that slot, the right toe in that slot, and you get into the cockpit. About like stirrups when you're riding a horse. All my equipment before I got into the plane was my parachute and

I also had to have two pads on the back of my back. The reason for that is that I'm so short and my feet are so short I couldn't extend to reach the brakes of the plane.

"So anyway, when I tried to get into the plane, I couldn't reach that first slot and I looked around and the mechanics looked at me and they started laughing, and believe it or not they lifted me into the cockpit. I was hoping no-one would see that but they all laughed and had a good time with it.

"I had my enlisted uniform on with my wings and over that I had the flight suit. The flight suit didn't have any insignia at all, just had the wings. One of the places I had to stop was McLelland Field. That's an Army airbase. I landed and went into the hangar. I had to pee so bad that I had to look out for a head. As you know, the head is another name for the latrine. There is one for the officers and one for the enlisted personnel. Well, I started for the enlisted men's head when a sergeant approached me and said, 'The officers' head is there,' and pointed to where it was. I said, 'Sergeant, I have to go and I don't care where.' He said, 'Didn't you just fly that plane in?' I nodded, and again he directed me to the officers' head. As I said, all I had over my uniform was my flight suit with no emblems or insignias except my gold wings. I then quickly unzipped my shoulder low enough to show my sergeant's stripes on my sleeve.'

"You talk about a confused sergeant. He sure was. Anyway, I barely made it. He didn't know that the Marines had enlisted pilots."

With December 7, 1941, and the American entrance into World War II, Daniels was in San Diego flying SBDs, Douglas Dauntless dive bombers. After a number of weeks, he was assigned to Squadron 144 which arrived on Guadalcanal in December 1942.

"What a hellhole it was. It was very rough on all of us. The temperature was 110–115 and the humidity you couldn't take it. Small boa constrictors, alligators, crocodiles, what they called the jungle rat. And other animals I never seen or heard of before."

But animals were not the only hazard on Guadalcanal. The Japanese were not the only enemies on that island where so many Americans had their baptism of fire. Illness and disease took their toll. "One of the worst things was what we call jungle rot. It was like a fungus that would start from the toes and work all the way up to your body. At that time, they didn't have proper medication to take care of this. However, they soon received supplies to combat it.

"It was nothing for at least fifty percent of the squadron to get malaria. Everybody was taking atabrine or quinine. Malaria out there was very bad. You'd be walking next to a fellow and suddenly he'd keel over. One hundred ten in the shade and we'd have to put him in his bunk, he'd be freezing. We'd put all kinds of blankets on him and after about ten or fifteen minutes, we had to take the blankets off. In those conditions, it was very, very rough."

Daniels noted the contrast between flying in Europe and conditions in the islands. In the former, the personnel found some semblance of civilization. They could return home from a mission, shower, eat, and go out on the town. Not in the islands. Compared to the more civilized conditions, the islands, such as Guadalcanal, were hellholes. Some of the men found the elements and nature worse than the enemy.

On Daniels's first mission, he, with ten or twelve planes, was to bomb enemy bivouac areas. They each carried a one thousand pound bomb, which was all the plane could carry. He encountered his first anti-aircraft fire. He described it: "At a distance those puffs of smoke were beautiful. As they approached us and we approached them, they weren't beautiful any more."

Although they met some fighter opposition, they didn't get close enough to fire on them. His gunner, an eighteen-year old named Riddle, flew for the first time with Daniels. They learned to respect and admire each other.

"We were both so proud. Here we were, a combat team of enlisted personnel. Me, as a tech sergeant, and my gunner as a Pfc. Can you imagine that? A Pfc. flying in combat. Maybe you don't know, but in those days, a Pfc. was the second lowest rank that the Marines had.

"We flew against the enemy many times, sometimes twice a day. Most of our targets were land based in bivouac areas and we received many raids from the enemy. The enemy dropped many bombs on our area. I never thought that I'd love a foxhole.

"After we left, we would scout around to see what damage was done, who got hurt, and tried to get back to normalcy again. It was very hard to take. The Japs in their bombs, they use nuts, bolts, and things of that sort to cut through a person if they ever hit. That part was war, but when we picked up those bolts and nuts and so forth, all were made in the United States. I understand that years before the war the Japs had imported all this material, mainly for this purpose which they had in mind."

Daniels's big day was February 7, 1943. He will never forget it.

"That day there were only fifteen dive bombers available and the few fighters in escort, not many! About two hundred miles from our base I came upon a sight that I'll never forget. There were twenty top notch destroyers that the Japanese had. In addition, there were quite a few Zeros which was their top fighter at the time."

Though the Americans were outnumbered, the bombers managed to select their targets. "It was just like you see in the movies. The anti-aircraft was very, very thick. I still don't know how we managed to get through it. I selected one destroyer for target and followed all their evasive turns all the way down."

Keeping one eye on the leveler and the other on the target, all he thought he could accomplish would be a near miss. This day he was carrying one 500-pound bomb and two 100-pound bombs. He dropped his bombs and the three of them hit the enemy ship midship. He angled his plane and saw that the ship was burning out of control. He put full maximum throttle and veered away.

When he pulled out, he was very low. That was a mistake. He shouldn't have pulled out so low. He was just inches above the water. His gunner yelled that flames from the destroyer were shooting up at them. As a result, he was the only pilot to score a direct hit. All the others got near misses, and, as Daniels says, they don't count. His hit was verified by the other pilots.

Returning to base, he and the gunner felt wonderful. When the news got around, other men came up to them, congratulated them, and shook their hands.

Daniels continued to fly in combat against the Japanese. He contributed to the campaign to drive the enemy off Guadalcanal and the Solomon Islands. "We finally defeated them there and they headed for the great big sea base at Rabaul. I flew one hop against Rabaul. That hop all hell broke loose. Rabaul was a big sea base controlled one hundred percent by the Japanese. Looking down from about 10,000 feet, it reminded me of a miniature Pearl Harbor."

A few weeks after sinking the destroyer, Daniels took part in a vital mission, one in which everyone contributed, even with just one plane left among all those participating. In that mission, his plane conked out, and Daniels doesn't know the reason even to this day.

The mission was over water, and on that day, the waves were particularly rough. His plane hit the water at one hundred five knots. As his plane had but a belly strap instead of a shoulder strap, his waist lurched forward and he hit the telescopic sight, causing his nose to split right down the center, in addition to injuries to his right arm and right eye. He began to bleed like a stuck pig.

Upon hitting the water, the gunner removed the collapsible two-man rubber raft and inflated it right away. Not long after entering the raft, they witnessed four or five sharks, not big, but about three or four feet long. Perhaps it was the smell of Daniels's blood that attracted them.

They started to row to several small islands that they saw sticking up in the water. To the downed airmen, they looked like giants. As Daniels described the situation, "The water was still quite rough and it seemed we weren't making any progress at all.

I couldn't give my gunner much help. I had a feeling of almost throwing up and almost passing out. However, I did not pass out. My gunner was not cut up at all. He was bruised quite badly." After what seemed like an eternity, they made landfall.

Apparently, the men in other planes of his squadron saw Daniels and his gunner go down and made mental notes of the location.

Within a short time, some natives appeared on the scene. "They were gibbering and very excited. They were equipped (I won't use the term 'armed') with darts about three or four times the length of the darts they use in English pubs. They looked like a small arrow. They threw these at various objects without too much accuracy. I believe they used them as a game, as like I said before, people in the pubs."

On seeing Daniels and the gunner, they started to chatter excitedly. Because he was so short, at first they thought he was Japanese.

By then, however, the natives noticed the gunner who was tall and thin. They knew right away that the crewmen were not "Japs." In fact, seeing the gunner, they broke into smiles. "A different look and attitude altogether. They took us to their native village. Two of their members spoke a broken French and a broken English. I say broken because I don't know what the hell it was. They seemed to have a better understanding after a while of what our situation was.

"I was still bleeding, but not very much. I was sick and weak. With my good hand, I put some of the bone fragments on my nose back to the center. Some of them were still on my cheek. One arm was practically useless. My left eye was shut completely and scars all over my forehead.

"While going to their village which wasn't very far—it could be measured in yards—I stopped on the way and started to gather white rocks. After a while we got the natives to help us get those white rocks. I'm sure they thought I was nuts. We picked up the white rocks and against a green background we spelled out the three letters of my name, D A N, in large letters.

"I surmised one of them in that vital mission radioed back to the base where I went down, or approximately where I went down, and I knew if that were the case, someone, somehow, would come out circling or looking for me. Quite a few hours later there was a plane that appeared. We were very, very happy.

They were picked up by a stripped-down PT boat that was used for the rescue of downed pilots. They said good-bye to the natives and boarded the boat. By that time, Daniels's head was "so swelled up you could hardly tell if I was a person or not. You could hardly see any hair at all. My ears were like two pieces of cardboard sticking out."

After considerable efforts to board the boat, the doctor went to work on him. They washed his head and started to clean him up. They laid him on a steel bunk and strapped him in tight, so tight that he couldn't move at all. It was almost as if he were in a straight-jacket. "Later, I found out the reason for it. The moment I was strapped in, they put full throttle on this stripped PT boat. Now you talk about a fast ride, that was it." They didn't want him to move at all.

Entering the harbor of the boat's base, he was transferred immediately to a moored hospital ship. There, Daniels was fortunate enough to be treated by one of the top doctors in the country, an eye, nose, and throat specialist named Dr. Shank. He operated on Daniels right away, stating afterwards that he probably would need at least a couple of other operations.

Although the squadron doctor suggested that the patient be returned to the States, Daniels insisted on staying in the forward area. Instead, he was transferred to the local hospital on the base, where he was able to recuperate and convalesce in about three weeks.

Having been checked out by the flight surgeon, he was back on flying status in about three weeks. Even his eyesight had been restored to its pre-injury 20-20. Daniels was delighted to hear the surgeon say, "'You're now on flying status,' which is something I wanted."

Abe Daniels got that destroyer single-handed. It was confirmed by coast watchers. "I sank that destroyer verified by the coast watchers before the islands were secure. Sinking a ship by yourself, confirmed before the islands were secured, rated a Silver Star. I take it back, not a Silver Star, but a Navy Cross. I didn't know what the hell a Navy Cross was. I thought they were trying to convert me to Christianity.

"My commanding officer, a captain by the name of Nelson, went to Headquarters and had that Navy Cross reduced to the DFC. His reason was as follows: all his pilots, he said, were officers except me, and not one of his pilots even got a near miss so he thought it wouldn't be right, me as an enlisted pilot to get the Navy Cross. The DFC was good enough, so he said.

"At the beginning of the war, everything was mixed up. They had men as commanding officers that didn't know a thing about it, and vice versa. When I heard about that, I sort of got a bad taste in my mouth.

"Later on, I found out that giving medals was more less a procedure. I know pilots that have got four or five DFCs. They never even fired their guns, they never saw an enemy airplane. All they did was fly over enemy territory and after so many hops, they got a DFC."

Returning to the States, Daniels was assigned to the Marine Corps Air Station at El Toro, California. He was given the job of training new pilots for combat duty. In addition, he received his commission as second lieutenant.

He enjoyed his stay at El Toro. Being assigned to live in the Hotel Laguna was a far cry from the Spartan and inhospitable conditions of the South Pacific. After flying, they would return to the hotel, put on their swim suits, take a swim, return, have dinner, then head out to the bar for a few drinks and a lot of socializing.

While there, he made the acquaintance of a number of celebrities. Some were in the movie industry, others were well-known athletes. Daniels was the instructor for Ted Williams, and he took up Tyrone Power for a hop. On one occasion, a man grabbed him, took him to the main dining room and ballroom, and "brought me to where the orchestra was playing. They stopped the orchestra from playing and this man started to introduce me to everybody that was there.

"Remember now, all this time I was feeling no pain. There were glasses of liquor given to me right and left, which I couldn't consume it all, naturally. However, the orchestra that was playing there that night was Freddy Martin. Then I found out that the man that grabbed me was none other than Merv Griffin."

Later, sometime in 1944, he was transferred to El Centro, California, a base where they trained gunners and some bombardiers. He was posted as the officer in charge of the new aerial gunnery school "because of my background and sincerity and being ex-enlisted they selected me for the job."

Under his command, he had thirty-five planes, mostly dive bombers. His primary job was "to make sure that each gunner graduated with the best ability there was to go overseas. My main job was to get these new, potential gunners ready, to teach them everything, particularly to let them know that their life depended on what they knew."

He had thirty-five officers under him and assigned individual jobs to each of them. His entire command consisted of 1,500 men. Daniels demanded perfection. "I have to have it that way. I was responsible for the pilots and gunners."

Though somewhat out of synch and chronology, Abe Daniels related a story of his service prior to the Second World War.

"While I was aboard one of the aircraft carriers, I don't remember now if it was *Yorktown* or the *Wasp*, I remember that aboard the carrier all the planes were loaded with bombs.

"Many hops were taken each day, fully loaded. I later found out this was called a neutrality patrol. However, I'm quite sure, fully loaded, if they did see any Nazi submarines or ships, I believe they would have dropped.

"Another time when I was in Pensacola, we were not at war yet and I was about two-thirds through my course in getting my wings. I was flying a biplane Curtis Hell Diver during that time. Nazi submarines were sighted off the coast of Florida. They called me up and told me I was going to fly a Curtis Hell Diver equipped with depth charges.

"Those days a depth charge was a 600-pound barrel affair attached to each wing. I had 600 pounds on one wing and 600 pounds on another wing. They sent me out over the water with instructions that if I see anything at all to drop those depth charges. Or to release them anyway. They might have given these instructions to the cadets or officer pilots. However, the enlisted pilots didn't receive those instructions.

"About two and a half hours patrolling out there I decided to come back. Well, naturally, I came back with my depth charges still intact and when I went in for a landing, you should have seen what happened on the field. The whole field dispersed. I didn't know why and didn't find out why till I landed and got out of my plane. Bringing those depth charges was a definite no-no which I didn't know.

"I had to report to the field officer immediately. It all worked out OK because they realized the enlisted pilots didn't get the word. They realized they neglected to tell us that."

Abe "Dan" Daniels eventually retired from the Marine Corps with the rank of lieutenant colonel. His awards and decorations include two Presidential Unit Citations, World War II Victory Medal, Distinguished Flying Cross, two Air Medals, Pre-Pearl Harbor Atlantic Neutrality Patrol on board the *Yorktown*, Asiatic-Pacific Theater Medal, and the Good Conduct Medal. Now (2002) in retirement, he resides in California.

Of all the things Abe Daniels is most proud is his acquaintance with some of the legends of Marine aviation. On Guadalcanal, and other places, he knew Pappy Boyington, Joe Foss, Marion Carl, the Jewish ace Harold Segal, and the recipient of the Medal of Honor, Kenny Walsh. They were not in the same squadron as Daniels, but on various occasions they flew cover for his formations of dive bombers.

His citation for the Distinguished Flying Cross is as follows:

"For action described in the following:

TECHNICAL SERGEANT A. M. DANIELS, (275212),
U.S. MARINE CORPS

For heroism and extraordinary achievement in aerial
flight against the enemy while serving with Marine Aircraft Group Fourteen, First Marine Aircraft Wing, in the
Solomon Islands Area,

Technical Sergeant Daniels displayed an unusually high degree of skill, courage, and devotion to duty.
On February 7, 1943, he participated in an attack upon
twenty enemy destroyers in the face of unusually heavy
and accurate anti-aircraft fire. His utter disregard for
personal safety was rewarded when his salvo of one five
hundred and two one hundred pound bombs hit the destroyer bridge causing it to burn furiously, and, it is believed, to be later sunk or beached. The superb airman-
ship, unyielding devotion to duty, and outstanding accomplishments of Technical Sergeant Daniels were in
keeping with the highest traditions of the United States
Naval Service."

Note: All the quoted citations are taken from a monograph (supplied by Daniels and sent to me) written by Abe Daniels entitled
Caribou to El Centro, A Reminiscence.

Chapter 35

Yogi

Captain Yonel "Yogi" Dorelis appeared as a featured celebrity on the Internet on the Jewish Marines website. His story was fascinating, and it is even more so at this time. The lead line on the website stated that "Captain Yonel 'Yogi' Dorelis is a Jewish patriot and a pilot. But what sets him apart from others is that he was an officer in the U.S. Marines, Navy, and Air Force." Now, having been privy to more information and facts about Captain Dorelis, his person and his story becomes even more fascinating.

His picture, lifted from the website, shows Yogi standing between the American flag and that of the Marine Corps, resplendent in his dress blue uniform of the Corps. Despite the fact that he is now a pilot in the U.S. Air Force, and has been the same in the Navy, one may assume that that photo speaks volumes of his interest and pride in being, or having been, a part of the Marine Corps.

His bio relates the following information about this marvelous person, father, husband, pilot, officer, veteran, and patriot:

"Yonel 'Yogi' Dorelis was born and raised in New York City, N.Y., After high school, Yogi attended college at SUNY (State University of New York) at Stonybrook. During college, Dorelis enrolled in the Marine Corps Platoon Leaders Course of Officer Candidate School. He spent two summers in the PLC program.

When Yogi received his degree in 1984, he was commissioned as a second lieutenant in the U.S. Marine Corps.

"In September 1984, Dorelis attended the Basic School, a basic training program that all U.S. Marine Corps officers must complete. He graduated in March of 1985. Yogi's dream was to be a Marine Corps pilot. He had just become a Marine officer and he was awaiting orders to flight school when the bad news came. Dorelis's company, along with three others, was told that there would be an additional 24-month wait before they would be sent to flight school. They were also informed that they would have to serve in MOSs that were lacking Marines. However, they were all given the option to switch over to the U.S. Navy if they didn't want to wait two years for flight school.

"Yogi says, 'Having completed all the Marine Corps training I was going to get, I chose that option along with about 130 fellow Marine officers. I still regret that decision a bit, but I really wanted to fly and was afraid my eyes would go bad in two years or something.'

"Dorelis was commissioned in the U.S. Navy as an ensign. He reported to flight school in Pensacola, Florida, and he earned his gold aviator wings in August 1986. Yogi's dream had finally come true. He was now a certified pilot, but in the Navy, and not the Marines. Yogi flew CH-531 helicopters and was stationed mostly in the Philippines and Norfolk, Va. During his time as a navy helicopter pilot, Dorelis was deployed to many exotic locations, including Japan, Puerto Rico, Italy, and Spain. Yogi mostly flew resupply missions for the fleet, but he also did some Special Operations work with the Navy SEALS and the Recon Marines.

"In 1991, Dorelis was discharged from the Navy, and he went back to New York. He began working in ticket sales in the theater business. He even studied a little acting as well. Yogi still wanted to fly helicopters, so he joined the Air National Guard. On one of his active duty periods, Yogi decided that he really missed flying full time. As a result, he requested extended active duty.

"In September 1998, Dorelis was commissioned as a captain in the U.S. Air Force. After seven years of broken service, Yogi was finally back to flying helicopters full time. Yogi's mission is very important and also very dangerous. Yogi replies, 'I fly the HH-60G Pave Hawk, and our mission is Combat Search and Rescue. Basically, our job is to go and get any downed aviators and return them to safety, regardless of where they are.'

"When asked about anti-Semitism in the military, Yogi answers, 'While I have had some of the same anti-Semitic experiences and dealt with them with a quick fist, overall the military has been great to me and my family and I would encourage any Jew who wants to test themselves, or follow a dream of being a Marine or any other military to DO IT.'

He senses that some anti-Semitic animosity does exist, but "I have been lucky. I have been asked some crazy questions about being a Jew, but I cannot truly say that no-one was ever hostile to me for it, at least not to my face."

"I have had several Jewish friends in my career in my time in the Marines, Navy, and Air Force. In my squadron now there are two Jewish pilots aside from me. I believe Jews are represented in the military in proportion to the Jewish population of the United States."

The fact of his being a Jew has had some impact on his attitude and determination as a military officer. "I felt that I had to be as tough or tougher and push myself harder because we are always portrayed as weak and soft and that was not me. I was a street guy before the service and always thought a Jew had to be tougher than the *goyim*. I had to be as good as the non-Jews and make sure that there was no doubt that the Jews could 'hack' it."

"Most Jews would consider Yogi a Jewish hero, but Yogi thinks differently. Yogi, a true embodiment of the virtue of modesty, simply says, 'While my career has been *highly* undistinguished, I have done OK and have enjoyed the leadership opportunities I have been given.'

"When asked whether being a *Jewish Marine* has had any impact on his success, Yogi answers, 'I will say this: any success I have or will have as a professional military officer is a direct result of my having been a Marine. I still carry myself as a Marine both in bearing and appearance and *being a Marine will always be my proudest accomplishment.*'

"Since returning to active duty in 1998, Yogi has been stationed in Nevada. He has also been deployed to Turkey, in support of 'Operation Northern Watch,' and to Kuwait, in support of 'Operation Southern Watch.' In fact, his sister unit made the pickups in Kosovo. He is married to a 'beautiful woman,' and he has two daughters (ages 15 and 10) and a horse.

"Captain Dorelis is a Jewish patriot, and he has an important message for *all* American Jews. 'I also want to say that it is important for Jews to serve in this nation's military. Those of our relatives who came here made a good life for themselves and their families and must take part in that way of life's protection. *The freedom we have and take for granted here in America was paid for in blood, and we as American Jews have an obligation to defend this nation.*'

"Captain Dorelis also has an important message for any American Jew who is discouraged by others from joining the U.S. military. 'Don't listen to the nay-sayers and whiners, for they will never know the pride being called 'Marine' for the first time, or the feeling of having a pair of wings pinned to your chest after a year or two of the hardest work you have ever done."

Attesting to the fact that military service is a definite asset and a positive influence on those who pursue a civilian career following active duty, Yogi states that "a few years in the military never hurt anyone and can give people the responsibility, discipline, and confidence it takes to succeed in today's competitive world."

In addition, he "wishes more Jews looked at it (the military) in a positive way and chose the military at least for an enlistment if not a career. Unfortunately, we really do need to protect and preserve our way of life and I would like to see more young American Jews contribute."

His lifetime wish to be a military pilot has been realized. He has held this wish since the age of nine years. Several of his relatives have served in the armed forces: Uncle Lester Beckerman, Paratrooper, WW II, Uncle Bernard Beckerman, U. S. Navy, WW II, and cousin Randy Beckerman, U.S. Army, Vietnam.

His most crowning moment in the military was becoming a U.S. Marine. His only wish is that "my timing was better and I could have remained in the Marine Corps and become an aviator, even though I got my wings, leaving the Marines will always be a bit of a regret. 'Once a Marine, always a Marine.'"

One of his most memorable times in the service was while he was stationed at Naval Air Station, Cubi Point, Republic of the Philippines. "I was there for almost three years. I was a CH-53E pilot flying logistic missions all over the islands and to naval vessels working or transiting the area. I loved it over there, the people were nice, I lived like a king. I had a maid, yard boy, seamstress, etc. I even went to a Passover Seder over there. It was fun and widely attended by the Jewish personnel over there."

Another momentous period was spent in combat operations in Afghanistan. He flew in twenty-three sorties in Afghanistan, and was involved in two high-risk missions to extract wounded soldiers during Operation Anaconda Operation Enduring Freedom."

The combat experience which he recalls the most vividly, is "the first time you realize people are really shooting at you. A defining moment to say the least. The best is the realization that you did your job, despite the fact that people were trying to kill you."

Captain Yonel "Yogi" Dorelis took part in the saving of six lives. "My unit (66th Rescue Squadron USAF) has saved twenty lives since Operation Enduring Freedom began."

As of September (2002), Captain Yonel (Yogi) Dorelis, USAF, is stationed at Moody AFB, Georgia, as a member of a helicopter rescue squadron.

Chapter 36

First Love

Lester Goldberg loved being a pilot so much that he considered making civil aviation his career. However, his wife Annette "would have been uncomfortable with that," and, as a result, he did not carry through with his plan.

Goldberg grew up in Washington, D.C., the youngest of three boys, all of whom served in the armed forces. One brother served in the Navy, another in the Army, and Lester in the Marine Corps. He left college in June 1942 to enlist, and took his preflight training at the University of Georgia in Athens, receiving his wings as a naval aviator in the Marine Corps at Pensacola in 1943.

While a pre-flight cadet at the University of Georgia, he met his future wife Annette—on the steps of the synagogue in Athens.

Prior to shipping out to his overseas assignments, he was stationed at El Toro Marine Air Station. From there, he served in the South Pacific and China as a fighter pilot, leaving the service in 1945 as a captain. He is a member of the Caterpillar Club, having bailed out from his plane in the South Pacific and been rescued by an American submarine.

Chapter 37

The Sergeant's Son

Captain Max Halpin, the son of a U.S. Army sergeant, began his military career in January 1942, "when my best friend and I applied for Officer Candidate School in the Air Force. A month or two later, Sam was accepted and, for some unknown reason, I never heard from the Air Force although my school grades were far better than Sam's. Soon after, I applied to the Navy for aviation training. I received my commission in the U.S. Marine Corps and wings in March 1943. Of the original sixty cadets in my class, thirty washed out and approximately fifteen survived the war.

"My next duty was transitional training in Opa-Locka, Florida, after which we went to Glenview, Illinois, where I qualified for carrier landing and takeoffs . . . I made the required eight landings and takeoffs consecutively—without a single wave-off.

"After a much-needed two week leave at home in Houston, I joined VMF-311, which we renamed 'Hell's Belles.' There I met all the other members of the squadron, including three who would become my closest friends: Bobby Fidler of West Virginia, killed on a night-training flight in July; Roy Neuendorf from Illinois; and Francis Clark from Detroit. Roy, Clark, and I were roommates all during our Pacific theater tour of duty.

"We check out in the F4Us, which were the first Corsairs assigned to a squadron in the States. At the same time, the first

F4Us sent overseas went to Major Joe Foss and his squadron on Guadalcanal. Our CO for most of the next year and a half was Major Harry Cooper. In August, we flew cross-country from Parris Island to NAS, Miramar, San Diego. In September 1943, we and our planes were loaded on a carrier bound for American Samoa. Upon arrival, we were chased into Pago Pago harbor by a Japanese sub. As we had to fly our planes to an airfield on Samoa and the submarine stayed just outside of the harbor, we were briefed on catapult takeoffs. None of us had ever done this. We were tied up at the dock with no wind over the deck. Some of our planes forward on the deck were taken off by cranes to make room for takeoff. After the deck was cleared, they were loaded back on the deck for their turn. Being shot off the deck was an experience not soon forgotten. I blacked out momentarily and came to flying between the masts of a two-masted schooner at anchor in the harbor. Needless to say, that shook me up a little.

"A week or so later, we flew to Wallis Island where more combat training followed. A couple of months after that, we proceeded to Kwajalein Atoll in the Marshall Islands. As we had twenty planes and forty pilots, we drew straws to determine who flew our planes and who went by ship. I went by ship to Kwajalein and then to Roi Island at the north end of the atoll, and was treated to all-night bombing by the Japanese on February 12, 1944. As our planes had not yet arrived and the runways were not completed, the bombers had a field day. Their last string of bombs was on the runway where the Seabees were working with their tractors. Casualties were numerous—the second string landed on our radar equipment and the third on our ammunition dump. Later, they demolished our tent area where I lost all of my personal belongings. All of our supplies were lost. In fact, we ate K-rations for two days until food was brought in by ship.

"When the air raid began at two in the morning, Francis Clark and I looked for a place to hide. You do not dig foxholes on a coral island with your fingers. We found a Japanese blockhouse, as our Marine ground force did not destroy everything. This blockhouse, approximately 10-by-12 feet, had 3-feet thick concrete walls, no windows, and a 6-inch thick wooden door which was still locked. We sat in the door opening when a nearby bomb exploded and took the blockhouse door off, which we looked for later and never found. Oddly enough, neither of us were scratched, even though we both were leaning back against the door. Clark and I went into the blockhouse for protection. I then noticed with my lighter lit that the blockhouse was full of dynamite and torpedo warheads. You never saw anyone evacuate a building as quickly as we did. At daylight, we went to the makeshift hospital to see if we could help. The place was filled to the rafter with some seriously wounded. The Japs also used incendiary bombs, and a fragment lightly grazed my arm which I did not remember happening. A corpsman applied an antiseptic to my arm and told me good-bye.

"More than once I came back from a mission with holes in my plane. The worst was when a shell went through my rudder and put a hole in it big enough to crawl through. As my hydraulic system was also shot out, I was cleared for an emergency landing on Roi. Not having landing flaps or brakes, landing was hazardous. Our island was only a half-mile square so there was not much runway on which to slow down. I finally was able, with a bit of luck, to veer off to my right into a ditch where my plane nosed down. Only my propeller was damaged on landing. With all the bombing, strafing, and search-and-rescue flight, I ended up with about eighty-three missions.

"Sometime in the middle of 1944 we had a surprise visitor. Charles A. Lindbergh joined our squadron as a representative of Vought, manufacturer of the F4U Corsair. With our help, he designed, made, and installed bomb racks which could carry two-thousand-pound bombs each. The F4U was a very powerful plane, and the first to take off with two-thousand-pound bombs was Lindbergh himself. His plane was airborne at the halfway point of our half-mile-long runway. He also flew on every mission we flew and engaged in mock dogfights with us. I am proud to have known him as well as eating breakfast with him for two weeks. Four thousand pounds of bombs carried by a fighter was something never done before. In fact, that was more weight than some of the Air Force medium bombers carried in the Pacific.

"In October 1944, my thirteen months of overseas combat duty concluded and we were relieved. I flew to San Francisco on a Pan American clipper. At the base mess hall where we were taken, we were treated to the best meal of our lives: steak and all the trimmings and all the fresh milk we wanted. After a couple of days, we were transferred to San Diego where we received all of our back pay and thirty-day leave papers.

"On arrival at Houston, I took a cab from the train station home. I never told my family when I would arrive. You can imagine the surprise on my mother's face when she opened the door and saw me standing there.

"Before returning to duty and after several dates with Rosalie (Dubinski), we became engaged and planned to marry in February 1945. When my thirty-day leave was up, I reported to Cherry Point. The normal course of events was twelve months combat duty, followed by six months in the States, and then twelve months' combat, etc. We were given our choice of duty following leave. Clark and I both chose Landing Signal Officer (LSO) School in Jacksonville, Florida, figuring that this could be good goof-off duty. Several weeks later, I asked the CO for time off to get married. I was turned down because I had taken all the leave I was going to get at that time. I informed Rosalie and said I would line up a rabbi and she should come to Jacksonville. As the Navy or Marine Corps had no rabbis in the area, I located one in the Army who agreed to perform the ceremony in his home on Saturday, February 17, 1945, and at 11 P.M., the knot was tired. Clark said 'Here!' for me about three days at morning muster and that was our honeymoon. Rosalie stayed with me for the balance of LSO training until we reported back to Cherry Point for reassignment. I was ordered to Columbia, South Carolina, to join a new squadron to prepare for overseas duty.

"Around April 1945, I took all my shots and physicals necessary for combat duty. The doctor told me that my tonsils had to come out. I told him I was going to take them to my grave. He told me they were infected that that if not removed, I could not go back overseas. I must have been crazy because I told him to take them out. A date was set and I went to the doctor's office. He sat me down in what looked like a barber's chair, with no assistant. He went to work on me with *me* assisting *him*. After the surgery, he told me to go outside and walk about one hundred yards to the ward building, where there were twenty-four beds with one unoccupied. All that night I heard, 'Corpsman, Vaseline.' It turned out that twenty-three beds were for hemorrhoidectomies and one, my tonsillectomy.

"Rosalie came to see me in the morning. Not being able to talk, I wrote her a note to go to the CO and ask if I could go home. I could not go through another night like the first one. The CO agreed and we went to our apartment in Columbia, which was about twenty miles from the base. The doctor told me to come back in one week for a check-up. When I returned, the doctor said my throat was infected and prescribed sulfa drugs. In another week the infection still had not cleared up and I was removed from my squadron shipping-out orders. When I finally recovered, I was reassigned to another squadron and more training. Japan surrendered and future combat was over.

"I had it pretty easy, as I was promoted to captain shortly before the war ended. Flying was limited and leave was easy to come by. This was good because I was able to drive Rosalie, pregnant with our first child, home to Houston in later summer, 1945.

"Both my brothers were radio operators in the U.S. Air Force during World War II, holding the rank of sergeant.

"My release to inactive duty came in November 1945. I was denied a discharge. Inactive Reserve duty lasted until June 1958, when I requested retirement. This was approved, without retirement pay, and I remain to the present day (2000) Captain Max L. Halpin, USMCR (ret.), 020547."

Chapter 38

Sam Levine, The Texas Marine

Sam Levine joined the Marine Corps three months after the Japanese attack on Pearl Harbor. After three months at Parris Island, he was transferred to NAS, Jacksonville, for guard duty.

When Levine learned that the Marine Corps was in the process of forming a new glider group, he volunteered for it. A corporal by this time, he was transferred with fifty other Marines for training at Mercersburg Academy in Mercersburg, Pennsylvania. After three months flying PT-19s at Hagerstown, Maryland, they were all transferred to Eagle Mountain Lake, Newark, Texas, not far from Fort Worth. Then, as Levine tells it:

"I ground-looped one day in a Waco biplane while doing some touch-and-go practice. Unfortunately, I turned over on my back, then I undid my safety belt and fell on my head, cutting my face enough for the sick bay officer to rush me to St. Joseph's Hospital. There, I met Ruby Suddith, a nurse who became my future wife, and we have been married for fifty-one years."

After receiving his wings as a Marine Corps pilot, Levine was transferred to Cherry Point for six months, then to NAS, Jacksonville, where he flew F4U Corsairs and did carrier work on the Atlantic Coast, "not only practicing carrier landings but patrolling certain areas to keep an eye out for German submarines."

Sent to China with VMF-153, MAG-15, 3rd MAX, Levine was posted at Peking to fly patrol over the China Wall in F4U

Corsairs. His CO was Colonel Harshberger, better known as "Iron John" Harshberger. Levine was transferred to Tsing-tao to check out twin-engine transport planes. His duty "consisted of flying mail, passengers, and cargo to Tientsin, headquarters of the 2nd Marine Division, and Peking MAG-15, and to Shanghai—American embassy people."

On one of his days off, his crew flew to Nagasaki where they learned there was a warehouse full of *samurai* swords. "Sure enough, it only took a fifth of whiskey and a carton of cigarettes to get into the warehouse. We all left with a bunch of *samurai* swords—I got six of them! These were swords that the Japanese had to surrender after they lost the war."

En route back to the United States for discharge, Levine landed first in Hong Kong, but a typhoon forced him to follow a group of Royal Air Force planes that "landed in Saigon, occupied by the French. They were fighting the North Vietnamese, so there were a lot of French Foreign Legion troops in town on R & R. Saigon was a beautiful town and we spent three days there!" Arriving next in Manila, the rest of the trip was easy and "we took our time on October 13th for Eniwetok, then on to Wake Island on October 15th." Landing nest at Ewa, they were met by MPs who escorted Levine and his crew to the CO, Colonel Evans, who then proceeded to "take us apart for two hours on why it took us twenty-five days to fly from Tsingtao, China, to Ewa, Hawaii, when it should have taken only five days." However, having delivered a reasonable explanation for the drawn-out trip from China to Hawaii, they flew back to San Diego where they were discharged.

On August 1, 1950, Levine was called back to active duty. Shortly after his squadron landed at El Toro, they all went to the OK Club and Bar at the officers' club. Shortly after they arrived, a general from the MAW entered. When everyone stood at attention, he said, "Relax and at ease, all I want to know is where the Dallas, Texas Squadron is." He then proceeded to their table and said, "I just wanted to shake hands with a real Texas Marine," and "he came over to me and shook my hand and walked away. The pilots in my squadron broke into a tremendous cheer and laughter. Since I was the only Yankee in the Dallas Squadron, they gave me the title, 'Sam Levine, the Texas Marine.'"

At El Toro, he was assigned to VMR-125, MAG-25, and checkout out as co-pilot of the R5D, the Marine version of the C-54, a four-engine transport. Levine then found himself at NAS, Barbers Point, Hawaii, the forward station of MAG-25. Later, at the forward station in Itami for a three-month tour of duty, Levine was billeted in a hotel close to the airport. One day, James Michener moved into the hotel to write his book *Sayonara*.

During Levine's tour of duty at Itami, he and his fellow pilots flew between Itami and Korea a minimum of four times every other day. "We would have as our cargo going to Korea ammunition, food, and mail for the troops—young Marines on the front lines. Coming back to Japan we would carry these young men for two weeks of R & R in Tokyo."

On one of the flights, his friend and copilot Blanco White said to Levine, "Go on back and talk to these young Marines just to make them comfortable," whereupon Levine sat with them on one side of the plane. Not long after, Blanco came back and sat with them on the other side. "Pretty soon we started our routine and I said, 'Blanco, what are you doing back here and who is up in the cockpit?' Blanco said, 'Heck, I thought you were up there!'" It turned out that they had the autopilot controls on, and the crew chief was sitting in the pilot's seat and turning the knobs on the autopilot if it needed it. Upon learning of this, "Blanco and I jumped up and ran into the cockpit. Later, I came back and told those kids not to worry, we were joking!"

One day, as he was approaching the runway of K-50, an airstrip on the coast of Korea, Levine made a pass at the K-50 tower. They gave the green light for him to land. As he made his approach, a Navy captain standing in the cockpit between Levine and the copilot said, "Captain Levine, if you are planning on landing, I order you not to and start flying to K-3." Levine then turned to the captain and said, "Sir, you outrank me on the ground, but I am captain of this plane and your rank does not mean anything on this plane. So if you want to watch from where you are, stand or get back to the cabin but we are going to land regardless." The captain had been worried about the snow on the runway. But they managed to land and "each wing just sliced about two feet of snow from the banks on each side of the runway." When they landed and pulled up to the operations hangar and deplaned, the Navy captain apologized.

While in Itami, Levine read a notice on the headquarters bulletin board in which all Jewish personnel were invited to a Passover Seder the following week. About fifty or sixty Navy and Army personnel and a Marine pilot took the bus and arrived at a "very big home on top of a hill and were greeted by our host, dressed in typical Japanese attire. It turned out that he was a Russian Jew who had made his way from Russian to Japan during World War II and the Japanese jailed him. After the war, he got out and married a Japanese woman. He was the owner of the biggest junkyard in Japan."

Levine finally returned to El Toro and, upon discharge, drove to Fort Worth, where he terminated his five years of active Reserve service (1950–55). Concluding his military career, he related, "So I ended up with a total time of ten years in the Marine Corps–from a private to a captain and a pilot."

He currently (2001) resides in Dallas, Texas.

Chapter 39

Modest Skyhawk

Lieutenant Colonel Myron Margolis, pilot, officer, gentleman, father, grandfather, and Marine is a modest, proud, private citizen who speaks fondly of his twenty-four year career in the Marine Corps. He waxes nostalgically of his experience as an officer and as a Marine. He found virtually no trace of anti-Semitism, and, in the one case he did, he dismisses it as inconsequential. He found the Marine Corps to be a welcoming and hospitable institution, one that he would heartily recommend to any young person of any background, status, and faith.

Originally, I mentioned that his would be a highly prized story for inclusion in this project given the fact that Jewish Marines, or officers, were not in great supply in Vietnam. He corrected me, pointing out that that was not exactly true. There were probably more than one might expect. The presence of Marines who happened to be Jewish, while not huge by any means, was very much part of the Vietnam experience.

Enlisting in the Marine Corps Reserve at the age of 17 in 1954 in Kansas City, Missouri, he completed basic training at Marine Corps Recruit Depot, San Diego. In 1959, he was selected for Marine Officer Candidate School, Quantico, after which he completed Basic School in 1960. Various professional schools followed including Hawk Missile School at Fort Bliss, Texas, after which he was selected for flight training. Graduating from flight school, he received his gold wings as Naval Aviator, and was stationed at various naval air installations in Florida, Mississippi, and Texas.

Reluctant to go into detail of his combat experience, he described his least memorable experience as "Getting shot at." His most unpleasant incident was in "Losing eight acquaintances in Vietnam due to combat."

His overseas assignments included Da Nang and Chu Lai in Vietnam during which time he underwent considerable combat as the pilot of an A-4 Skyhawk, experience which he preferred not to go into detail. The fact that he served seven years on active duty, and seventeen years in the Reserve, plus receiving the following medals and decorations speak for themselves:

Five Air Medals, Navy Commendation with Combat V, Vietnam Service Medal, National Defense Service Medal, Vietnam Cross of Gallantry, Navy Unit Citation, USMC Reserve Medal, and Vietnam Campaign Medal.

Chapter 40

The Very Model of a Modern Marine, Flyer, Officer

Currently (2001) residing in Palm Beach, Florida, Colonel Marvin Schacher, USMCR (ret.) commanded Marines in combat on both land and in the air During World War II.

Born in the Bronx and raised in Far Rockaway, New York, Colonel Schacher is a graduate of Vanderbilt University, Nashville, Tennessee, and the Brooklyn Law School. Immediately following graduation in November 1940, he enlisted in the Marine Corps and became a member of the first Reserve Officer Candidate (ROC) class at Quantico.

According to Schacher, "We remained at Quantico to continue training as members of the 4th ROC and graduated in June, 1941, receiving our commissions as second lieutenants. At that time, I was ordered to the Fleet Marine Force as a platoon leader in E Company, 2nd Battalion, 7th Marines, 1st Marine Division, then stationed at Parris Island, South Carolina.

"We became a part of the 3rd Marine Brigade in March 1942, and embarked for the Pacific that month. I was named executive officer and, shortly before landing on Guadalcanal with the rank of captain, I realized the dream of every Marine officer—becoming the commanding officer of a rifle company, in the opinion of most, the best job in the Corps. When I climbed down the cargo net for the last time, in command of my 250 Marines, I knew what being an officer was all about.

"The first night at Guadalcanal we barely got off the beach. No time to dig in when night fell, as did the rain. We were lying out in the open on the wet ground. Shortly after dark, the Jap fleet moved in and launched an artillery attack on our position. A baptism of enemy is terrifying. I felt no different than the rest until a frightened man called, 'Captain, Captain, we're being shelled and I'm scared.' That was all I needed to snap to and realize there were 250 men who depended on me. My fear immediately vanished. I gave reassurance to that Marine and continued to reassure the others. I suddenly understood what command was all about.

"The next day our company moved to a forward position. We halted while there was still sufficient light to allow us to use our machetes to carve a field of fire to our front, but I still had a company of nervous, trigger-happy Marines. A cow wandered into the area and took over 100 rounds of rifle fire. Anything that moved got shot. On the second night, one of my own men was shot. On the third night, I resolved to put an end to that and, waiting for dark, I walked the entire company front 1,200 yards. Again, with my heart in my mouth, I made it back and forth. After that, things settled down to patrolling all day, holding off the Japs all night. Casualties ran high, injuries frequent. The smell, the noise, the screams were always there.

"Late in October 1942, I left Guadalcanal and returned stateside. In November, I assumed command of F Company, 2nd Battalion, 21st Marines, 3rd Marine Division, at Camp Pendleton preparing for the next invasion—that of Bougainville.

"After Guadalcanal, I requested a transfer to flight training, unaware that the Marine Corps at that time was looking for about seventy-five ground officers to become Naval Aviators. I was approved, and orders arrived transferring me to Dallas for flight training in February 1943. I then went to Pensacola for final flight training and was designated a Naval Aviator in October 1943.

"After completing a course in aerial photography, I was transferred to multiengine flight. In March 1944, I joined the 4th MAW and in July sailed overseas to Kwajalein where I joined VMR-353 as executive officer.

"During my time with VMR-253, I flew supply and evacuation missions. We flew off makeshift runways, frequently under enemy fire.

"At Kwajalein, I was advised that we were to be furnished with the new and larger R5C-type Curtiss Commando plane. We sent back on R4D Douglas Dakota with each arrival. It became my custom to wait at the landing strip to welcome each pilot and crew. On one such occasion a Curtiss Commando rolled to a stop and out stepped my new pilot. He saluted and announced, 'First Lieutenant Tyrone Power reporting for duty.' I hid my surprise, thinking to myself, 'We're trying to run a war and they're making movies.' Then I recalled that screen idol Ty Power was indeed a Marine and had, in fact, successfully completed flight training. He turned out to be an outstanding officer, an excellent pilot, and a generally fine person.

"The squadron moved up to Saipan in February 1945. This involved breaking camp and establishing another—all the time continuing flying, most of the time within fighter-plane range of Japan. Our only defenses were pistols and a cloud cover in which we could evade the Jap fighters. Fortunately, their time on station was limited by fuel supply. We all went through this evasive action from time to time. My luck ran out in March of '45 when a *giretsu* (Japanese commando plane) caught me attempting to land on Yontan airfield, Okinawa. Its machine guns brought me down on fire, but we all escaped without injury.

"VMR-353 participated in supplying blood plasma and ordnance. During the battles for Iwo Jima and Okinawa, the squadron brought in the evacuated and the recently wounded to the Navy hospital at Guam. On each flight, I carried twenty stretcher cases or forty sitters, or any combination. I had on board only one Navy corpsman to care for the wounded, some of whom were hit minutes prior to takeoff. At no time during the war did I ever feel a similar sense of accomplishment than bringing those wounded out of danger.

"My initial flight into Iwo Jima was on steel matting. Our takeoffs were low, over enemy positions. Bullet holes in the wings and fuselage were common.

"I received the Air Medal for this service. In July 1945, I left VMR-353, once again returning stateside, and was ordered to MAB, El Centro, until the end of the war.

"When the war was over, I transferred to the Marine Corps Reserve until I completed thirty-two years of service. During that time, I organized and commanded the first Marine Corps Reserve unit—the first of several to follow and from whose ranks were furnished many lawyers required by the Corps.

"I commanded numerous Reserve units, both air and ground. I returned to active duty each year to maintain my flying skills and also attend many armed service schools.

"I have served as a member of four boards involved in the selection and promotion of lieutenant colonels to the rank of colonel. My file contains a letter of commendation from Lieutenant General Rathvon McC. Tompkins for that service.

"In 1950, I became an active member of the Marine Corps Reserve Officer Association (MCROA), and subsequently president of the Karl S. Day Chapter in New York. By the mid-1960s, I ventured into the national scene, first as a member of the National Board, and then as second and first vice president. I took one year off, 1968, but in 1969 I attended the national convention along with approximately 1,200 other officers.

"In 1962, a group of five Reserve officers formed the Marine Corps Scholarship Foundation organized by Brigadier General Martin F. Rockmore who served as its first chairman of the board. I served as its first president for six years. The Foundation sponsors the annual Leatherneck Scholarship Ball and continues to flourish, having contributed millions of dollars for scholarships to Marines and Marine Corps families.

"In September 1970, General Leonard F. Chapman, Jr. (then Commandant) ordered me to active duty in Vietnam. I went as a member of the Marine Corps Reserve to observe and incorporate the lessons the Marine Corps was learning, and carry my observations back to the Reserve program. I participated in combat with both the division and the wing flying missions, accompanying forward patrols. Upon my return, I completed my tenure as president of MCROA, after which I transferred to the Retired List on July 1, 1971.

"I look back with pride on my years with the Corps. I have served my country and my Corps to the best of my ability. I have no regrets and leave with a loud 'Semper Fidelis.'"

Chapter 41

Ace

Major Harold E. Segal served as a Marine pilot from 1942 to 1946 and became one of the Corps' premier aces with a total of twelve planes to his credit.

He was born in Chicago on September 1, 1920 and grew up in New York City. After graduation from Long Island High School in 1939, he attended Pratt Institute in Brooklyn for two years.

With war imminent, Segal lost no time in getting into it. Before the outbreak of the war, he enlisted in the U.S. Navy for flight duty, was appointed an aviation cadet in March 1942, and completed flight training at Pensacola, Miami, and Jacksonville, Florida. He chose service in the Marine Corps, was commissioned a second lieutenant, and became a Naval Aviator in October 1942.

As a member of VMF-221 in the New Hebrides, he was awarded his first Distinguished Flying Cross for "heroism and extraordinary achievement in shooting down seven enemy in the Solomon Islands area from June 25 to August 8, 1943. His citation states in part:

"As a member of a flight of flyers, First Lieutenant Segal intercepted a formation of enemy aircraft over the New Georgia area, and, in the ensuing action, show down a Japanese bomber and a Zero. During a patrol flight on July 11, he joined another plane in an assault against fifteen hostile bombers with escort, and, despite his crippled engine, valiantly attacked against tremendous odds, shooting down three Zeros before attempting to take off for his base. Followed and strafed by enemy fighters while making a forced water landing, he was eventually picked up by our surface craft. On August 6, while escorting a photographic mission over hostile territory, he destroyed two enemy fighters which attempted to intercept, and, although his plane was badly damaged by shellfire, succeeded in bring it safely to base."

In the action of July 11, he was wounded. His citation for his second Distinguished Flying Cross reads as follows:

"Flying as wingman, First Lieutenant Segal took part in numerous raids, fighter sweeps, task force covers, strafing missions, and patrols deep into enemy territory. Accompanied by one other plane while flying cover for a task force on November 17, he attacked six Japanese bombers, then diving on three of the hostile aircraft, sent two crashing into the sea, then pressing home his attack against the third, succeeded in destroying it."

Another of his awards was the Air Medal earned for meritorious achievement in the Solomon Islands and Bismarck Archipelago. In less than a month, he downed two enemy planes for a total of twelve. His citation for this military operation reads as follows:

"Participating in a daring run over Buka Passage on 8 January, Captain Segal rendered valuable assistance in the strafing of two Japanese barges which resulted in casualties to numerous enemy personnel and severe damage to the vessels. Intercepted by a vastly superior number of hostile enemy fighter planes while flying escort for our bombers during a strike over the Rabaul area on 24 January, he immediately engaged the enemy in fierce combat despite the tremendous odds and shot down two of this hostile aircraft from the sky."

Combat duty over for the present, Segal returned to the United States and assigned to MCAS, El Toro, February 1944, to April 1945. The next months saw his return to the Pacific theater, where he joined VMF-115 in Mindanao, Philippines, and subsequently earned his Distinguished Flying Cross, and his second, third, and fourth Air Medals for aerial missions carried out from May to August 1945.

Overseas service still not completed, he was transferred to Manila and then to China. The war now concluded, he returned to San Diego on January 31, 1946. He was released from active duty as a captain in March 1946 while attached to the Brooklyn Navy Yard. Remaining in the Marine Corps Reserve, he was promoted to major in September 1951 and honorably discharged on August 7, 1958.

PART X

Generals

Chapter 42

Lieutenant General Robert Magnus

Now in his fourth decade of service as a Marine, Lieutenant General Robert Magnus is stationed at Headquarters, Marine Corps, Washington, D.C., as the Deputy Commandant for Programs and Resources. He received confirmation of his appointment to his present grade and was promoted in July 2001.

Born on April 28, 1947, in Brooklyn, he moved in 1952 to Levittown, New York, where he received his public school education. Always an avid reader, he attended Island Trees High School and was a member of the wrestling team, the National Honor Society, and the Spanish Club. He went to synagogue at Hicksville Jewish Center where he was *bar mitzvahed*.

In 1964, General Magnus received basic training as a Naval Reservist at the Philadelphia Naval Base and then drilled at the Naval Reserve Center, Freeport, New York. During the summer of 1965, he received active training aboard the USS *Orion* at the Naval Base, Norfolk, Virginia, after which he was discharged as a seaman (electronics technician striker) and commissioned a midshipman in the Naval ROTC. He joined the Marine Corps and entered OCS in 1968, and received his commission as a second lieutenant in June 1969 upon graduation from the University of Virginia at Charlottesville with a bachelor of arts degree in history. Shortly thereafter, he completed The Basic School at

Quantico. He then reported to the Naval Air Training Command, where he was designated a Naval Aviator.

In 1971, General Magnus was given a helicopter squadron assignment with HMMT-402, New River, for CH-46 training, followed by duty with HMM-264 as the S-2 (intelligence) staff officer in preparation for deployment on his first Sixth Fleet Landing Force cruise aboard the USS *Inchon*. In 1973, he transferred to H&MS-15 SAR (Search and Rescue) Detachment, Task Force Delta, Royal Thai Air Force Base, Nam Phong, Thailand, as S-3 (Operations) staff officer.

He remembers with great satisfaction rescuing a Laotian pilot near RTAFB Udorn, Thailand, after his T-38 aircraft crashed. The year 1973 was also memorable for a religious reason. Along with fellow servicemen, General Magnus attended a Passover celebration in Bangkok hosted by the Israeli ambassador after a terrorist attack and guarded by hundreds of Thai Army commandos. In 1974, General Magnus was assigned as Training Officer, Stations and Operations Engineering Squadron, MCAS, Quantico, where he was released from active duty in October 1974.

In December 1975, he returned to active duty to serve as Aviation Safety Officer, HMM-263, deploying for his second Sixth Fleet cruise, this time aboard the USS *Iwo Jima*, and then as Aviation Safety Officer, MAG-26. He also served as Assistant S-3/Weapons and Tactics Instructor, HMM-261, where he made his third Sixth Fleet deployment, again aboard the USS *Iwo Jima*, then as Assistant S-4 Officer and Assistant S-3/Weapons and Tactics Instructor, MAG-26.

In 1980, Magnus reported to Headquarters, Marine Corps, to serve as Aviation Training Devices Officer and H-46/Assault Medium Lift Requirements Officer, Aviation Weapons System Requirements Branch, Aviation Department. In 1985, he attended the U.S. Marine Corps Command and Staff College, and was reassigned as S-3 officer, MAG-29. In 1986, he became Executive Officer, HMM-36, and assumed command of HMM-36 for his fourth Six Fleet deployment, once more aboard the USS *Iwo Jima*. In 1989, General Magnus attended the National War College and later reported to the Joint Staff where he served as Chief, J-4 Logistics Readiness Center, and as Executive Assistant to the Director, Joint Staff.

In 1993, he returned to Headquarters, U.S. Marine Corps, as Head, Aviation Plans, Programs, Doctrines, Joint Matters, and Budget Branch. That same year he received a master of science degree in business administration from Strayer College, Washington, D.C. In July

1994, he was promoted and became the Assistant Deputy Chief of Staff for Aviation, Headquarters, Marine Corps. In 1999, he became a major general serving as Commander, Marine Corps Air Bases Western Area, MCAS, Miramar.

General Magnus's personal decorations include the Defense Superior Service Medal, the Legion of Merit, the Navy Achievement Medal, the Joint Meritorious Unit Award, and the National Defense Service Medal with bronze star.

His late uncle John Magnus fought in the U.S. Army under General George S. Patton during the invasion of Nazi-occupied Europe.

Chapter 43

Major General Harold W. Chase

Major General Harold W. Chase had distinguished careers as a Marine Reserve officer, an educator, an author, and a public official.

Born February 6, 1922, in Worcester, Massachusetts, General Chase attended public schools in his hometown, then Phillips-Andover Academy, and Princeton University from which he received three degrees (B.A., 1943; M.A., 1948; and Ph.D., 1954—the latter two in political science).

He enlisted in the Marine Corps and was commissioned the following year. After receiving parachute and other training, he was transferred to the 2nd Battalion, 26th Marines, with whom he served on Iwo Jima where he was twice wounded. Remaining in the Reserve, he returned to active duty during the Korean War. In 1969, he completed a thirteen-month tour in Vietnam where he served as III MAF Psychological Operations Officer.

His decorations include the Legion of Merit, two Purple Hearts, and the Republic of Vietnam Honor Medal, 1st Class.

A colonel when a member of Volunteer Training Unit (VTU) 4-52, Chase was promoted to brigadier general in the Reserves in 1971, and by 1974 he was a major general and assistant director of the Marine Corps Reserve. In 1977, during the Carter administration, he accepted the post of deputy assistant secretary of defense for Reserve Affairs, a position he filled until 1980.

General Chase was a founder of the Marine Corps Command and Staff College Adjunct Faculty and usually spent several weeks each summer on active duty working on studies or academic programs.

From 1947 to 1966, he served in numerous academic capacities: as instructor; assistant professor; associate professor; visiting, civilian, and resident professor at the University of Delaware, Princeton University, Columbia University, the University of Chicago, and the National War College. He was also assistant director at the Woodrow Wilson School, administrator of the Schools Program for Princeton University, and administrator of the Independent Research Program for Students at the National War College.

In addition, he had been a featured lecturer at forums for adult education; appeared on panels; and served as a member of committees and commissions at universities and state level within the United States. In 1961, he was the first recipient of an annual prize for Distinguished Teaching by faculty, alumni, and students of the Liberal Arts College of the University of Minnesota in Minneapolis where he was professor of political science for more than twenty years and acting vice president for academic administration in the mid-1970s.

General Chase was still on the faculty there but had begun a four-month teaching stint at the University of California at San Diego, a month before he died on January 12, 1982. He was buried at Arlington National Cemetery on January 19, 1982.

General Chase was author or editor of twelve published books and numerous articles. Among his best-known books are *Corwin's Constitution and What It Means Today; Federal Judges: The Appointing Process;* and *Constitutional Interpretation,* a widely used casebook.

In 1964, he edited with G. T. Mitau *Proximate Solutions: Case Problems in State and Local Government;* with Paul Dolan, *The Case for Democratic Capitalism;* and with Allen Lerman, *Kennedy and the Press* and *Essays on the Constitution.*

In 1982, the Major General Harold W. Chase Essay Contest,

endowed by contributions from the family and friends of the late general, was launched. Prizes in the Chase Contest are termed "Boldness and Daring Awards," and the theme of the contest is change. To be eligible for consideration, all entries must "challenge conventional wisdom" by proposing some change to existing Marine Corps policy, practice, or custom. Authors must have strength in their convictions and be willing (i.e., bold and daring enough) to stand up and say, "Here's something we can do much better than we are now doing," and go on to make their case.

The winner of the Chase Contest receives a Boldness and Daring Plaque and $750 for the 1,500–2,000-word essay; second place, a suitably inscribed plaque and $375; honorable mention, $100 to an unlimited number of entrants. The Marine Corps Association administers the contest.

General Chase's two sons served in the Marine Corps—Colonel Eric L. Chase, USMCR (ret.), and Bryce S. Chase, who was a private first class. Both practice law in New Jersey.

Chapter 44

Major General Melvin L. Krulewitch

Melvin Krulewitch was a Renaissance man who considered himself a Marine first. "Major General Melvin L. Krulewitch has crowded a remarkable range of activities and accomplishments into his lifetime—ranging from lawyer, Marine in three wars, bibliophile, philanthropist, author, aspiring politician, painter, and chairman of the New York State Athletic Commission (during the Cassius Clay-Sonny Liston era)."[1]

Versatile, personable, convincing, suave, educated and urbane, he was as comfortable in a corporate board of directors meeting or a courtroom as at the post slop chute and PX.

To round out his talents, he could lay claim to being a linguist, a capability which served him well in his military career.

While Krulewitch wore many hats, that of the military provided him the most satisfaction and pride. At the outbreak of America's entry into World War I, Krulewitch joined a military-style group at Columbia University, New York City. After some elementary training, "July 4th, (1917), we marched in the Litchfield parade, and I went down to the recruiting station on 23rd, between Fourth and Madison Avenues, climbed the rickety stairs to the second floor, and enlisted in the Marines. I still had a year to do in law school.[2]

---

[1] Krulewitch, Melvin, *Now That You Mention It*, Quadrangle/New York Times Book Co., 1973, front cover.

[2] Ibid., p. 24.

At recruit training at Parris Island, his company was under the direct supervision of a senior DI, Sergeant Horsh Skoda, a regular Marine and veteran of China, Nicaragua, and Haiti. Each day, he would preside over a conglomerate of "ridgerunners, hayshakers, crackers, muleskinners, clodhoppers, punks, college boys, and clerks,[3] setting them off on a daily ten-hour grind that ended with a prechow shower and cleaning of shoes. Krulewitch described evening chow as "slop consisting of sowbelly, boiled and greasy, speared by a dozen forks as the KP detail banged down the platter in the center of the mess table with coarse barracks bread to sop it up. Dessert was blackstrap, a by-product of the first grind of sugar cane, and not too bad when scraped on a crust of bread and washed down with black coffee."[4]

His company spent the last thirty days on the rifle range. During that period, Krulewitch underwent a transformation from New York City slicker to that of the Marine. "The heavy felt hat was no longer at the back of the head or hanging over the bridge of the nose, but straight and square."[5]

Three more months of training awaited Krulewitch "in the mud of Quantico, at the new camp on the Potomac, before they were ready to shove off (December 1919) in the 133rd, commanded by Captain Francis Burns. Then he embarked on the USS *Von Steuben* and, after three days at anchor in New York City upper bay, sailed for France.

Krulewitch, now a corporal and a bayonet instructor, settled in among the fields surrounding the hamlet of Chatillon-sur-Cher, Department of Loire et Cher. He speaks fondly of these three months at Chatillon—training in the best of British and French techniques, chasing after French women, and, "For most of us, it was a flashback into history—ancient *chateaux* peasants in wooden, shoes, *pissoirs* in public view, and universal wine drinking.[6] *Le bon temps* that the Marines enjoyed came to an abrupt

---

[3] Ibid., p. 27.

[4] Ibid., p. 27–28.

[5] Ibid., p. 29.

[6] Ibid., p. 35.

halt with the frenzied gasping of a Marine running toward Krulewitch with the word that they were moving up to the front.

Following muster and receiving provisions and ammunition, "We fell in and the entire population of the village lined up across the company to see us off as we marched down to the railroad station.[7] After heading into boxcars marked "*40 Hommes and 8 chevaux,*" they stowed their equipment and rations, slung their rifles, and began their "high adventure."

Arriving at Fontainebleau along the Paris-Metz road, they could already hear the guns at the front less than forty miles away. Krulewitch and his comrades were assigned as replacements for the dead and wounded of the 6th Marines. Krulewitch did not have to wait long for his baptism of fire. In his listening post one hundred feet in front of the line, he thought, "In my mind as we looked up at the stars were thoughts of the past and present—not the future. A year ago, I had been in the middle of a busy social and college life; that other Krulewitch had been able to go and come as he pleased. But then reality asserted itself as my relief broke in with a soft sibilant call, and I crawled as silently as possible back to the line.[8]

Soon he experienced the hail of a heavy German box barrage—first, a crescendo of shell screams, bursts of yellow and red auroras, "showering a rain of death." Not only were the members of his unit the targets of horrendous artillery, but objects of the horror of a gas attack. "Instead of tearing bursts came the plop-plop of a different kind of shell and, with it, the smell of mustard and horseradish. 'Gas! Gas!' and we put on our masks. This was the attack that cost us literally hundreds of casualties."[9]

As Lieutenant Clifton B. Cates, Krulewitch's commanding general at Iwo Jima in 1945 and a future commandant of the Marine Corps, related:

> "I had not gone over twenty feet from my foxhole when I heard a salvo of shells heading our way. From the whistle,

---

[7] Ibid., p. 42.

[8] Ibid., p. 46.

[9] Ibid., p. 43.

I thought they were gas shells, and when they hit with a thud and no detonation, my fears were confirmed. Soon I smelled the gas, and I gave the alarm to the men, and they all put on their masks. By this time, there was a steady stream of incoming shells—gas, air bursts, shrapnel, and high explosives; I reached for my gas mask, but it wasn't there. Naturally, I was petrified. I tried to find my hole where I had left it, but I became confused and couldn't locate it . . . It kept us for hours, and we suffered rather heavy casualties, both from shell fragments and gas, as many of our masks were defective. Heroes were made that night."[10]

Krulewitch described the attack in detail, highlighting the difficulty he had with his gas mask. Although he came through unscathed, men all around him were wounded and gassed. A writer for *The New York Times Magazine,* Pierce Frederickson, recounted, "For the next twenty days, the Brigade fought in the woods rock to rock, one German machine gun to the next, only to find that for every machine gun they captured, two more were positioned to take the Marines on the flank. The Germans went to mustard gas and a Columbia college boy named Mel Krulewitch remembers that they put down a neat barrage and then sent in gas shells. When it was over, Krulewitch led out the eleven men left in a company of more than two hundred."[11] After that, Krulewitch made sergeant.

By the end of June, the woods had been secured. Now an old-timer, Krulewitch was ordered to take out a detail to set up double-apron barbed wiring in German territory. Krulewitch was hit in the leg, left, thigh, and left chest. He reached inside his shirt and pulled a piece of shrapnel in the shape of a horseshoe out of his left rib cage.

At the Aid Center, a gutted church, he was treated for his wounds and then transferred to a field hospital set up to receive

[10] Ibid., p. 47.

[11] Op. cit.

casualties of the 2nd Division. Greasy, infested with lice, and covered with mud, he was bathed before being shipped out with other wounded to the base hospital at Bordeaux.

After a stint as B2 (not fit for combat) and a tour of guarding German prisoners, Krulewitch decided to go over the hill in order to rejoin his company, the 78th. After a forced march of fifty miles to Leffincourt from dawn to moonlight, Krulewitch's battalion received orders to rejoin the division near Montpellier and prepare for the last battle of the war.

The 78th Company captured Belleau Wood on June 25, 1918; achieved victory at Soissons to receive from Petain the *fourragere* of the *Croix de Guerre;* broke through the citadel of Blanc Mont, and participated in the great drive against the *Kremhilde Stellung* (a so-called impregnable 14-mile belt of defense of the Germans) and its approach to the Meuse.

On November 10, 1918, amid rumors of an armistice, the 78th–now online, wet, cold, hungry, exhausted, and sick–waited for orders. Then Second Lieutenant Robb ordered each man to draw four grenades, two extra bandoleers of ammunition, and advised them to stand by.

Reduced from a force of two hundred men to fifty-four within ten days, they found themselves at a crossing of the Meuse. Then they moved to the attack just before dawn, November 11, 1918, Krulewitch's twenty-third birthday.

After an attack during the crossing, enemy shelling began to increase in tempo. Frequent cries of "First aid!" were heard. Ambulances bounced across the uneven terrain. Morale was high. No deaths were suffered.

Suddenly, they heard the unmistakable approach of a whizbang–and they all froze. "Each knew from experience that this particular high explosive had his name on it. Even if cover had been available, no one could have reached it in time. Fascinated, immobile, they could only count to the end."[12]

The high-speed shell landed in the center of the company. Each soldier braced for the inevitable, but "nothing happened.

---

[12] Ibid., p. 58.

For that little group of men came the war's greatest thrill and my best birthday present–the shell was a dud."[13]

The war was over.

On the Marine Corps' birthday, November 1, 1927, Krulewitch was back in the Corps as a Reserve second lieutenant. After promotion to first lieutenant in 1932, he soon received promotion to captain, and, when his company was transferred to the 1st Battalion of the 19th Reserve Regiment, he was promoted to major–thus having gone from second lieutenant to major in five years.

For a year prior to December 7, 1941, Krulewitch had been trying to get back into active service, but it was deemed impracticable for the time being. After a few false fits and starts, in one of which he would be ordered to active duty in the Philippines, on December 26, 1941. Later, Lieutenant Colonel Melvin Krulewitch was ordered to active duty at Marine Barracks, Boston. With 724 officers and men, and seven other detachments, there was little to do and certainly none of the action he wanted. His unit put out a fire on a destroyer loading ammunition, and herded German prisoners (fifteen hundred members of the Afrika Corps) arriving on the *Queen Mary*.

On July 19, 1943, Krulewitch was ordered to Camp Elliott to report for duty with the 4th Marine Division. "I was on my way at last," he thought.

At Camp Pendleton, his division participated in landings on Aliso Beach on the base; field problems at Las Pulgas Canyon and command-post problems near the tent camps; pillbox assaults at Windmill Canyon; and night attacks at the Santa Margarita Ranch.

According to Krulewitch, "Operation Flintlock" was the code name for the 4th Marine Division's mission to seize, occupy, and defend the islands of Roi and Namur, the islets of Ennuebing and Mellu, and the atoll of Kawjalein.

At division headquarters, the commanding general announced to the staff, including Lieutenant Colonel Krulewitch, that the next objective of the 4th Marine Division was to seize,

[13] Op. cit.

occupy, and defend the fortified island of Saipan. After a week of rehearsals during the middle of May 1944, the division sailed for the Central Pacific.

Aboard the transport USS *Leonard Wood*, Krulewitch arrived at Eniwetok. A month later, he and his division sailed for the Marianas where they stormed ashore on June 15. After thirty-eight days of battle, they seized the island of Tinian.

One day, a mortar shell came down on his patrol and exploded right in the middle of the road. He was hit. "A small fragment had cut through my dispatch case, mashed a pack of cigarettes, and been stopped by the metal tube of an antichap petrolatum issued to protect the face and lips against the heat of the tropics. I picked out the sizable metal splinter and held it up to the goggle-eyed patrol. 'Still hot!' I said, and put it in my pocket (I still have it)."[14]

On February 10, 1945, D-Day, H-Hour, the Marines hit the beaches at Iwo Jima. Krulewitch was ordered by General Cates to organize a new unit for combat patrolling. They were soon "Mel's Marauders" and cleaned up his area of operations. After a futile attempt by the enemy on the night of March 15 and early on March 16 to break out of a trap, Krulewitch received the message: "The commanding general of the 5th Amphibious Corps has announced that all organized resistance on Iwo Jima has ceased," and Krulewitch was ordered to return with his troops and detach them, back to their respective battalions.

Never at a loss to defend the Marines, Krulewitch was in a meeting in the Radio City suite of the Bulova Watch Company with former Army Colonel Harry Henshel of that company and General of the Army Omar N. Bradley, who was appointed chairman of the board, when Henshel slyly remarked to the general, "'Our war in Europe didn't need the Marines.' Rising to the bait, I told him, 'You had all you needed for that show—a Marine lieutenant and a platoon. The others were busy.' This did not go over well with the General."[15]

But another conflict was brewing—the war in the Middle East

---

[14] Ibid., p. 116.

[15] Ibid., p. 147.

between the Arabs and Jews over Palestine. Though Krulewitch was not an avowed Zionist, at least politically, his sympathies lay with the Jews. Unwilling to stand on the sidelines, in a purely civilian capacity he went on a mission on his own to inspect the situation firsthand, having been convinced to do so in February 1948 by Teddy Kollek who was procuring arms, men, and supplies for the Haganah. He told Krulewitch that "the British are slated to pull out and leave the country in a few weeks. Around us are thirty million enemies and we stand like the English in 1941. We need your help."[16]

Henshel and Krulewitch arrived in Palestine on March 31, 1948. Briefed by Moshe Dayan and a Haganah commander, then with Ben-Gurion, they set about the country observing, discussing, recommending, criticizing. Krulewitch's report, at least in part, read: "My judgment, based on personal observations, that while some of the Jewish outposts and settlements may be lost in an all-out Arab invasion, Haganah will successfully defend itself against the main attacks. If it acquires heavy weapons and planes, it can win an offensive war against any combination of its enemies."[17]

He was not only sound in his military judgment, but prescient as well. He said, "Diplomatic necessity may require, even command, a return of some of the occupied territories, for which Israel must grow, it cannot do so where it exists at the vital expense of its neighbors. Surrounded by ninety million enemies, Israel must have peace with security within its frontiers."[18]

On his return from Jerusalem, he reported to his old comrade in arms of both world wars, Clifton Cates, Commandant of the Marine Corps, and presented him with a beautiful silver and jeweled Arab dagger. They discussed the possibility of sending U. S. Marines to Palestine. Krulewitch and Henshel both argued against it. At the culmination of arguments in and out of the Senate and the House, they won out. Marines were never sent.

---

[16] Ibid., p. 148.

[17] Ibid., p. 168.

[18] Ibid., p. 169.

With the outbreak of the Korean War, Melvin Krulewitch was recalled to active duty and ordered to Korea on December 16, 1952.

Reporting to his old friend from the late twenties and now commanding general of the 1st Marine Division, Major General Edwin A. Pollock assigned him to headquarters near the railhead at Munsan-Ni as sort of an assistant to Bill Buse, his chief of staff.

Krulewitch's first duty was to inspect the main line of resistance. He was able to see the desolate terrain laid waste by the previous battles between North Koreans, Chinese, and the Americans and their allies. Colonel Lewis W. Walt, USMC, invited Mel for a walk through the area occupied by his regiment, the 5th Marines. While being shelled, Krulewitch picked up the nose cap of a mortar shell with Russian inscription, A11RNH. Although Mel was wearing armor, "Lew took care of the elderly and shunted me into a foxhole with the remark, 'This is no place for a Belleau Wood veteran.'"

The highlight of Krulewitch's Korean tour was a visit to the front lines of the 1st Marines where he got more than a glimpse of the ordeal of that winter of 1952. The regimental CO, Colonel Hewitt D. Adams, USMC, invited him to the assembly point of the patrols. He joined the group there and they all moved out in darkness to the outpost. Adams had gone off somewhere else, and Krulewitch followed the troops only a few ahead. Invisible to sight, although close to touch, they stumbled down the craggy heights toward the valley between the Main Line and COP Vegas.

In the distance, they could "hear the faint rustle of moving bodies, but whether they were Chinese or not I could not tell. Even in 15-degree-below weather, I had begun to sweat in my longjohns, field uniform, and parka, and black terror took hold of me."[19] As it turned out, he now could detect the smell of American sweat and muttering of English. "The Marines approached. They were returning from Vegas but had gotten lost in all the twisting and turning, confused by the black, starless night and bitter cold. After a whispered word of identification, we joined forces, a colonel and three pri-

19 Ibid., p. 176.

vates in a valley that could easily spell death for the four of us."[20]

Although they all were lost, they managed to find their way back to the main line of the 5th Marines. The temperature had reached 17 degrees below zero, and they had reached the limits of their endurance. They "fought that rugged, craggy, perilous terrain with the cold clawing at our guts, our hearts, and our breath. We sobbed as we struggled up the steep, bitter, bruising pitch of hill, very close to the stumbling, tripping, cursing limit of our strength."[21]

The four Marines collapsed and could go no further. Krulewitch found himself begging, cajoling, pleading, cursing for them to get up and continue. He no longer was their superior officer; he was once again a sergeant with his troops–using their language and pulling the men forward to safety. Together, they held each other up, supported one another, and moved over the last stretch to the high ground of their lines. They "lurched and blundered over the crest into waiting arms, warmth, the bunkers, and the nectar of black coffee. It was a while before I realize that the gasping, wrenching, heavy breathing was mine."[22]

"I returned to Division Headquarters after dawn and went to the officers' galley for still more coffee, pitch black, bitter, and hot. The General was up. They were bringing him his eye-opener and a bucket of hot water for his bath and shave. When he saw me, he called out, 'Hi, Mel. Everything OK?'

"'Aye, aye, sir,' I replied."[23]

But Krulewitch's military career still had not run its course– two more missions lay ahead. In 1958, he undertook an assignment to Morocco "to get the lowdown on the French, Spanish, and American situations in order to let us know if there's anything the Corps should know in advance." [24]

He performed his last mission in February 1972. Ordered

---

[20] Op. cit.

[21] Op. cit.

[22] Op. cit.

[23] Op. cit.

[24] Ibid., p. 190.

back to temporary active duty by the Marine Corps for the Memorial Day Service at Belleau Wood, Renaissance man that he was, he delivered the following address in French:

"We return after fifty-four years to these woods, where, in the flower of our youth, we withstood the murderous attacks of the enemy's best regiments. We beat him at his own game and then we counterattacked and resolutely and unflinchingly imposed our will on him.

"Closely adjoining these woods, we endured the poisonous, suffocating gas attack of June 12, 1918, when our company, the 78th, was reduced from a strength of two hundred officers and men to a remnant of eleven men, of whom I happened to be the senior in command. We were all wounded, bloodied, gassed, burned, and weary to the bone, but every one of us refused to be evacuated.

"Here we made our stand, and in that moment of decision we did not fail our fallen comrades. We held these woods and their surrounding area against every violent counterattack during the succeeding days, and as we moved forward, we left behind bodies of our beloved comrades.

"I have come back to Belleau Woods.

"We loved France in springtime and the flowers were as beautiful then as now. There is a true nostalgia among all of us who knew France in our youth, and whose friendship and affection for this country have never changed.

"The *muguet* whose fragrance we enjoyed on that May day in 1918 brought luck to some of us—it's just chance and fate that we are here today—but to our comrades who lie so peacefully in this eternal city, brought the fulfillment of their destiny.

"Say not that these young men who rest around us were cut off in their youth. Life is not measured by years, but rather by accomplishment. To them was granted the opportunity to give their all for freedom, and in that moment of supreme dedication they reached the highest summits of devotion. Let us never forget them, because in their reflected radiance shines the eternal light of freedom."[25]

---

[25] Ibid., p. 250.

Major General Melvin L. Krulewitch, USMCR (ret.), veteran of World War I, World War II, and the Korean War, died at the age of 82 on May 25, 1978, following an apparent heart attack.

Melvin Krulewitch commanded the Headquarters Battalion of the 4th Marine Division at Kwajalein, Saipan, and Tinian, and led the 4th Division's Support Group; and commanded the 4th Provisional Battalion on Iwo Jima. He was promoted to brigadier general on September 28, 1955, and to major general in the Marine Corps Reserve upon his retirement on September 1, 1956.

Among his personal decorations are the Bronze Star Medal with Combat V, and gold star in lieu of a second Bronze Star Medal at Iwo Jima, the Purple Heart with gold star in lieu of a second award, the Organized Marine Reserve Medal, the World War I Victory Medal with three battle clasps, the Army of Occupation of Germany Medal, the Korean Service Medal and the United Nations Service Medal. In addition, he wore the ribbons and decorations of three special battle commendations received by units with whom he fought: the individual French *fourragere* at Soissons, the Presidential Unit Citation at Saipan, and the Navy Unit Commendation at Iwo Jima.

After his retirement, General Krulewitch continued to be active in Marine Corps Reserve and public affairs. He paid special attention to wounded veterans at the St. Albans U.S. Naval Hospital, St. Albans, New York, making frequent visits to wounded Marines there and addressing them on numerous occasions.

Always supportive of the Corps and director of the 1st Marine Corps Reserve District, he helped organized various functions honoring distinguished guests and retired Marine officers, and received and entertained foreign dignitaries.

Among those he was privileged to honor were the commandant of the Korean Marine Corps; the commandant of the Chinese Marine Corps NCO Schools; the admiral commandant of the British Royal Marine Corps; General and Mrs. S. M. Chang, Chinese UN Representative and his wife; the British Joint Warfare Establishment and Presentation Team headed by Air Vice-Marshal Le Cheminant; the commandant of the Royal Netherlands Marine

Corps, Major General A. M. Liujk; the Netherlands ambassador to the UN; and Lord Carodon, the permanent representative of the United Kingdom to the UN.

Krulewitch was a member of various military organizations, including the Marine Corps Reserve Officers Association, the Navy League of the United States, and the Military Order of the World Wars (MOWW). In 1969, he became the first Marine to serve as commander of the New York chapter of the MOWW.

General Krulewitch's son, Peter, graduated from the alma mater of his father, Columbia, and, while there, joined the Platoon Leaders Class Program. He was not commissioned, however, and was honorably discharged as a corporal after five years of Reserve service.

Chapter 45

Major General Larry Taylor

Major General Larry Taylor retired from the Marine Corps on October 1, 1997, after completing thirty-eight years of cumulative service, including five years active and thirty-three years in the Reserve.

Having received his gold wings as a Naval Aviator, he served as a squadron pilot in HMM-264 and 263 in 1964 and 1965. During that period, he participated in operations during the Dominican Republic crisis with the 6th MEU. In August, 1965, he transferred to the 3rd Battalion, 8th Marines, as a forward air controller/air liaison officer. While serving as a platoon commander of the Air and Gunfire Platoon, 2nd Marine Division, he completed his active duty in December 1966.

For all of 1967 and most of 1968, General Taylor served in Laos and Vietnam as a pilot for Air America, flying the Sikorsky H-34.

After returning to the United States in late 1968, he began his Selected Marine Corps Reserve Career, flying the H-34, the UH Huey, and the AH-I Cobra helicopters, and serving in a variety of staff positions at the squadron, wing, and division levels. He held the following command billets: Commanding Officer, Marine Attack Helicopter Squadron 773, (1980–82); Commanding Officer, 4th ANGLICO (1982–84); Commanding General, 2nd

Marine Expeditionary Brigade (1992–93); and Commanding General, 4th MAW (1993–96).

General Taylor's professional education includes: Strategic Intelligence Course at the Defense Intelligence Agency; Aviation Safety Command Course, U.S. Naval Postgraduate School; NATO Air-Ground Operations Course in England; Marine Corps Command and Staff College; and Joint Flag Officers Warfighting Course, Air University, Maxwell Air Force Base, Alabama.

General Taylor graduated from the Georgia Institute of Technology in his hometown of Atlanta with a degree in industrial management. He completed his military career while serving in Central and South America as Deputy Commanding General, Marine Forces South, based in Panama.

In civilian life, he was a captain with Northwest Airlines flying the Boeing 747/400. At his retirement in March 2001, he had accumulated over 22,000 hours of combined military and civilian flight time.

An active member of the USO Council of Georgia, a Fellow of the Inter-University Seminar on the Armed Forces and Society, and the Marine Corps member of the Executive Council of the Reserve Officers Association of the United States, he also chairs the Greater Atlanta Marine Corps Coordinating Council.

General Taylor relates that "in my senior years I have taken up competing in marathons. Having competed in nineteen . . . I was the senior Marine to complete the Marine Corps Marathon in '93 and '95. I am usually timed with a calendar instead of a stopwatch."

Chapter 46

Major General William J. Weinstein

Soon after William J. Weinstein of Detroit became a lawyer, he felt war was coming and enlisted in the Marine Corps in July, 1941 to fight Hitler and Stalin. (After the war, it was discovered that forty-nine members of the immediate family of his Polish-born father were murdered by the Nazis.) He was made Pfc. and assigned to the 4th Officer Candidates Class.

Weinstein was at Quantico for training when the Japanese bombed Pearl Harbor on December 7, 1941. "The base at Quantico took on an emergency aura. We trained night and day, and on January 31, 1942, those of us who had made the grade were commissioned second lieutenants and assigned to the 7th Reserve Officers Class which also was to be trained at Quantico.

"The Marines needed new lieutenants in the field as quickly as possible, and on April 1, 1942, segments of my class were sent to the 1st Marine Division at Tent City in North Carolina (now Camp Lejeune), the Artillery School at Quantico, and the 2nd Marine Division units at Camp Elliott. (At the time, the entire U.S. Marine Corps consisted of less than 60,000 officers and men. At the end of World War II, that number had grown to over 500,000 officers and men.)

"In April 1942, I was ordered to the West Coast where I joined the 2nd Battalion, 6th Marines as a leader of an infantry platoon.

The 6th Marines had just returned from duty in Iceland and were 'salty' Marines.

"Promotions were unusually fast during 1942 and 1943, and I found myself in June of 1943 promoted to the greatest rank in the Corps, 'Captain,' and assigned to the best possible position in the Corps—the command of an infantry rifle company, B Company, 1st Battalion, 23rd Marines, 4th Marine Division, FMF.

On January 1, 1944, Weinstein's entire division left San Diego and was the first Marine division to leave the United States and go directly into combat without stopping at an interim base. His infantry company was to land on Roi, one of two principal islands in Kwajalein's northern chain. Captain Weinstein's rifle company was initially embarked on an APA. Before the landing, the company was transferred to an LST.

"I found that the tractors [LVTs (landing vehicles, tracked)] carrying my two assault waves were loaded in the well (the 'belly' of the ship that had two large doors to permit the tractors to drive directly into the water), and my third and fourth waves of tractors were loaded on the main upper deck and had to be lowered into the well by one elevator."

After a number of tense moments occasioned by the LSTs malfunctioning elevator, Weinstein's company eventually landed on the beaches.

"Fortunately for my rifle company, the naval bombardment and naval air strike had been so effective that there was little opposition, and the forward elements of my company pushed across the island of Roi—which measures approximately 400 by 450 yards—within five hours. We suffered no casualties. I had landed with the second wave at H-Hour + five (minutes). The regiment on our right (the 24th Marines) was not as fortunate. They met considerable resistance on the island of Namur and lost a number of courageous officers and men."

As the 4th Division streamed across the Pacific toward Roi and Namur, each APA carried approximately 1,400 officers and men. On each ship, the Marines had a Protestant and a Catholic chaplain. Men of the Jewish faith had but one chaplain in the entire division (approximately 18,000 officers and men), and he could be on only one ship. "Our APA had no Jewish chaplains, and no Jewish services were scheduled when we departed," reported Weinstein.

[After he had been at sea for a week, Weinstein was approached by] "Four enlisted Marines, none of whom were in my rifle company. Their spokesman, Pfc. Bernard 'Jinx' Shaffman, with some trepidation in his voice, said: 'Sir, we're of the Jewish faith and we have a question for you. Sir, are you Jewish?'

"I was somewhat taken aback by the question and replied, 'I sure am.'

"The Pfc. then said, 'Sir, we're going into combat, and the Protestant and Catholic men aboard are having services, and we wondered if we could have Jewish services.'

"I gulped, and said, 'Absolutely. I'll check to see if we can hustle up some prayer books and have Jewish services.'

"Luckily, I had been *bar mitzvahed* as a youngster and had some instruction in Hebrew. I contacted the Catholic chaplain of our battalion, a saintly and beloved man, and he said 'Yes, Bill, I've got a number of prayer books furnished by the Jewish Welfare Board (JWB) and, if you like, I'd be glad to conduct the service for you.'

"I thanked him profusely but said, 'I think the Jewish Marines would be too surprised to see the Catholic chaplain conduct their services, and I assure you we'll manage somehow, but thanks so much.'

"I contacted the ship's captain and asked for a time and place for our services. He was most agreeable, and soon thereafter over the loudspeaker came the announcement: 'Jewish services will be held on the poop deck at 1930 hours on Friday.'

"As Friday approached, I wondered if we would have a *minyan*. At 1930 on Friday, I went to the poop deck and, to my chagrin and surprise, I found forty-six enlisted men—my congregation!

"I said hopefully, 'I need a volunteer to lead the services,' and looked around. They were all outstanding and well-trained Marines. Not one volunteered.

"In desperation, I passed out the prayer books and announced: 'Alright. I'll try. Turn to page 3 and we'll start with the *Oshreh* (an opening prayer for the service). I started the prayer in a low tone, but as I strained my ear, I could not hear my congregation praying. I immediately stopped and turned around, faced them, and asked, 'How many of you can read Hebrew?'

"Approximately twenty men raised their hands, at which time I realized that my assumption was wrong about every person of the Jewish faith having had at least the equivalent amount of religious education as I. Many had little, if any, such education. It seemed that my congregation was a mixture of Orthodox, Conservative, Reform, and agnostic Americans of Jewish background who wanted and needed their faith very badly at a critical time in their lives.

"'OK, then,' I said, 'we'll conduct the services in English, but when we come to the portion of the service that highlights our faith, it will be said in English *and* Hebrew. If you can't read Hebrew, read it phonetically. That prayer is the *Shema*—'Hear, O Israel, the Lord our God, the Lord is One.'

"I conjured up some type of sermon for each service, but my sermons were mainly nothing more than pep talks in my congregation for us to prove that Americans of the Jewish faith were darned good Marines and would give a good account of themselves in combat.

"Thus began our Friday night services that continued until our division landed on Roi-Namur. After the battle, where the casualties were basically light, we boarded the APA to return to our training base at Maui in Hawaii.

"These same Marines, my congregation, sought me out and many said, 'We'd be hypocrites if we didn't have services going back to Maui and thank God for having sustained us throughout this battle. We did, and it has a lasting impression on me for the remainder of my years, and I shall never forget them.

"I had command of this same rifle company (B Company, 1st

Battalion, 23rd Marines) for the battles of Saipan and Tinian in the Marianas Islands in the Central Pacific. We continued Jewish services for the troops before and after these battles. But, unfortunately, we lost many wonderful young Marines of all faiths, including a number of my congregation."

"My rifle company landed on the left flank of the 4th Marine Division on Saipan with the mission of securing that area until the large gap in our beachhead could be closed in contact with the 2nd Marine Division whose units had landed on the adjacent beaches far to our left.

"The Japanese had the high ground to our front (Mount Fina Susu) and were looking down our throats. We were subjected to intense artillery barrages all day and night. Our casualties were heavy, but we held our ground. The next day, as we attacked to our front in our mission to capture Mount Fina Susu, we discovered the Japanese artillery emplaced hub to hub at the mountain's base. It took our battalion six days to capture the mountain and the 'Palm Grove' on its reverse slope. At the end of this phase of the operation, I had one officer and myself, and ninety-eight enlisted men left in my command. (My rifle company had six officers and 205 enlisted personnel when we landed on Saipan.) I also had 'earned' my first Purple Heart, as I was shot during our assault on the 'Palm Grove.'

"Approximately six days later, in the late afternoon, my rifle company encountered a mammoth cave which appeared to be some type of supply area. We Marines had been taught three sentences in Japanese: 'Don't be afraid,' 'Come out with your hands up,' and 'Take off your clothes.'

"I stepped to the mouth of the cave and shouted in Japanese, 'Don't be afraid. Come out with your hands up.' After repeating the sentences three or four times, to my amazement, a Japanese officer appeared with his hands up. Although he spoke no English, I was able to understand that there were many other Japanese in the cave, but I couldn't understand anything else. I reached for my radio, contacted my battalion headquarters, and requested a Japanese interpreter to be sent to the area ASAP.

Within twenty minutes, Lieutenant Howard M. Moss of Elizabeth, New Jersey, arrived. Moss was a Japanese specialist assigned to the Marines and spoke Japanese.

"After a briefing by me as to what had occurred, he began shouting into the cave in Japanese. 'Come out. We have food, medicines, and we will treat you fairly.' The Japanese officer reappeared and spoke to Lieutenant Moss, and told him the Japanese personnel in the cave were leery—that if they surrendered, the Marines would kill them. Moss assured them that they had nothing to fear from my Marines, that they (the Japanese) would be treated fairly and would be fed and housed. The Japanese officer went back into the cave and, within ten minutes, reappeared with thirty-four dirty, emaciated, exhausted soldiers who surrendered to us. This was the largest contingent of live Japanese I had ever seen.

"As I was standing talking on the radio, reporting to my battalion headquarters, unbeknownst to us, one Japanese soldier, incensed that his comrades surrendered, had secretly, with a Nambu machine gun, climbed into a crevice in the cave hidden from our view and opened fire.

"My radioman, my runner, and I were exposed but the fanatic Japanese soldier did not shoot at us. Instead, he shot and killed twenty-two of the surrendered Japanese soldiers before I could crawl to safety to contact my half-track (looks like an armored truck, but had a 75 mm cannon mounted on it) commanded by Lieutenant Russell Paquette, then assigned to support my company. We were finally able to maneuver the half-track into position, fire its cannon, and, fortunately, on the first shot, kill the Japanese machine gunner. We then gathered up the remaining twelve Japanese soldiers and, as dusk was descending marched to our assigned area. We were then placed in battalion reserve. Unfortunately, we still had our Japanese prisoners with us, and it was not a comfortable night for my rifle company nor myself. We guarded those prisoners until dawn when the Military Police finally arrived to escort them to the prisoners' stockade at Division Headquarters.

"The III Amphibious Corps Commander (on Saipan), Marine General Holland M. ('Howlin' Mad') Smith, relieved the 27th Army Division commander and ordered the two Marine divisions to stretch their lines, join forces, and continue northward to capture the remainder of the island. My company was to attack . . . at 0700 that morning, and each Marine rifle company would replace an army battalion on the front lines. My company now had approximately thirty-seven men and two officers. We were assigned a front of approximately 1,200 yard, a *battalion* front!" (A normal frontage for an attack by an infantry rifle company was approximately 250–400 yards.)

In attempting to relieve the army units in his assigned section, Weinstein was unable to find a knowledgeable army officer to brief him.

"I then knew I was in a terrible bind—I hadn't the slightest clue as to where the front lines were, where the flanks were, and most important, what the enemy situation was . . . I made the hard-nosed decision. Form a skirmish line, head north toward Mount Tapotchau (my objective) as best we could. We didn't have enough personnel to cover 1,200 yards of frontage . . . but took our assigned objective within hours. We later drove north to the sea with little or moderate opposition . . . I shall never forget the Japanese soldiers forcing civilians to jump from a precipitous cliff into the water, to their death, before our Marines were able to destroy those crazed soldiers.

"The island of Tinian lies directly to the south of Saipan in the Marianas chain in the Central Pacific. The 4th Marine Division landed at the northern beaches of the island on July 24, 1944. At first glance, everyone would have agreed these beaches were much too narrow to land one Marine division, let alone two such massive war machines. The beaches assigned to the 4th Marine division were only 65–135 yards wide, hardly large enough for one rifle company. There was an excellent military reason, however, that justified the use of these beaches. The adequate and well-designated landing beaches at the southern part of the island were used by the U.S. naval forces to feint a landing there by deploying small landing craft from APAs in the area without troops in them to trick the Japanese into strongly defending the southern beaches while the real landings were miles to the north. The landing was almost under impossible conditions, but Tinian will always be held to be an outstanding example of U.S. Marine ingenuity and innovativeness in amphibious operations.

"As a result, the Marines found light to moderate opposition in making the landing. My rifle company was assigned the mission to protect the right flank of the division, and we found ourselves on the coral reef of the island. We couldn't dig in because the coral reef was nothing more than sharp, hard rock and our shovels were absolutely useless. We spent the first day aligning our front lines, setting up our machine guns and mortars, and just laid down on the coral rock and hoped for the best.

"Throughout the first night, the Japanese, who finally awoke to the fact that Marines had landed on the narrow northern beaches, moved their forces from the southern beaches, a distance of approximately seven miles. Throughout the first night, the Japanese forces counterattacked our front lines with everything they had: tanks, mortars, and the fanatic infantry.

"In the morning on D-Day +1, my company was ordered into the attack. In our attempt to move forward, it was necessary to climb over hundreds of dead Japanese soldiers stacked in front of our lines, none of whom ever were able to pierce our battalion's front lines.

"As my company approached the town of Tinian, located on the southern part of the island, we were in the attack. As we moved forward, I noticed movement in a bush approximately 100 yards to our direct front. I cautioned company Gunnery Sergeant Norvell Mills, who was alongside me at the time, and we both lifted our carbines and shot into the bush. When we approached it, we finally saw a Japanese officer on the ground, dead, holding his binoculars and his sword, and in his holster was his pistol. The officer had been shot in the head and in the area of the heart. Apparently, Mills and I had both shot the officer."

When Weinstein returned to the United States, he brought three souvenirs from that battle with him: a large Japanese flag with much writing on it, the Japanese officer's sword, and his binoculars. Weinstein assumed the flag was a "regimental flag," and had it cleaned and put away. In 1947, he asked a Japanese client of his to translate the writing. The flag turned out to be a department-store banner advertising the sale of merchandise. Now, only the sword hangs next to Weinstein's Marine Corps sword on a wall of his home in Michigan.

"As we prepared for the invasion of Iwo Jima, I was transferred to the 1st Battalion, 25th Marines, where on Iwo Jima, was given the assignment of Battalion Operations Officer.

"While the first six days on Saipan were most difficult for the Marines establishing our beachhead, Iwo Jima was literally hell from beginning to end. We landed on February 19, 1945, and secured the island on March 18, 1945.

"I was with the headquarters unit of the battalion and will always remember February 19, 1945, as a beautiful, sunny day with a calm sea and nary a cloud in the sky. My amtrac contained the battalion commanding officer, Lieutenant Colonel Hollis Mustain, one of the Marine greats of World War II. (Lieutenant Colonel Mustain was killed in action on D + 1 on Iwo Jima by enemy artillery as he was inspecting our front lines.)

"Our amtrac was in the fifth wave. We could see the assault rifle company tractors in waves running to the beach. We could spot no resistance by the Japanese. As the third wave hit the beach, all hell broke loose. The Japanese were hidden in their fortifications, and, after the naval bombardment and air strikes lifted, they opened up with their artillery, mortars, machine guns, and rifles and swept the beaches with fire. The beaches were made up of black volcanic ash approximately 10–15 deep. We could see, while still in our tractors, that we were in for one tough fight. When our tractors finally landed at H + 25, the issue was in doubt. We had suffered serious casualties; the assault companies were spread out and had lost contact with each other.

"The sand on the beach made walking difficult, but that wasn't my problem. The enemy fire was so intense that I had to literally crawl from foxhole and foxhole and direct the men so that our front lines were kept intact. (I was awarded the Bronze Star Medal with Combat V for these acts.)

"Our front-line commanders were more than able to obtain some semblance of a beachhead on D-Day. The battle for a fight for yards, not miles.

"Our division made a turning movement to the right after the landing, and eventually we found that we facing 'Turkey Knob'—a Japanese defensive position that consisted of cement blockhouses containing Japanese machine guns and infantry. We used everything we had: tanks, flamethrowers, tank flamethrowers, infantry, but breaching these Japanese defenses was not going to be easy. Our tanks carried 75mm cannons which we found were useless against the cement blockhouses. These cannons were antiquated, low-velocity weapons that could not penetrate cement more than a fraction of an inch per round.

"The flamethrowers were effective, but attempting to move them up into position where they could fire was most difficult. They were met with a hail of enemy artillery, mortar, and small-arms fire. Again, we were fighting for yards every day.

"After the Battle of Iwo Jima, the 4th Marine Division returned once again to the island of Maui to regroup, obtain replacements, and retrain for the final push—the invasion of Japan. The Marines who had survived the four amphibious operations that were still in the 4th Marine Division were considered by all to be the 'old salts'of the Corps. We trained hard and finally, in July of 1945, we conducted practice landings on the beaches of Maui before embarking upon the naval ships for the invasion of Japan. We knew the Japanese soldier to be a fanatic who had been indoctrinated to fight no matter what the odds were against him. So the thought was constantly in our minds that this battle would be the toughest of them all.

"In August 1945, as I was sitting on a sandbag, watching a movie one night at the regimental outdoor movie area, the film was interrupted by an announcement over the public-address system telling us of the dropping of the atomic bomb on Hiroshima.

"A cry went up from the 2,000 men at the outdoor theater—the Marines with wild with joy. Within days, another bomb had been dropped on the city of Nagasaki, Japan. Again, the reaction of our troops on Maui was one of joyful excitement. The peace treaty was signed shortly thereafter.

"Ironically, many years later, as Mrs. Weinstein and I were on a tour of China and Japan in 1987, we arrived in Japan. I was then a retired major general in the U.S. Marine Corps Reserve. We were met there by a group of Japanese boys and girls with petitions in their hands, asking for our signatures. I read the petition requesting in effect that all atomic weapons be destroyed and never used again. The young man who made the request for my signature repeated the slogan over and over: 'No More, Nagasaki, No More Nagasaki.'

"I looked at him and said, 'I'll sign your petition, but you have to add one more phrase to it: 'No More Pearl Harbor. No More Nagasaki.'

"The lad, with a quizzical look on his face, asked, 'What's Pearl Harbor?'

"Have your teachers teach you the real history of World War II that finally led my country to use the atomic bomb, and you'll understand.

"However, it was during that visit in 1987 as I looked at the faces of the young Japanese boys and girls when I realized it was not fair for me to hate—that it was their parents and their grandparents who had fought the war and believed the propaganda their country had fed them, much of which was not true. I duly rearranged my thinking about the Japanese people.'

"After the war, I attended services to celebrate the Jewish New Year and Yom Kippur held by the Jewish chaplain in the city of Kahului on the island of Maui in October 1945.

"Hundreds of Marines of the Jewish faith were at the services to ask for repentance and to thank the good Lord for sustaining us throughout the battles of the Pacific and permitting us to return to our families in the United States. After the services were over, the rabbi and Lieutenant Colonel Melvin Krulewitch, who was serving in the 4th Marine Division headquarters, asked if I would accompany them back to the division officers' mess to break the fast. (Jews are required to fast for the entire day of Yom Kippur until sundown.)

I gladly accepted the invitation and returned with the Jewish chaplain and Colonel Krulewitch to the division officers' mess to find, to our dismay, that the menu for the day was ham!

"I turned to the rabbi and said, 'Look, Rabbi, we don't have to eat here. You can eat at my battalion's officers' mess, and I think we've got steak for dinner!'

"The rabbi looked at me and said, 'Look, if it was meant to be, it's meant to be. Under Jewish law, we all have dispensation to eat whatever we need in order to sustain us. This is especially true under these circumstances while we are serving in the armed forces of our country.' Thus, I had my first meal of ham and it was the first and last meal I ate 'of the forbidden fruit.' There were only two things that I could not eat and still cannot eat to this day because of my religious training as a young man—one is ham and the other is lobster; and truly, I can't understand why I cannot do it. It seems that although I have tried, the food sticks in my throat and I just can't swallow it.

"Many years later, in 1969, I attended a ball in New York City given by the Marine Corps Scholarship Fund. There were two other generals present—one was our Commandant, General Leonard Chapman, and the other was Major General Melvin Krulewitch. It was great seeing him again. He had remarried a wonderful lady. I had followed his career while practicing law in Detroit. I knew he had run for mayor of the City of New York. I knew he had been a boxing commissioner for the State of New York, but General Krulewitch was just one great Marine who had served his country in many wars.

"As the war ended, I was offered a regular commission in the United States Marine Corps—but chose to return to civilian life and continue my military career in the active Reserve—when I returned home in 1946. The Korean War broke out in 1950, and I volunteered for active duty. I was told the Marines were only interested in junior officers, lieutenants and captains. In 1948, I had been promoted to the rank of major.

"In 1951, while the Korean conflict was at its height, the Marine Corps decided to reestablish its active Reserve throughout the United States. I applied for a billet in a newly formed battalion in Detroit, Michigan, and was made its Executive Officer. In 1954, after being promoted to lieutenant colonel, I was given command of the battalion.

"After four years as commanding officer and a stint in a Volunteer Training Unit, I was promoted to colonel in 1962 . . . . I was then given command of the 13th Staff Group duly formed at Detroit, Michigan, which, in effect, was a regimental staff group capable of operating a Marine infantry regiment. We conducted summer camps at Coronado and Twentynine Palms, California, and Little Creek, Virginia.

"While training at Twentynine Palms in 1965, the commanding general, William Jones, said to me, 'Bill, the Vietnam War is on, and we're getting more and more involved. One of these days you're going to be called out to active duty and no doubt you'll be assigned to the Judge Advocate duty of our Corps.'

"I turned to General Jones and said, 'Sir, you can't afford me as a lawyer—my fees are too high. But you can afford me as a Chief of Staff of an infantry division or as an infantry regimental commander.'

"The general laughed and said, 'Bill, come on, you're still gung ho. We shall see.'

"In the summer of 1966, while attending an attorneys' convention in Miami, Florida, Major General Sydney McMath, USCMR, former Governor of Arkansas and one of the outstanding trial lawyers in the United States at the time, sought me out in the coffee shop of the hotel to inform me that he had just left

Washington, D.C., and the Commandant of the Marine Corps at the time, General Wallace Greene, had briefed him to the effect that the Marine Corps Reserve would be mobilized. He then informed me that he would command the 4th Marine Division (the Reserve division) and that I was selected to be one of the regimental commanders of the division.

"I was about to start some important litigation, and I said, 'Well, I've got to leave Florida immediately and return to Michigan and wind up my practice. How much time do I have?'

"'You have approximately ten days,' he replied. General McMath then turned to me and said, 'Oh, let's go up to my room and listen to President Johnson. He's about to go on the air to announce the calling up of the Reserves at 11 A.M.'

"Later that morning, I appeared at his room. The television was turned on and President Johnson made his speech. He finally said, 'I will *not* be calling up the Reserves at this time.' General McMath looked at me in disbelief and said, 'My God, I just left Washington yesterday. The Joint Chiefs had met. The President had approved it. My God, he's changed his mind!'"

As a result, Bill Weinstein never got the opportunity of leading a regiment in combat.

"Years later, when I was a brigadier general, the Commandant ordered me to make speeches (from time to time) throughout the Midwest on the issue of Vietnam. Invariably, as I finished each speech, someone in the audience would raise his or her hand to ask the question, 'When was the last time you were in Vietnam, General?' And I would have to answer, 'I have never been to Vietnam.' This was always followed by a snicker in the back of the audience, and I was most disturbed about the situation. Finally, I called General Greene to inform that I would prefer not to make any further speeches unless he would send me to Vietnam. After I related the background to General Greene, he agreed, and, in April of 1969, I was ordered to Vietnam.

"I was briefed as to the situation at FMFPac, Headquarters on Oahu in the Hawaiian Islands and flew into Vietnam. I was ordered there as the FMFPac Deputy Commander. I spent approximately ten days in Vietnam where I was given a small staff and permitted to go anywhere I wanted. I visited all the front-line units, and spoke to the officers and men. When I left Vietnam, I was debriefed at FMFPac, Headquarters on Oahu.

"In August of 1970, I was the Assistant Division Commander of the 4th Marine Division. I was assigned the responsibility by Marine Corps Headquarters of conducting the largest amphibious operation exercise by a Reserve unit in the history of the Corps to be known as HIGH DESERT. Approximately 22,000 officers and men, Marines and naval personnel, were assigned to the exercise to be conducted at Camp Pendleton. General Lewis W. Walt, Assistant Commandant of the Marine Corps, together with a number of Marine general officers and Navy admirals, were there to observe the entire operation. At the conclusion of the exercise, General Walt declared the exercise 'an outstanding success,' and further stated that he was impressed by the Reserves to the extent that he could not tell the difference between the Reserve Marine and the Regular Marine.

"In May 1975, after having served stints as Assistant Base Commander, Camp Lejeune, North Carolina, and as Deputy Commander, Fleet Marine Force, Atlantic (FMFLant), I was retired at a ceremony at Eighth and I, Washington, D.C., with the then Commandant of the Marine Corps, General Robert Cushman, the Marine Band and the Marine Drum and Bugle Corps, and all the Marines present turned out in their blues and whites to render me the honor of a parade in front of the Commandant's home."

Major General William J. Weinstein was decorated with the Legion of Merit with gold star in lieu of a second award, the Bronze Star Medal with Combat V, the Purple Heart with gold star in lieu of a second award, two Presidential Unit Citations, the Asiatic-Pacific Campaign Medal with four bronze stars, and other medals and decorations.

"To this day, remnants of my old rifle company I fought with in World War II still meet each year to reminisce, tell our sea stories, and rekindle the flame of camaraderie that existed all these years. I take great pride in having served in the 23rd and 25th Regiments of the 4th Marine Division with so many excellent officers and men. The enlisted personnel were mostly teenagers when they served their country in World War II, and they were truly outstanding. Their courage, tenacity, and bravery can never adequately be described in words.

"When I returned from World War II to the Detroit, Michigan, area to resume my life, I began the practice of a small law firm. My legal trial career lasted from 1946 until my retirement from the practice at the age of 76 in 1996."

Weinstein received the Distinguished Alumnus Award from Wayne State University Law School in 1968.

"I had two wonderful, great, exciting careers—one in the law and one in the military."

Author's Note:

I received an unsolicited letter from a Mr. James "Red" Kelley of Tewksbury, Massachusetts, as follows: "(a stand-out) is the former Captain William Weinstein, now Major General William Weinstein. Bill was my section leader on Iwo Jima. He was the battalion intelligence officer, S-2, for the 1st Battalion, 1st Marines—a former lawyer from Detroit and still a great lawyer today. He was without a doubt the best line officer I have ever seen in action and he did a great job on Iwo. After our CO was KIA, D + 1, Weinstein was told to take over the position of operations officer for our battalion."

At the end of June, 2002, I received a call from his long-time friend, Colonel Sylvan Kaplan, that General William J. Weinstein had passed away.

Chapter 47

Brigadier General Martin F. Rockmore

Born on September 5, 1917 in Brooklyn, Brigadier General Martin F. Rockmore, USMCR (ret.), graduated from James Madison High School there in 1934. He received his B.A. degree in economics upon graduation from Saint Lawrence University, Canton, New York, in January 1939.

A month later he enlisted in the U.S. Marine Corps Reserve as a second lieutenant and was assigned to Company D, 3rd Battalion, USMCR.

Called to active duty on November 8, 1940, he was assigned as a company officer of Company I, 3rd Battalion, 7th Marines, and served at Guantanamo Bay, Cuba; with the 1st Marine Division, FMF, while aboard the USS *George F. Elliott,* and at New River. In February 1942, he was reassigned as CO of Company E. 2nd Battalion, 1st Marines, at New River.

With this unit, he was ordered overseas in May 1942. His company landed in the assault wave on Guadalcanal August 7, 1942, and played a major role in the Battle of the Tenaru. He later participated in combat as Operations Officer, 1st Marines, 1st Marine Division. During this period, he received a meritorious promotion to major and a regular commission in the Marine Corps. For conspicuous gallantry and intrepidity during the seizure and occupation of Cape Gloucester, New Britain Islands, December 26, and 28, he was awarded the Silver Star Medal.

General Rockmore later served as Regimental S-3 with the 1st Marines and Assistant Chief of Staff, G-3, with Headquarters Company, Headquarters Battalion, 1st Marine Division.

Upon his return to the United States in June, 1944, he served as Instructor, Tactical Section, Reserve Officers' School and later, Instructor, General Subjects Section, Platoon Commanders School, Marine Corps School, Quantico. He served in the latter capacity until he resigned, as a major, in December 1945.

General Rockmore was reappointed a major, USMCR, with rank from May 3, 1943; promoted to lieutenant colonel, February 1, 1950; and to colonel, July 1, 1958. He retired November 1, 1959, and was advanced to the rank of brigadier general for having been specially commended in combat.

He conceived and founded the Marine Corps Scholarship Foundation in 1962 after reading about a Marine who could not afford to send his to college. Within a few years, hundreds of young men and women were able to attend college because of General Rockmore's foundation.

In addition to the Silver Star Medal, his awards and decorations include the Navy Unit Commendation, the American Campaign Medal, the Asiatic-Pacific Campaign Medal, and the World War II Victory Medal.

General Rockmore died on June 27, 1992, at his home in Chesterfield, Missouri, and was buried in Arlington National Cemetery with full military honors.

PART XI

Marines . . . The Pride Is
Permanent

Introduction

It will take the reader but a few moments to inquire, perhaps to be perplexed, as to the order in which the stories of the following Marines is presented. There is an obvious absence of order or chronology in which they appear.

It is not, however, done with some absence of logic or afore-thought. The task of obtaining the names and stories of most of the participants was, at best, difficult. Some participants were eager to collaborate, others were reluctant, and a number, for a variety of reasons, had no wish to disclose their histories.

The responses of the following participants, nevertheless, were received in divergent time frames; some received very quickly after they learned of the project; others were sent belatedly. The accounts which follow are presented, more or less, in the order in which they responded, or, in the case of deceased veterans, when their stories were uncovered.

They have been Marines. Each of them continues to carry that title proudly. No distinction is made among the following participants. They were, and remain in perpetuity, holders of the proud title of U.S. Marine.

Chapter 48

Marines

Harold A. Cohen, Bronx, New York, enlisted in the U.S. Marine Corps, in 1942. Upon completion of boot camp, he was sent to MCAS, Cherry Point, and subsequently to the Supply School, Naval Training Station, San Diego. Following graduation, he had duty at various bases, principally MCAS, Mojave, California, and MCAS, Goleta, California.

From the last base, Technical Sergeant Cohen was deployed overseas, joining MAG-24, with its dive bombing squadrons, in Bougainville.

General MacArthur, impressed with the close air support tactics employed by these squadrons, requested the attachment of MAG-24 to the 6th U.S. Army for the invasion of Leyte in the Philippines. During that period on Leyte, MAG-24 was attached to the 8th U.S. Army for the invasion of Mindanao. While there, and with the surrender of the Japanese, Cohen was sent to Peking, China, where MAG-24 set up an airbase.

After several months in China, Cohen was returned to the United States for discharge at Great Lakes NTC.

Cohen enlisted in the U.S. Marine Corps Reserve, leaving after one year to join the U.S. Army Reserve. He retired in 1972 as a CWO-3.

Harold Cohen is the recipient of the Good Conduct Medal, the Navy Unit Commendation Ribbon with star, the American

Campaign Medal, the Asiatic-Pacific Campaign Medal with 5 bronze stars, the World War II Victory Medal, the Navy Occupation Service Medal, the China Service Medal, and the Philippine Liberation Ribbon with one bronze star.

Second Lieutenant Herman Drizin was the son of Jacob and Lena Drizin, immigrants from Russia. As the son of immigrants he felt that he had a special loyalty to his country, and rendered the ultimate sacrifice in defending it.

He graduated from Frankfort High School in Philadelphia, followed by three and a half years at Villanova University where he was a star basketball player. With the outbreak of the war, he enlisted in the Marine Corps Reserve on April 11, 1942 while still in college, and was assigned to the Marine Detachment, Navy-12 unit as a private. Called to active duty in the summer of 1943, he took basic training at Parris Island from November 1943, to January 1944.

Following boot camp, he was assigned to the Candidates Attachment at the Training Center, Camp Lejeune, North Carolina, and, in February 1944, became a member of the 46th Officers Candidates Class at Quantico. With graduation on May 3, 1944, he was commissioned a second lieutenant in the Marine Corps Reserve, and, later, completed the Reserve Officers Course at Quantico.

In October, he joined the 17th Replacement Draft after having been assigned as a platoon leader with the 2nd Training Battalion, Infantry Training Regiment, Camp Lejeune. Departing the United States as a member of E Company, 2nd Battalion, 23rd Marines, he sailed from San Diego on November 10, destination Pearl Harbor. In January 1945, he embarked with his unit aboard the USS *Mifflin* for Saipan, and re-embarked aboard LST-761 for Iwo Jima on February 15.

He participated in the invasion and capture of Iwo Jima until March 6, 1945, when he was killed in action. He was buried in the 4th Marine Division Cemetery on Iwo Jima. After the war, he was returned to the United States at the request of his parents, and re-interred in Har Yehuda Cemetery, Philadelphia.

Lieutenant Herman Drizin was posthumously awarded the Silver Star Medal, the Purple Heart, as well as the Presidential Unit Citation, the American Campaign Medal, the Asiatic-Pacific Campaign Medal, and the World War II Victory Medal.

Marine Major Irving Schecter (later to be promoted to colonel), then 27, of Smithtown Branch, landed on Tinian with his rifle company, took over a narrow beach section of cliffs and coral boulders. Theirs was the left flank of the entire landing force and it had to be held. Soon after their landing, they were raked by hostile fire as they tried to establish a beachhead.

In the morning, Schecter and his men were expecting a Japanese counterattack. The enemy poured down on the small beachhead with rifles, machine gun fire, and grenades, threatening to overrun the Marines by sheer weight of numbers. His men replied with their own fire to prevent the larger Japanese force from overrunning them. After a heated battle which lasted for hours, Schecter's force suffered many casualties and were severely reduced in numbers. Assisted by a relief force sent to their assistance, they forced the enemy back to their own lines. Schecter's force held their ground, Major Schecter moving constantly among them.

The Japanese counterattack was broken as more than 400 enemy dead lay in front of Schecter's defense position. Huge quantities of enemy weapons were captured.

For his gallant part in this action, Major Schecter was awarded the Navy Cross. The citation for the award declared: "By his heroic action Major Schecter was responsible for eliminating a serious threat to the success of the entire operation and contributed greatly to making further organized resistance by the enemy virtually impossible."[1]

---

[1] Kaufman, I., *American Jews in World War II*, Dial Press, New York, New York, p. 224–26.

Major Schecter found himself deep in combat with the invasion of Saipan. He was once again in the forefront of the hostilities. Always exposed to intense hostile fire, always leading his men, he continued to expose himself to withering enemy fire, continually guiding his men skillfully, all the while directing accurate fire on the enemy. Although his unit suffered many casualties, he continued the fight and directed the evacuation of the wounded until they were relieved.

In addition to the Navy Cross, Major Schecter received the Silver Star, Bronze Star, Purple Heart, and the Presidential Unit Citation.

In his classic award-winning book of U.S. Marines in World War II, *Semper Fi, Mac*, the author, Henry Berry, commends Schecter for his loyalty, bravery, and dedication to the Corps and country, and singles him out as a person most to be emulated and admired. He says that, "Irving Schecter is another World War II Marine who was decorated several times for bravery yet who hardly seems to fit the mold of a fire-eating Chesty Puller."

Buck (a Marine Corps sobriquet) fought in three campaigns as a rifle company commander and was decorated after each campaign. He received the Silver Star for bravery on the Marshall Islands, the Navy Cross for heroism at Saipan-Tinian, and the Bronze Star for bravery at Iwo Jima. He was also wounded on Saipan.

Mr. Schecter is currently (1998) the president of the Bank of Smithtown on Long Island and quite active in his own law firm in the same town. If one ever makes a wrong turn in Smithtown, Buck is a good man to know.

Buck serves as a model for all Marine Corps Reserve officers. He had never planned to be a military man. A graduate of the University of Iowa, he later received a law degree from New York University and was about to hang out his single when the threat of American involvement in World War II convinced him to enter the Marine Corps. He could have easily obtained a job in the Corps's legal department but that wasn't why young Mr. Schecter had joined the Corps. He would be the last one to brag about it, but Buck joined the Marines specifically to fight for his country. And he did.

Mr. Schecter retired from the United States Marine Corps Reserve a few years ago with the rank of colonel. But he still looks as though he could lead a company into combat."[2]

Another former Marine whose military experience has proved to be of inestimable benefit is Louis Burg. Enlisting as a recruit in August 1942, he completed boot camp at Parris Island. He feels as if the military has inculcated in him a positive manner, pride in what he is and what he does, and promotes a certain camaraderie among friends, colleagues, and acquaintances.

Brooklyn-born Louis Burg was graduated from the City University of New York with a degree in accounting; and Brooklyn Law School with a law degree. After completion of boot camp, he entered pre-commissioning training at Duke University, Durham, North Carolina, and Camp Lejeune, then Officer Candidate School at Quantico. After receiving his commission as a second lieutenant, he was stationed at Lejeune before being transferred to Camp Pendleton.

A rather unusual incident happened to Lieutenant Burg and his wife, Lil, while assigned to a training battalion in 1944. He and his wife lived off base in Jacksonville, North Carolina, with a southern family.

At first they were very cold to the Burgs. With the passage of time, however, they became more open, and more friendly.

As Burg says, "When I was assigned overseas and we left the tenancy, they confessed that they would not have rented to us had they known we were Jews.

"After getting to know us, they said they were sorry we were leaving and corresponded with us for a long time afterward and asked if one of their children could come to visit and stay with us in New York. They didn't know any Jews before that except–to use their expression–'Goddam New York Yankee Jews with horns.' (That's all one word as they pronounced). That's what they had learned."

Later assigned to the 24th Marines, 4th Marine Division, Burg was transferred to base headquarters in Maui and assigned as an infantry platoon commander. He and his platoon soon hit the beaches at Iwo Jima. Wounded by mortar fire in the left leg, he recovered at the hospital on Saipan and was subsequently awarded the Purple Heart.

Describing an ecumenical experience in which the camaraderie and pride of belonging, Burg says, "I happen to be a Kohen (a high priest descendant of Aaron, the brother of Moses). As such, I am not permitted to go into cemeteries or be in the same room as a deceased, except G-d forbid, in the case of my own family members. I honor that custom out of respect for the departed.

"One day on Maui, my company commander ordered me, on short notice, to be a funeral officer, assemble a firing squad to honor a dead Marine, march to church, be pall bearers, etc., that very afternoon at a nearby church.

"Not knowing if this is proper for a Kohen (I was the only Jew involved), I telephoned the Jewish chaplain in the 4th Marine Division. His clerk, however, told me he was in Honolulu on liberty. I then tried to call the regimental Protestant chaplain, but he was already in the church in preparation for the funeral. I therefore did the only remaining thing possible. I called the regimental Catholic chaplain for advice as to whether it would be irreligious or disrespectful for a Kohen to be present where the deceased was non-Jewish.

"'Nah,' he immediately responded. 'If we can eat meat on Fridays,' Father Banning said, 'you can do it.' (Meat was OK on Fridays for Catholics during WWII).

"So there you have it – a Catholic advising a Jew on a Protestant matter. Truly, a co-operation among religions."

A first lieutenant and being an accounting by training, he became the Auditor of the Fleet Marine Force Pacific (FMFPac).

His two brothers also served during World War II—one was a lieutenant colonel in the engineers; the other, an enlisted man who worked on classified projects in New Mexico.

Louis Burg is a life member of the 4th Marine Division, having served as adjutant general for several years. He was chairman of the annual reunion of the 4th Marine Division held in September 1998 in Anaheim, California, and served as vice president of the local association chapter in 1999.

Miranda (Randy) Bloch Brooks had a very interesting background even before joining the Marine Corps. She was born in Jerusalem on Suleiman Road, Jerusalem, next door to what was then Notre Dame de France convent. In 1982, it became the Notre Dame de France Hotel.

Her grandfather's house was in ruins as a result of shelling and rocket attacks. Her mother and her aunt were also born in that house. Her grandfather, Abraham Solomiac arrived in Palestine in 1888, later to become the Postmaster General of Palestine and the Consul of Russia. Golda Meir and Miranda's mother were school classmates. Miranda Bloch arrived in the United States when she was two years old.

After joining the Marine Corps, she was selected to participate in Marine Aviation. As such, and because she was on flight duty status, she received flight pay of fifty percent over her basic salary. As she was a sergeant at the time, she made $78.00 per month, plus $39.80, for a grand total of $117.00, and "I thought I was a millionaire."

Before her discharge, she attended Radio-Radar School at Norfolk Naval Air Station, then back to Cherry Point. She was discharged on December 15, 1945, "very sadly, as were most of us. But we were proud to have been 'Pioneers' for women not only going into the military, also 'Rosie the Riveter' in the commercial world, and things have never been the same since."

Readers may recall the name Bloch. It made front-page newspaper reports in the wake of the rescue at Entebbe by Israeli commandos. Dora Bloch, of the same family name as Miranda, was the woman the commandos had to leave behind. Dora Bloch's sons related the fact that her body was found in a forest three years later, tortured and burned.

Miranda's father, Isaac, arrived in Palestine during the First World War, as an aide to General Allenby, the commanding general of the British forces. There, Isaac met and married Miranda's mother.

It took a lot of doing to get Miranda Bloch into the Marines, "I fought World War III to get into the WWII Marines with my father and I lost! So, I had to wait until I did not need his signature and enlisted on September 30, 1943, in Washington, D.C . . . . after I graduated from West Philadelphia High School." She was sworn in on November 10, 1943, the 168th birthday of the Marine Corps, on the steps of the Library of Congress.

After eight weeks of boot camp at Camp Lejeune, she was assigned to an experimental class of Aircraft Radio Repair with twenty-nine other women. They repaired radio gear from planes that had crashed. These were then re-installed in other airplanes. Eventually, Miranda Bloch was one of the few women authorized to fly in those planes to be sure that the radios were in proper working condition. The planes were mostly the Marine or Navy equivalent of the B-25 bomber, or PBJs. They wore the alpaca-lined leather jacket commonly used by the pilots, seat parachute, and the Mae West orange-colored vest which, inflated, enabled the wearer to stay above water. "We wore the same 'Boondocker' shoe boots as the men, and I always said that if we had to ditch in the ocean, those boondockers would carry us right down to the bottom of 'Davy Jones Locker.'"

Miranda has a lasting admiration for the Marine Corps. "We had to enlist for the duration of the war, plus six months, so that none of us knew how long we would be in the Corps. But I loved every minute, even though I had never been away from home."

Proud to have served her country as a U.S. Marine in time of need, Gloria Press Borochoff said, "I know that we were very proud to be part of the war effort. It was a tough one but we were very young and will have proud memories of our service years."

She met her husband, Marvin Borochoff, while on active duty. He had returned to the United States after three years aboard a minesweeper in the South Pacific. They were married seven weeks before the end of the war. Her sister, Eleanor Press, was a member of the WAVES, and served at Hunter College, New York City, as a storekeeper.

Gloria Press entered the Marine Corps in October 1943, and completed her boot training at Camp Lejeune, North Carolina. After a strenuous training session in unusually cold weather, she was assigned to Cherry Point, North Carolina. Her next duty assignment was in San Diego, at the Marine Corps Air Depot in Miramar.

Press was attached to the office of Major Gooding as a stenographer. He had been assigned to Miramar after having completed a tour of duty in the South Pacific. His job was to supervise the Construction and Maintenance School to enable the Marines to construct housing for the troops landing in the jungles of the South Pacific. Specifically, they had to provide troops with Quonset huts with electricity, plumbing, sanitation, and mosquito netting. Since the Marines were often unable to get the help they needed from the Seabees, they had to do the job themselves. Therefore, they assembled their own crews at the depot to speed up the production of facilities which supported the landings on the islands of the South Pacific.

One of the benefits of that station was that the personnel were close to Hollywood. They were able to enjoy first-run Hollywood shows at the base. It was a big morale booster.

Gloria Press Borochoff describes the celebration in which she participated fifty years after V-J Day: "A heartfelt memorial interfaith service was held in mid-August 1995 in a Palo Alto, California church. Hundreds of veterans, families, and friends attended followed by socializing at their Stage Door Canteen, with big band music (recorded), refreshments, and pictures of all theaters of war, Europe and the South Pacific. Nostalgic conclusion to a miserable world war."

Jack Seeler "loved the U.S. Marine Corps. Wanted to be a lifer. But wounds prevented my dream."

Jack was wounded on Saipan and received the Purple Heart. Not satisfied with extensive combat in the Pacific during World War II, he reenlisted for Korea, achieved the rank of platoon sergeant, received the Silver Star Medal, and was awarded two Purple Hearts for wounds in that war.

After boot camp at San Diego, he trained at Camp Pendleton. Boot camp was more than he had bargained for. However, he more than survived. He was "scared to death. I never thought I would make it. God knows, I wanted to be a U.S. Marine." He says that he never knew or saw a Jew in the Corps until he met Harold Nebensall in New Zealand.

He admired this man very much and remembers much of his life. Harold spoke a number of languages, including French, German, Yiddish, and Japanese. One day, the two visited a shop in Noumea, New Caledonia. On entering the shop, the "owner said to his daughter in French, 'Watch out, all Marines all thieves.'"

Later, "a group of drunken PT boat men asked us where the best whorehouses were. He told them they were in the back of the shop and he pointed to the Governor's Mansion. We sat and watched this crew wreck the shop and pound and yell at the door of the Mansion. Harold never cracked a smile, but I did mention that strong drink made buffoons of most men."

Before departing for combat on Tarawa, Saipan, and Tinian, he was attached to Intelligence, 6th Marines, 2nd Marine Division, at Camp Paikakariki, New Zealand.

Recovering from his wounds in the hospital, "I finally knew I was not going to die."

David Rosenthal enlisted in the Marine Corps Reserve on April 30, 1940 while attending San Jose State University, San Jose, California. That summer he attended the Western Platoon Leaders Class at the Marine Corps Recruit Depot, San Diego. Subsequently, he was a member of a Reserve organization and in 1941, again attended the Platoon Leaders Class in San Diego.

In April 1942, Rosenthal was commissioned a second lieutenant and ordered to the Basic School at Philadelphia Navy Yard.

After Basic School, his first assignment was at Camp Elliott, California. This was early in World War II and the Marine Corps was short of officers. He was given command of F Company, 6th Marines.

He left San Diego with the Second Marine Division on November 3, 1942, arriving in Wellington, New Zealand. As Rosenthal had majored in Law Enforcement and Police Science in college, he was transferred to the 2nd MarDiv Military Police Company, where for a period, he served as company commander. While in New Zealand, he participated with the 2nd Parachute Battalion in jungle operations.

In 1943, he served as platoon commander with I Company, 3rd Battalion, 2nd Marines. In Auckland, New Zealand, he was one of the officers helping to organize the Fourth Base Depot. They served on Banika, Russell Islands, until they were attached to the First Marine Provisional Brigade as the Fifth Field Depot and landed with the liberators of Guam on D-Day, June 21, 1944.

During his free time, Rosenthal studied Naval Courts and Boards and often defended enlisted Marines and sailors accused of violating naval regulations. As a result of his lengthy experience, Rosenthal was ordered to act Judge Advocate on Guam where he served until the end of World War II.

At the end of the war, on leave in New Zealand, he married his wife, Marion, who later joined him in the U.S. In October

1946, Rosenthal became disabled and was placed on the retired list at the rank of captain.

Rosenthal's father was an officer in the U.S. Army in World War I.

In the October 1998 edition of *Leatherneck* Magazine, the following article appeared:

"Former Captain Louis L. 'Louie' Goldstein died at his home in Calvert County, Maryland. He was 85.

"Known as 'Mr. Maryland,' he had recently announced his campaign for an 11th consecutive term as State Comptroller, a post he won more than 40 years ago. He served 60 years in state politics.

"Goldstein enlisted at age 29 and reported to Parris Island, South Carolina, after the Japanese attacked Pearl Harbor. Aside from his age, he was unique in that he was also a member of the House of Delegates of the State of Maryland, a lawyer, a member of the bar, and in the midst of a state senatorial campaign at the time.

"'I felt it was my duty to serve my country,' he told *Leatherneck* Magazine in 1990. Goldstein chose the Corps because 'of the association I had with the Marines when I was handling acquisition for the land on the Chesapeake Bay that was used for amphibious training at the Solomons during World War II.'

"He returned to Maryland's political scene four years later as a first lieutenant after having served with the 3rd Assault Company, Third Marine Division on Guam and as a member of General MacArthur's staff investigating war crimes in the Philippines. Over fourteen months, his team of officers and interpreters collected evidence eventually used to convict Lieutenant General Masaharu Homma for the Bataan Death March and General Tomoyuki 'Tiger of Malaya' Yamashita, supreme commander of Japanese forces in the Philippines, of war crimes. Both were executed in 1946.

"He left the Corps as a captain in the Reserve. He later said,

'Without a doubt my service in the Marines had its impact on my success. It taught me the necessity for making decisions, no procrastination, no equivocation, and no vacillation: make the decision. You handle men and women with different personalities, ethnic backgrounds, from all over the United States. So you learn leadership, simply the knack of getting people to think the way you want them to think, and Marines are good at that.'"

Colonel Paul DePre, USMC (ret.) responded to a request in the July/August 1999 edition of *Follow Me* for information about a Marine named Israel Aronowitz. This is his response:

"Although I do not recall Aronowitz personally, I surely recall his name. We were both serving in the 1st Battalion, 10th Marines, when he was killed on D-Day in the landing on Saipan on June 15th, which is my birthday.

"Fortunately, I and others in my LVT got ashore that day without being hit. Being in my eighties, my memory is not always too reliable, but I recall that the LVT or LVCP in which Aronowitz and others were approaching our assigned landing beach was hit by enemy shellfire, killing him and two other Marines whose names I do not recall.

"He and the other two Marines were not buried initially in the division cemetery. A roadway paralleled the shoreline not too far from the waterline, and the three bodies were buried across from and quite near the roadway. I recall there were one or two small trees nearby, a few feet from the gravesite.

"Initially, three crosses were erected over the common grave. This is where I heard about Aronowitz. Prior to the landing as a 2nd lieutenant, I was assigned the additional duty as Battalion Graves Registration Officer. This function entailed plotting the grid coordinates of the burial sites of any 1st Battalion men so the site would be recorded for later removal to the Central Division Cemetery. I submitted my reports to the Regimental Graves Registration officer. After the battle, we knew where our men were buried and the additional duty terminated.

"This was an essential function, for, in earlier battles, our men, with the best of intentions, would shovel dirt over a fallen comrade because, in the tropics, flies would swarm over the remains. But, as the battle progressed, the men who did this were subsequently killed or moved on with there being no record of where the bodies were buried.

"Word soon got to me that Aronowitz had told someone that if he 'got it,' he wanted a Star of David over his grave. His wish was granted, and a Star of David replaced one of the bodies in the grave. Not knowing the actual position of the bodies in the grave, the Star was placed between the two crosses. Within a few days, we displaced and moved into the town of Garapan. I never saw the triple gravesite again."

In a letter to the 2nd Marine Division Association newspaper regarding the July/August article, "Placing the Star of David Front and Center," Ken V. Quarternik wrote that he was witness to the same incident involving Israel Aronwitz (or Aronowitz). His letter is as follows:

"I was attached to Co Battery, 1st Bn, 10th Marines. I was in the landing craft on D-Day, June 15, 1944, that was hit by a Japanese shell that killed Israel Aronwitz and two other Marines. In addition, six Marines were wounded and three walked off that craft not injured. I was one of the three. The shell hit the port side at the .30-caliber machine gun.

"I feel that Israel Aronwitz saved my life that day. I was on that gun in front of the Amtrac when we got the word that we would hit beach. Aronwitz asked me if he could take my place, but I said, 'No.' However, he continued to insist until I gave in because my friend Bill Lee of Coffeeville, Kansas, hollered at me to come sit with him in the back of the Amtrac. I finally did so, and we took off to the beach. Aronwitz was happy and I was glad to be with my friend.

"Just as the Amtrac came onto the beach, there was a loud explosion. I was in a daze (shellshocked), and I noticed a chaplain had come in to help with the killed and wounded Marines. The three dead Marines were placed near a dusty road by the Amtrac just off the beach. Other Marines helped the wounded off. Bill Lee, me, and another Marine got off and joined our company.

"I think about that incident often. I feel that Aronwitz saved my life by taking place on the gun. I have prayed for him many times, and I am sure he got the Star of David he wanted. May he forever rest in peace.

— Ken V. Quarternik"

On the occasion of Hanukkah, 1996, Bernie Kessler sent a letter to his children, grandchildren, and "the many generations that shall remember," in which he tried to explain his participation in the defense of his country:

"There are many ways of serving—this is but one of them . . . . Whatever way you choose, may you feel secure in the knowledge that you responded as did Jews throughout history—in defense of basic human rights and privileges [Kessler's father served in World War I].

"For me—I believed that I served to make a better world . . . . We can make it a little better in some way. While it is for each of us to find that way, I tried to find mine in two wars."

Although he was actually drafted into the Navy, he begged to get into the Army, "claiming second-generation family tradition," but nothing worked. "The officer gave me one way out of the Navy—volunteer for the U.S. Marines. I looked at the great uniforms the two Marines were wearing and decided that was much better than the Navy and I became number fifty-six of the sixty volunteers they accepted that day, February 1, 1943—the first day in the history of the Corps that they accepted draftee volunteers."

Eight days later, Kessler was at Parris Island.

He was smart enough to memorize the eleven general orders for guard duty very quickly and was chosen to be guidon bearer. That was great, "except that I couldn't see too far ahead and always had the guy behind me keep me in a straight line and avoid road hazards."

When given another eye examination, "they discovered my defective vision and sent me to the base hospital to get a thorough eye exam and confirm the defect." After his eye test, he was issued two pairs of glasses, released back to his company, and reassigned to a new platoon.

Not long after, when the Navy ruled that all draftee volunteers in the USMC had to be fit for combat duty, Kessler was told that he would be discharged from the Corps in about two weeks. As a result, Kessler's father "visited the USMC in New York City and was told there was nothing they could do to counter the Navy regulations. They kept him waiting two hours until they discovered he was there trying to keep 7me *in*—not get me *out.*"

Kessler ultimately received an honorable discharge from the Marine Corps in May 1943. After trying to enlist in the Army, he was brushed aside and told to go back to his draft board and was inducted into the Army in June 1943. He received his commission in the Army Transportation Corps upon graduation from OCS in November 1945

In the summer of 1951, Kessler participated in the building of Thule (Greenland) Air Base as part of the DEW line (a 3,000-mile-long network of radar stations north of the Arctic Circle, maintained by the United States and Canada for providing advance warning of the approach of hostile planes or missiles-*D*istant *E*arly *W*arning). Assigned as Army Liaison Officer to the staff of Rear Admiral T. F. Brittain, Kessler was responsible for coordinating lighterage assignments to all cargo vessels in the convoy. The staff commander was a Marine lieutenant colonel and his assistant, a Marine major. Then it all came together. "During one conversation they mentioned 'pogey bait,' and asked if the Army used that term for candy. I told them we did not but I've used it since my boot camp days. And then all the good stuff happened. I gave them my service background with dates and all and showed them my USMC dogtags—I always carried them but wore the Army tags. Relationships changed dramatically. I received a very nice recommendation addressed to General Whitcomb and at the conclusion of my assignment was sent back to my barracks ship on the admiral's yacht. We exchanged signal messages on the date of our departure from Greenland and I concluded my greetings with 'Semper Fi and God speed.'"

In 1952, Kessler served as adminstration officer for Pine Tree Sites on the DEW Line in Newfoundland and Labrador. He separated on July 24, 1952.

Having recovered from the adversity faced during his initial months in the Marine Corps, his pride in being a Marine was largely responsible for his success. He says:

"I consider my entire military experience as very positive. It served as a maturing ground and I walked away with habits and ingrained working ethics that served me very well when I entered the corporate arena. The three and a half months I spent in the Marines has always been a highlight of my military experience. To me, like millions of other kids from the city streets, the demands of military life, especially Marine boot camp, can be overwhelming. I sympathize with those who for one reason or another could not cope. It taught me the value of inter-dependent relationships and commitments. It taught me how to function in a highly structured society—and how to assume responsibilities when called upon. Above all it prepared me for the management function in which decision-making is part and parcel of the process. For all this training, I have been enthusiastically grateful."

Steve Judd trained at Parris Island for twelve weeks after enlisting in the Marine Corps from New York City at the age of 17.

When his outfit, the 5th Defense Battalion, departed Parris Island for Guadalcanal, Judd stayed behind and became a member of the 11th Defense Battalion which left for Camp Lejeune. His unit was next assigned to Onslow Beach at Camp Lejeune to watch for German submarines.

Shipped overseas, he trained first in British Samoa, then on New Caledonia, and was sent next to New Zealand to join M Company, 3rd Battalion, 6th Marines, 2nd Marine Division. He recalls "wading in the water six hundred yards from the beach on Tarawa while the Japs were shooting—running across the airfield and it was dark. I jumped into a large shell hole and I was alone. I whispered for one of my buddies. I got an answer. I felt around, and there were bodies all around. I touched their legs and they had leggings, and then I knew they were Japs, but they were all dead. Just about that time, my buddy found me and I joined up with the rest of the platoon."

The division sustained a huge number of casualties in the battle for Tarawa in the Gilbert Islands, after which the remaining members, including Judd, went to the big island of Hawaii for the process of rebuilding. "I was in the B/1/18 Assault Demolitions and Flamethrower Section."

On May 15, 1944, they boarded LSTs for additional training prior to departure for Saipan and ran into terrible weather at sea. Some men were lost over the sides. On May 21, when Judd was asleep in a truck, he heard two quick explosions. When he jumped up, the motor and the windshield were gone, as well as their LST loaded with napalm, gasoline, ammunition, and all their TNT and dynamite. Judd swam to shore—no top, no shoes, dungarees shredded, steel plates flying over. Then, someone grabbed him and got him to the pier.

He was covered with oil and smelled awful. After an Army truck picked him up, he got cleaned up. A couple of days later, Judd heard an announcement that all Marine stragglers were to report to their units immediately. On May 23 or 24, they boarded new LSTs—all the others had been lost.

Other members of Judd's family served in the military. His father was in World War I, and his brother was a career officer in the Air Force who retired as a colonel.

Steve Judd was discharged from the Marine Corps as a corporal.

A native of Boston currently (2000) residing in Hyannis, Massachusetts, Nathan Kashuk joined the Marine Corps in 1943 at the age of 17. Upon enlistment, he was told he would have the opportunity to become a pilot, but that was not to be.

The boots were under orders to shave daily. One day he decided to skip shaving. His DI slapped him across the side of his head. This "taught me a lesson—to obey orders without question."

With recruit training completed in February 1943, he underwent further training in Samoa, New Caledonia, and New Hebrides. Although Kashuk had never driven any vehicle before, the Corps taught him to drive a one-and-a-half-ton truck, and, "ultimately, I drove everything the Corps had (except tanks)."

He joined the 2nd Marine Division in New Zealand where he was assigned to the 2nd Motor Transport Battalion. For a couple of months, he drove a two-and-a-half-ton 6 x 6 truck, after which he was transferred to a line company.

Kashuk participated in the invasion of Tarawa in November 1943. He described it as "one of the bloodiest battles in Marine Corps history," and, "remember, this was only a four-day battle." After a respite on the island of Hawaii, he participated in the invasion of Saipan in June 1944. From there, Kashuk participated in the invasion of Tinian in July and into August 1944. There, he came down with jaundice. He described the ordeal of treatment and recuperation from the illness: "The Navy medical people were there to get us back to health, and they guarded their own facilities. That perhaps was more frightening than combat, as they were very trigger-happy, and didn't know very much about the security that should have been in use." From Tinian, his unit returned to Saipan and established a base for the division where "we trained for our invasion of Okinawa in June of 1945."

His best experience was the moment that Japan surrendered. "My buddies and I threw one of the biggest binges one could

imagine. We could buy extra beer and some of the more inge-
nious amongst my group were able to concoct a very potent
alcoholic drink."

Marine Corps experience had a positive overall effect on the
life of Nathan Kashuk. "I guess I grew up real quick. I learned
the importance of discipline, and more important, it taught me to
make decisions that could affect my future. It also taught me how
to get along with others, and not to discriminate against anyone
different from myself."

Many Jewish-Americans continued in the footsteps of their
fathers and grandfathers. Military service was a tradition in a
number of families, and that of Murray Sklar was no exception.
He worshipped his dad. He was "my hero who fought in the
Mexican border wars against Pancho Villa, and, because he was
Regular Army, was among the first troops sent over in WWI."

Murray Sklar reported for active duty with the Marine Corps
on July 16, 1943. He completed boot camp at Parris Island, and
was awarded the Marksman Medal with the rifle. His only anti-
Semitic incident turned into a bit of a triumphant and bizarre
event. When a fellow boot called him a "dirty Jew bastard," the
platoon, to a man, jumped in to his defense, and "said they would
arrange for his transfer if he didn't like my presence." He noted
that this incident "was both a 'hurt' and a wonderful sense of
belonging."

Having completed boot camp, he was sent to the 2nd Marine
Air Wing at Cherry Point, where he was trained as a radio/radar
operator, and promoted to private first class. He joined Marine
Air Assault Warning Squadron 5, and went on to Advanced Infantry Training at Camp Pendleton. Once, on a night exercise, a
group of six became separated from the main force and were lost
in "the darkest, loneliest spot I ever imagined." Sklar fell into a
small ravine where he cut his hand, but managed to follow the

stream back to the main road where they hooked up with the main body and completed the exercise.

He participated in the assault on Saipan, then in the invasion of Okinawa in April 1945. With the first incoming rounds, Murray remembers being terribly frightened, and "prayed that if G-d would protect me I would be as true to my faith as I could and which I have done." They were under constant air attacks, one of which killed twenty of their people. Murray had a poncho covering his foxhole, from which he was blown out and briefly knocked unconsciously. He remembers waking, just lying there, wondering if he were dead, feeling to see if he had his limbs. "The poncho was perforated with shrapnel, yet I received not a scratch."

In time, the Japanese attempted to penetrate the Kadena airstrip. Murray and his men force-marched from Yontan to Kadena. He relates the ensuing battle:

"The Japs were still jumping out of transports. They landed on the strip and we took positions on the runway. The Japanese were being picked off like ducks in a shooting gallery. I had no idea how bad that firefight was until some forty odd years later I read William Manchester's book, 'Goodbye, Darkness,' where he covered that particular engagement in a paragraph. As you know, in such an encounter you are concerned with your buddies on either side of you and now knowing—or caring, what is the big picture."

Murray describes a delightful incident: "At another time, slogging off patrol and trudging back to the main group, a person claps me on the back and says, 'How goes it, son?' 'Okay,' I reply, turned around and recognized General Vandegrift checking on his Marines. Of course, in a combat zone there was no saluting or other recognition given."

On another occasion, just after the Bomb was dropped on Japan, a Catholic chaplain called Sklar to take him to Holy Day services aboard one of the Navy ships in the harbor. When Murray told the chaplain that he couldn't attend because he was scheduled to go on patrol, he was informed that everything would be taken care of. At the base, one of his buddies who he had befriended for over two years asked him why he had not participated in the patrol. "When I explained to him what happened, he asked me incredulously, 'You're a Jew?' When I replied in the affirmative, he exclaimed, 'Gee whiz, you're just like me!' I asked him, 'What did you expect, horns?' He repeated just as amazed, 'No, but you're just like me!' Such was the comment from a farm boy brought up not too far from Cincinnati, Ohio."

One experience that had more impact than others was the time that he was called to the tent of his CO and handed a letter from his high school biology and homeroom teacher that she had mailed to the Commandant of the Marine Corps. In the letter, she described Murray as a "very worthy lad," and suggested that he take courses from the Marine Corps Institute. In the battery of tests at boot camp, he "was amazed at my IQ scores, and the Kuder Preference Tests which showed my interests in the field of engineering and music." This information encouraged him to use the GI Bill to attend the Citadel, Charleston, South Carolina, for two years. Whereupon, he transferred to Newark College of Engineering where he became a mechanical engineer with a master's degree.

Just prior to the dropping of the atomic bomb, Murray Sklar was training for the invasion of Japan. Murray, too, was spared from the likelihood of being seriously injured, or worse, by this quick and merciful culmination of the war. In reality, his ship, en route to the invasion, turned around, and "we were one of the first boarded and sailed to Treasure Island, California, under the 'Welcome Home' banner flying from the Golden Gate Bridge . . . we watched astounded as brand new aircraft were pushed into the 'drink' to make room for the Marines being returned to our beloved America."

In December 1991, Murray Sklar returned to Hawaii to celebrate the fiftieth anniversary of the bombing of Pearl Harbor with the Pearl Harbor Survivors Association. There, he laid a wreath on behalf of the Marine Corps League on the USS *Arizona* with New Jersey Senator Frank Lautenberg. During the taxi ride returning to the airport, he mentioned that he went to Jungle School there. "The driver excitedly told me he was one of the instructors and proceeded to turn off the meter while he took us around the course, now overgrown, and pointed out the various obstacles. He turned the meter back after the tour to take us to our destination.

As so many of his Jewish Marine comrade-in-arms, he continues his ties with the Corps. He is past Commandant of the West Hudson Detachment of the Marine Corps League in Kearny, New Jersey, having served as the yearbook chairman, adjutant, and scholarship chairman. In addition, he has served as New Jersey State Officer of the League, and continues to be active in the Jewish War Veterans of the United States.

Charles Jacobs joined the Marine Corps in January 1942. He soon got used to the discipline of soldiering and was looking forward to shooting a few Germans. He was disappointed in that, and was sent to the South Pacific to even the score with Japan.

After boot camp at Parris Island, he was sent to Camp Lejeune and assigned to the 7th Regiment which was part of the 1st Marine Division. The Marines in the South Pacific were called the FMF (Fleet Marine Force). The 7th Regiment was detached from the division and sent to Western Samoa (British) as the 3rd Marine Brigade. This was where the Allies thought the Japanese would attack next in their quest for domination in the Pacific. Before the Japanese could hit Samoa, the 1st Marine Division, without the 7th Regiment, landed on Guadalcanal in August 1941. "In September, the Army relieved my unit on Samoa and we were sent to Guadalcanal as reinforcements. We landed on the island with no opposition since the rest of the division was already there.

"We were sent to the center of the lines with the 1st Regiment on our left and the 3rd Regiment on the right. When we inquired as to who was out front, we were told no-one except the Japs. At night, 'Washing-Machine Charlie' came over to disturb our sleep and drop a few flares and a few bombs. Ships out in the ocean shot big shells at us. My first foxhole on Guadalcanal, dug in a naval bombardment, was two feet deep and less than three inches. Yes, I was scared.

"We did patrols and got battle experience. Marines got killed and we all knew what war is all about. I was wounded on a patrol that was ordered by a man who had no business being an officer. He got word that the Japanese were coming down the beach in company strength. Our battalion commander, 'Chesty' Puller was at a divisional meeting. His second in command ordered A Company to the Higgins boats to halt the enemy advance. It was an utter disaster. The enemy was in battalion strength. We were hung out to dry. I took some shrapnel in the leg, but managed to get to the beach. The boats were circling in the bay. Hinnett stripped and swam out to the boats. The sailors pulled him aboard but refused to go to the beach to rescue us. Hinnett picked up a wrench and threatened to brain the coxswain. That boat headed for the beach and the rest followed. I was back on duty in ten days with the shrapnel still in my leg.

"I was privileged to serve under "Chesty" Puller, my battalion commander. I also served with John Basilone, who received the Congressional Medal of Honor. I mention this because I was one hundred yards from him the night he fought so bravely. I was lucky that night no Japanese came near my position.

"In December, wracked with malaria, jaundice, and a badly infected leg wound (all three which kept me from standing), I was evacuated from Guadalcanal to the hospital ship *Hope* and sent to Wellington, New Zealand, to a naval hospital. The iron was removed and I recovered quickly. At Passover, I met a rabbi who talked my rabbi in Troy, New York, into becoming a rabbi. This man assigned me to a lovely family for Passover.

"I was discharged in January 1946, and in September 1947, I married Lillian Dunn. We have three children and six grandchildren. We flew my old rabbi who was no longer in Troy back to Troy to marry us. He remembered his old mentor well.

"After Guadalcanal I was in one more campaign on Cape Gloucester. It was not much better than Guadalcanal. The war had started to go our way and we had better chow. The rest was the same.

"After the Cape Gloucester campaign, I was rotated back to the United States. I was sent to Colgate University for pre-OCS. World War II ended while I was at Colgate.

In 1997, Marvin Hoffman visited the places that were so much a part of the young Marines of World War II, but were denied to him. What he was able to do as an older person, he was not called upon to do in his prime. He visited Guam, Palau, Peleliu, and a few other islands in the Pacific where the fighting raged. "On Palau, there are still tanks rusting in the middle of the jungle and the old airstrips still remain. I walked on what they called 'Orange Beach,' saw the reef they (the Marines) had to cross to get to the beach. That was a very moving moment for me. Off the beach on Guam, there are still tanks sitting out in the water about a hundred yards offshore which I guess were hit in the assault."

Although he served more than three years, from 1943 to 1946, he was not called upon to participate in combat against the enemy, despite repeated requests for transfer to combat duty. Each time he was to be rebuffed by refusal to honor his requests.

Having undergone boot camp at Parris Island, he received no further training. At boot camp, his senior DI, Staff Sergeant Travezant, was "one tough SOB, but fair." The assistant DI "kept needling me as 'one of the New York people' and other remarks which were anti-Semitic. I had a fight with him behind the barracks and broke his nose. The sergeant *knew* what was going on but I was never court-martialed or given *any* kind of punishment." Punishment, however, was meted out after his escapade in an empty ward in the hospital, where he was caught with a woman Marine. He received a deck court-martial and was busted from buck sergeant to Pfc.

He was stationed at Cherry Point and Edenton, North Carolina, both of which bases he considered good assignments, with lots of beer drinking. Also pulled guard duty at Portsmouth and Norfolk Navy Yard. At Cherry Point, he was part of a PBJ crew in a training squadron where the officers were very unhappy being there. They were eager to get into combat, and further irritated over the fact that they were training others for action.

Hoffman, too, was very proud to have served in the Marine Corps. He was disappointed, however, at not being assigned to combat duty. He wanted action very badly. "I was really gung ho at that time, so I was very disappointed."

His older brother served with an armored division on D-Day in Europe, while his younger brother served with an army unit in Paris.

Marvin Hoffman was "Absolutely proud to have served in the military because I wanted to do something for this great country of ours. It was an experience that gave me structure and discipline and a patriot which I still am."

Gary Greenstein held similar evaluations of military service. He said that the "military gave me confidence. Made me more mature." He was proud to have served in the Marine Corps. "Very much so. It makes me feel I paid my dues to be an American citizen."

Born and raised in Wilmington, Delaware, Garry Greenstein graduated from DuPont High School in 1947. From there, he graduated from the University of Delaware, followed by completion of law school at the University of Pennsylvania.

Law school was followed by Marine Officer Candidate Course at Quantico, graduating with his commission as second lieutenant. He completed Basic Officer School after five months.

His assignments consisted of Tracked Vehicle School for one

month at Quantico, C Company, 3rd Tank Battalion in South Camp, Fuji, Honshu, Japan. Later, he was assigned to the Pentagon for one year working on navy claims.

During his military service, he had the pleasure of visiting Japan, Okinawa, Hong Kong, Paris, London, Bermuda, and San Francisco.

While in Japan and Okinawa, he had the opportunity to become friends with the navy chaplain, Rabbi Turetsky, and attended religious services several times.

One incident that remains vivid in his memory is the following: while he was stationed at the 3rd Division Legal Office in 1955 as a second lieutenant on Okinawa, he had the duty as Junior OD once a month. Early one morning, he went to Division Headquarters (a Quonset hut) where a staff sergeant made up a cot for him. One night at dinner in the enlisted mess he made a comment about the food in the OD log. He went to sleep about 2100 hours. The next day he ate in the same mess and made comments about the food in the log once again.

The third time when he reported at 1700 hours, he was shown a map on a big easel. It had a celluloid overlay which showed a circle about three hundred miles northeast of Okinawa. It was a map for plotting a typhoon in the area. They were in Condition 4, which meant typhoon in the general area: Condition 1, right on top of them.

He described the situation: "I could see from the map that the typhoon was going away from us, and I was to call the Air Force periodically to get a fix on it. About 2100 hours, I called and it was still moving away from Okinawa. I went to sleep confident that there was not going to be any trouble.

"At 0500 hours the telephone rings. 'Kadena AFB weather Condition 2.' What happened to Condition 3? "We lost track of the typhoon. How soon before Condition 1? Ten minutes.

"I didn't panic, but began calling the duty officers of the Marine Corps units on the island and giving them the news.

"Then I called the CO and told him. He was a lieutenant

colonel. He said he would call the general and then come to the office.

"In about ten minutes people started coming to division headquarters. I waited around until time for breakfast and then left. After that, I went back to my room and stayed there for three days until the typhoon left."

This incident proved to be a most pivotal one in Garry's military and subsequent professional life. He realized that he didn't have to be worried at all about being Junior Officer of the Day because, "I knew if something happened, I could handle it." As an obvious spin-off of his Marine Corps experience and training,, and as a future first lieutenant, he was confident he could handle any situation.

Garry makes a very interesting and touching observation of one of the Corps' true legends, "Chesty" Puller. In his biography, he said, in so many words, that intolerance had no place in his command. "On Guadalcanal, he had three company sergeants, one Polish, one Italian, and one Jewish. They were all fine men, and he doesn't tolerate ethnic slurs."

Paul Zonderman is one of those former Marines who consider the Marine Corps motto of Semper Fidelis not just a saying, but a way of life. He is one who considers the Marine Corps as an important phase of his life, one which helped shape his thinking and outlook on life. Marine Corps training "was perhaps the most challenging thing I've done in my life. I'm proud of it. It served us well. Aside from Vietnam, I enjoyed the military experience—after training. I still feel patriotic, and would do it again despite hindsight." Also, "My military experience has given me a quiet pride and a confidence and a 'never quit' attitude which has served me well. Sometimes even today, when situations look bleak, I remind myself that nobody is shooting at me. It's funny, but even now when it rains, I still appreciate being under a roof and dry."

He is the third generation to have served. His father was a World War II veteran of the Army, and his grandfather served during the Spanish-American War. Most of his memories of the military are good ones, although, "There are memories, good, bad, sad, and funny."

Paul was a Marine officer with a specialty as a legal officer. He completed the Platoon Leaders Program-Law in 1962, and was commissioned as a second lieutenant. His request to enter law school was granted. With that, he entered the Reserve and received his law degree in June 1964. Now married, he started his three years of active duty commencing in January, 1965, as a first lieutenant. After six months at Officers Basic School in Quantico, he received the MOS of 4405, Trial/Defense Counsel in General Courts Martial. After a brief orientation at the Naval Justice School in Newport, Rhode Island, he reported to MCB, Twentynine Palms where he was promoted to captain.

Duties as legal officer in Vietnam provided no more immunity to enemy fire than it did to other support troops: The front lines were as much to the rear as to the front. Assigned to I Corps, first in Da Nang, then in Phu Bai, he served with the Division Legal Office, 3rd Marine Division, Judge Advocate. In addition to being a legal officer, Zonderman had been trained as a line officer.

Generally speaking, anti-Semitic activity wasn't much of a problem with Zonderman. "Being an officer and a lawyer, I was generally treated decently on the surface." But, how about under the surface? He apparently found some anti-Semitic sentiment among his fellow PFL trainees. He found more among them than at his duty stations. He relates one incident that could be interpreted as anti-Semitic: "During training, I was one called to my DIs office. I pounded on the door and he said, 'Louder, Zonderman. Where do you think you are, in a synagogue?' That told me instantly that he was aware that I was a Jew in the Marine Corps."

While he did not detect much overt anti-Semitism, "In the active duty assignment world, there wasn't much on the surface, but you got the feeling that you weren't one of the 'good old boys.'"

His awards citations include the Vietnam Campaign Medal with device, the Vietnam Service Medal with 2 bronze stars, the National Defense Service Medal, the Presidential Unit Citation, and the Republic of Vietnam Meritorious Unit Citation (Gallantry Cross Medal with Palm).

He doesn't talk much now about Vietnam. His circle of friends isn't interested. "They weren't when I came back, there aren't many now who are curious." That doesn't bother him. "I know how my pregnant wife and my parents were worried; and I know I paid my dues."

In 1943, Bob Klein's boot platoon came mostly from Maine, Pennsylvania, and Florida. His was the last platoon to be made up entirely of volunteers: Drafting of Marines began right after that time. During the first week, the recruits were beginning to get to know each other. One late afternoon, while waiting for chow call, a Hispanic kid shouted: "Which one of you is the Jew? I know we have one because the DI said so." "There was no answer from me or any other person." Bob was "sort of stunned at the question."

They had been given their dogtags, and Bob had noticed the letter "H" on his. He didn't even understand what that meant. On the way to chow, he was walking with a friend from Philadelphia, Jack Binswanger. Jack asked him if he had indicated his religion on his application for enlistment. Jack replied that of course he had. But Binswanger had not, because it might cause trouble in the Marine Corps. Bob never saw him again.

The recruit who had asked who was the Jew didn't give up. Finally, Bob decided that he had nothing to hide and challenged him. "He got real tough with his language and wanted to fight me. Things happened so fast that my memory on what transpired at that moment is not clear." With that, Bob got off his bunk, or was pulled off by his challenger. Bob remembers that the others started yelling in order to stir things up. They were finally stopped

by the DI before things got out of hand. Whereupon, he sent out
for boxing gloves for each of them. The DI took the two of them
behind the hut and ordered them to swing away. The result was
"There was no winner, just two arm weary kids. After that, there
was no more fuss from the Hispanic."

Bob learned at least one thing from this incident. One, he
learned to prevent the dogtags from making noise by placing
adhesive tape around the periphery of each metal tag. He made
sure that the edged tape went high enough to cover the "H"
which he learned meant "Hebrew."

The aftermath of the story took place some time later at New
River, Camp Lejeune, North Carolina. At that time, the men began to realize that they were missing personal belongings. It was
agreed that there must have been a thief in the group. Later, the
thief was discovered. A group of men threw him down a stairway
of five stories that resulted in his death. It turned out to be the
Hispanic kid from Bob's recruit platoon with whom he had fought.

Bob Klein went on to join A Company, 20th Marine Engineer
Battalion of the 4th Marine Division and fought at Roi-Namur
and Saipan. His outfit was the first to go directly from the United
States into combat. His last year and a half was spent in naval
hospitals, the hospital ship *Good Samaritan*, New Caledonia,
Oaknoll, and lastly, at the Philadelphia Naval Hospital.

When Jerry Blank was drafted in October 1943, he had the
choice of services—and he chose the Marine Corps. His recruit
platoon must have broken a record: "We were seven Jews. Four
of us including myself made corporal right out of boot camp."

Jerry's Marine career followed much the usual schedule as
others during World War II: boot camp, Camp Lejeune for Field
Telephone School, infantry training in Jacksonville, North Carolina. Arriving with the 8th AAA Battalion in Kaui, Hawaii for
further training with combat wire, his job was to provide antiaircraft guns with communication to the command post.

He hit the beach on April 17, 1945 at Nago Harbor, Okinawa, and saw action between Nakadamari and Ishikawa until August 16, 1945. Some fighting continued even after V-E Day.

His most unpleasant incident occurred while manning a quad .50 machine gun, expecting a last ditch Japanese landing while on Okinawa. "I was lucky that they never made it." He remembers vividly the bombing of Ie Shima from a high point on Okinawa when Ernie Pyle was killed.

With the end of the war in the Pacific, Jerry was transferred to the 1st Joint Assault Signal Company of the 1st Marine Division. They boarded the USS *Leon* APA 48 on September 20, 1945 and landed in Tsientsin, China on September 30 to disarm the Japanese troops there. In fact, of all the places that Jerry visited, Tsientsin was the most interesting. He had the chance to see old China before Mao Tse Tung changed it. He saw old Mao himself in the British Concession at the Victoria Restaurant. "I was carrying a loaded carbine."

Among his unusual incidents, the first was while aboard ship in the middle of the Panama Canal in May 1944. An announcement came over the ship's loudspeaker: "Now hear this. Jerry Blank and Larry Bronson report to the forecastle." It happened that it was Friday at sunset. Eight navy men needed two more Jews for a minyan. "Right there I knew I would return home in one piece."

His brother, Sidney, served four and a half years with the Army. He saw action on New Guinea, was well decorated, and remains alive and well today (2001).

Jerry is proud of a number of things. One, he is proud to have served in the military because he "helped my country when we needed all the help we could get." He admired Lou Diamond, 'the famous Marines' Marine. He was a real Marine, and a kind person. I met him at Parris Island the day I got there. He helped me with good advice."

Jerry was awarded the American Campaign Medal, Asiatic-Pacific Campaign Medal with bronze star, World War II Victory Medal, and the China Service Medal.

His overall evaluation of the military is that "it made me a better and stronger person. Better able to handle tough situations."

In 1944, Harris Nadley told a lie. And it's a lead pipe cinch that he's been proud of it ever since.

In that year of his enlistment in the Marine Corps, he was not yet eighteen and he did not have parental permission to join up. So he lied: He told the recruiters he was eighteen and was accepted for enlistment. His recollections of the Marine Corps are virtually entirely positive: His training was excellent, he had two great DIs, and encountered only one incident of anti-Semitism. A recruit called him a "God-damned Jew." He most likely regretted that mistake because Harris "hit him in the nose with my fist and thus settled the matter 'amicably.'"

Following boot camp, he trained in infantry tactics at Camp Lejeune, North Carolina. Later, he shipped out to Guadalcanal where he joined 6th JASCO, 6th Marine Division as a radio operator for a naval gunfire team. He was wounded in action in the invasion of Okinawa on June 4, 1945, when a "mortar shell blew me away." At that moment, he experienced a "big noise, then silence." He wrote of the excellent medical attention he received. For this action, he received the Combat Action Ribbon. Shortly after the termination of hostilities, he was shipped to Tsingtao, China, where he ran the Armed Forces radio XABU.

When the war ended, Nadley stayed in the Reserve and was eventually released to inactive duty as a captain. He received a B.S. degree from the University of Pennsylvania in 1950 and an M.B.A. from Harvard University in 1952.

He served as a board member of the U.S. Naval War College Foundation, Newport, Rhode Island, and as a regional vice president for the Greater Philadelphia area.

Irving Labes joined the Marine Corps early in World War II from Boston, Massachusetts, and went through recruit training at MCRD, San Diego. It was at Pendleton that "we really became combat-ready Marines. Although an expert rifleman, my weapon was a Browning automatic rifle. It was fine as far as I was concerned, and I was proud to be able to 'up and on shoulders' with the BAR while the others hoisted only M-1s."

At Mare Island, California, he had the good fortune of meeting Charles Laughton, Brian Donlevy, and Robert Taylor, who were on location for a movie, *Stand by For Action,* which took place on a destroyer. He said that "It was amazing to hear and see they were just like anyone else. They could swear and curse with the best of the gyrenes."

"I stood out from the rest for a few reasons: most of my outfit were Texans, or from other southern states, and, of course, I was a Yankee, and Jewish at that. They called me Boston, but showed little or no prejudice."

While on mess duty at Pendleton, he was assigned to officers' mess. One day, he served Colonel James Roosevelt's table, and "though he didn't lower himself to talk with a mere enlisted man, it was a memorable experience."

Reminiscent of Leon Uris's book *Battle Cry,* the 9th Marines with Labes arrived in Auckland, New Zealand, and trucked to Pukekohe. "We had great liberty in Auckland, where steak and eggs cost one-and-a-half shillings and people were very nice to us. They thought we were filling in for their men who were then fighting with the 8th U.S. Army in Europe.

"We marched sixty miles with full pack. This was the roughest thing we had done so far. But very few fell out—probably bravado and pride kept us going. If Major Asmuth could do it, so could we. As expected, he was called 'Back Asmuth,' but not to his face. Warm beer and strong-tasting mutton were hard for some, but I grew to like both."

Arriving in Guadalcanal, his unit set up camp in a coconut

grove, went out on combat patrols in the jungle, and trained even harder than in New Zealand. One night, they were scheduled to see the movie *Stand by For Action*. Since Labes had met the actors, he looked forward to seeing it. But just as the film started, they had their first Condition Red—their initiation to enemy fire. They scattered while the bombs fell.

"There were many wet trousers that night, and, to this day, the sight of a full moon leaves a queasy sensation in my innards."

They shipped out in October on the Coast Guard transport *Hunter Liggett* and stopped at Efate, Gilbert Island (former name of Kiribati), for a final practice landing. They disembarked at Empress Augusta Bay, Bougainville, and went ashore in landing craft in very rough surf. Wading ashore under enemy shelling, they participated in one of the first contested landings of the Pacific campaign. Unable to get further than a fetid swamp, they stayed the night there, drinking swamp water laced with iodine. A few days later, they made their first contact with enemy soldiers and suffered a great many casualties. Though they "gave more than we received, we made it back to our lines with our wounded, but left about a third of the platoon in a jungle clearing. I learned to respect the Japanese and their use of two very effective weapons—the Nambu machine gun and the knee mortar (Japanese Model 89–1929–50 mm Heavy Grenade Discharger)."

Not long after, Labes himself was wounded and had to be evacuated to Guadalcanal to a field hospital equipped to treat severe burns. He was then sent to the Navy Base hospital at New Caledonia where he remained for several months. Returning to his unit on Guadalcanal, and "back with my buddies, I began to feel like less of a lost soul."

His regiment sailed from Guadalcanal on June 2, 1944, en route to his second combat landing. From his LST, he witnessed the "Marianas Turkey Shoot," during which numerous Japanese planes were shot down by U.S. carrier planes. Labes says that "It was aptly named, for the many, many enemy planes shot down. Whenever Zeros and bombers attacked, we would all join the

Navy deck guns with our small-arms fire, cheering wildly whenever one was shot down."

Labes was wounded once again. On Guam, on August 8, while repulsing a *banzai* attack, a grenade landed in the foxhole where he and his buddy Parks and a war dog handler were posted. Labes's partner was also injured, but the handler was untouched. However, "his dog, a Doberman, was found dead, lying with the many dead Japs in front of our position. After the grenade explosion, Parks lobbed grenades while I used my BAR, a fantastic weapon." For Labes, "with wounds to both legs, the war was, in effect, over."

Irving Labes took permanent leave from the Marine Corps as a corporal. To him, "the military experience was good considering the friends made, and bad considering the death of too many friends. It was no more difficult for me than for any other combat Marines. I was one of the lucky ones., and for that I am grateful."

Philip Laden of Philadelphia enlisted in the Marines at the age of 17. Following recruit training at Parris Island, he was sent for three months to Sea School at Norfolk.

His next assignment was as orderly to the admiral aboard the flagship of Cruiser Division 6, the USS *Astoria,* after which time the admiral moved his flag to the USS *San Francisco.* There, Laden became orderly to Admiral Husband E. Kimmel, "one of the fast-rising stars in the U.S. Navy. Kimmel later became CinCPac—Commander in Chief, Pacific Fleet. He had the misfortune of being made the scapegoat for the Japanese attack on Pearl Harbor." His ship, with Phil Laden, was privileged to be among those invited to open up the Golden Gate Bridge in 1936 by sailing under it.

Phil Laden was "always imbued with the idea of seeing the world, and as soon as I graduated from Simon Gratz High School, I enlisted. They only took one enlistee a month from the Philadelphia area—I was told that in 1936 there were more policemen in New York City than there were Marines in the world." Out of the many incidents that he experienced, one of the most memorable was his promotion to Pfc. in 1939 after three years of service. But to compensate for that, "I was one of only two out of the entire FMF then." Another notable moment was "getting my field commission (permanent). I was so proud."

In 1941, he was a member of the 6th Marine Regiment stationed in Iceland when the Japanese attacked Pearl Harbor. He was then transferred to the West Coast. A staff sergeant when he joined the 22nd Marines, Laden served in the Pacific for three years and received a battlefield promotion to second lieutenant.

Laden eventually achieved the rank of first lieutenant and served as intelligence officer of the 2nd Battalion. He then attended Japanese Language School on Maui where he learned enough of the language in two months to be able to interview prisoners.

"While on Fleet maneuvers, a yearly triangle event—Long Beach to Alaska to Pearl Harbor and back—we happened to arrive at Pearl Harbor the first night of Passover and the word went out throughout the Fleet that the Chief Rabbi of Hawaii invited Jews from the Fleet to join a *Seder* at the Royal Hawaiian Hotel.

"Of course, I eagerly volunteered and, out of 27,000 men in the Fleet, just I and one sailor showed up. We were treated royally, and I was amazed at how many Jews from the neighboring islands showed up."

Another time, I was ashore in Colon, Panama, and one of my uniform buttons came loose. I saw a tiny tailor shop on a side street and walked in. There was a bearded old man reading the *New York Daily Forward*. He could speak only Spanish and Yiddish. But I got the button sewn. I've run into Jews even on Samoa."

His wartime experiences were many and memorable. He doesn't know how he managed to survive with so many people around him being killed. He says that, "I sent my runner (a kid of about seventeen) ahead of me while we were pinned down on the beach and he stepped on a land mine about fifteen feet in front of me and was blown to bit." His most unpleasant incident was in "Learning that my best buddy, a Marine from Boston, who I went with all through Sea School, ship, Fleet Marine Force, and Iceland, was killed by a sniper on Bougainville. Also, visiting the wife of a fellow Jewish Marine from Camden, New Jersey, and telling about seeing her husband killed."

His most unpleasant time was "visiting the family of my sergeant when I returned to Philadelphia Naval Hospital. He died in my arms."

In the *Philadelphia Evening Bulletin* of March 15, 1944, a new item appeared which read: "First Lieutenant Philip P. Laden, of 347 S. 5th Street, knocked out a Japanese pillbox with hand grenades on the beach of Eniwetok." According to Laden, "It was the first news my family had of me for months." He fought through three landings, twice in the first wave. But he had the "misfortune of coming down with dengue fever and amoebic dysentery, and ended up in the Naval Hospital, New Caledonia."

Although he had been commissioned in the field two-and-a-half years previously, he "never had an officer's uniform until I got back to San Francisco. The lieutenant's bars came off a dead officer."

Laden's two brothers served in the armed forces during World War II: Milton, a sergeant in the Air Corps with combat duty in North Africa and Italy; and Hyman, a lieutenant commander in the Navy aboard a carrier.

Laden "never regretted Marine Corps days and would have stayed in and retired as perhaps a major or lieutenant colonel. I particularly loved serving aboard ship. There are no foxholes or K rations there. And clean sheets, too. My actual combat experiences were up close and I lost most of my friends. I had a very interesting and eventful nine years in the Corps.

Marco Meyer enlisted in the Marine Corps on April 7, 1942. He completed recruit training as a member of 336 Platoon, USMC,

MCRD, San Diego, then entered into another six months accelerated training prior to going overseas. Having graduated from Aviation Ordnance School, Memphis, Tennessee, he trained on the .20 mm Oerlikon machine cannon, .30-caliber machine gun, 50 mm machine gun, .50-caliber auto pistol, 30.06 rifle, the BAR, and the carbine.

Going overseas, he went to Guadalcanal with the 1st Marine Air Wing, Russell Islands, Miramar, and North Island, San Diego. He participated in the invasion and defense of the

Russell Islands from March to November 1943. As armament specialist and gunner on crash boats operating from Banika, Russell Islands, he saw action during various times from March 21, 1943, and November 18, 1943.

During this time, Guadalcanal and Banika had come under heavy bombing attacks by Japanese forces. Defending the ground units were Marine fighter pilots flying F4Fs and F4Us. Meyer was a crew member on one of the crash boats whose mission was to rescue downed pilots and capture the Japanese ones whenever possible. That, however, never happened: They went down with their planes. Although the crash boats tried to locate enemy pilots, they would find only debris at the sites of the downed planes. On the other hand, the American pilots always parachuted when they were able to do so. "We saved most of them. And the pilots were most appreciative. They supplied me with whiskey when they had it." Meyer never got whiskey rations, and was able to get a cupful, or dram, only from the officers' supplies. "So I appreciated back at the pilots. I offered to pop a Jap for them if they drove him across my guns. One F4U pilot, a lieutenant colonel—he couldn't have been more than twenty-three—told me, 'Hey, Sarge, you got it wrong. Take the second plane. The Jap will be on my tail."

Marco Meyer left the Marine Corps as a master technical sergeant. His overall experience and personal evaluation of the military was very positive. He was proud to have served in the military because he "helped keep the Japs from the United States."

Former Staff Sergeant Joseph Leifer, currently (2001) residing in Lincolnwood, Illinois, enlisted in the U.S. Marine Corps mid-December 1941, and reported for duty February 16, 1942. After completing recruit training at San Diego, Leifer was shipped to NAS, Jacksonville, Florida, for Aviation Machinist Mate (AMM) School. In November 1942, he sailed for Samoa, attached to VMF-111, 1st Marine Air Wing (MAW), later the 3rd, then the 4th. After ten months in Samoa, he became crew chief and was transferred to Funafuti, Ellice Islands. After being transferred to Nukufetau, he landed at Betio Island in Tarawa Atoll, Kwajalein, and on the Marshall Islands. After being wounded during an air raid on February 12, 1943, he was shipped to Pearl Harbor and back to the States to Great Lakes Naval Hospital near Chicago. He was transferred to Klamath Falls, Oregon, for six months and completed his active duty at Glenview Air Station, Illinois. He took a COG (convenience of the government) discharge instead of finishing regular service, and on August 16, 1945, completed three and a half years in the Marine Corps.

Syracuse, New York native, Paul Maloff enlisted in the Marine Corps, and subsequently saw combat on Roi-Namur, Saipan, Tinian, and Iwo Jima. He was a forward observer serving with George Battery, 3rd Battalion, 14th Marines of the 4th Marine Division.

After attending Telephone School, he made Pfc. and left the Corps with that rank. His decorations include five medals, like everyone else in the 4th Marine Division who made the four landings.

When the Bomb ended the war, the division was on the island of Maui. "About seventy days later, we boarded the aircraft carrier *Shamrock Bay* and sailed to San Diego and were trucked to Camp Pendleton, about seventy miles north.

While at Camp Pendleton, Kay Kyser came down to entertain the troops. Maloff and his foxhole buddy, Ken Jackson, got two empty buckets. "We knocked on the door of the movie house and told the Marine who opened the door that we were on a special butt detail. He let us in. The place was soon filled with officers." Jackson and Maloff were the only ones with no rank in the place. Kyser looked out and saw all the brass:

"I came here to play for the non-coms. Are there any here?" The two raised their hands.

He called us up on the steps. We went up with our buckets.

"How did you get in?" he asked.

"I told him Special Butt Detail."

Then he asked, "How many butts did you find?"

"We both tipped the buckets over. No butts dropped out."

"That was our ticket in," we said.

"He sat us down on chairs on opposite ends of the stage. Ginny Sims came out and sat on my lap and sang her first song. Then she walked across the stage and sat on Jackson's lap and sang a song to him. It was a day we will never forget.

Paul Maloff was particularly proud of his Marine Corps experience. Most of his memories are good ones and they persist to his day. One, in particular, is of March 10, at 0700, when "we were shelled. People were killed right next to me. I think about it every day."

One sorry incident was the following: One day, "I was called into regimental headquarters and along with two Italian boys was told I could not go to radar school because my father was from Russia and not an American citizen. The two Italian lads lost their lives on Tarawa. They sent me to telephone school. It was ok for me to be cannon fodder. But the bastards did not trust me."

In response to a letter Maloff sent to a state senator of New York, he was informed that, "The suspicion that you were subjected to during World War II, resulting from your Russian heritage is truly unfortunate . . . Many mistakes were made, but there is no excuse to compromise bedrock principles of acceptance and diversity . . ."

Reminiscing about the advice "our tough drill sergeant told us one day," he recommended that when in combat, if one should see a shell land, "you should go where the shell landed, because a shell never lands in the same place twice."

However, "One early morning on Iwo Jima, a shell landed no more than five yards from me, killed a Pfc. instantly. I covered him with a poncho. One minute later another shell landed right in the middle of the poncho. The Pfc. was killed twice. But he did not feel it the second time. The drill instructor most likely never was in combat."

His memories of the Marine Corps are mostly warm and still vivid. "I've slept at eighteen homes of guys in my outfit. All welcomed me with open arms. I went to Ken Jackson's wedding fifty-two years ago, and went to Bud Morgan's fiftieth wedding party four years ago. One of the guys from Cincinnati said many times he was going to piss on my grave. His doctor gave him four weeks to live about a year ago. He was a retired detective. Used his service revolver and blew his head off . . ."

He admired a number of people with whom he served: Captain Bill Brown, Staunton, Virginia., who died in 1998; Lieutenant Frank Webber, Miami, Florida, also died in 1998; Sergeant Jules Klein, also passed away in 1998; Ken Jackson, North Scituate, Rhode Island; Tom Bryly, Albany, New York; and Colonel Joe McCarthy, who died in 1996. These men, in combat with Maloff, were, "great leaders."

Oscar Haimowitz was one those who served prior to the entrance of the United States into World War II having joined up at the age of seventeen. Boot camp at Parris Island was "excellent for a seventeen-year old." Most of his assignments were in the States, with such posts as Headquarters, Marine Corps, Eighth and I Streets, Washington, D.C., with the Drum and Bugle Corps of the U.S. Marine Bans; Philadelphia Navy Yard, Portsmouth Naval Prison, and Honolulu, Hawaii.

He found practically no anti-Semitism in his almost eight years in the Corps. In the one incident he encountered, "a Polish anti-Semite called me a 'kike' and we put on the gloves. I didn't knock him out nor did he drop me. I put up a good account and not only he, but the others, respected me thereafter as a Jew."

All of his duties and stations were good ones. He "did guard duty at the Capital when President Roosevelt was sworn in." His comments about the military are very positive. In general, Sergeant Haimowitz's experiences were "excellent. It gave me responsibility, self-pride, accept anyone on the basis of their integrity, honesty, loyalty. Glad to get out after seven and a half years."

Haimowitz served until 1938, reentered in 1942 for his second stint, and was discharged with the rank of sergeant in 1946. After his time in the Corps, he spent his grandchildren's inheritance visiting a number of countries, including Argentina, Austria, China, France, Italy, Russia, and Spain. He made *aliya* for three years in Israel.

He was awarded the Good Conduct Medal, the American Campaign Medal, the Asiatic-Pacific Campaign Medal, and the World War II Victory Medal.

Haimowitz divides his eighty hours a month as a volunteer at Cedars-Sinai Medical Center, Los Angeles; the Beverly Hills Police Department; fire departments; public library; and public school kindergarten.

Milton Geller was one of those men whose experience in the Marine Corps has had a deep and lasting effect on his life. It provided a positive experience which "provide me with a personal esteem which gave me leadership qualities and confidence in my abilities. These were carried through my entire career as

.an electrical engineer. I was proud to have served in the Marine Corps, and received the high esteem in which the American public held any former Marine."

He enlisted in Yonkers, N.Y., March 1946, after the termination of the Second World War. After boot camp at Parris Island, he attended the Electrical Material School at the Great Lakes Naval Station. Graduating from there, he was assigned to Headquarters Battalion, 2nd Marines, 2nd Marine Division, Camp Lejeune. He remained there till the expiration of his enlistment in November 1947. He was required to leave active duty because the Marine Corps was in the process of reducing its manpower and releasing anyone who was on a two-year enlistment.

His MOS was Radio Repairman. He made rank of corporal, and served at Parris Island, Great Lakes, and Camp Lejeune.

During his entire period of military service, "he met one coreligionist. I never went to any religious services. I never hid the fact that I was Jewish and never experienced any expressions of anti-Semitism whether directly or indirectly."

Clearly, his military experience was a positive one. His experiences in the Marine Corps "were more than I had anticipated. I never felt left out, cheated, or disappointed in my tour of duty. I was always an accepted participant both on and off duty, on and off base, especially while on duty."

He was very candid in stating that one of his reasons for enlisting was to take advantage of the educational benefits of the GI Bill of Rights. "I had completed one semester of college and was committed to return. If I had to do it again, I definitely would have done it."

"I consider myself one of those who is once a Marine, always a Marine."

Ed Segal would like to turn the clock back fifty-seven years. At the outbreak of World War II, Ed was eighteen years old, in his freshman year at Marietta College, Marietta, Ohio, and had always admired the Marine Corps. "I decided to enlist instead of being drafted into the Army."

He actually considered his Jewish background to be a benefit to him in his military career. "I had been brought up in a good middle class Jewish home and being an only son received all the benefits of the same."

Although he may not have been prepared for boot camp at Parris Island, it didn't take him long to find out what was expected.

At first, he found the food and toilet facilities to be miserable. However, soon adapting to the stern life at PI, no less than anyone else, he began to get used to way of life he had elected.

He experienced his share of anti-Semitism, especially at the hand of "southern rednecks who had never been in close contact with any Jews." From July to September 1943, he "sweated out and took whatever my DI dished out." He qualified as a Sharpshooter with the MI and even began to enjoy the Spartan life of a U.S. Marine.

His college background enabled him to be assigned to Cherry Point and placement with a Marine Air Wing. Not long after some months of training and guard duty, he was assigned to a VMB bomber squadron. He actually became "anxious to go overseas and did not wait long."

After some time training on the west coast base of Miramar, he shipped out from San Diego in 1944. Arriving at the South Central Pacific area, his first stop was Hawaii, later to Eniwetok, then to Saipan, Iwo Jima, and finally Okinawa, where they were caught in a typhoon.

His squadron participated in night bombing missions with rockets, destroying Japanese shipping. Religion awakened in these hazardous times. He said, "I must say that I did do some praying especially while in these combat areas." Modest as he was, he admitted that "in my opinion, I was in a safer situation than the Marines who landed in the invasions such as

Guadalcanal, Tarawa, Wake Island, but am still proud to be a member of the U.S. Marine Corps. I held the rank of Pfc.

Ed recognized some of his heroes of the war. They included "Pappy" Boyington, John Basilone, "Chesty" Puller, and Ensign Colin Kelly. "They say once a Marine, always a Marine. And I believe that is true with me."

Ed's father served in France with the American Expeditionary Force in the First World War. He was engaged in combat in the Meuse-Argonne and Chateau-Thierry battles and was "lucky to have survived in that terrible war."

Some of the greatest heroes of our military have been those born outside the United States. Not the least among that elite group is Sergeant Samuel Glucksman of the U.S. Marine Corps. Born in Austria, he fought with such distinction in the First World War that he was declared by Colonel O. B. Forbes, Director of the Veterans Bureau, to be one of the war's great heroes. Colonel Forbes personally congratulated him upon his return to Washington, D.C.

As Sergeant Glucksman was too modest to tell his own story, he was questioned closely by officials of the Veterans Bureau. Glucksman fought in seven major engagements—Verdun, Belleau Woods, Chateau-Thierry, Marbach, St. Mihiel, Soissons, and Blanc Mont. When his company of two hundred fifty went over the top in one of the engagements, Glucksman was only one of twelve to survive the battle. On October 3, 1918, Glucksman single-handedly captured twenty Germans.

In another engagement, Glucksman went out to get water for his comrades who were at Triangle Farm without food or water. During this time, he captured a German soldier who had been firing at his comrades with a machine-gun. As the Washington Star of March 17, 1922, reported the action: "Instead of bayoneting the gunner, Glucksman forced him to lead the way to the rest of the advance party. Coming to a shellhole some thirty feet in depth, although painfully wounded, Glucksman crawled among them with a hand grenade and forced them all to go over the top and into the hands of other members of his unit.

When his wounds were dressed, he rejoined his unit in the process of advancing. Although he was ordered back to the hospital, he remembered that his men still needed water.

Whereupon, he took canteens from the debris on the field, filled them with water, and staggered two kilometers to provide his fellow Marines with the needed relief. Then, he was forced to return to the hospital.

Sergeant Glucksman is the recipient of the Victory Medal with five battle clasps, five gold stars, and silver stars for special mention in general orders. He received the Navy Cross, the *Croix de Guerre* with gold star, and the Distinguished Service Cross.

The Washington Star hailed Sergeant Samuel Glucksman as, "A rival for York," and described him as "One of the greatest heroes of the war."

Bob Applebaum's personal letterhead stationery is adorned with an American flag. Hardly surprising considering his record of participation in three wars in the service of his country.

He joined the Marine Corps at the age of eighteen and completed boot camp at MCRD, San Diego. Since he had spent a year and a half at a military academy, he was appointed right guide. He was also excused from much of the close order drill as he had already mastered it.

The rest, as he says, was pretty easy.

Following boot camp, he trained at Camp Elliott, near San Diego, as a member of the 2nd Marine Division. Transferring to the new base at Camp Pendleton, he was assigned to the12th Marines of the 3rd Marine Division.

Not long thereafter, he shipped out to New Zealand in January 1943. There, along with the training for forthcoming combat, he, with the others, enjoyed the great liberty and hospitality of the people of that country. Soon, he was transferred to regimental headquarters, 12th Marines.

Departing New Zealand, he disembarked on Guadalcanal for more training in the summer of 1943. He landed on Bougainville on D-Day on November 1, 1943. As a member of the Artillery Survey Section of the 12th Marines, he participated in the ensuing combat on that island, departing Bougainville the end of December to return once again to Guadalcanal.

After fifty-five days aboard an APA, he landed on Guam on July 21, 1944 for more training, departing in February 1945 for the invasion of Iwo Jima.

After the campaign on Iwo, he returned to the States where he was stationed at NAD, Dover, New Jersey, then to Brooklyn Navy Yard, where he was released from active duty.

After some time in the Reserve, he returned to active duty in August 1948. With the outbreak of the Korean War, he found himself stationed in Washington, D.C. After nine months at Parris Island at a drill instructor, he shipped out to Korea for thirteen months. There, he was a member of E and F Batteries, 11th Marines, as gun chief on 105 mm guns. In 1955, he went to Japan with the 1st Battalion, 12th Marines, once again to participate in another landing, this time more relaxed from the previous one, on Iwo Jima in February 1956.

After tours of duty in California and Okinawa, with training in the Philippines, he was stationed first at Camp Pendleton, then at MCAS, Yuma, Arizona. He retired in 1964.

But his retirement was to be short-lived. Recalled to active duty in 1968, he was sent to Vietnam, as a member of Headquarters Company, 3rd Battalion, 9th Marines, 3rd Marine Division, as S-4 Chief. After a year in Vietnam, he returned to Okinawa with the 9th Marines and spent his last year on active duty at Camp Pendleton. He retired once again in 1970 as staff sergeant after twenty-two years of active service.

Erwin Small, now Dr. Erwin Small, Doctor of Veterinary Medicine, MS, couldn't have had better advice. His brother, on a destroyer off Iwo Jima participating in the bombardment of the island, advised him to keep his butt down.

Dr. Small was probably influenced in his decision to become an animal doctor because he was a war dog handler, one of the first to train in the use of the animals in combat.

Small was a member of one of the first War Dog Platoons. Following boot camp at Parris Island, he was sent to Camp Lejeune, North Carolina, for training with the War Dog Training Program, a specialized group of Marines that trained scout and messenger dogs.

Doberman Pinschers and German Shepherds were the breeds of choice. Small ended up with a young shepherd named "Pal." Once training was completed, they traveled cross country to the old World Fair Ground in San Francisco, followed by additional training at Moffett Air Force Base, California.

Subsequently, they were identified as the 7th War Dog Platoon, and after landing on Maui, Small was attached to H & S Company, 25th Regiment, 4th Marine Division.

After several more months of training, they shipped out for, as Dr. Small says, "a combat mission of unknown location. When we finally saw land again, it was the shores of Iwo Jima. According to our CO, this was going to be a cakewalk and our biggest headache would be later."

Of the many memories that Dr. Small still holds, one of the most tragic was the death of one of his closest friends. "He was a tall, straight as an arrow individual, from the Kentucky hills. We used to play basketball whenever possible. There was little or no action, so we took a walk to visit his brother in another company. On arrival at Headquarters, we were informed that his brother had been killed in action the day before."

Small, and the other dog handlers, were always assigned to the periphery for night guard duty. One particular night, his buddy's telephone line was not functioning. At that moment, "He left his foxhole to investigate and was shot and killed by another Marine who apparently failed to challenge and assumed he was the enemy." That meant two brothers were killed on Iwo. Small asked rhetorically: "Can you imagine the grief of that poor mother living in the hills of Kentucky receiving a visit by the Marines informing her that both boys were killed on Iwo Jima. I am sure, like most of us, she had never heard of Iwo Jima."

Dr. Small was recalled to active duty during the Korean War. He was assigned to the 2nd Battalion, 6th Marines. While participating in a Mediterranean cruise as part of a reinforced battalion of the 2nd Marine Division, Small was acting First Sergeant for the company. With several companies aboard, the schedule for chow had to be very precise. They were assigned designated times and would have to stand in lines for hour that stretched around the deck.

One day, arriving at the gangway leading to the mess deck, First Sergeant Small asked one of the Marines returned from chow, "What did you have for chow?" He said, "steak."

But when Small reached the line, he was served Vienna sausage. The same scene was repeated the next evening. A Marine told him they were having chicken. But when Small got to chow he was served Vienna sausage. Whereupon, Small stopped the chow line and talked to his CO. They both went to the colonel where Small repeated his story. They finally ended up before the ship's captain. After he heard the story, he called for the ship's commissary officer. And Small repeated the story.

Thereupon, a young Navy lieutenant J.G. had to break out sufficient meat to feed the company of two hundred. "He ended up thawing out sufficient chops to feed the troops. The galley crews were up all night cooking and cleaning and then had to prepare breakfast within an hour. For the remaining 15–20 days aboard, whenever I appeared in the mess line, they always made sure I was satisfied."

Lastly, Small relates the story of an interesting challenge facing each Marine returning from liberty: They had to salute the flag and the officer of the deck in the presence of the chaplain who asked if "we had contact. He paid no attention to our response but gave each of us a penicillin tablet."

The citation for the Navy and Marine Corps Medal awarded to First Lieutenant John B. Cohen reads as follows:

"For heroic conduct in rescuing four men from drowning off Namur Island, Kwajalein Atoll, Marshall Islands, on 6 June 1944. Aware of the danger from heavy surf and jagged reefs, First Lieutenant Cohen led four volunteers to the rescue of the struggling men. Braving the rough seas which at one time swept him into the open sea, he resolutely continued his efforts until all four men were recovered and taken to safety. By his courage and initiative, he was instrumental in saving the lives of these men and his prompt actions were in keeping with the highest traditions of the United States Naval Service."

However, those familiar with his background, dedication, training, and outlook on life would hardly be surprised. This was exactly what they would expect from such a man. As a boy, he was "very interested in Scouting, receiving the highest awards." In fact, he received the highest—the Eagle Scout. He was proud to be a Marine. At Quantico, he was a member of a "great football team, made of some of the best in the country, both pro and All-American, of which I was one (honorable mention)." He never experienced any anti-Semitism in the Corps, "maybe because I was quite large and well built."

He was commissioned after Officer's Training at Quantico. His DI, Dombrowski, taught them well. He was an old-timer, having served in China and Nicaragua. Cohen was among a group of "Ninety-day wonders. Ten of us won regular commissions out of three hundred. I was one of them. Our colonel, Clovis Coffman, swore me in with great ceremony at a poker game."

As a second lieutenant, "I was the senior officer at the startup of the 1ˢᵗ Airdrome Battalion. Can you imagine at age twenty-two in command of a few hundred or more young new Marines?"

At that age of twenty-two, he got married. They lived on the base at New River, beautiful quarters—for a while. But soon, he had orders to leave. He participated in the landings at Roi-Namur, Kwajalein, Saipan, and Tinian, where he managed to survive relatively unscathed.

His least memorable experience was "the heat of the islands. The ocean temperature was hotter than the land. There was nowhere to cool off." He had the pleasure of making the acquaintance of a number of great people of whom Jack Fey was the best. He became the President of the University of Vermont, and later the CEO of Equitable Life and one time chief clerk of the Supreme Court.

He remembers many wonderful experiences, and he was blessed to "have so many great officers under me. We still get together occasionally."

They even conspired to keep their beer cold. "We made arrangements with some of the 'fly boys' to take our beer up and bring it back cold."

The Marine Corps experience had a profound effect on his personal and professional life. The military "was very important in my later years. I always seem to attract bright and loyal people in my business. Somehow, they all believed in my leadership which came from the Corps and the fact that as a boy I was an Eagle Scout."

John Cohen has had a "helluva life" indeed: Marine Corps officer, decorated for bravery, combat veteran, business executive (Distributor of Columbia Records, founder of a large music firm, President of the National Recording Industry). Perhaps he may be forgiven for his for his "horrendous" typing. But he does pretty well on the computer, "where you get second changes."

John B. Cohen concludes with a very understandable, "I've had a helluva good life!!!"

Ed Miller is an enigmatic person: a bit cynical, perhaps a bit fatalistic, somewhat confused, but no less a hero. He survived Iwo Jima. For Ed Miller, there was no most memorable incident. His experiences in the Marine Corps were among the most vivid, and interesting, if not convoluted. At each stop along the way, from boot camp to discharge, his life was full, varied, frantic, unpredictable, and fraught with danger.

He had a shot at Officers Candidate School. Among his most memorable experiences was that of witnessing Rabbi Gittlesohn deliver his Iwo Jima Cemetery oration, "The Purest Democracy." Other memorable experiences included "Facing down an anti-Semite aboard the return ship from Iwo. An unknown Marine brandished his bayonet shouting, 'I'm gonna kill all the niggers and Jews!' I offered him to start with me." Others included being sworn into the Corps, Bob Crosby and band aboard an APA flagship, conducting a Seder aboard an APA, and the Danny Kaye show in Japan.

There are a number of unpleasant incidents: watching the communication wiremen pulling teeth from the mouths of dead Japanese and Koreans, the Iwo Cemetery, and seeing Danny Ginsburg's star.

Heroism, if not modesty, runs in Ed Miller's family. His older brother was in the 69th Divison of the Army. At first, his distaste for the elite led him to refuse a commission. However, he was a hero at the Battle of the Bulge. When his CO was killed, his brother saved his platoon from German tank fire, was almost fatally wounded, and did, in fact, receive and accept a battlefield commission.

At Parris Island boot camp, most of the recruits were from the northeast and New York. One of the recruits in his platoon was Adolph Ochs Sulzberger, later to be the publisher of the *New York Times*. One kid from Kentucky probably was not yet ready for the Marine Corps: He cried all night, wet his bed, and departed.

Ed Miller's boot camp was not exactly a case study in success: The DIs were tough, but civil. Ed "barely passed rifleman. Barely passed physical requirements. Failed Morse code. Left a private."

However, things began to look up after training at Pendleton and Hawaii. From Hawaii, he shipped out on an APA, the 7th Fleet Command ship. Admiral Halsey and the Bob Crosby band were on board. The downside was that the ship's hold was too hot, driving the men to sleep on deck, except when it rained.

En route to Iwo, the Protestant chaplain invited him to make the Passover Seder for the Jewish troops. "The JWB provide the haggadahs and the food. Rabbi Gittlesohn had offered my name."

Arriving at Iwo, he was assigned to "Replacement Unit, Iwo Jima." For two days, he ferried supplies to the beach, and returned the wounded to the ship's infirmary. On the third day, he was assigned to the 26th Marine Communication Platoon. There, he met a replacement who soon was to become his buddy and teammate, Pfc. A. G. R. Budde. Not only did they run wire to their own line companies, but ran into Japanese wire as well. Both Budde and Miller were assigned to E Company, in charge of walkie-talkies and radio communication with Regiment. Every night, they did their line duty past Motoyama Airfield. They had the unforgettable experience of cheering the raising of the flag on Suribachi.

His evaluation of the military, or Marine Corps, experience is a bit tortuous, confused, perhaps contradictory. He was proud to have served. "But fate put me in a Marine uniform.

I was serving in World War II, fighting the Axis. We had *esprit de corps*, but much was false. The bravado covered up the SNAFUs and incompetence of the brass that cost thousands of lives. Of Iwo! How could one be proud of the killing of unarmed Japanese and Koreans trying to surrender? Or proud of the wiremen who used their pliers to pull out the gold teeth of warm corpses?"

As Ed Miller climbed black sand dunes on Iwo, he passed

dead Marines and Japanese; he saw dead bodies floating off the beach. He was a witness of "stacked filled body bags that lay across the path from our message center. Aboard the APA, he heard the dead, and the trauma victims being 'deep-sixed every midnight." He found Lieutenant Ginsburg's Star.

Ed Miller never felt left out or cheat. That is, not beside Iwo. He had a great travel experience, met all kinds of people across the U.S. and the Pacific. "I did my best as a proud Jew, *sans* horns, and a credit to the Corps."

For heroic actions on Iwo Jima, 1ˢᵗ Lieutenant Gene Hochfelder, received the Silver Star. Presumably modesty prevented him from describing the heroics which warranted that award. But he does explain that he was one of only two Jewish officers in the Marine Corps paratroops and was one of only two officers out of thirty-six battalion officers (nineteen original officers plus seventeen replacements), to survive Iwo Jima without being killed or wounded.

The resume of J. Gene Hochfelder is an impressive record of personal, professional, and military achievement. It includes his awards and decorations which include the Distinguished Service Medal, the Silver Star Medal, the Bronze Star Medal, the Presidential Unit Citation, and the New York State Letter of Commendation.

His wife, Carol Ostrow, could boast of being an off-Broadway producer, and they stake claim to five children, thirteen grandchildren, and three great-children (as of 2001). His professional record is equally impressive with various executive positions in the clothing and securities industries. His other affiliations include positions in a number of charitable and religious organizations.

Born in New York City on April 27, 1922, Gene Hochfelder graduated from Lawrence High School on Long Island in 1939 and attended The Wharton School, University of Pennsylvania,

Philadelphia. After graduation, he entered the Marine Corps as a private.

Following recruit training at Parris Island, he was selected for OCS and Parachute School, Quantico, Virginia. He received his commission as second lieutenant in August 1942, and was duly qualified as a parachutist after training at El Cajon, California.

Shipped overseas in the 27th Replacement Battalion, he landed at Guadalcanal, and was then transferred to Bougainville prior to being assigned to a unit. Having been overseas only three or four months, Lieutenant Hochfelder "had no desire to go back to the States and then come back again to the war." As a result, he was transferred to a "Parachute Airborne Supply unit in which he served a few months, dropping supplies to our troops in Bougainville."

Hochfelder return to the States and was assigned to the 5th Marine Division at Camp Pendleton. He was appointed H & S (Headquarters & Service—later to become the Headquarters Company) Company Commander in the 1st Battalion of the 26th Marines. He landed on Iwo Jima on February 19, 1945. "Although our battalion had thirty-six casualties among our officers, I survived without injury and served for thirty-seven days on Iwo Jima." For heroic action on Iwo, First Lieutenant Hochfelder received the Silver Star Medal.

Upon his return to Hawaii, he was placed "in charge of writing the citations of all our brave Marines," and trained for the projected invasion of Japan with the 5th Marine Division. However, with the end of the war, he landed at Sasebo, Japan, three days after the second atomic bomb, and was placed in charge of an advance that occupied Kyushu, the southernmost island of Japan.

Hochfelder "entered the Marine Corps and was ultimately discharged as a Captain and a Company Commander."

A story that made headlines all over the country in 1943 was the ordeal of Harvey Weinstein. This man was kidnapped by three employees of his Lord West Tuxedo Company in New York City and held in an underground dirt dungeon for thirteen days. However, his abductors failed to remember that he was not only their employer, a man of almost seventy, but a Marine.

At the time of his kidnapping, he was sixty-eight years old, a far cry from the young, lean eighteen years he was when he enlisted in the Marine Corps. Shortly after his ransom was paid, and his rescue was effected, did he first calmly ask for a cigarette, then credited his survival to his Marine Corps training. "I could never had survived without it," he told the New York City Police Department Chief, Raymond Kelly, another former Marine.

He had been buried in a steel covered pit where he was kept alive on fruit and water. The dungeon was seven feet wide and fourteen feet deep, shaped like a gallon plastic milk bottle. In addition, he was shackled during the entire time of his ordeal.

Upon his rescue by two New York City detectives, he said, "The Marine Corps training I received, including living in foxholes and coming under fire in World War II, helped me to keep my mind clear while imprisoned in that total darkness."

Harvey Weinstein enlisted in the Marine Corps on August 1, 1943, and served for almost three years. He was wounded on October 9, 1944 on Peleliu when a grenade shattered his left arm. Peleliu was a campaign noted for its unique cave warfare, a place where thirty-four Japanese emerged after two and a half years after the end of the war.

Weinstein was born on Valentine's Day, 1925. "No wonder all of New York City and his fellow Marines love the guy."

In an article printed in the 6th Marine Division Newsletter, March 4, 1994, Jerry Steigmann said: 'In a special appreciation conference with former Mayor David Dinkins, also a Marine, and Commissioner Kelly, Weinstein donated $10,000 to a Police

Charitable Fund. He was trained on Parris Island as I. He also played basketball on the same James Madison High School as Larry Baxter, my teammate on the 22nd Regiment team in Tsingtao."

In the article, Weinstein said that he attended his first reunion of the Third Amphibious Battalion in New Orleans. There, he met his former commanding officer, who said, "When I got you, you were just a big dumb kid from Brooklyn. But two years later, you were one tough Marine."

Weinstein credits Lieutenant Colonel Arthur Parker for his survival. Speaking again of Weinstein and linking him to his Marine training and commitment, Steigmann says, "Marine training to the very end. He makes us all that prouder of our Marine heritage. Survival during difficult times is what bonds us."

———————

Prior to joining up, the most difficult thing that Howard Gherman did was to light his cigarette. The match was the heaviest thing he ever lifted. It may be a stretch to say that the Marine Corps needed the likes of Howard Gherman. But he sure needed the Marines.

When he broke the news at dinner one night in 1958 that he had enlisted in the Marine Corps, his mother "gagged, and my father who was an ex-Air Force colonel with political clout said he would see what he could do to get me into the Air Force." His father didn't get the picture. Howard wanted to join the Marines.

He shortly found out that Parris Island was not Pleasure Island, especially in mid-August. The first weeks were a nightmare. His bunk was positioned where he could see the lights from the main gate and he thought to himself, "God, what have I done?"

He hated every moment of it.

He was assigned one week in the chow hall. One day while working in the women Marines' mess hall, he was in the line putting potatoes on "the little darlins' trays as they came through." He recounts that, "Out of the dead silence, I heard a woman DI scream out—'Listen, bitch, quit looking up. There's five thousand miles of cock on this island, and you ain't getting' one fuckin' inch until you get off. If you get off.' At that point, I was getting a little salty and could not help the laugh. Our DI pulled me in the back of the kitchen, whacked me across the mouth with this huge hamlike hand and began to convince me that I didn't pack the gear to be a Marine."

At graduation from boot camp in the Marine Corps birthday, 1958, Sergeant Perry, late of the Frozen Chosin, tossed him another unflattering assessment of his talents to be a Marine: As Howard was loading on the bus to leave PI, he approached him and said, "I remember when you first got here you had to drag that seabag. Now you tossed it up on your shoulder with one hand. However, you fuckin pussy, you still don't pack the gear. It's no wonder you're going to wingwipers school 'cause you couldn't cut it at ITR."

Then, things began to change. Maybe he was really beginning to shape up. Howard evaluated the training as "excellent," and "I did become a well-disciplined man."

Arriving at Jacksonville, Florida, to become an air controller, things didn't work out too well. "It was wisely decided that I didn't have the skills for a radar operator," and, consequently, now that he was "squared away," reported to the Guard Force and spent some time on the gates.

From Jacksonville, he was transferred to Naval Air Station, Glenview, Illinois, with MACS-22. There, he was the squadron CO's driver and squadron right guide. Although he admits that he did not measure up to being a grunt, "I did and do love the Corps." He has but two career regrets: one, that he didn't pursue a law degree, and, two, that he didn't stay in the Corps. "To this day, I can see myself retiring as a CWO4 ((I don't know why) or a sergeant-major."

Today, his wife thinks he's nuts because he has a Marine Corps League license frame, a Marine Corps emblem decal on his car, wears a baseball cap with a Marine air wing emblem on it with a Pfc. stripe.

In his book, *Iwo Jima, Legacy of Valor,* Bill D. Ross describes three events involving Jewish Marines. In the first "There was a sergeant of Marines, Herbert Kielson of the little community of Laurelton in Queens. He enlisted as a boy of eighteen back in 1938, and two years later, at the World's Far in San Francisco, won the heavyweight championship of the Marine Corps. Later, in 1941, he was gunnery instructor at San Diego, but he pleaded for a transfer to combat duty. On January 2, he telephoned home across country in a jubilant voice, "I'm shoving off."

That was the last the family heard of him until the official word arrived that he died on March 23, 1942, on a U.S. cruiser of wounds suffered in action somewhere in the Pacific. They brought this young, once strong body back to Laurelton, perhaps the first to be returned to the U.S. for burial from the Pacific theater. "More than one thousand neighbors, including young men in uniform, attended the funeral service in Laurelton's Jewish center. He lies in Mount Judah Cemetery, Cemetery Hills." [1]

Max Clark of Galveston, Texas, wounded twice at Bataan and Corregidor, received the Silver Star and the Purple Heart. He was born on July 9, 1897, in New Britain, Connecticut. Originally, he enlisted in the Army at Fort Slocum, New York, in September 1916, and served overseas from September 1917 to August 1919. He was wounded by a shell fragment and in 1919, he discharged as a first sergeant. In addition to the Silver and Star and Purple Heart, he also received the French *Croix de Guerre* and the *fourragère.* He was first reported missing, then killed in action.

Clark re-enlisted in 1920 and was made a staff sergeant before being discharged in 1921. In 1925, he was commissioned a second lieutenant in the Officers' Reserve Corps until 1936.

[1] Ross, Bill D., *Iwo Jima, Legacy of Valor,* p. 26.

In 1937, he resigned from the Army and received an appointment as a captain in the Marine Corps Reserve, attached to the Fleet Marine Force Battalion at Galveston, Texas.

Clark was ordered to active duty in 1941 and sent to Shanghai, China. Remaining with the 4th Marines, they were sent to the Philippines. In January 1942, on Corregidor, he was promoted to major.

There he was killed in action. He was posthumously awarded the Navy Cross for distinguished service at Cavite Navy Yard and the Sangley Point Naval for Station for "working day and night, to the limit of human endurance, salvaging war materials and explosives from the stricken and burning areas—materials desperately needed for later use by MacArthur's men on Bataan."[2]

Lastly, an amusing anecdote in a not-so-amusing setting: "Corporal Eugene S. Jones, on his way with a flamethrower platoon, thought the island looked like a giant pinball machine, what with the streaking rockets and fireballs from exploding shells. "Biggest fuckin pinball machine you ever seen,' was the shouted answer to the eighteen-year-old from Sergeant Herbert Ginsburg."[3]

Seymour "Sy" Brody was another Marine whose service had lifelong meaning and an important influence on his adult for several reasons: One, it was another experience that broadened his mind and his life; secondly, "Boot camp was a demanding experience, but I came out in the best shape of my life, and when it was over, I never felt in better physical shape"; third, he was proud for having served in the Marine Corps; fourth, "I chose the Marine Corps because it was a small military force and I wouldn't be lost in the shuffle"; and lastly, "The experience made

[2] Ibid., p. 63.

[3] Op. cit.

me a better person as it made me look at life a little more seriously."

After enlisting in the Marine Corps, Brody took boot training at New River, North Carolina. While at New River, other than being a "demanding experience," he had one anti-Semitic incident with another recruit, but "That disappeared after we were matched up in a boxing bout."

After New River, Sy was transferred to Camp Pendleton, California, where he joined the 1st Marine Division. With the division, he landed for more training in New Zealand, preparatory to the invasion of Guadalcanal. He participated in the defense of Guadalcanal, the invasion of Bougainville, and in the campaign on Guam. During the invasion of Bougainville, he was a BARman where he was point man as they moved toward the Japanese lines. Nothing special happened except that he came close to being killed on a number of occasions. He remembers the mud and insects on Bougainville as being particularly unpleasant.

He most admired the Seabees who built facilities as they moved ahead in combat. Another experience on Bougainville that he recalls vividly is the earth tremors "which was scary as nobody controlled it. We had after shocks for about thirty more days."

Other members of his family served in the armed forces of the United States: His father served in the Army in World War I, a brother served in the Navy in World War II, another brother was a soldier in the Korean War, and two sons-in-law served in the Army in Vietnam.

Returning from overseas, he was assigned to Quonset Naval Air Station, Rhode Island. When he returned to Brooklyn, he received "a tumultuous reception from my family and the people on the block."

Michael Harac was obviously more of a man of action, and less one of words. Even though language was his principal occupational forte, he remains terse and laconic.

Although he was born in Brooklyn, New York, he lived in South America as a young boy. After service in the Marine Corps, he worked as an architectural draftsman, studied tropical architecture in Puerto Rico and Miami, and practiced commercial and residential architecture in Florida, Puerto Rico, and Panama. Married to the former Mimi Mitrani, he has two children, Lani Sara and Seth Morris, and currently works as a medical facilities architect. He is one of the featured writers of *Soldier's Heart, Survivors' Views of Combat Trauma,* and author of *Shore Party and Other Tales of War.*

He joined the Marines at eighteen, right after high school. Having completed boot camp at Parris Island, he was transferred to Camp Lejeune. He was trained as a Spanish language interpreter with the 2nd Interrogation/Translation, then shipped to Vietnam.

One anti-Semitic encounter remains firmly in his mind: "A fellow Marine of higher rank was provoking me with anti-Semitic talk. I responded with talk, which turned out to be offensive to him. Being of higher rank, he ordered me to do some menial task. I didn't refuse, but before I did, I went to report the incident to the staff sergeant, who was located in a separate room in the barracks, he being the highest ranking person at that time and place. He turned out to be Jewish. The end result was that the sergeant had a talk behind closed doors with the anti-Semite. To this day, I don't know what he said, but I could imagine and he basically begged me to accept his apology. And I could also imagine what would have happened had I not accepted."

There were a number of persons he admired in the Marine Corps, namely the Jewish Navy chaplain and a black Marine whom he had befriended. To this day, he retains the friendship of the chaplain's assistant.

Some of his memorable experiences include service in Vietnam as a supply specialist with the 3rd Marine Division in 1966–67, participating in an amphibious landing in Portugal, travels to Spain, Thailand, and Okinawa.

Michael Harac, Corporal, U. S. Marine Corps, was proud to have served his country in the premier 911 military force.

Evelyn Levine Nyman was quick to point out that she experienced no incidents of anti-Semitism. Most of her experience in the Marine Corps was very positive.

Completing boot camp at Camp Lejeune in January 1944, she was assigned to Washington, D.C. and the Naval Annex in Arlington, Virginia. Then, she went to school for training in Inventory Taking, after which she received promotion to buck sergeant.

Her next assignment was at Parris Island working at the PX, the NCO Club, and the Officers Club.

A number of her family served in the military: her husband and father-in-law were members of the Army, and her daughter served in the Air Force.

One day, while having lunch at the Officers Club, after taking inventory, Tyrone Power came in and spoke to her and her friends at their table. She admired the rabbi at Parris Island for being very friendly and compassionate. The first time she flew in an airplane was on her first furlough home.

Summing up her military experience, she says that it was "a very good experience, and would enlist again if I were a young person—but it was good to become a civilian." One positive experience of the military was the discipline she was required to accept. What she does regret, however, is the fact that she did not have the chance to go overseas.

Born July 13, 1921, in Philadelphia and raised in Pittsburgh, Pennsylvania, Jacob Marks was drafted into the Marine Corps on May 6, 1943, and completed recruit training at Parris Island. Having had a double hernia as a child, his physical activities in school were limited. Because of this, he never learned to swim. As a result, he had "one helluva time passing the swimming test, but managed to struggle through it after having to stop halfway and holding onto the side of the pool until I could catch my breath." Besides, "the DI threatened to stomp on my hand if I didn't let go and finish the swim."

Marks graduated from recruit training as a private first class in the upper 10 percent of the platoon, after which he was transferred to drafting school at Camp Lejeune and graduated as a corporal. From there, he was placed in charge of construction crews at Camps Lejeune and Pendleton. At Pearl Harbor, he was detached and assigned to Task Force 36 to do map work, after which he was transferred to 5th Amphibious Corps for both map work and drafting.

During the sea voyage from Hawaii, Marks acted as lay chaplain on board ship. Julius Mark, chief chaplain in the Pacific area (who became chief rabbi at Temple Emanu-El in New York City after the war), explained *Kaddish* to him, showed him how to conduct services, and supplied him with prayer books for the Jewish religious services on Saturday mornings. "It was quite a thrill to have services piped down, knowing the religious services of a handful of Jews were being respected."

Another chaplain learned to play *Ain Kelohenu* on the violin so he might add something to the service. "He also loaned me candles for the Friday night service. I was treated royally in that respect. What was most amazing was that officers and enlisted men came to me with questions and problems. There was little I could do to console them, but it was very gratifying to be in that position."

Marks was the only draftsman on Iwo Jima, doing map work for the engineers, 5th Amphibious Corps. His responsibility was to maintain the progress map showing the positions of the day-to-day work of the Seabees and the engineers. In addition, he had to keep records of the desalination and distribution of water.

He was very resourceful. In some of his escapades, others laughed at him when he took it upon himself to gather and save rainwater. However, their ridicule ceased when they learned that he had enough fresh water to wash, sponge bathe, and shave, "while they had to use a mixture of fresh and sulphur water. The laugh was on them, since they came begging for a little water to shave with."

His foxhole, dug deep enough to be the envy of his mates, and made as comfortable as could be under the circumstances, was protected with sandbags all around. He even had enough space to set up a box which he used as a desk. He wrote letters home by candlelight. One day, the CO, Colonel Litz, ordered him to share his foxhole with others on a rotation basis. This pissed him off no end. One night, he shared the foxhole with the Engineer Section captain who proceeded to ask Jacob if he knew the difference between friendly artillery and incoming shelling. Jacob tried to explain that once in a foxhole it made no difference. Whereupon, the captain insisted in explaining the difference and then went to sleep. That night, they experienced heavy incoming artillery. Jacob could hear the shells falling closer and closer to the foxhole. It was such a fearful experience that he developed a duodenal ulcer, which never did heal, and caused him to develop Barrett's syndrome (cancer of the esophagus). Ultimately, this was removed in 1996 at the Miami Veterans Hospital.

With the end of the war, Marks saw occupation duty in Japan. He was quartered in a Japanese naval barracks in Sasebo. Most of the men were waiting to be returned to the States. As Marks was short of points, he was assigned to MP duty with the rank of sergeant.

Marks's two brothers, Joseph and Leonard, also served in the armed forces during World War II. Both were engineer-gunners—Joseph served in Europe; Leonard in the China-Burma-India theater.

Famed jazz/swing drummer Bernard (Buddy) Rich had a formula for dealing with anti-Semites: He knocked them on their butts. Although he had been classified 3-A, Rich joined the Marine Corps anyway in 1942. He served stateside as a judo instructor. Making a common observation that he was the only Jew in his platoon, he "wasn't used to hearing stuff about the Jews don't know how to fight, the Jews don't do anything but make money, the Jews started the war, and so forth. After the first dozen beefs, I didn't hear any more talk like that."

He was the son of vaudeville performers who made him a part of their act before he was 2; he was only 4 when he appeared as a drummer and tap dancer on Broadway. He led his own age band by the time he was 11, and subsequently performed as a drummer with such big-time bands as Jimmy Dorsey, Tommy Dorsey, Harry James, and Artie Shaw.

He was born in New York City on June 30, 1917, and died in Los Angeles, April 2, 1987.

Herman Kaufman had a curious reason for joining the Marines. A number of his childhood friends decided to join the Navy. Six of them attempted to join, but only three were accepted. Being the brave and different he enlisted in the Marine Corps on April 19, 1942, a year after graduating from high school in Illinois. His boot camp at San Diego was the quick wartime basic training designed to get them out and into combat as fast as possible.

He was then transferred to Camp Elliott for further training. He made a number of friends there, except one man who was anti-Semitic. Not only that, he killed another Marine. There was a bit of a mixup in his religious preference: Although a Jew, they gave him Protestant dog tags until it was determined that he was actually Jewish.

His division, the 1st Marine Division, was shipped to Wellington, New Zealand, where they stayed for seven months. Kaufman wound up in the hospital with the malaria he had contracted on Guadalcanal.

Tarawa in the Gilbert Islands was especially difficult and perilous. Going ashore was exceptionally difficult because of the coral which impeded the movement of the Higgins landing boats. To make things worse, the tide was out. Consequently, they had to wade ashore for about a quarter of a mile, resulting in the death of quite a few men killed and wounded even before they landed on the shore. One of his Jewish buddies was killed in this landing.

Afterwards, they were shipped to Hilo, Hawaii, for further training. During their six months there, he came down with another attack of malaria and ended up in the hospital once again.

Leaving the hospital and Hawaii, they embarked for the campaign at Saipan and Tinian. He volunteered to handle the .30-caliber machine gun on the front line, even though he knew nothing about that weapon. Although he repented for doing that, and called himself "stupid," it turned out well as he wasn't killed or injured. At Saipan, he found himself in a demolition company blowing up the Bank of Saipan, where he promptly confiscated about a million dollars of Japanese yen. He was heavily engaged in combat, finding himself the target of enemy sniper, mortar, and artillery fire. "We were on Tinian dug in for the night. A mortar round landed next to the foxhole and killed one Marine and injured the other Marine." On August 2, near the end of the island was where he saw women and children committing suicide by throwing themselves off the high, steep hills. They had been told that if they were captured, the Marines would rape and kill them. It was on Tinian where he was wounded when a Japanese hand grenade landed close to him. Shrapnel stuck him in the shoulder and face. "The medics took good care of me."

With Tinian now secured, Herman had had two years of overseas duty and had been engaged in four island battles. After a thirty-day leave, he was stationed at Klamath Falls, Oregon, for four months, after which he reported to Mare Island, California, where he guarded American prisoners at the naval prison, mostly deserters and homosexual sailors and Marines. "It was the worst duty I ever had. I was at Mare Island until the war ended. I was discharged in the summer of 1945."

His resentment at not having been promoted when he should have did not change his opinion of his service in the Marine Corps. He continues to believe that it has had a positive effect on his life. One of the ways that the military affected him was to endow him with the belief that we should "try to get along with your fellow man. Don't take things for granted."

Ralph Black's military experience, too, was of great lifetime value. Born and raised in New York City, he enlisted in the Marine Corps not long after the attack on Pearl Harbor. However, due to the huge number of enlistments and the difficulty to house and train so many people initially, he wasn't called to active duty till May of the following year.

He trained at Parris Island. While he hated it, in retrospect, he feels that it was a good experience. Ralph found some incidence of anti-Semitism during his three-year career in the Marine Corps. Once, at Parris Island, he and his tormentor faced down each other in a fight. After that, although the anti-Semitic incidents continued, he was left alone. He qualified as a sharpshooter with the Springfield .03, and later, as an expert with the pistol.

Following boot camp, he was sent to Quantico for telephone school, after which he transferred to Camp Lejeune and joined the 4th Marine Division. After nine months, he was sent to Camp Pendleton for five months.

The 4th Marine Division, with Ralph Black, hit the beaches at Roi-Namur, Marshall Islands, for a two-day operation, then Tinian, and finally, Iwo Jima. After two days on Tinian, he was wounded and taken to the hospital ship for treatment. Even his stay on the hospital ship was short-lived. A severe storm was approaching and the ship had to depart for open sea. His stay was shortened by the order for all walking wounded to leave the ship and remain on shore.

One of his most pleasant experiences took place on Maui. It turned out that his tent mate had been a golf pro. They both played on the nine-hole course provided for the members of the division. Until recently, he held a ten handicap, now drastically reduced to nine.

There were two occasions in which he felt disappointment: the first was the refusal of the Marine Corps to award him a citation for action he performed while on a lone night patrol on Iwo Jima, and the second, he felt wronged by not being promoted to corporal. He did eventually receive his promotion upon his discharge in 1945.

As with so many other Marines, he found his military experience "fabulous." Although he would not particularly wish to go through it again, "I wouldn't have missed it for the world."

Danny Blank and Elaine make a twofer: They both were in the Marine Corps. Not only that, but they both found a very rewarding experience during their time in the Corps. Elaine says that, "I thoroughly enjoyed my tour of duty and met many interesting people. Enlisting in the Marine Corps was an excellent choice." After all these years, they continue to maintain their strong relationship with the Marines. "Beside our love of traveling and cruising, we look forward to attending our Marine reunions: Danny's 1st Marine Division, China Marine Association, and my Women Marines Association. We've also belonged to the local Marine Corps League and JWV at large."

Elaine Sevell joined the Marine Corps at the age of twenty from York, Pennsylvania. Boot camp was at Camp Lejeune from December 14, 1943 to January 31, 1944. She thought that being in the South was going to be nice and warm, but "Little did we know that winter was the coldest and snowiest in years. So, we were caught without hats, gloves, and scarves for the first two weeks.

Following boot camp, she attended a three-month quartermaster course at Camp Lejeune. She was then stationed at Quantico, until her discharge from the Corps on December 7, 1945. At Quantico, she was in charge of the Book Storeroom in the Marine Corps Schools Building, issuing TMs and FMs to officers in the Command and Staff School and Advanced Field Artillery School. She made Pfc. right after quartermaster school and was promoted to corporal a year later.

She notes that "most women enlisted during World War II out of patriotism and to 'Free a Marine to fight,' which was the motto at that time. She never found anti-Semitism to be a problem at all during her entire two-year tour in the Marine Corps.

At first, her transfer to the base commissary was a disappointment. But it turned to be great, "since we were usually secured by 2:30 P.M. and often went across the street to the base pool, hours before it got crowded."

Many people can relate the story of the Four Chaplains who went down with the SS *Dorchester* when they handed their life jackets to soldiers without them. The Jewish chaplain was Rabbi Alexander Goode in whose first confirmation class in 1939 was Elaine Blank. The military affected her general outlook on life. It gave her a "great deal of respect for our fighting men and the sacrifices they made, so we will still live in a free country." Three uncles and many cousins have served in the military, plus her husband. She was particularly proud to have served in the military and "to have been part of such an elite corps and historical background." She remembers the day at Camp Lejeune, in a regimental review, "with the famous Women's Reserve Marching Band, planes flying above in a picture perfect day in the spring of 1944. This was an unforgettable experience."

Daniel Blank provides the male side of the family Marine Corps. An obviously suitable match, they both retain their interest in the Marine Corps, and admiration for all their personnel.

For Dan, "boot camp was probably the best learning and

physical training experience that happened to me so far, during July and August of 1945. During this time, in addition to the usual military training, I learned to empty coal bins and then fill them back up; had an M-1 at the ends of the top of my finger tips, while squatting until I dropped (not the rifle). If I did, I would've had to sleep with it."

They drilled in the summer heat of 110 to 115 degrees, even when the C rag was up on the parade ground. On one occasion, four boots passed out in front of Blank, and they marched over them into a puddle of hot water in the sand. Showing no mercy, the DI stood under the only tree calling out commands. One day, in the afternoon, while he was in a treed cove "boringly waiting with about five hundred guys for our turn at the grenade ground, I broke out in song and the next thing I knew, others joined in with me."

A number of things remain fixed in Dan's mind. He will never forget "the saying on a sign at a large Quonset hut, where gear was turned in after boot camp. 'The person that knows *how* will always be his boss.'" A bad experience was the time when "we were readying our M-1 rifles for return to the QM. I was cleaning my rifle butt with steel wool, when another boot approached to borrow it, with the understanding that he would return it when finished. He then made a vulgar and insulting remark to me as a Jew. A confrontation ensued. I don't know what would have happened if the DI hadn't come in to investigate all the shouting going on."

Completing boot camp, he was sent to Camp Lejeune on temporary assignment while awaiting shipment overseas. They were originally destined to go to Guam for special training for the invasion of Japan. But, along with so many others, he was spared this ordeal by the dropping of the atomic bombs.

Blank joined the 1st Signal Battalion, 1st Marine Division, for service in North China. When they arrived in Tientsin in December 1945, they were billeted at the Temple of the Japanese Girls School. As the war terminated before he had the chance to enter into combat, he had a close call while on a double date with Joe

Cavallero in a gondola. A shot came out of nowhere, and Dan shot back with his .45. That was the end of the incident.

One of the incidents that Danny recalls was his participation in an honor guard for a Marine who died at sea of "Japanese Sleeping Sickness." As Dan had no knowledge of the deceased's religion, he felt that, as a Jew, he was obligated to be present.

On another occasion, Dan helped the baker make a chocolate cake. Someone had switched the unmarked cans. The next day the fish had a feast. One day, Blank persuaded the baker to make some pizzas, since he had a number of Italian friends. He cautions everyone, "Never wake a Marine in the middle of the night. I nearly got my throat cut until I held the pizzas under their noses."

Overall, he rates his Marine Corps experience as great. He would do it again if given the chance.

Jake Silverfarb states that, "It's a shame that such a small segment of the U.S. population serves in the military these days, because they lose a true appreciation of what it means to be an American. It is even more sad that more Jews don't join the military (we have done our share in wartime, but our volunteer rates are low), after all America has done for us. The United States has provided a haven for Jews and we have flourished here; more of us should be serving our country."

Jake muses with some thoughts: "I sometimes talk with friends from college and high school and we compare life experience. It doesn't take them long to realize that I have probably seen more of the world and experienced more of life in one random year since joining than they have in their entire lives."

At the age of thirty-two (2002), Jake Silverfarb is a captain. He entered the active military world as an officer after having completed the requirements as a member of a Platoon Leaders Class consisting of two summer training sessions at Quantico. Following his commissioning, he attended OCS which was, "extremely demanding physically. I thought I was in great shape showing up—boy, was I wrong!" His strongest recollection of OCS was his CO, Colonel Wesley Fox, veteran of the Korean War and recipient of the Medal of Honor in Vietnam. "This man who was older than my father could outrun ninety percent of the candidates. Remember we were twenty-year-olds in the peak of condition."

Completing Officers Basic School, Jake was assigned an MOS of Artillery and transferred to the Officers Artillery Training School at the army base at Ft. Sill, Oklahoma. In his class of one hundred forty lieutenants, twenty-five were Marines. Of the top thirty spots in class rankings, twenty-five were Marines. "The Army students would ask us how we did it; the simple reason was our senior officers told us if we did not finish in the top third of the class, horrible things would happen to us. This taught me, if used in the right context, fear can be a powerful motivator."

Jake Silverfarb served on active duty for six years, during which time almost half of it was spent overseas or training for overseas duty. He took part in Operation Restore Hope in Somalia in late 1992 and early 1993, the Unit Deployment Program on Okinawa (including exercises in Japan and Korea), and in 1996, served as a staff officer for a Marine Expeditionary Unit (MEU) on deployment aboard ship across the Western Pacific and Middle East.

While his combat experience was limited to Somalia, Jake relates that compared to the Gulf War, "Somalia was a virtual bloodbath." He was assigned as liaison officer to the Pakistani forces. It is interesting to note how the Pakistanis, Moslem as they are, treated Silverfarb, Jewish as he is. As he states, "not once was a Jihad launched against me. They were actually nice guys and good soldiers, though their ideas and methods were about one hundred years old. Living with them is how I imagined the British Raj to be."

He encountered no overt anti-Semitism during his service. However, it was another Jewish officer who provided a humorous anecdote, unrelated to anti-Semitism, but otherwise comparable to a situation which could be labeled as Jewish in character. Jake's first commanding officer was a Captain F. He was a tyrant who loved to abuse new lieutenants, not too different from others who loved to do the same. But he reveled in taking "a perverse pleasure in breaking our spirits." Silverfarb arrived a month prior to his departure, and "he confided to the battalion chaplain that 'It's a good thing I'm leaving. There isn't enough room in this battery for two Jews.' That next month couldn't have passed fast enough."

Jake Silverfarb's pleasure and pride in serving in the Marine Corps is obvious and genuine. He "had a great time in the Marines. My experiences and friendships I have made have been invaluable. The loyalty we have for one another is something civilians just do not understand and has been something I have missed in my various civilian jobs."

Jake Silverfarb was especially grateful for the opportunity he had to travel and visit places throughout the world. With the MEU in the Pacific, they visited the Philippines. His Reserve unit participated in the Battle Griffin 99 in Norway, which he enjoyed immensely. He said that

"After many years of training in hot climates, it was nice to do some cold weather training."

He expresses his respect and admiration for the officers and NCOs with whom he has worked. About "ninety percent of the men I served with were outstanding individuals; that includes men both higher and lower on the chain of command. With two glaring exceptions, all my commanding officers have been great men. The examples that they set have been guidebooks for myself in any endeavor. It is no wonder that so many fortune 400 CEOs are former Marines."

For Ed Kaufman, boot camp was tough, but bearable. It took from November 1943 to January 1944 to complete, but "we felt like a million dollars when it was over." His platoon had "about twenty Jews, so we didn't have any trouble to talk about."

Ed returned to Parris Island many years afterwards to see the camp. He could not find the wooden barracks they were in nor the roads "we paved by marching all day on them. The sand was gone and grass and brick was there instead."

After boot camp, Kaufman was stationed at Cherry Point and Memphis. Then, overseas, he served on Peleliu and Guam.

Ed Kaufman loved the Marine Corps. He would have liked to have stayed in after the war, and, in fact, wishes he was still in the Corps now. He is reminded of the time at boot camp, while they were doing close order drill. A Marine and Kaufman were leading the platoon.

Suddenly, he "looked back and saw the platoon going the other way. It was a Laurel and Hardy scene."

He remembers fondly several incidents: While on the train proceeding to Los Angeles, they were feted with wine, women, and song. "It was great." Once, he nearly shot another Marine "while on guard duty as he came out of the jungle about three a.m. He wouldn't stop and give the password until he heard the bolt slamming a bullet into the chamber." Also, during the crossing of the Pacific, he and the other Marines nearly lost their lives when a torpedo crossed the bow of their troopship.

He relates his pride in being a Marine with the following story:

"If you ever go to Washington, go to the Marine Barracks at Eighth and I Street. You will see a show that beats any branch of service. You see the Marine Band, Drum and Bugle Corps, and Silent Drill Team in which they play the Marines' Hymn. It makes you proud that you wore that uniform.

"We stood in line four or five hours to get tickets to the Kravitz Theater as the Marine Band was going to play there. After the concert, they played the usual songs of each branch of service. When the Marines Hymn was played, the roar nearly tore the building down. And you ask why we are so proud? There's the answer."

Lastly, "there is much which can be told. But the memories come in spells." He relates a most unusual story: "I worked near a fellow for twenty-five years, and one day we were talking and I mentioned my serial number and he stopped me and asked me to repeat it. 902549. He told me that his was 902548. We were in the same platoon, but never knew it until then. Semper Fi!"

———

In June (1999), James I. (Moon) McMullen, of Johnstown, Pennsylvania, wrote that "your book would not be complete without adding Jack Stein." He and Jack Stein served together in the 24th Marines during the battles of Roi-Namur and Saipan. They were both wounded on Saipan, and, after hospitalization, were reunited on Maui to prepare for the battle of Iwo. He concluded his note with, "He is a credit to his race."

Jack Stein's tour of duty in the Marine Corps is somewhat typical of most of the others.

He had a certain respect for the Corps even prior to his enlistment in World War II. Much the same training, admiration for the Corps and its personnel, the battles in the Pacific, wounds, and his good fortune to return home in one piece.

After enlisting from his hometown of Hewlett, Long Island, he trained at boot camp, Parris Island, for eight weeks, which, "was quite a change from my previous life. I think I adapted well and managed to survive."

Following boot camp, he was selected for communications and was sent to Quantico for school, although, "I don't know why. I did make Pfc. after completing the course."

He was then assigned to the First Separate Battalion, later to be reclassified as the 1st Battalion, 24th Marines, 4th Marine Division. There, he encountered some anti-Semitism from two other Pfcs. "I wound up having fights with both of them and they then got off me although we never became friends."

He entered combat with the division when it landed in the Marshall Islands, Saipan, Tinian, and Iwo Jima. Stein did not make Tinian and Iwo because he had been wounded in the shoulder on Saipan and spent some time in the hospital. "I guess I was lucky."

He recalls vividly going over the side of the transport ship and into the LCVP, with both of them bouncing up and down on the waves. "Whenever I see that in the movies or TV, I wonder, did I really do that? I guess I did."

As with so many other Marines, he met many fine people during his service and still keeps in touch with some of them. Many of them have passed away, and he waxes philosophic when he remarks that he will join them in the not-too-distant future. He had a "terrific platoon leader, Lieutenant (later Captain) Tom Kerr. He still lives in Philadelphia, and I see him occasionally."

His younger brother, Michael, served in the Army Tank Corps in Europe. He, too, survived the war, managing to get out of his tank in time when German planes strafed them.

Stanton A. Kessler, B.A., Amherst College (1955), LLB, Harvard Law School (1958), Pfc., United States Marine Corps (ret.) 1959, Chief Counsel's Office, IRS, Washington, D.C., 1959–64, Mayer, Brown, & Platt, 1964—, was impressed. As he drove up to the sentry post at Parris Island at 0715, September 7, 1995, the Marine at the gate looked sharp. Dressed in a khaki shirt and tie, white cover and blue trousers with the Marine Corps red stripe down the sides. Kessler, too, was sharp: in business clothes and tie. None of the casual dress of the other civilian occupants in the cars ahead of him. Kessler pulled up to the post, the sentry cocked his head down at a 45 degree angle and said, "Are you here for graduation, Sir?" Kessler replied in the negative saying that he was a guest of General Humble. The sentry snapped to attention. "Yes SIR!" he said. "Go right in, SIR!" Kessler was directed to Headquarters. He was back. And almost aghast that someone at Parris Island greeted him with "Sir."

It wasn't exactly like that at boot camp. He reported to Parris

Island in December 1958, after receiving any number of cautionary reproaches from friends and family, plus a bottle of Kaopectate from his mother.

Before reporting to camp, however, Kessler walked around Charleston for a while. He had some time to kill. After a while, he drifted into a bar in the Fort Sumter Hotel. "After I'd had a couple of drinks, a young, very sharp looking Marine sergeant sauntered into the bar and sat down a few bar stools away. I told him I was waiting for the bus to take me to Parris Island. He winced. 'You poor son-of-a-bitch,' he said. 'What do you mean?' I said. 'They start yelling at you the minute you get off the bus,' he said, 'and they don't stop until you leave. From time to time they punch you out. I wouldn't go through that shit again.' I ordered another drink."

Kessler probably wouldn't go through that shit again, either. He wouldn't want to be called "maggot" again, either. He wouldn't want to be a recruit at any boot camp again, much less at Parris Island. But he was justifiably proud of the fact that he was a boot, and a successful one at that.

The day of Kessler's graduation, they were all together in their dress greens, waiting to assemble for the march to the parade ground. He saw Sergeant White walking toward him. "I made sure my hands were not in my pockets. He stopped in front of me and said, 'Kessler, you're going to make it.' 'Sir, yes Sir,' I said, and he turned and walked away. 'I have never received a compliment that I've cherished more.'"

Things and lessons learned in the Marine Corps are permanent. Kessler learned that "every Marine uniform will always have the edge of his 'blouse' (shirt), the front edge of his belt buckle and the fly on his trouser in perfect alignment (the 'Marine Corps line'). To this day, I do not leave home without checking the Marine Corps line of whatever it is I'm wearing."

The day he returned to visit Parris Island for graduation, "Various speakers talked about the history of Parris Island and the camaraderie that exists among all Marines. One said, 'Once a Marine, always a Marine,' and asked those in the stands who had formerly served in the Corps to stand. General Humble turned in his seat and gestured for me to stand. I stood. I would have anyway. I was proud to be a Marine."

His fantastic experience in the Marine Corps had a positive overall and lifelong effect on Sumner Warshaw. "It made me organized and disciplined in everything I do." And, "I'm proud to have served with the best branch of the military. People highly respect Marines."

Warshaw joined the Marine Corps from Chestnut Hills, Massachusetts, not far from Boston, and did his boot camp at Parris Island. Boot camp was a positive experience for him, as "This experience changed me from a boy to man. Our DI did an excellent job of transforming us into Marines."

He completed Radio Operators School at Camp Lejeune and received a double promotion to the rank of corporal. At that time, radar was secret. Warshaw enjoyed the work very much.

However, "My counterpart of another team hated me only because I was Jewish." Following Radar School, he spent a month in a guard company at Lejeune, "guarding the beach against possible saboteurs." From there, he was transferred to Treasure Island, San Francisco, then to the Fleet Marine Force in the Pacific, hitting such places at Oahu, Eniwetok, Marshall Islands, and Okinawa. On Okinawa, he participated in action against the enemy, manning his radar station and received the Presidential Unit Citation for his action in manning a 90 mm AAA gun.

Traveling cross-country by train provided a welcome break for Warshaw, but "three days of seasickness on a troop transport going to Okinawa" was a very unpleasant time. He was aboard this ship for thirty-five days. "He also became seasick in a landing craft going ashore at Okinawa."

Most of the unpleasant incidents were those related to anti-Semitism: "In Hawaii, a fellow Marine on seeing a wallet that I carried for coins only said, 'You must be Jewish.'"

At Camp Lejeune during the Korean War, "I had just had a Marine Corps emblem tattooed on my arm. On seeing it, a fellow Marine said, 'I never heard of Jews being gung-ho.'"

In Hawaii during World War II, "On hearing that I was from Boston, a fellow Marine said, 'I wouldn't go there. It's full of Jews and niggers.'"

Flying in the face of some unpleasant behaviors of some of his fellow Marines, Warshaw's Marine experience was a positive one. He was recalled to active duty at the beginning of the Korean War and spent a year at Camp Lejeune as a corporal, training with two AAA gun battalions. Although past prime age, "I would join up again, if I could. It was a fantastic experience."

Jewish-Americans, not unlike others, dream of pursuing certain careers—even in the military. Some, like Jerry Steigmann, had this dream, and just to prove that dreams do materialize, "Many years ago, as a youth, I dreamed of becoming a Marine, travel to Hawaii, and the mysterious Far East." His dream came true—he made it come true. It may have taken a war in the Pacific to make it happen.

With the outbreak of World War II, Steigmann was still underage. But his dreams persisted. In May 1943, he was a high school dropout, not yet eighteen years of age, and soon to be subject to the draft. "My yearning for advantage led me to apply to the local draft board and request active military service with the Marine Corps." The members of the draft board, a bit incredulous, looked at him, patted him on the back, and said, "Finally, a live one." He was inducted into the Marine Corps on May 29, 1943. And, "four years later on the same date, my daughter, Inez, was born."

Jerome Steigmann describes himself as a "World War II Marine, pursuer of Amelia Earhart, and a New York City Police Department forensic evidence detective." In retrospect, Jerry credits the Marine Corps for helping him to become a rough, tough detective in the NYPD.

Having signed up for the Marine Corps, he was sent to Parris Island for boot training. He completed it on August 13, 1943. Despite his rough and tough demeanor, he still found a lot of anti-Semitism. He didn't even tell his parents that he volunteered for the Marine Corps until he received his orders. At Camp Lejeune, he found anti-Semitism to be rampant.

The usual fearful welcome awaited the newly arrived boots at Yemassee, South Carolina.

They were greeted by "Tobacco-chewing flannel-mouthed yokel drill instructors who probably never wore real shoes until they joined the Marine Corps." Arriving at Parris Island, they went first to the delousing chambers, then to the Quartermaster for shoes and ill-fitting uniforms.

Boot camp was tough. Living in Quonset huts, hot and unbearable. His fellow recruits were mostly from New York, Pennsylvania, and Massachusetts, ranging from coal miners to street-wise men. "Some of them paired off in groups, and tried to intimidate other Marines who were loners . . ." When the drill instructors discovered any problems, "they would dump the innocent Marines out of their beds, paddle them, and make the entire unit put pails over their heads and march on the darkened drill fields." Failure to understand or comply with orders resulted in scrubbing hot kitchen ranges with emery cloth to make them spotless. It was widely believed that their food and drinks were spiked with saltpeter.

He graduated from boot camp on August 13, 1943 after which the members of his platoon were shipped to various units stateside and overseas.

As with some of the others with "special qualifications," Steigmann was transferred to Camp Lejeune, where he trained to be an Intelligence Specialist and a Japanese linguist.

Sent to the Pacific, he participated in the invasion of Anguiar, Palau, and in the initial occupation of Japan. He was attached to the Army G-2 in counter-espionage and counter-sabotage work.

In the course of his assignments, he interrogated Japanese prisoners of war and island natives, and searched for evidence that Amelia Earhart may have crashed her plane on one of the Palau islands. In Hawaii, he worked as an undercover operative conducting counterintelligence work. In addition, he assisted the Army Graves Registration units in the identification of deceased American and Japanese troops.

Steigmann participated in his share of combat. The most dangerous assignment was attempting to enter caves on the islands to try to convince Japanese troops to surrender. He participated in the invasion of the Palau Islands with the 7th AAA Battalion.

His CO was a Major Dewey, a pre-World War II Marine and a real gentleman who agreed to share Jerry with the Army intelligence people. Dewey requested his temporary transfer, and the Army G-2 "gladly welcomed my assistance."

At the time, a number of Japanese-American soldiers were participating in these operations. There was a fear that they might be taken for Japanese soldiers, or prisoners, so there was some concern for their safety. One of Steigmann's duties included "Protecting the Nisei soldiers from other American troops who thought that the Nisei were Japanese Army infiltrators. I interrogated POWs, translated maps and diaries, and other documents."

His last duties in the Pacific included being "a member of Navy Task Force 31 in the initial landing in the Tokyo Bay area, August 1945, and the capture of His Imperial Majesty's ship, *Nagato*, plus the surrender of the Yokosuka Naval Air Station, which act symbolized the complete surrender of the Japanese Navy."

Collaterally, he participated in the liberation of "Allied POWs, rounded up suspected war criminals, and other occupation duties."

In Japan, he found the easiest assignment while in the Marine Corps: investigating brothels. There, he enjoyed the company of the most memorable person he met in the military, Toshiko-Shii, the daughter of a Japanese colonel.

Other than the widespread anti-Semitism that he encountered, he found his experience to be very positive and of great value to his future professional and private life. He doesn't resent not being promoted to Pfc. upon graduation from boot camp, which, as he said, "every guy gets out of PI boot camp." He experienced a number of religious events including attendance at Passover Seders in combat areas, and a positive image of Jewish chaplains who provided religious guidance.

As a footnote to the Steigmann story, his grandson is following in the footsteps of his granddad: He is currently in the Marine Corps on his second enlistment.

The first morning at San Diego Marine Corps Recruit Depot was eventful. He was greeted with bugles blowing, drums beating, and the DI yelling at the new bots to rise and shine. For Albert L. Schear, St. Louis, Missouri, boot camp lasted seven weeks—three weeks at MCRD, three weeks at the rifle range, and the last week back at the Depot.

Schear was then assigned to Aviation Ordnance School at Norman, Oklahoma. Upon graduating with the rank of private first class, he was first sent to the camp at Kearny Mesa, California, processed and shipped overseas. Landing first at New Caledonia, he was assigned to Marine Air Group (MAG) 14 on Guadalcanal. Then to Green Island for nine months, then to VMF-223 on Bougainville.

On January 24, 1945, Albert witnessed "the worst accident I have ever seen" on Guiuan (Gee-Wan) Samar, Philippine Islands. "A little after 0930 a pilot from VMF-222, while taking off, blew a tire and careened wildly into his squadron's revetment area. The plane caught fire and exploded, setting off .50 caliber ammunition. Fourteen were killed and more than fifty wounded seriously. I still think about this today, over fifty years ago."

Though Schear was in a combat area for nineteen months straight, with no R & R, he "did not fight the enemy face to face or otherwise." He departed the Philippines in March 1945 with the rank of sergeant, and sailed on the USS *Admiral Capps*.

Aboard the ship were women, children, and men over the age of sixty. Being a Marine meant pulling guard duty all the way to San Francisco. He was still on guard in the beer hall on Bogue Field, North Carolina, when the war ended on V-J Day.

During his thirty months in the Marine Corps, he had the opportunity of seeing Second Lieutenant Tyrone Power and Byron Barr (Gig Young), a hospital corpsman on the *Capps*.

Although he was glad to have served in the Marine Corps, he was also glad to get out. He said, "I was glad to have served in the Corps. I think I am a better person for it."

Bob Weinberg was even more enthusiastic of his service in the Marine Corps. He was extremely proud to have been a Marine. He "would not enjoy being home while everyone else was serving. It was the thrill of a lifetime." Also, "being in Marine aviation was much easier than in the line company. I think that's why I am alive today. Loved the experience."

Enlisting in the Marine Corps at the age of nineteen from Port Chester, New York, he trained at Parris Island. It was pretty rough because, "After Parris Island, any place was great." Thirty members of his platoon of sixty recruits were killed in the battle of Tarawa. Ten of his platoon were assigned to Marine Aviation. "So we lived." There were two Jews in his platoon, one of whom was wounded on Tarawa.

He never had any problems with anti-Semitism.

Initially, Weinberg was assigned as flight clerk in VMF-216, a fighter squadron in the South Pacific. On Guam, he was transferred to the Headquarters Squadron where he became a flight photographer on PBYs flying over enemy territory in the Marianas chain of islands. On landing, he developed and printed the photos for Intelligence.

Having been a Boy Scout served him well in the Marine Corps.

He had reached the rank of Eagle Scout before entering military service. "Scouting made boot camp somewhat easier, as I knew how to march and drill."

Service in the military gave him a greater appreciation of life. It "made me enjoy every day I'm alive. I still feel that way."

Leonard Sobel enlisted in the Marine Corps on May 20, 1942, at Utica, New York, and completed recruit training at Parris Island. Sobel's training as a field telephone linesman was completed at Quantico, after which he was promoted to Pfc. At Casual Company, Camp Lejeune, he ran into trouble and received a couple of summary courts-martial.

Sobel left California to join the 22nd Marines at Maui, which was preparing for the combat for Eniwetok. He later joined the 5th Amphibious Group on Oahu. He shipped out for the invasion of Saipan and Tinian. Then, Sobel and a few others were sent to Guam to join the 3rd Amphibious Corps.

There:

"Some Seabees and a native boy came to our camp and said that they had seen a Jap go into a cave where the Seabees were working, and this was interrupting their ability to work and they asked us to go get the Jap or Japs out. Private Leon Somers and I were the only ones in camp and we did go into the cave. Leon went in first and I covered him. The Jap swung a saber at Leon. Leon grabbed it and pulled it away from him. Leon dropped his flashlight, the Jap fell to the ground and popped a hand grenade at us, and we threw two back. The cave was full of smoke, and Leon and I flew out of the cave to wait until the smoke cleared. The Seabees treated Leon and me for some injuries we received. After a short time, Leon and I went back into the cave and found that the Jap was dead."

Later, on Guam, "We were camped near where there must have been a battle. There were Jap bodies scattered around, and Marine bulldozers had dug a deep ditch and were pushing the bodies into it. The stench and the flies were absolutely horrible. It was impossible to eat our rations with all the flies. We had to eat with one hand and shoo the flies away with the other. My buddy Leon Somers became very sick from the flies. Also, we had no shelter and we slept on the ground.

"After the incident with the Jap in the cave, I was hit with dengue fever. It healed and later I was hit hard with jungle rot. There were no doctors in our area, only two corpsmen that operated out of a tent near us. When I went for treatment for jungle rot, they covered all of the infected areas with gentian violet and bandaged my arms, legs, and body as best they could. I received this treatment for some time and finally they gave me the medicine and bandages and told me that there were no doctors available and there was nothing more they could do.

"A short time later, we received our orders to pack up and return to Oahu. As soon as we started to leave our area, my jungle rot started to heal and by the time we arrived at the coast, the infections were drying up very well."

His unit, working in teams, set up telephone poles. Then, their task was to climb the poles and pull the telephone lines up and tie them to the top and get down quickly to avoid snipers. Sobel volunteered to finish getting the lines back on the poles. While he was pulling up a telephone line, one of the safety lines loosened and Sobel fell to the ground. Taken to the hospital at Pearl Harbor, he was informed that he had a dislocated shoulder and fracture of the left femur. He was returned to the States by plane for treatment.

Sobel spent about a year in eight hospitals. The last one was at Bainbridge where he was processed for a medical discharge with a fifty-percent disability.

"When I had returned to Oahu after Iwo, I had been overseas almost twenty months and could not get a stripe. I had now decided that the Marine Corps was never going to forgive me or allow me a promotion due to my bad record. I don't think this had anything to do with religion."

The year in the eight hospitals was "my best duty in my four years in the Corps. By the way, when I was flown back to the States, my sea bag was lost and everything I owned was gone. Since I was in the hospital, I did not need much clothing, but I did eventually receive a new issue.

"At Bainbridge, a corporal was mustering me out and he said that he had some good new for me. All Marines getting a medical discharge were entitled to one promotion."

Sobel earned the Presidential Unit Citation with bronze star, the American Campaign Medal, the Asiatic-Pacific Campaign Medal, and the World War II Victory Medal.

Chicago native Mike Singer was 15 years old when he enlisted in the Marine Corps at the outbreak of World War II.

After completing recruit training at MCRD, San Diego, he was assigned to the 1st Marines,

1st Marine Division, and landed on Guadalcanal in 1942. He later participated in campaigns on Cape Gloucester (on the western end of New Britain) and Peleliu (in the Palau Islands, a former name of the Republic of Belau).

On Peleliu, while under the command of "Chesty" Puller, Singer was advancing behind a Sherman tank when a machine gun in a Japanese pillbox opened up and he was shot in both legs. With bullets flying around him, Singer had to lie where he fell for many hours. It was almost nightfall before medics could rescue him. After initially recuperating aboard a hospital ship, he returned to the States for several more months at Sampson Naval Hospital, Sampson, New York.

Singer received the Silver Star Medal, the Bronze Star Medal, and three Purple Hearts.

His two brothers fought in the Battle of the Bulge. One was killed and the other wounded.

The Illinois State Commander of the Veterans of Underage Military Service, Singer currently (2001) in Flossmoor, Illinois.

In April 1944, Jack Stearn volunteered for the draft. He had already been in the Army. Arriving at Grand Central Palace, New York City, where all inductees were sent, he was told he was returning to the Army. As he had no intention of going back into the Army, he enlisted in the Marine Corps.

After a night on the train to Parris Island, he was "deposited with the rest of the group in beautiful downtown Yemassee." Then were then taken to Parris Island, where a "gentle, loving DI suggested we disembark from the bus." He lined the up, and commanded the group to march straight ahead. Stearn managed to keep in step, but the boot in front of him was out of step. "Suddenly, a body hurtled towards me. It was the DI who kicked the boot in the ass and encouraged him to get in step."

After recruit training and further training at Camp Lejeune, Stearn was integrated into the

17th Replacement Draft, transported to Camp Pendleton, and a week later boarded the *Jean Lafitte*. "All the guys from the boot platoon were with me and—lo and behold—so was my DI. The old DI spent time explaining why he had been on my back so much. I told him to relax, it was all part of training and making Marines of us."

In Maui, a lieutenant called for volunteers for the scout and sniper platoon. When Stearn said, "No way," his name was called and he reported front and center. The lieutenant told him, "I understand you know how to read maps. You're in the scout and sniper platoon."

One day, the lieutenant took him and others on a wild-goat hunt on Mount Haleokala to toughen them up. One of the sharpshooters shot a kid which they promptly barbecued.

Not long after, they set sail aboard the USS *Bayfield*, destination Iwo Jima. After a stop at

Kwajalein, "the brains in charge informed us it was to be a five-day affair after all the bombardment the island took.

"It was quite a show to watch the shelling, the best display of fireworks I'd ever seen. We were in the 9th wave. I had an ocarina with me and I began to play the Marines Hymn, until I was told to jam it."

Upon hitting the beach, he found two half-tracks laying on their sides, "forming a wedge toward the front. My buddy, L. L. Stevenson and Carl Rothrock and I dug in between the half-tracks. The Japs used them as aiming points and shelled us all night."

His platoon performed security duty around the headquarters of the 24th Marines for a few days and cleared away some of the dead bodies. "One night, Washing Machine Charlie flew over our position. I had fallen asleep. Suddenly, I felt an explosion and the foxhole caved in on us. Besides dropping two bombs, Charlie dropped a flare. I was able to dig myself out as did Rothrock and all we could see of Stevenson was his two feet. He usually slept on the bottom with his poncho over his face. We scrambled to dig him out. The foxhole was home to three shook-up Marines."

In the morning, they moved up to attack a ridge. They began their advance after a barrage from Marine artillery. "I was zig-zagging from hole to hole when I jumped into a hole in which someone had defecated. I came up covered with crap and I forgot to zig-zag when I got shot in the shoulder."

With that, the war was effectively over for Jack Stearn. Ending up back at Camp Lejeune, he was told that he was slated for occupation duty in Japan. However, as he had the points to be discharged, he was transferred to Quantico and within a month he "was given my ruptured duck and sent home."

He admired a number of people, some of whom remain friends today. His scout and sniper platoon consisted of thirty-five men. "It took a long time to locate some of them, but I found nineteen. I've been in touch with seven. But time has taken its toll on our own ranks as well as the war."

After the war, Stearn tried to join the National Guard. But as he was a police officer, they turned him down. He sums up his service with, "I like the military and I think it wouldn't hurt the youth of today to spend a few years and obtain discipline and learn how to get along with others in a structured society."

While Pritikin may not be a totally recognizable household name throughout the country, it does have some readily identifiable features. Leonard isn't sure, but he believes he is a part of that well-known family of health advocates. He wanted to "stay in for thirty," but the fortunes of war intervened and thwarted his ambitions from being carried out.

Pritikin enlisted in the Marine Corps Reserve more than a year before the outbreak of World War II. When he was called up in June 1941, he was assigned to Platoon 58 and appointed squad leader. Then he found out that he did not have to attend boot camp. The day after he was posted to the Marine Guard at the Great Lakes Naval Center, the Japanese bombed Pearl Harbor, and Pritikin was in the war.

As a corporal, he was assigned to D Company, 1st Battalion, 3rd Marines. Arriving in San Diego, he boarded the SS *Lurline* and landed in American Samoa on September 14 to relieve the 8th Defense Battalion. At the end of May, he joined the 3rd Marine Division which was forming in New Zealand. After a period of intense training, they left for Guadalcanal, where they went ashore on August 7, exactly one year after the initial 1st Marine Division landing. During the training on Samoa, he was trained as an instrument corporal doing the setup for indirect firing or mortars and machine guns. On Guadalcanal, he was promoted to section leader of heavy water-cooled .30-caliber machine guns. On September 20, while they were test firing all weapons preparatory to invading Bougainville, a clover leaf of 81 mm mortar shells landed one thousand yards short right into his gun section. Six men of his No. 1 gun were killed and he with ten others, were hospitalized. After a week in a coma, Pritikin was placed on the Hospital Transport USS *Tryon* for the trip to Espiritu Santo, New Hebrides, where he spent a month. However, he never set foot on the island as both his shin bones were shattered, along with other shrapnel wounds. On November 5, he embarked on the SS *Matsonia* at the Mare Island Hospital where he landed on November 17. He remained there till January 10, 1945, when he was discharged on physical disability. His medical disability foreclosed any thoughts he had had about remaining in the Corps for thirty years.

One day, on Guadalcanal, he and his working party were finishing their job and were heading back to their base when they passed Father Kempker, the Catholic chaplain, sitting in front of his tent. Pritikin stopped and asked the priest if he needed any work to be done. He replied that "he would sure appreciate a load of gravel for a floor." Whereupon, Pritikin "commandeered a dump truck and sent for a load of gravel for a floor, and I went to Battalion supply for a wall tent, and he had his chapel built by a Jewish corporal. When I was wounded, he was right there for me before I passed out."

Despite his love and admiration for the Marine Corps, there was one incident in which he felt disappointed, or cheated. He had planned to stay in for thirty years. The day after he was wounded, the promotion rates came through. Instead of drawing platoon sergeant pay, during his sixteen and a half months in the hospital he still drew pay as a corporal. He felt cheated.

Pritikin admired a number of men in the Marine Corps. Those he admired the most were Lieutenant Colonel George Van Orden (later a general), and Lieutenant Emil J. Dadics, who saved his life by his quick action in putting tourniquets on both legs. He retired as a colonel.

Pritikin kept in touch with him until his death around 1977.

An article in the February 1995 issue of *Leatherneck* contained copy and pictures of the horrific action that took place fifty years previously on Iwo Jima. The article had the headline of *The Cost and the Reward*. It related that "The price paid by the

Marines was the highest of any single battle in the history of the Corps. In the thirty-five days of combat from D-Day to the fall of the Gorge, 5,931 Marines were killed in action, died of wounds, or missing; 17,272 were wounded; 2,648 suffered combat fatigue: total Marine casualties: 25, 841.

Jack Groskin was one to survive that ordeal. And he would modestly say that it was only a miracle, or perhaps a stay of execution mandated by the hand of the Divine. It was there that Admiral Nimitz issued his now famous communiqué, the last of the campaign, in which he saluted the will of those who fought and died in that conflict: "Among the Americans who served on Iwo island, uncommon valor was a common virtue."

Jack Groskin, only one of the Americans who served on Iwo with uncommon valor, survived. In a photograph in the February issue, *Leatherneck,* 1995, he is prominently shown among a group of Marines at rest, "kneeling to the right of a Japanese solider who was killed by a mortar as Groskin's unit, Company G, 2nd Bn, 23rd Marines, moved inland from Yellow Beach. The photo was taken by a combat photographer on D + 7, but it wasn't given to Groskin until G/2/23 was on its way back to Maui after the Iwo campaign."

Jack Groskin, Syracuse, New York, enlisted in the Marine Corps in 1942. Boot camp at Parris Island "was difficult, but I enjoyed it." Part of the reason he "enjoyed it" was due to his excellent physical condition, and the sports he played at high school—football and basketball.

Slated for overseas duty, he reported to Camp Pendleton for infantry training. Following the Saipan campaign, he joined G Company, 2nd Battalion, 23rd Marines, at Maui, Hawaii, whence came the odyssey to Iwo Jima. He was among the first assault troops to hit the beach on D-Day. His "worst day was D + 3 when each man had to race across the airfield one at a time. He was the only Marine that the Japanese laid in with mortars, all landing behind him. Honorably discharged with the rank of corporal on February 18, 1946, he earned many medals." But modesty prevented him from naming the ones he received.

The closest he came to losing his life in combat was on Iwo. His most distasteful experience was seeing his buddies die. His religious experiences in the Corps included going to services on Friday night, and he particularly admired the officers with whom he fought. His most favorable experience was "getting out of Iwo Jima alive."

Returning home from the war, he was warmly welcomed. "My father and two sisters made a party for me." He was proud to have contributed in protecting his country, and not untypical of so many Marines of all walks of life, the Marine Corps "taught me discipline."

With the Shimanoff family, currently residing (2001) in Ashland, Oregon, one gets not just two, but three: in addition to being Brooklynites, Jimmy and Adele, a husband-and-wife team of Marines, their son Perry who was commissioned a second lieutenant in the Marine Corps on the day he graduated form the University of California (UCLA). In fact, his proud father had the honor of pinning on Perry's gold bars shortly before Dad departed for Vietnam.

Jimmy Shimanoff joined the Marine Corps at the age of 17 in 1944. Following recruit training at Parris Island and attending radio school, he was sent to Panama on a ship that escorted foreign vessels through the Canal. "After making one hundred trips, the thrill was gone. In 1992, my wife and I took a cruise through the Canal. It was exactly the same, except that now they were using Japanese equipment instead of American."

With the end of the war, Jimmy reenlisted in the active Reserves and was stationed with an aviation unit at Floyd Bennett Field, Brooklyn. It was there, in 1947, that he met his future wife, Adele. She had gone to a dance one Saturday night with some other women Marines. After a courtship of two months, they were married. One problem remained: he had promised her a five-carat ring. He quickly and adroitly solved that by giving her a ring surrounded by four carrots. Yet another problem persisted: "Adele had been a sergeant and I was still a corporal. She has never let me forget it."

After moving to Detroit, Jimmy joined an instructor-inspector (I-I) detachment. In June 1950, there was a budget cut, and, because Jimmy already had three dependents, he was once again a civilian. However, two weeks later the Korean War broke out and his Reserve unit was called to active duty. He was sent to Camp Pendleton where he was promoted every year. By 1953, he was a master sergeant with the 4th Marines and became "the youngest sergeant major in the Marine Corps."

While on maneuvers in June 1953, he received a field commission as second lieutenant. This was, however, "really a letdown after having been a sergeant major. There is nothing lower than a second lieutenant, figuratively speaking." After completing The Basic School at Quantico, he returned to Pendleton and became the CO of a DUKW (amphibious vehicle used to ferry troops and cargo between ship and shore) company. Returning to Camp Lejeune as a captain after fifteen months on Okinawa, he was transferred to a motor transport unit. His daughter was born at Lejeune and his family of four children was complete.

Next came Quantico, which offered the Shimanoffs the opportunity to get together every Friday evening with other Jewish Marines and their families. "Since we did not have a resident Jewish chaplain, the men took turns conducting services and a different family hosted the *Oneg Shabbat* (a celebration in honor of the Sabbath that takes place on Friday evening or Saturday morning and usually includes a program of songs, a lecture, and refreshment each week). We enjoyed being with other Jewish families."

Jimmy's next year was spent at Junior School (for captains and majors). Upon completion, it was back again overseas to Iwakuni, Japan, where he taught English to Japanese students.

Completing his tour of duty in Japan, he was stationed at Albany, Georgia. "It was there that I learned about the Bootstrap Program for military personnel to earn their college degrees while on active duty. Through the years I had taken many college courses and had accumulated three-years' worth of credits. The commanding general at Albany was instrumental in getting me involved in the program. I attended Park College in Parkville, Missouri and earned my bachelor's degree." Years later, while in Grants Pass, Oregon, he returned to graduate school and earned a master's degree in business administration.

By the time Jimmy completed his year tour of duty in Vietnam, he was a lieutenant colonel. After a few months at MCAS, El Toro, he retired from the Marine Corps in 1971, after a twenty-six year career, during which he had been promoted through every rank from private to lieutenant colonel. Upon his retirement, he received the Legion of Merit for performance of outstanding service.

He takes great pride in his Marine Corps service. "Every day I hoist both the American flag and the Marine Corps flag on my front deck." He is a life member of the Marine Corps League and served as Commandant of the Rogue Valley Detachment. He has given speeches on such civic occasions at Memorial Day, Veterans Day, and the Marine Corps Birthday.

"It will be Semper Fi until the day I die."

Adele Shimanoff, nee Berres, enlisted in the Women's Reserve in March 1945. Recruit training at Camp Lejeune was much "like summer camp except with a little more discipline and some marching thrown in. I loved it. I was in the 50th training battalion.

After finishing recruit training, she was sent to Headquarters, U.S. Marine Corps, Washington, D.C., in the Rehabilitation Office, where she was trained as a counselor for Marines being discharged from the Corps. She attended school at Parris Island and enjoyed it immensely; however, upon returning to Headquarters, she was assigned to do secretarial work, a job she considered a disappointment.

From Washington, she was transferred to New York, where she was able to live at home. On August 23, 1946, all Women Marines, with the exception of nearly one hundred at Headquarters, were discharged. As she did not want any part of getting out, she soon joined the Reserve. She and a few other women decided to form a Volunteer Training Unit so they could visit various Marine units in a semiofficial status. "It was there at Floyd Bennett Field, that I met Corporal Shimanoff. He was very good-looking, a terrific dancer, and he was Jewish. Two months later, we were married, and fifty-four years later, we are still together."

Adele had joined the Women Marines Association in 1965 while living in California, but upon moving to Oregon, discovered there was no chapter—so she formed one. She has since served as its president three times, as well as vice president, treasurer, and a national officer and attended many Association conventions. She is also a life member of the Marine Corps League. She and many of her women Marine companions have remained close friends for over fifty years.

Not to be outdone by either parent, son Perry joined the Marine Corps and was commissioned a second lieutenant in June 1970 after graduating from UCLA. During his first summer of Platoon Leaders Class at Quantico, he and his unit were waiting for their physicals in the hot sun when a sergeant instructor started screaming at him for no apparent reason. When the DI asked Perry where he was from, he answered, "Georgia." In return, the DI "started in with 'Is your father a redneck farmer? Does he live in a broken-down shack?' I finally summoned my voice and replied, 'No, Sergeant, he is not a redneck farmer—he is a lieutenant colonel in the Marine Corps,'" whereupon the sergeant refrained from picking on Perry and started in on someone else. "That night in the barracks, the story circulated, and everyone started claiming their father was on active service in the Marines."

Perry became an infantry officer. As a platoon honor graduate, he was selected to attend the Army's Ranger School (with four other Marine officers) at Fort Benning, the largest infantry post in the United States, located south of Columbus, Georgia. The eight-week course focused principally on patrolling skills. From there, he was transferred to Okinawa as platoon commander in L Company, 3rd Battalion, 4th Marines. When he was promoted to first lieutenant, he became the executive officer, and then the CO of L Company. Aboard the USS *Duluth* for nearly six months, he was CO of all Marine troops for two of the six, "much to the chagrin of the Marine captains who were in staff billets."

The *Duluth* remained in the waters around the Gulf of Tonkin, the result of which the troops received the Vietnam Service Ribbon. As they were fired on by North Vietnamese while aboard ship, the sailors, too, received the Combat Action Ribbon.

Perry's roommate at The Basic School was a graduate of the U.S. Military Academy, West Point. They had been friends since ninth grade and served as best man at each other's wedding. Although Perry was in for only three years as a Reserve officer, in 1971, he was selected to participate in an exchange with the Royal Welsh Fusiliers and went to Hong Kong for seven weeks. He says that he was selected for the program because the Regimental CO knew his dad in 1954. "Hong Kong was terrific, since the British Army put their officers on a pedestal—I had my own BOQ suite, a corporal to oversee my uniforms and other logistics, and my Fusilier platoon was always taking me on adventures in Hong Kong and the remote islands."

Once, Prince Juan Carlos of Spain visited Quantico, and Perry was asked to escort one of his nieces. He "was told in no uncertain terms to be a model citizen. She (the niece) wanted to ride in a tank, which I was able to surreptitiously arrange. I did get a nice hug at the end of the evening."

Perry, who resides in San Carlos, California, still stays in touch with his Marine buddies. Although Perry never intended to make the Marine Corps his career, it served as a wonderful exposure to the real world. "'We never promised you a rose garden' still applies today. I remain in decent physical shape, and, in part, the Marine Corps instilled the body/mind dichotomy that I rely on to this day."

Perry Shimanoff found the Marine Corps to be one big organization in which it helped to know people. He was unable to understand how some people were able to be promoted. Once, when returning from Okinawa, they stopped in Hawaii to refuel. The commanding officer of the Marine base at Oahu arranged to drive and visit with Perry, "which always impressed the hell out of me. He eventually became the Assistant Commandant and even today we stay in touch. I had gone to school with his kids in the late '60s."

As did so many Jewish servicemen during the Second World War, Perry, too, always volunteered for the "duty" on Christmas. He generally found the Marine Corps very accommodating on Yom Kippur ("even though the senior officers were mostly negligent regarding any Jewish holidays") Once, aboard the *Duluth*, the ship's chaplain gave Perry a bottle of wine and "all my platoon commanders and I celebrated an abbreviated Sabbath ceremony in my stateroom. After a quick prayer, we drank all the wine from little paper cups—I required each lieutenant to wear a makeshift yarmulke before indulging."

In keeping with the Shimanoff family tradition, Perry, too "always tried to do the best job possible, and the Marine Corps reinforced such skills as discipline, hard work, professional leadership, etc. As the owner of a small consulting business, I attribute much of my success to my three years in the Marines."

―――――――――

Attesting to the lifelong effect and pride accruing to Marines and former Marines, Norman Gertz's stationery emblazons the emblem of the globe and anchor.

Enlisting in the Marine Corps in December 1942, he completed boot camp after which he reported to Camp Lejeune where he was an instructor at the radio school. From there, he received orders to the 4th Marine Division at Camp Geiger, where they stayed till the division was shipped to Camp Pendleton to prepare for the invasion of the Marshall Islands. They shipped out from San Diego directly to the islands—the only operation that embarked form the USA and went directly into combat. Subsequently, he stayed with the Division through the campaigns on

Saipan, Tinian, and Iwo Jima. Gertz was a sergeant on Tinian when he received a field commission. He went to Iwo as a second lieutenant.

In 1945, they were on Maui for Passover. His battalion commander was Lieutenant Colonel Melvin Krulewitch. He "arranged for us to have a seder at the Maui Grand Hotel. To my surprise the owner of the hotel was sitting at the table with yarmulke on also."

Shortly after Iwo Jima, Gertz was ordered back to the States and spent several months as an instructor at the Troop Leaders School at Camp Pendleton. With the end of the war, Gertz was transferred to the Marine Air-Infantry School at Quantico. This was essentially for aviators, but there were about ten ground officers in the class of one hundred. He was the only Jewish member of the class composed of officers who had been commissioned in the field. Following this program, he was transferred to Marine Barracks, Naval Air Station, Quonset Point, Rhode Island, till his release from active duty in 1946.

With the outbreak of the Korean War, Gertz was recalled to active duty in 1951, and assigned to the 3rd Marine Brigade at Camp Pendleton. This was the nucleus of what was to be the 3rd Marine Division. It was his "pleasure to serve under the legendary Chesty Puller who was Commanding General at that time."

Gertz recalled that there was no Jewish chaplain at Camp Pendleton. Friday night services were held at the Ranchhouse Chapel and a rabbi from San Diego came in to conduct services. "A bountiful *kiddush* was provided by nearly local families. I was enjoying the most delicious guacamole and asked the lovely lady what made it taste so good. She confided in me that she made it with 'schmaltz.'"

Gertz later became affiliated with the Reserve program and served in a variety of billets including commanding officer of a howitzer battalion for two years. As the Marine military aide to the Governor of Rhode Island, John A. Notte, he accompanied him to many events and often represented him when he was not available. He flew with him to visit the local Reserve unit while training at Camp Lejeune accompanied by the Adjutant General of Rhode Island, Major General Leonard Holland.

Some of his other assignments included CO of a special ground training unit assigned to the Intelligence Branch of the Development Center at Quantico and AO2F at Headquarters, Marine Corps. This unit was part of the Marine Support Battalion, Naval Security Group, which oversaw the radio battalions which provided signal intelligence for the Marine divisions and had teams assigned to Navy security activities all over the world.

It was during this time that he made the acquaintance of a young captain named Al Gray who later became Commandant of the Marine Corps, "much to my pleasure."

Schools completed by Norman Gertz included Marine Air-Infantry School, Naval Justice, Communications Officer, Command Staff College, phases I and II, Amphibious Warfare School, and other short-term courses.

Norman Gertz received promotion to colonel in August 1967, at which time he "was doing assignments with the signal intelligence activity and traveled to a number of units in the field. One very interesting experience was a visit to the activity at Key West during the Cuban crisis."

He notes that "through the years the Marine Corps never failed to issue a Marine Corps order annually to all commanding officers alerting them to the dates of the Jewish High Holidays and to make every effort to allow Jewish Marines to observe the holidays."

Pride is as permanent with Colonel Gertz as with so many others. He makes that clear when he says that, "All things considered, I have always felt fortunate that I had the experience of all those years and the opportunity to work with such outstanding people in the Marine Corps and learn so much from my association. I have made some lifelong friends as a result."

Bob Brooks wrote to cite two of the most outstanding Marines that he knew: two Marines of the Jewish faith, Sam Winer and Werner Heumann. Werner Heumann's story is more bizarre and interesting that even Bob knew.

Werner Heumann was a refugee from Germany. He and his three brothers escaped from the Nazis in 1933, but his parents did not. They perished in the Holocaust.

Werner tried to join the armed forces as early as 1939, but he told his sons that he was rejected by each of the services. He felt that the Army didn't want him because he was a Jew. Having been turned down by the Army, he tried to join the Marine Corps. While he was originally rejected, ostensibly because of his height of five foot five, he was persistent and kept returning to the recruiting office until one day, the recruiter told him, "You want to get in so bad, you stupid SOB, I'm gonna let you in."

Before he entered into combat, he received his citizenship a few days before Pearl Harbor, the day of his birthday. One year after the attack on Pearl Harbor, he had been in the Corps for close to a year. Now a member of Carlson's Raiders, he earned four battle stars for Midway, Guadalcanal (thirty day patrol), first wave on Bougainville, and regimental reserve on Iwo Jima, where he lasted two days, earned the Silver Star and the Purple Heart. As a sergeant, he was the leader of a machine gun squad.

His son remarked that all during his time in the Marine Corps, he was torn with concern about his parents, where they were, and how they were. He also noted that "his Corps experience stayed with him his whole life, especially his Raider affiliation. He never talked much about combat, but it's clear he saw more than his share. He told me once (while he was dying) that he had his best time on Iwo and when I asked him why he said it: he said it was because he knew exactly what he was supposed to do, and considering the mayhem of that battle, only another Marine might truly know what he meant."

Werner Heumann was a professional soldier, or Marine: his

experience with Carlson shaped him. "He knew what he was doing, why he was doing it, and how it had to be done."

Arriving at Parris Island, Norton Garfinkel was greeted by none other than Lou Diamond, fresh from Guadalcanal, "and now in charge of the recruits their first day. Inspirational to see a real Marine, and even more for me as a Jew."

Norton Garfinkel was a twenty-three-year-old man with two children in a platoon composed of the usual teenagers. As it turned out, this wasn't too bad all. With his years of college already under his belt, maturity, plus good scores on the range and some leadership skills, he made corporal quickly. In fact, it was quickly recognized that he had officer potential at a time when the losses of lieutenants and captains at Tarawa were horrific. When he faced every field officer in his regiment, "and as I was shaking like a 'dog shitting razorblades,' the colonel asked me if I would like to be an officer. Then I had to tell him why I thought I would make a good one." "Wonder of wonders," he was promoted to sergeant.

Graduation from Parris Island provided at least one surprise, if not a big laugh. Sam Winograd, a member of Garfinkel's company, ordered a Sam Browne belt to wear over his uniform. "When he showed up for the graduation parade and inspection, it was quite proper to wear it, but the captain remarked, 'and here we have Same Browne with his Winograd belt.'" "Really clever, but with a tinge of anti-Semitism. To be fair, there was none once we got rid of the enlisted instructors."

Transferred to Camp 3 at Camp Pendleton for infantry training, Norton scored very high on several field exercises, the result of which he was kept behind as an infantry instructor while the rest of his class went overseas.

It wasn't too long, however, before his turn for overseas combat came up. He "finally hit Okinawa as Marines were cleaning up around Naha airfield. On a cave clearing assignment, he just missed getting killed. "We were throwing Bangalores into caves followed by flame throwers to flush out Japs who had been coming out at night and lobbing mortars. A fellow officer and friend working a couple of levels above and ahead of me hit a cave filled with the Japs' explosives, picric acid, very volatile. Blew the side of the mountain where he was working out and killed the whole fire team. I do believe now in guardian angels because my Marine experience was exceptional and since then have been spared on many occasions."

As an officer now, he was automatically placed in the Reserve and called up for duty for Korea in 1951. However, it was determined that his physical condition was not acceptable. Besides, at that time, he had three children and owned a restaurant.

As a member of the "Shanghai Marines" regiment, 6th Marine Division, he was among the first troops of any kind to land in Japan following the surrender on V-J Day. They took over the Yokosuka Naval Base in Tokyo Bay and secured it for the senior military commanders arriving for the signing of the treaty on the *Missouri* on September 2.

Lieutenant Garfinkel assumed a number of side duties with the occupation of Japan. He was Motor Transport Officer, Commissary Officer, BOQ, and he was right in saying that "I didn't know there was such a person as Shoe Repair Trailer Officer."

Though Lieutenant Garfinkel was married, he could not help but observe the lines that "went around the block for 'geisha houses': not the real thing, just brothels. Venereal disease got so bad that if they went off base for liberty they had to use a prophylactic to get back in whether they had done anything or not. Really funny to see a room full of Marines massaging their privates under the eyes of the Shore Patrol and the Marine MPs."

After twenty years in the restaurant business, Norton Garfinkel decided to enter a real and honest profession—teaching cooking to vocational high school students. "Long before anyone started sending cookies to our troops (other than WWII), I got fed up with anti-Marine stories re Vietnam. As a lesson in caring, and a lesson in patriotism, my class baked fruit cakes and sent them to Marines."

Not unlike many Jewish-American Marines, his comments about the Corps strike a common chord. He got so much out of the Corps: "A can-do attitude, problem-solving, improvising." "Loyalty to my group: my Corps, my platoon, my fire team, my foxhole buddy." His success can be attributed, at least in part, to his experience in the Marine Corps. Norton Garfinkel is "the one and only Marine who was a Jewish inductee (yes, it's true) commissioned out of the ranks." In addition, he "became principal of the school and earned a doctorate in Educational Administration, due in no small measure to my brief stint as a Marine."

Rosabelle Cohen of Chicago actually started out to join the WAC. When she went to the recruiting office, the recruiter asked her whom she worked for. Rosabelle answered, "Joseph Weidenhoff, Inc." The woman recruiter asked her if he is a "Jew-man." Whereupon, Rosabelle looked her in the eye, ripped up the application form and walked out. While storming out of that office, she saw a poster which said, "Free a Marine to Fight," and "when I got off the elevator there was a recruiter with seven hash marks and a smile ear to ear and before I knew it, I was sworn into the Marines."

Rosabelle Cohen has been hospitalized in a veterans hospital in California. Her Marine heritage and training have been essential in her fight to recuperate from Legionnaires Disease. While she has been hospitalized for eight months (as of 5/99), she credits much of her determination to get well and fight for her life to her military experience.

She trained at Camp Lejeune for twelve weeks. Later, she reported for duty at Camp Pendleton where she worked at the message center. She was fortunate enough to have open gate liberty. Once, when she was returning to camp to go on the midnight shift, she had some time to wash her hair and put it into curlers. The phone rang and it was the CO wanting to know if she was sleeping. She replied that she had a headache and was closing her eyes to relieve it. When he asked if she had some coffee brewing, Rosabelle replied that she had just put on a fresh pot. He said he would be right over.

"Ten minutes later, he came and I was more embarrassed that he saw me in curlers than to think I was asleep."

While she was stationed at Pendleton, she had liberty in Los Angeles. She was walking down Vine Street in Hollywood to meet a friend for breakfast. Two Marine lieutenants approached her. She dutifully saluted, they returned the salute, and the one nearest her said, "Good morning, BAM." "I looked at him straight in the eye and said, 'Go to hell, you HAM.' His buddy said, 'What's a HAM?' I said, 'Same as a BAM, only the "H" stand for Half, and I'd rather have it all, brother.' He laughed his head off while the other who addressed me turned red as the braid on his hat! I went back to camp and told all the gals and they cheered me and started to do the same whenever the men called them BAMs. That slowed down references to 'BAMs thereafter.'"

She had one particularly unpleasant incident. While she was on mess duty, the officer in charge of the detail refused to allow Rosabelle to escort the flag for a fallen Marine. In addition, she did not grant permission for her to spend a ten-day visit with her family.

Otherwise, the Marine Corps provided her with "a wonderful experience while I was serving—but glad to get out when it was over. The military affected her very positively. "It made me feel I could handle anything in life. Prepared me to be self-sufficient and use my experience in the Marines to continue to be a teletype operator for twenty-two years at Lockheed Aircraft."

She spent her most pleasant times at Camp Pendleton. One of her favorite pastimes was meeting friends for dinner in Carlsbad, California. The most difficult, or most distasteful, assignment she had was "Handling the 'eyes only' orders for shipping out of the 4th Marine Division to Iwo Jima."

She was very proud to serve her country in the Marines. "It

taught me a wonderful profession. Proud to release a fellow Marine." She "admired the men and women in the service for the sacrifice they all made to serve our country."

———————

After completion of his training in New Zealand, Nat Berman arrived in Guadalcanal for his first taste of combat. No sooner had they arrived on the firing line, they were held up by a Japanese machine gun nest. "It was extremely hot, no water, or chow, and in despair, Sergeant West, an old Iceland Marine, shouted, 'Why are we fighting this f—g war? I'll tell you why—it's because of the Jews. You'll never find them here on the firing line—they're either in the Army or Quartermasters!' This sergeant was right next to me and I was absorbing the same hardship that he was."

During boot camp at San Diego, Barney Ross was the athletic instructor and matched Nat with a guy from Chicago, a Leo Block, a pretty tough guy, also Jewish, and also a friend of Ross. The day after the match which lasted exactly twenty-seven seconds of the first round (Block cold-cocked Berman), Nat questioned Barney about that mismatch. Barney said, "I was the only guy that would look good going up against him!" Although Nat could throw a good punch for his five-foot-eight size and had red hair, the fact that he was Jewish meant nothing to most of the guys in his platoon.

Having completed the usual training and qualifying as a Sharpshooter, Berman was assigned to I Company, 3rd Battalion, 6th Marines, and assigned to a weapons platoon, manning a light .30-caliber machine gun. Training at Camp Elliott, they had night problems, bayonet course, judo, and "crap like that." Soon, they received the word that they were shoving off to New Zealand. They had a rough trip on a Dutch merchant ship named the *Brastagi*. It was a difficult voyage with numerous general quarters being sounded. A number of enemy planes were supposed to have been spotted, but none proved to be true.

After more training in New Zealand, they landed at

Guadalcanal for their first taste of combat. Regular enemy artillery fire, sniper fire, and "Washing Machine Charlie" were featured. Originally, they were instructed to refrain from firing their weapons at night. Rather, they were to lob grenades and use their knives. They had a password every night with the letter "L" in it. The reason being that the Japanese couldn't pronounce "Lawnmower," "Lalapalooza," etc. It was on Guadalcanal that the only member of I Company *not* to get malaria was Nat Berman. Then, they turned Guadalcanal over to the "doggies" and "shoved off for New Zealand again."

After more training, Berman and I Company boarded the USS *Harris* for their next campaign on Tarawa. Reaching their objective, the tide was so far out that they had to wade into the surf "with rifles and machine guns firing at us. Fought the fight as valiant as any Marine. Burkett and I captured five Jap Imperial Marines and took them to the Battalion CP. There were only *eight* prisoners taken, and we got five of them." There were 4,000 Japanese on the entire atoll, and Berman's company and the rest of the Marines suffered heavy casualties. In recognition of this battle, they received the Presidential Unit Citation.

At this time, Berman was transferred to Headquarters Company because he had typing ability. "It was good duty after almost two years in a line company and just drawing cartoons and clerical work. It was gravy, but didn't last long as we shoved off for the landing on Saipan."

Berman never did land at Saipan. On the eve of the battle, he came down with the mumps, and was unable to walk. Pangs of guilt invaded Nat Berman "as they were bringing the wounded aboard and I saw many from my company."

After eleven days on board ship, they shoved off again for Hawaii. While there, he received word that he was eligible to return to the States because he had been overseas for more than two years. They arrived in San Diego, and Berman was assigned to Marine Barracks, 8th and Eye Streets, Washington, D.C. While there, he "drew cartoons for *Leatherneck* Magazine, Marine Corps

Institute, and assigned funeral details for Arlington National Cemetery.

Nat Berman received his discharge in Washington, D.C. right after V-J Day in September 1945.

———————

From September 30 through December 7, 1941, Platoon 154 was the last platoon to complete boot camp at Parris Island, South Carolina, prior to the attack on Pearl Harbor. On that day, Private Sidney A. Sadin received orders to his first duty station.

His first tour of duty was at Naval Mine Depot, Yorktown, Virginia. He was assigned to guard duty, guard clerk, and weekend shore patrol. When he volunteered for transfer to a raider battalion, "My CO obliged me to take the place of Sergeant M. Innocently, I asked, "In the PX or the brig?" I reported to the PX officer.

Toward the end of World War II, Platoon Sergeant Sadin was on Guam with the 15th Regiment, 6th Division, preparing for the invasion of Japan. When the atomic bombs were dropped on Japan, we were rerouted and sailed for Tsingtao, China, which was occupied by Japanese troops.

Duty in China was interesting. But his request to extend his duty there was denied. He was returned to the States and civilian status. After five years of active duty, the Marine Corps was in his veins.

During the Korean War, Gunnery Sergeant Sidney A. Sadin was recalled to active duty and assigned to Camp Lejeune. He was assigned to be an instructor at Supply School and the Naval Field Medical Research Laboratories. There were now two gunnery sergeants in the company: one had to go. The other gunnery sergeant, Herbie Sweet, received orders for Korea. Eventually, this led to his selection as Sergeant Major of the Marine Corps.

After a short tour of duty at Supply School, Sadin received orders to report to Marine Corps Institute, Washington, D.C. as head of the Science Section. When released from active duty was pending, Sadin was offered a promotion and tenure at MCI. However, a career beckoned as a research pharmaceutical chemist in civilian status.

After discharge from active duty, Sadin maintained association with the Marine Corps Reserve by joining a rifle company in New Rochelle, New York. He was company first sergeant for sixteen consecutive years. His final tour of duty was with Headquarters Company, 2nd Battalion, 25th Marine Regiment in Garden City, New York. In the final count, he served a total of nearly thirty years. His date of discharge for retirement was June 1, 1974.

Following careers as a pharmaceutical chemist, certified as a brew master, and executive in a laser company, he recently retired as a chemist consultant.

First Sergeant Sidney A. Sadin, USMC, retired, is a member of the West Point Retiree Council. He also volunteers at the Hospital Pharmacy, U.S. Military Academy, West Point.

Nate Sadowsky served in the Army before joining the Marine Corps. As others, he feels that the two have very little in common: the others simply just don't shape up.

He served in the Army from 1938 to 1939 and, was, in fact, a retired captain. But he says that "The Marine Corps is first in my memory." He is extremely proud of his military service, and feels bad that more members of the Jewish faith have not found it attractive enough. As he says of his country, "Nowhere have the 'Chosen People' had the freedom they have here. I have a number of friends that are retired from the Israeli Defense Forces, and have visited them several times. They know what 'Security' means."

When he received his draft notice, he chose to go into the Marine Corps. His previous experience in the Army was not the best. As a result of his past military experience, and in contrast with so many others, Parris Island was not that bad at all. He was selected for squad leader.

Just one point separated his qualification as Expert with the M-1 rifle. Other weapons were as easy as the M-1. Following boot camp, he returned to Parris Island for DI School.

Getting away from there, he joined the 43rd Replacement Company at Camp Lejeune where his commander was 2nd Lieutenant Billy Cumba. They remain close friends to this day. At Lejeune, Sadowsky was assigned as machine gunner on the Model 1917 water-cooled machine gun.

Following Camp Miramar in California, he shipped out to Noumea, Caledonia. They experienced a severe storm at sea which made a lot of people seasick—but Sadowsky was not one of them. Upon landing at Noumea, his unit was sent to camp, whereupon he lost his "faithful M-1," and was issued a carbine. Soon, they departed for Pavuvu, in the Russell Islands, to join the 1st Marine Division.

The first few nights in tents near the 1st Marines, they got acquainted and heard some wild stories. He was assigned to Fox Battery, 11th Marines, as a machine gunner.

His unit landed on Peleliu in the thirteenth wave, and "as we were climbing out of tracked landing craft, someone yelled, 'Sniper.' Everybody opened fire on the tree that was close, and sure enough, it was a Jap soldier that was the sniper."

"That night was my baptism of fire. No one moved around, and about 2 A.M., someone yelled, 'I'll get you, you dirty SOB.' The next morning we learned that it was Jim Borsius (?) that woke up, saw a Jap soldier coming at him with a bayonet. He took the rifle away, and shot the Jap with his own rifle. That night we had a 'Banzai' attack, and I found out that a carbine wasn't as good as they said it was. Can remember putting five slugs in the Nip's chest, and he kept right on coming. Dropped my aim to his leg, and then he fell down. He might have been dead before he hit the ground, but that caused me to pick up a BAR. It was my constant companion after that."

Although one of the first things they did was to get rid of their gas masks, there came a time when they wished they didn't. Once, while troubleshooting their wire, someone yelled, "Gas!" and Nate looked around for his mask. Later, they determined that it was in fact somewhat of a gas attack: "The Japs were using picric acid in their detonators, and that was the gas scare."

On maneuvers on Guadalcanal, he was sent out to troubleshoot some wire. The Kunia grass was soaking wet and so was Sadowsky. While holding the wire for taping, someone rang through on the phone. "That was a shocking experience to say the least. As my phone was connected, I really told the person off, and it turned out to be Lt. Colonel Woods. Needless to say, the splicing was finished very quickly and I disappeared."

It was here that he experienced his first taste of anti-Semitism. It was the custom that the first person to reach their truck was given the assignment of "riding shotgun." One evening, Sadowsky got there first, and a corporal told him, "You goddam Jews always try to beat everyone." Sadowsky "came out of that truck like a cannon shot, and the result was that they had to stop at the hospital and put some stitches over his eyes." But it was the corporal who got dressed down, and not Sadowsky. That evening, "the Commo wanted to know what had happened. After telling him, the Commo got real 'pissed off' and told the corporal that because of people like him, we were fighting a war."

Although he had picked up some jungle rot on Peleliu, he refused to remain on board ship when they reached Okinawa. "You can't dig a foxhole in a steel deck," said Sadowsky. He went ashore in the eighth wave. It was real scary: no gunfire, no mortars, very quiet. They heard their first shot about thousand yards inland. On the third day of the campaign, Sadowsky tried to get some treatment for his jungle rot. The doctor began to chew him out: "The people on the ship had been looking for me, and were ready to report me MIA. The doctor told the corpsman to take me not only to the shore, but to see me aboard ship."

He was then deposited at the hospital on Saipan. Ten days later he was sent to the hospital on Guam. While on the LST returning to Okinawa, he noticed that he had worked on that ship while it was being built. "One of the sailors didn't believe me, so I took him down to the bilges and showed him my number stamped on the plates." It was during this trip that his jungle rot deteriorated so badly that the corpsman told the skipper that he had to be put ashore.

With that, the war ended in Europe. Sadowsky was shipped back to Guam, and finally to Iehia Heights, overlooking Pearl Harbor. The war ended there. "That night Pearl Harbor was a mass of rockets, flares, and anything the swabbies could get their hands on to light up."

He served in Korea as well as in World War II, was a Commo for a field artillery unit and met many fine people. He "was awarded an honorary rank in the Queen's Battery, 16th New Zealand Field Artillery, and honorary captain in the RAF, and has made many valued friendships while both in and out of the service."

Nate Sadowsky is now more than eighty years of age. He is retired from the Army, Civil Service, and draws SS. He was awarded the Purple Heart, Asiatic Theater Campaign Medal with two stars, Korean Ribbon with two stars, American Defense Ribbon, and "the one I prize the most is the Presidential Unit Citation with two stars, while with the 1st Marine Division. There are, of course, the Sharpshooter badge, CBI, one for being good."

Obviously proud of his country, his Corps, and his military service, he waxes a bit nostalgic over the old times. He looks out on today's military, and harbors some reservations about it. He says that, "Without the military this country would not survive, and people of all faiths should do all they can to keep this country going. I am an advocate of a strong military, and we don't have enough people in Congress that have a military background."

There is much about Nate Sadowsky that must go unspoken. He is most proud of the contribution he has made and the people with whom he has served. As he says, "There is so much that still comes to mind. Could have made a real career out of the military. Have thirty- seven and a half service, and married a wonderful gal the second time around that had twenty-six years in the Army. She died on Erev Yom Kippur in 1998, and to say that I miss her is putting it mildly. Most of the members of the 1st Marine Division knew her and they miss her, too."

Not a few of the Jewish-Americans who served in the Marine Corps made it their career. Among them was Colonel Sidney J. Altman, of the Bronx, New York.

Following his graduation from New York University in 1940, he entered the Marine Corps on February 1, 1941, completed the Officer Candidate Course at Quantico, and received his commission as second lieutenant in the Marine Corps Reserve in May 1941.

He was then assigned duty at Quantico, Commanding Officer, Barracks Detachment, then Executive Officer, 15th Provisional Company, and Commanding Officer, 11th Battalion, Reserve Officers Course. Integrated into the regular Marine Corps, he was promoted to captain in August 1942.

During World War II, Captain Altman served as CO, Company E, 2nd Battalion, 21st Marines, in the campaigns on Bougainville and Guam. It was during these that he received the Silver Star Medal, the Bronze Star Medal with Combat V, and the Purple Heart Medal for wounds sustained in battle. Returning to the United States for hospitalization, he became an instructor at Marine Corps Schools, Quantico.

From February 1945 until June 1949, Captain Altman was assigned duties in the Recruiting and Officer Procurement Program, serving as OIC, District Headquarters, Recruiting Station, El Paso, Texas, and other posts in California and New York. He was promoted to major in August 1947.

Major Altman returned to Quantico in July 1949, to serve as Assistant G-3, Marine Corps School. He also completed the Amphibious Warfare School, Junior Course. Then, he was assigned a tour of duty as Assistant Training Officer, Troop Training

Unit, Pacific, Coronado, California. In January 1951, he was promoted to lieutenant colonel and a year later, he was assigned duty as Commanding Officer, 18th Replacement Draft.

As a member of this unit, he sailed for Korea, where he served as Commanding Officer, Military Police Company, Headquarters Battalion, 1st Marine Division, Division Provost Marshal, and Battalion Commander, 3rd Battalion, 1st Marine Regiment. He was awarded the Legion of Merit with Combat V for his service in Korea.

Returning to the United States in December 1952, he completed a tour of duty as Camp Special Services Officer, Camp Lejeune, then attended the Armed Forces Staff College, Marine Barracks, Naval Base, Norfolk, Virginia. He returned to the Fleet Marine Force in July 1956, where he assumed command as Battalion Commander, 3rd Battalion, 7th Marines, and Assistant G-3, 1st Marine Division. His additional duties included assignment as Assistant Chief of Staff, G-3, 1st Marine Provisional Brigade.

In August 1959, Lieutenant Colonel Altman was assigned as Deputy Commanding Officer/Inspector, Marine Corps Component, U.S. Naval Advisory Group, Republic of Korea Navy, with additional duty as Adviser to the Chief of Staff, Republic of Korea Marine Corps. He was promoted to full colonel in October 1959.

After two years, he was assigned as G-2 of the 1st Marine Division, Camp Pendleton. In May 1962, he was appointed Commanding Officer of the 1st Marine Regiment, 1st Marine Division, serving in this capacity until March 1963, when he was appointed Assistant to the Director for Long Range Objectives Group, Office of the Chief of Naval Operations, until June 1966. Later that month, Colonel Altman was transferred to Camp Butler, where he served briefly as Division Inspector, at which time he assumed the post of Chief of Staff, 1st Marine Division (reinf), FMF, in July 1966.

Colonel Altman's decorations and awards include the Legion of Merit with Combat V, the Silver Star Medal, the Bronze Star Medal with Combat V with Gold Star denoting subsequent award, the Purple Heart Medal, Presidential Unit Citation, Navy Unit Citation, American Defense Service Medal, American Campaign Medal, Asiatic-Pacific Campaign Medal, World War II Victory Medal, National Defense Service Medal with one bronze star, the Korean Service Medal, and the United Nations Service Medal.

Colonel Sidney J. Altman, USMC, retired from active service on May 1, 1968.

Sam Singer, now of Florida, wished to relate the following story of perseverance, determination, and guts:

"It was a time long gone when the war years were upon us (1943). With my overwhelming need to escape the confines and the iron-handed demands of my mother, I enlisted in the United States Marine Corps.

"Upon arriving at Parris Island, South Carolina, I immediately began the ten-week basic training program that would attempt to transform a raw recruit into a fine-tuned Marine. The drill instructor that would be responsible for accomplishing this transformation was Gunnery Sergeant Gregg, who had engaged the enemy in battle at Guadalcanal and returned victorious. He was a line noncommissioned officer who proudly wore his sixteen years of hash marks on his sleeve, along with three rows of campaign ribbons and medals on his chest.

"Basic training proved to be extremely challenging. Wake up call was at 5:45 A.M. At 6:15 A.M., we marched in close order drill to the mess hall. I can still remember the large sign that hung over the 'belly robbers' who doled out the food: 'BEWARE . . . Take all you want but eat all that you take!' After several occasions of witnessing what happened to those who did not heed the rule of the mess hall, I came to the realization that enlisting in the Corps proved not to be the escape that I wanted but only a transference to a place with stricter rules and that demanded iron-clad obedience at the high level.

"Each day Platoon 683, made up of sixty recruits, would fall out on the company road and in cadence would attempt to march in unison. With his swagger stick in one hand and a bull horn in the other, Gunnery Sergeant Gregg continuously insulted and harassed us as he shouted out his commands. Insults and harassment were daily occurrences as this was used to help identify those capable of withstanding the rigors of basic training and the Marine Corps. By the fourth week, I began to realize that Gunnery Sergeant Greggs' sole purpose was to remove the civilian-psyche makeup of each of us to re-mold us into the image of what the United States Marine Corps, past and present represented.

"It was late one hot afternoon when we returned from a twenty-mile hike. Carrying a full pack and with my M-1 rifle resting on my right shoulder, I was relieved when the platoon was brought to a half and the command 'at ease' was given. As Gunnery Sergeant, with his full military bearing, walked through the ranks, he once again faced the individual recruits and harassed each one with insult and condemnation. As he moved close to me, I sensed the fear inside me begin to build. Before I knew it, there he was, Gunnery Sergeant Gregg, with his swagger stick in hand, staring me down.

"'You're a Hebrew boy, how come I can't get to you? You march like a latch on a s—t house door during a hurricane. ANSWER ME SON! How come I can't get to you? ANSWER ME!'

"With sweat pouring down my face and trembling with fear from within, I mustered up all my courage, stood at attention and blurted out my response. 'Sir, my mother was tougher.' From that moment on, Gunnery Sergeant Gregg never approached me or demanded anything of me.

"At my platoon graduation, I was one of twelve Marines awarded a Pfc. stripe. Having received this, I would get an additional $4.00 a month in pay as well as the respect from those who were not awarded the stripe. But, most importantly, I knew that the stripe was a symbol of Gunnery Sergeant Gregg's accepting me into the Corps."

"I was a proud, not quite eighteen-year-old high-school graduate who, along with many of my Jewish friends, enlisted in the services of the U.S. Armed Forces. I chose the USMC and to this day, believe that my thoughts about the elite training I would receive would better my chances of survival. Indeed, the training was demanding. Yet, here I am at the ripe age of 75 writing to you in the comfort of my home. Needless to say, I survived. I can surely attest that a lot of my own survival has been due to the training.

"It was July of 1943. After boot training at Parris Island, and a ten-day furlough, I was assigned to report to the Marine air base at Cherry Point to await entry into a technical aviation training program. My entry into the program never happened as the urgency to form fighter and bomber squadrons became more immediate. I was then assigned to ground defense to VMB-433, a Marine bomber squadron that was shipped out to El Centro, California. After several months of training, on May 18, 1943, my squadron shipped out on the HMS *Brastagi*, a Dutch merchant vessel that had been transformed into a troop carrier.

"After many days out to sea, we entered the Pacific theater of war. Guadalcanal had been captured along with a partial occupation of Bougainville (we had control of the airstrip). Just about Bougainville, VMB-433 disembarked at Espiritu Santo in the New Hebrides, scaling down Jacob's ladders to establish a beach position without resistance. The beach master immediately arranged working squadrons. Within days, a tent city was established along with Seabees contracting Quonset huts for approximately 500 officers and enlisted men. This would be VMB-433's home for the next three months.

"Life proved to be tolerable. There was daily training for the pilots going out on 'dry runs' to practice synchronizing bombing raids. After three months, we moved further north to a tiny island on the Equator called Emirau, located in the Admiral Archipelago. Now in the northern Solomon Islands, along with other Marine fighter and bomber squadrons, our sole purpose was to contain large segments of Japanese troops from attacking our forces from Rabaul which was located on the island of New Britain. This continued for twelve months."

Corporal Samuel Singer participated on active duty in the Marines from August 1943 until his discharge on March 25, 1946. He participated in the campaigns in the Northern Solomon Islands, Mindanao, Philippine Islands, and Espiritu Santo.

Not unlike many of his contemporaries of the greatest generation, Joel Krensky dismisses his participation in World War II with the usual modesty so predictive of his comrades in arms. While it is true that his service is absent of the extraordinary achievement of so many, the mere fact that he served on Iwo Jima attests to his courage, patriotism, and eagerness to participate. "I was not involved in any of the actual fighting . . . the only activities were frequent air raids, many typhoons, plus alarms by enemy planes and subs while at sea."

He says that "We Jews were represented in the USMC during time of conflict, World War II. My primary reason, and in fact, my only reason for joining the Marines was because I felt that a presence in the Marines was where I belonged.

"I enlisted at age 19, passed my physical in August 1942, and was sworn in on September 14, 1942, at the world's premier of the movie *Wake Island* with William Bendix and cast . . . on the stage of the Metropolitan Theater (now called the Wang) in Boston.

"I went off to Parris Island with a platoon to avenge Wake Island which was taken by the Japanese shortly after Pearl Harbor."

During boot camp, he encountered only one isolated act of anti-Semitism. His platoon was selected to march as Honor Guard for Brigadier General Moses who received a promotion to Major General.

Following boot camp, he was sent to Camp Lejeune for a six weeks course in supply. During that time, he studied navy regulations, threw dummy hand grenades, and ran the obstacle course. The top ten men in his platoon were promoted to corporal. Three members of the platoon were Jewish and all attained high grades. After Lejeune, he was transferred to Cherry Point Marine Air Station, assigned to VMB 612, MAG 61, 3rd MAW, and prepared for service in the Pacific. His squadron was the first to experiment with Tiny Tim rockets. There is a plaque in the Smithsonian Institution that describes this event.

Shipping out of San Diego, Krensky was appointed NCOIC in charge of all life rafts aboard ship. En route to their destination, they stopped at Eniwetok, continued on to Saipan, where he was assigned as beach master unloading ship using small craft. There, his CO, Lt. Col. Cram, offered him a field commission, which he politely declined.

Departing Saipan, he moved out to Iwo Jima aboard LST 748. He remained on Iwo for about three months. Following Iwo, he arrived on Okinawa where he stayed for about six months. After the second bomb at Nagasaki, he departed Okinawa through the China Sea, and headed to Midway for a stopover. Boarding the USS *Hendry*, an attack troop carrier, he finally returned to San Diego. There, he was discharged on December 26, 1945.

"In all, I spent about three months at sea during my 'grand tour' of the Pacific. I was discharged at San Diego on December 26, 1945. Uncle Sam paid five cents a mile back to point of enlistment, which was Boston. Five of us took a long cab ride from Los Angeles to New York for the final leg of our journey."

Krensky's awards include the Navy Unit Citation with Star, Asiatic-Pacific Ribbon with two Stars, Combat Action Ribbon, Good Conduct Medal, American Campaign, World War II Victory, and the Cold War Certificate. He maintains affiliation with the Marine Corps Heritage Foundation, Marine Corps Association, Marine Corps League, VFW, American Legion, and the Jewish War Veterans. He continues to be active in the Marine Corps League's "Toys for Tot" program and received a plaque and certificate for his participation in these activities.

Today, he remains active in business and military activities.

He continues to be chairman of his travel firm, Colpitts World Travel, Dedham, Massachusetts. As such, he leads large groups to conventions and conferences to all parts of the world. Now, after a half century of travel, "Krensky is cutting his international trips down to three or four a year. 'I pick and choose now,' he says. 'I want to spend more time with my grandchildren and with my hobbies. I love gardening, woodworking, and reading, especially military history.

"His interest in military history dates from his days as a Marine. He enlisted after the outbreak of World War II and saw both the fierce fighting on the Pacific islands of Saipan, Iwo Jima, and Okinawa, and the aftermath of the bombing of Nagasaki.

"Rather than spoil his penchant for travel to distant places, these experiences with death and destruction abroad only increased his interest in international travel and helped fire his determination to do whatever he can to relieve poor conditions wherever he finds them."[1]

"In all, I spent about three months at sea during my 'grand tour' of the Pacific. I was discharged at San Diego on December 26, 1945. Uncle Sam paid five cents a mile back to point of enlistment, which was Boston. Five of us took a long cab ride from Los Angeles to New York for the final leg of our journey."

On Marv Goodman's nineteenth birthday in August 1942, he and his best friend—both of whom were about to begin their third year of college—went to the Post Office Building in their hometown of Portland, Oregon, to sign up in the Navy's Officer Candidate program for college students. It was an extremely hot day and the line to join the Navy was clear out the door and down the hall. Goodman told his buddy he had no plan to wait in a long line and left him there.

Down the hall on his way out, Goodman passed the Marine Corps recruiting office and noticed it was empty except for a sergeant. Goodman had heard about a Marine Corps Officer Can-

[1] Medical Meetings, Nov/Dec/2001, p. 78.

didate program for college students, similar to the Navy's, so he approached the sergeant and inquired about it. Goodman says the sergeant dropped his pencil, his mouth flew open, he smacked the palm of his hand against his forehead and said, "And what make you think YOU could be a MARINE?" Goodman responded, "Well, you silly SOB, what makes you think I COULDN'T?" Goodman says, "I was hooked, but didn't realize it." Several days later, he was sworn in.

In July of 1943, he was called to active duty in the V-12 unit at the University of California, which consisted of Navy and Marine officer candidates. Upon graduation from college in February 1944, he and about forty other V-12 graduates were shipped, in a railroad boxcar, to Marine Corps boot camp at Parris Island.

Marine boot camp is a humbling experience. Goodman and all the other V-12ers went through normal Corps boot camp training—but with a difference. As each of the 72 men in these platoons of V-12ers was a potential officer candidate, the drill instructors "made it as miserable as possible for these 'collich boys,' with the intent of weeding out those who might not be qualified for officer training." Some men were dropped from the officer program.

As time passed, Goodman notes, "You begin to think 'I have taken everything you have handed out and can handle anything else you have to offer.' We began to walk tall, with newly found self-respect. By the time we completed boot training, with Pfc. stripes on our sleeves, we were cocky, self-assured Marines, looking to take on the world. The system had worked! Again!"

After boot camp, Goodman and several hundred others were sent to Camp Lejeune to train and wait for a turn at Officer Candidate School at Quantico. Shortly thereafter, due to the loss of so many young officers in the Pacific, the group was designated the Special Officer's

Candidate School and began officer's training. The graduates were commissioned second lieutenants in September 1944. No other group of Marines has ever been commissioned as platoon leaders without having trained at Quantico.

After brief further training at Camp Pendleton, Goodman was assigned to the 27th Replacement Draft and sent to Hawaii. In Hilo, he became a Shore Party platoon leader. One day he ran into his former Parris Island corporal drill instructor, now a sergeant. "He didn't know me. A triumph! It is an objective of every man in boot camp to keep the drill instructor from ever learning your name—so you would almost never be singled for anything."

In January 1945, Goodman and his platoon boarded a troop ship, bound for Iwo Jima, a forty-two-day voyage. By chance, he was on the same ship as the men in the famous photograph of the flag raising on Mt. Suribachi, and he observed this event while on the beach. After several days of unloading supplies and equipment under almost constant fire on the beach, his platoon was broken up and the men were assigned to various front line units, as replacement.

Goodman was assigned to G Company, 3rd Battalion, 26th Marines to replace a first lieutenant who was a regular, a mustang, and a former drill instructor, and had last been seen charging an enemy cave with a grenade in one hand and a pistol in the other. The company commander greeted Goodman with the following statement: "I don't know who you are or where you came from, but wherever that is, there's plenty more like you. Do not lose any of those NCOs. They are the best in the business." They were all former parachute troopers and this was their third campaign together.

On his first day on the front line, Goodman was in command of a rifle platoon, a machine gun section, and several corpsmen, seventy-two in all. Almost immediately, they ran into a complex of meanly defended caves, connected by tunnels. Goodman came upon a large cave in front of which was a mound of earth as high as the mouth of the cave. He saw three of his men lying against the mound. He ran forward to take charge and flopped on the mound between two of the men. The man on his right was dead. The man on his left held a BAR. Goodman held his carbine in his left hand, his right on the trigger, ready to fire. Suddenly, a giant Japanese head and shoulders rose from behind the mound, directly in front of his carbine, no more than a foot from the muzzle. He pulled the trigger. Nothing! The enemy ducked instantly. Goodman's carbine was full of sand from the beach and he hadn't had an opportunity to clean it.

The BARman rose and fired a burst. He quickly ducked and said, "I got some." All this occurred in no more than thirty seconds from the time Goodman arrived on the mound. Then, from the other side of the mound came grenades. Luckily, they were not fragmentation grenades meant to kill, but concussion grenades meant to stun. The body of the man on Goodman's right shielded him from most of the effect of the grenades. He and the two men then backed off while a demolition team and flamethrower were employed to destroy the cave entrance.

As this was happening, Goodman was talking to his platoon guide, an experienced Texas outdoorsman. From the corner of his eye, the guide spotted an enemy soldier trying to escape from a previously unseen entrance to the cave. He raised his M-1 rifle and fired a single shot, hitting his target. He had executed a "snap shot," using his rifle sight without adjustment. Goodman called it breathtaking marksmanship.

After eight days and nine nights on the front line, Goodman's unit was relieved. He had twenty-eight men left. Many of his NCOs, including the platoon sergeant, were casualties. He and Goodman were sitting side by side in a foxhole, when the sergeant was hit with shrapnel. After two days of rest, they received twenty-six replacements, many of whom were cooks, bakers, and bandsmen—not well trained as infantrymen—and were sent back to the front.

This pattern of time on the front line with many casualties followed by a brief interval of rest went on for a month. Every single NCO in Goodman's rifle platoon was a casualty. Just one NCO from his machine gun section was unhurt. Goodman's runner became his platoon sergeant due to his experience (three campaigns) and leadership qualities. He celebrated his sixteenth birthday on Iwo Jima.

After thirty-six days, Iwo was secured and Goodman's 5th

Marine Division returned to Hawaii to prepare for the invasion of Japan. Ships were actually loaded in Hilo harbor when the atomic bombs were dropped. Loading continued and the division sailed on schedule. Once at sea, Goodman learned that his division was to have been one of the first to land on the beaches of Kyushu on D-Day of the invasion. Instead, they were the first Americans ashore in the occupation of Japan in Kyushu.

After serving in Japan for one month, Goodman and his battalion were sent to the Palau Islands to supervise the evacuation of over 50,000 Japanese troops who had been bypassed by previous battles. Returning to the States in 1946, Goodman was released from active duty as a first lieutenant.

With the outbreak of the Korean conflict, he was recalled to active duty with the 6th Marine Division at Camp Lejeune as a company commander. Shortly thereafter, he was transferred to Junior School at Quantico.

The school was like Staff and Command School, but for lower-ranking officers, in grades from first lieutenant through major. It covered all aspects of command at the battalion and regimental levels. While in school, Goodman was promoted to captain.

Student activities were assigned alphabetically. Goodman recalls "the guy immediately before me was a red-haired fighter pilot, just back from a tour in Korea. He was USMC, a captain, friendly, rather quiet, very self-confident and did extremely well in all class work. On the page of the class photograph, his photo and mine are side by side." Later, after release from active duty and working in his civilian job, Goodman read that his classmate had broken the transcontinental speed record in a fighter plane. His name was John Glenn.

After graduation, Goodman was asked to write a field manual on small infantry unit tactics. Upon completion of that assignment in mid-1952, he was released from active duty.

Goodman attended a 5th Marine Division reunion in Atlanta in 1995, on the fiftieth anniversary of the landing at Iwo Jima. He recalls that while waiting for one of the activities to begin, he went to the bar for a drink. There, he was joined by two young

Reserve Marines and another older man about his age. It turned out that this other man had been a Navy corpsman assigned to Goodman's platoon on Iwo. The corpsman thought he recalled that he and Goodman had shared a foxhole once. It had been hastily dug in the dark, and they had to endure an unbearable odor in this foxhole through an awful night. Goodman confirmed the incident, agreeing that in the morning they found the cause of the smell. It was a decomposing enemy soldier whose arm was sticking out of the side of the foxhole.

In an article of the Bergen County Record of August 26, 1999, notice was made of the death of

Joseph Gold. Six weeks after receiving France's Legion of Honor, Joseph Gold passed away at a Tenafly (NJ) nursing home. He received this honor eighty years after his service as a foot Marine. He "'was thrilled to get the medal and had looked forward to it for weeks,' said his son, Arthur Gold of Englewood Cliffs." "'It really meant a lot to him,' Arthur Gold said Wednesday. 'We talked a lot about it.'"

Joseph Gold served with the American Expeditionary Force in World War I and participated in the battle of Belleau Wood and others of that conflict. "Despite his advanced years, Gold held on to many memories of the war. On the day of the medal ceremony, he regaled a room full of reporters with a hummed version of the Marine Corps anthem and with tales about crawling through trenches on his belly." Gold said "that he was glad people still remembered soldiers' sacrifices and still wanted to hear their stories." "'If you don't talk about it, you forget it,' he said in an interview before the ceremony.'"

His family had been alerted to the decision by the French government to mark the 80th Anniversary of the end of the war by awarding the Legion of Honor to all living World War I veterans who had fought on French soil.

Gold, a native of Cleveland, Ohio, enlisted in the Marine

Corps at the outbreak of World

War I, and served in one of the first units sent overseas. He was wounded in the hand by a bayonet while engaged in hand-to-hand combat with the enemy. Joseph Gold died at the age of 107. He was the oldest former Marine at the time of his death.

And lastly, the quintessential Jewish-American Marine, a young man from Brooklyn, Private First Class Bernard Siegel, who enlisted to defend his country in time of need and was killed in the first wave to go ashore on Saipan.

PART XII

Postscript

Chapter 49

Postscript

Dennis Prager, philosopher, author, educator, advocate, ethicist, and talk show host said that man's greatest gift is gratitude. It doesn't simply humble us—it ennobles us. Gratitude empowers us to appreciate what we have and challenges us to accept the fact that we are always in debt to others—our parents, forefathers, and our country. In practical terms it invites us to subordinate our own ego and ambition to acts which transcend earthly and temporal things to causes that are greater and more important than our selves and our possessions.

Gratitude is an essential ingredient to the formation of character. "Character begins with gratitude. And the great challenge for America is that gratitude and wealth are sometimes at odds. The more we have, the less grateful we are. The easier our lives become, the more we may forget how lucky we are to be free. Our parents struggled to make certain that our lives would be better than theirs. But, by giving us more, they may have prepared us less for those moments when our bank account will not help us." (Bob Kerrey, *Parade* Magazine, May 12, 2002, p. 17.)

It was precisely this sense of gratitude that empowered so many of our young people to take a stand against the evils that plagued the free world at so many stages of our history. Those who would risk life and limb in the early '40s, realized that their gratitude to parents and country enabled them to enlist willingly, if not eagerly, in the struggle against those who would challenge the rights of all people to live in peace and freedom. Their gratitude and character could not permit them to allow others to do what they had to do themselves.

And no group of people felt more obligated to share in that struggle than the Jews. Whereas the entire world was at risk, no one was more in jeopardy than the Jews. They in no small extent, and in no less measure, flocked to the colors to combat what was commonly perceived as the forces of evil and those who would threaten to extinguish the very society to which we are all so indebted for our lives, our homes, and our sacred honor.

Those who joined willingly in the struggle, perhaps more than those were coerced, did so out of gratitude. They felt the obligation to participate. They would not allow others do to their dirty work. And most took pride in their endeavors.

All those who joined in the crusade were proud of their participation. They were, and continue to be, an integral part of a great crusade. Their participation was wanted and appreciated. Their willingness made the struggle that much easier.

Of those who volunteered to be part of those crusades, great and small, and that which continues to this day, no one can be more grateful than those who volunteered for the elite forces of the military—SEALs, paratroops, Special Forces, and others. They should be rightfully proud of what they did and continue to do. They demonstrate their pride and character tangibly, visibly, and often at the risk of life and limb.

Jewish-Americans have demonstrated this pride in the U.S. Marine Corps. Virtually every man and woman who has been part of the Corps, inclusive of conscripts, have shown that pride and character. Despite the hard times, difficulties, and obstacles, that they, as others, have overcome, they are proud of what they were and continue to be. Even those far removed in time from their service continue to demonstrate their pride, gratitude, and character.

Although Jews as a group are rather uncomfortable with concepts such as patriotism, they continue to bask in their pride as former Marines: they stand straight and tall at the sound of the Marines Hymn and the National Anthem. They revel in talking about their time in the Corps, and most agreed that, despite what some may consider lost opportunities and time, their service in the Corps was well spent, productive, educational, and, in many cases, essential. Some would argue that it was a better educational opportunity than college itself. It taught them much that they could not have ever otherwise learned—at least not on their own. Their service provided a base for the formation of character building, formation of virtues such as self-confidence, integrity, perseverance, punctuality, personal appearance, and loyalty; lessons which unfortunately are not often learned at school or at home. Many young people matured and began to accept responsibility: lessons that we learned quickly and intuitively—if not at the bark of an obviously intolerant drill instructor—lessons that carried over into their personal and professional lives. For the most part, they were better people for it, and they have no problem expressing their gratitude and pride.

In her incisive article critical of present-day suburban education, Kay Hymowitz *(Commentary*, June 2002, p. 41) recognizes Elinor Burkett's *Another Planet: A Year in the Life of a Suburban High School*, in which so many contemporary ills and shortcomings are encapsulated, in which academic challenge, excellence, tough love, and originality are all but eviscerated. Not much effort is required to achieve. Teacher apathy is almost as strong as that of students. She quotes the author as saying that "Burkett is surprised to run into one class goof-off, who, after graduation, had enlisted in the Marines. He finished basic training with a perfect score on his final exam. 'In boot camp,' he tells her, 'they kick your butt if you don't try your hardest.'"

Sid Klein's service in the Marine Corps affected his overall outlook on life. It empowered him to acquire self-confidence, a can-do attitude that he can accomplish anything he sets out to do. "Finish the job. No patience with whining—be they kids, adults, male or female." "Better believe it. Especially love it when no-one believes that a Jew would join the Marine Corps."

Jake Silverfarb expresses his gratitude saying, "It's a shame that such a small segment of the U.S. population serves in the military these days, because they lose a true appreciation of what it means to be an American. It's even more sad that more Jews don't join the military after all America has done for us. The U.S. has provided a haven for Jews and we have flourished here. More of us should be serving in the military."

Semper Chai tells the story, at least in part—a paradigm, a microcosm, of what we did—and hopefully, will never cease to do. American Jews have always been a part of our history. You'd never know it, though. Perusal of our school texts reveal little of what we have done. In some cases, you'd never even know that we were ever here. One reads of highly fragmented, cursory, and distorted Jewish participation in our history. Other than a token mention of Dr. Salk, Haym Salomon, Samuel Gompers, Albert Einstein, or Emma Lazarus, one is likely to believe that we did nothing at the least, or very little at most. Certainly, scant mention is made of the Jews in the military. You'd never know that Jews have always participated in the military, sizable numbers during wartime, even during unpopular conflicts. It is conceivable that many, if not most, Americans have no idea of Jewish participation in the military, let alone in that of the Marine Corps.

Such was the backdrop for the genesis of *Semper Chai*. In a conversation with a gentile acquaintance at our sports club, it became evident that he knew nothing of this subject. He had no idea that Jewish-Americans even served in the Marines.

This man was educated, well-established, and fairly successful. If he was this uninformed, it was easy to imagine how the general American public would be.

It was time to set the record straight: and if I could contribute to the effort, so be it. I accepted the project not only as a challenge, but as a trust.

Semper Chai is an obvious play on the words, *Semper Fi* from Semper Fidelis, the motto of the Marine Corps. It combines Semper (which is readily identifiable), and Chai (Hebrew for life), which is not generally recognizable. There were those who said that the title was most appropriate and liked it, and those who took exception to it. Resisting the temptation to change it and sticking to the guns that I probably acquired during my short stay in the Marines, the title stayed. I hope that it becomes universally accepted and understood.

The sub-title *Marines of Blue and White* refers to the so-called national colors of Israel—colors which long pre-dated the creation of the State of Israel. Though they are Marines of red, white, and blue, and always will be, the Jewish colors are meant to distinguish them from others. After all, the book is about them: It sets them apart from the others. The blue and white make them just a bit more identifiable.

If there is a common thread among the participants of this book, it can be summed up in one word: Pride. "Once a Marine, always a Marine" is not the cliché that is so often portrayed. It's not just a slogan to these people. Virtually no-one expressed regret in their service. On the contrary, they all bask in the title of Marine, they take pride in their service.

To me, their performance is humbling. I am proud of my service: I signed up willingly, if not eagerly, and even volunteered for wartime service in Korea. But my service pales in comparison to most of them. I confess to periodic pangs at the wisdom, or lack of, my decision to depart the Marines. I can't help but contemplate whether or not I should have left.

But, I, too made my contribution: less than many, more than most. And, though I could have and should have done more, I am encouraged by the fact that I did what I did, willingly, if not enthusiastically.

As for the Jewish aspect of the military, specifically that of the Marine Corps, it is a coat of many colors. Most Marines don't give a damn what religion a person professes, or doesn't profess, for that matter. Character is important, pride is relevant, and performance is essential. Despite some obvious anti-Semitic episodes, Edward Lev (Chestnut Hills, Mass.) finally realized that his buddies didn't give a damn about him being a Jew. If anything, he felt that his Jewishness was a big plus. He was something special among a special breed of people. He, as others, learned that bigotry existed. It probably always has and always will. People are people and you can't break their prejudices easily. You just have to learn to cope with it. Just as prejudice exists outside the military, there is no reason to believe that it doesn't within. But don't make too much of it. It exists among all groups, no exception. However, all in all, anti-Semitism, and probably other prejudices, is less extant in the military than in civilian life.

The pride continues today. As it does with all of our thirty or so members of the Semper Fi Honor Detail, even we, men and women in the twilight of our lives, carry on with our mission and our tradition. Our Semper Fi Military Honor Detail renders military honors to deceased veterans being interred at Riverside National Cemetery. While age, illness, indifference, and personal obligation take their toll, they soon dissipate upon donning our dress blue uniforms. Shoulders heretofore sagging straighten up, chins jut out, chests swell, guts are sucked in, heads are held higher, and heaven forbid that a button be caught open, a couple of whiskers appear on your face, or a shoe is not gleaming to a high gloss. They, or we, are twenty years old again. Even our speech retrogresses to that of our barracks and field of fifty years ago. We are serving once again. We are again Marines—and no one can take it away.

Pride!

> *He that publishes a book runs a very great hazard, since nothing can be more impossible than to compose one that secures the approbation of every reader.*
> Miguel de Cervantes (1547–1616), *Don Quixote*, Part II, Book III, p. 466.

Index

Rabbi Jon Cutler

Abe Daniels **
Sammy Davis
Paul DePre
Larry Diamond **
Leland "Lou" Diamond **
Leroy Diamond **
Yonel Dorelis

Herman Drizin *
Alfred Drucker
Dr. Harold Dymond **

Edward Eiland **
Nat Elliott
Lloyd Evans
Jack Feinhor **
Joe Feinhor
Marvin Feinhor **
Dr. Edward Feldman
Ralph Finkel
Albert Finkelstein *
Martin Flaum *
Benis Frank
Wilbur Franks
Arthur Friedman
Mark Friedman
William Friedman *
Howard Fuller

Norton Garfinkel
Abraham Geller **
Milton Geller
Norman Gertz **
Howard Gherman
Daniel Ginsburg *

Rabbi Roland Gittelsohn
Saul Glassman
Samuel Glucksman **
Joseph Gold **
Murray Gold *
Ira Goldberg *
Lester Goldberg
Louis Goldstein
Marv Goodman
Frederic Green
Louis Greenberg
Ben Greenburg
Garry Greenstein
Jack Groskin **
Sheldon Gross
Irving Grossman **
Mark Haiman
Oscar Haimowitz
Max Halpin
Joseph "Red" Hecht
Ed Heffron
Werner Heumann **
Rich Higgins
Robin Higgins
Gene Hochfelder
Marvin Hoffman
Irwin Howard

Sy Ivice **

Alan Jacobs
Charles Jacobs **
Dick Jessor
Ben Johnson **
Kingston Jones
Tom Jones
Steve Judd **

Arnold Kaplan
Nathan Kashuk
Ed Kaufman
Herman Kaufman **
Bernard Kauffman **
Bill Katz **
"Red" Kelly
Bernie Kessler
Stanton Kessler
Herbert Kielson *
Bob Klein
Sid Klein
Joseph Kohn
Dr. Sol Kozol
Maurice Kranzberg
Joel Krensky
Melvin Krulewitch **
Peter Krulewitch
Irving Labes **
Phil Laden
Edward Leavitt
Howard Leavitt
Robert Leavitt
Ben Leffler **
Joseph Leifer **
Abe Leon
Sam Levine
Joseph Lowit

Lt. Gen. Robert Magnus
Paul Maloff
William Manchester
Myron Margolis
Jacob Marks
Abraham Marovitz **
Sam Messing

Marco Meyer
Ed Miller
H. R. Mitchell
Don Mollica
Murray Moskowitz **
Ralph Most
Joseph Murgida
Robert Mussari**
Harris Nadley **
Mike Nechin
Gerry Newhouse
Rabbi Joel Newman
Don Niederman
Erwin Novy

Berl "Bo" Olswanger **

Cantor Ivan Perlman
Leonard Pritikin **

Ken Quarternik

Herman Rabeck **
Arnold Raxton *
Buddy Rich
Barry Rice **
Brig. Gen. Martin Rockmore **
Rabbi Milton Rosenbaum
Donald Rosenberg
Edward Rosenberg
Elliot Rosenberg **
David Rosenthal
Barney Ross **
Meyer Rossum **
Meier Rothschild **
Dr. Richard Ruben
Abe Rubinstein

Sidney Rubinstein
Stanley Ryback

Sidney Sadin
Nate Sadowsky **
Bill Sager
Elizabeth Sager
Oscar Salgo *
Jerry Sander *
Jack Sands
Pete Santoro
Marvin Schacher
Bill Schaefer **
Harold Schainberg
Albert Schear
Irving Schecter **
Burton "Bud" Schwartz **
Goldie Schwartz
Jack Seeler **
Ed Segal
Harold Segal**
Jacob Sheiker **
Oscar Sherman
Adele Shimanoff
Morris (Jimmy) Shimanoff
Perry Shimanoff
Bernard Siegel *
Jake Silverfarb
Rabbi Hillel Silverman
Mike Singer **
Sam Singer
Murray Sklar
Ted Sklaver
Louis Slep *
Dr. Erwin Small
Ronald Sniegowski
Leonard Sobel **

Rabbi Samuel Sobel **
Allen Soifert *
Leonard Sokol *
Jack Stearn **
Jack Stein **
Phil Stock
Marty Sucoff
David Swerdlow **
Maj. Gen. Larry Taylor
John Terrence
Herman (Steve) Trevor **

George Ward
Sumner Warshaw
Bob Weinberg
Richard Weinberg
Harrold Weinberger **
Leo Weiner
Harvey Weinstein **
Maj. Gen. William J. Weinstein **
Sam Winer
Alan Wolf
Herbert Wolf **
Leonard Wollman **

Sam York **
David Yush *

Aaron Zeff
David Zeitlin **
Harris Zimmerman
David Zimmermann
Jack Zimmermann **
Terri Zimmermann
Paul Zonderman

*Killed in action

Table of Personal

Decorations

Congressional Medal of Honor
Samuel Margulies (Gross)

Navy Cross
Samuel Glucksman
Meier Rothschild
Irving Schecter

Distinguished Service Cross
Samuel Glucksman

Silver Star
Herman Abady
Stewart Burr
Max Clark
Norman Cohen
Leroy Diamond
Herman Drizin
Edward Feldman
Albert Finkelstein
Ira Goldberg
Werner Heumann
Martin Rockmore
Gene Hochfelder
Barney Ross
Irving Schecter

Mike Singer
Herman (Steve) Trevor
David Zeitlin

Distinguished Service Medal
Eugene Hochfelder

Distinguished Flying Cross
Abe Daniels
Harold Segal

Legion of Merit
Sidney Altman
Victor Bianchini
Harold W Chase
William Weinstein

Bronze Star
Sidney Altman
Victor Bianchini
Phil Bogatz
Edward Feldman
Frederic Green
Mark Haiman
Eugene Hochfelder
Melvin Krulewitch

Ben Leffler
Ivan Perlman
Irving Schecter
Mike Singer
Samuel Sobel
Herman Rabeck
Meyer Rossum
Harrold Weinberger
William Weinstein
Jack Zimmermann

Air Medal
Victor Bianchini
Alvin Clark
Myron Margolis
Marvin Schacher
Harold Segal

Meritorious Service Medal
Ernest Brydon
Edward J Leavitt

Navy and Marine Corps Medal
John Cohen
Herman Rabeck

Croix de Guerre
Max Clark
Samuel Glucksman

Navy Commendation Medal
Murray Bromberg
Rabbi Jon E. Cutler
Edward J. Leavitt